THE WAR TO END ALL WARS

The War

End All Wa

to End All Wars

*The American Military Experience
in World War I*

• Edward M. Coffman •

THE UNIVERSITY PRESS OF KENTUCKY

Published by The University Press of Kentucky

Scholarly publisher for the Commonwealth,
serving Bellarmine University, Berea College, Centre College of Kentucky, Eastern
Kentucky University, The Filson Historical Society, Georgetown College, Kentucky
Historical Society, Kentucky State University, Morehead State University, Murray
State University, Northern Kentucky University, Transylvania University, University
of Kentucky, University of Louisville, and Western Kentucky University.
All rights reserved.

Editorial and Sales Offices: The University Press of Kentucky
663 South Limestone Street, Lexington, Kentucky 40508-4008
www.kentuckypress.com

11 10 09 08 07   8 7 6 5 4

Library of Congress Cataloging-in-Publication Data

Coffman, Edward M.
    The war to end all wars : the American military experience in World War I /
    Edward M. Coffman.
        p.   cm.
    Originally published: New York : Oxford University Press, 1968.
    With new pref. by author.
    Includes bibliographical references (p.   ) and index.
    ISBN-10: 0-8131-2096-9 (alk. paper).—ISBN-10: 0-8131-0955-8 (pbk. : alk. paper)
    1. World War, 1914–1918—United States. I. Title.
D570.C6   1998
940.4'0973—dc21   98-15563
ISBN-13: 978-0-8131-0955-8

This book is printed on acid-free recycled paper meeting the requirements of the
American National Standard for Permanence in Paper for Printed Library Materials.

Manufactured in the United States of America.

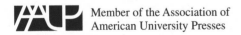 Member of the Association of
American University Presses

To Anne

Preface

"The war" meant the World War when I was growing up in the 1930's. My father and most of the other middle-aged men in my hometown were veterans, and I was fascinated by their war stories. Parades and ceremonies on Armistice Day also helped keep the memory of that war alive. In the 1940's, World War II eclipsed what then became known as World War I in the nation's consciousness. Over the next four decades, the Cold War preoccupied Americans, with the experiences of the Korean War and the Vietnam War further dimming memories of 1917 and 1918.

This book originally appeared in 1968, and that golden anniversary of World War I came at a time when the Vietnam War was reaching its nadir. Approximately a third of those who served in World War I (almost 1.9 million) were still living then, but a people sickened by a war they watched on television paid little attention to them. They had become, as my father in his last years said, "the forgotten men." Twenty-five years later on Armistice Day, now called Veterans Day, only one American family attended the memorial service at Romagne, the largest American military cemetery in Europe, where the dead from the Meuse-Argonne campaign are buried. During this eightieth anniversary of the war, only some four thousand veterans survive. What they and their comrades did so long ago certainly deserves to be remembered.

Although many American historians were enthusiastic about the war during 1917-1918 and a few later wrote about it, virtually none showed any interest by the 1950's when I began my graduate studies. Nor did I, initially, as the Civil War then captivated me. After considering at length a Civil War topic for a dissertation, however, I came across an obituary in the morning newspaper which changed my mind. The death of Peyton C. March, who as Chief of Staff was the top-ranking American soldier in the last months of World War I, evoked a desire to learn more about March's accomplishments during the war. Preliminary research turned up relevant personal papers of March and other key figures at the Library of Congress and his office files at the National Archives. I also corresponded with or interviewed quite a few people who had been closely associated with him. During my research I had a virtually clean slate as there were hardly any other scholars in the entire field of the American participation in World War I.

Before I completed *The Hilt of the Sword: The Career of Peyton C. March,* former Wisconsin governor Philip F. LaFollette, a friend and World War I veteran, suggested that I write a history of the war. He also put me in touch with Sheldon Meyer of Oxford University Press, who was then planning a series on American wars. As it happened, the series did not materialize as only *The War to End All Wars* and Charles B. MacDonald's *The Mighty Endeavor: American Armed Forces in the European Theater in World War II* were published.

I conceived of this book as a comprehensive history of the American military experience in World War I. I wanted to deal with the administrative and logistical aspects of the War Department and the strategic and diplomatic matters at the high command level, but I also wished to describe how the draft worked, what the training camps were like, and how the generals' plans affected the men in the trenches. I planned to devote separate chapters to the sea and air wars. As it happened, they were among the earliest I wrote. Originally, I thought I would do more with the two expeditions to Russia but time and space limited that coverage.

I used some of my previous research on General March, and the experience gained from those months in the Manuscripts Division of the Library of Congress and the Modern Military Branch of the National Archives facilitated my efforts to locate other relevant material for areas not covered in the earlier book. My discovery of the Hugh A. Drum Papers in an attic in his grandson's home was a particular boon to my understanding of the high level staff work in the American Expeditionary Forces (AEF). Again I talked with people who were there. Listening to Douglas Campbell describe dogfights as planes swooped within fifty feet of each other or Lieutenant General Charles D. Herron explain how he as a division chief of staff worked with his commander, as well as many others' accounts, certainly taught me a great deal about the war.

When I wrote about the battles, I leaned heavily on the superb maps and terrain descriptions in the American Battle Monuments Commission's *American Armies and Battlefields in Europe*. At the time, I had never seen the Western Front. In the late spring of 1990, I finally got to France, where Paul Jacobsmeyer, an excellent, well-informed guide and congenial companion, took me over the American battlefields. As we retraced the operations of the AEF, we depended on those Battle Monuments maps. They are invaluable to anyone who studies the operations of the AEF or visits those battlefields; hence I was pleased when the Army's Center of Military History recently reprinted this long out-of-print book and its maps.

Near Belleau Wood, Paul and I stood where the Marines had begun their attack and saw the poppies swaying amidst the waist-high wheat in the fields that those Marines crossed exactly seventy-two years before. There was wheat also on the fields near Soissons where the First and Second Divisions fought. Appropriately, it was a gloomy day in the Argonne Forest when we found the vestiges of foxholes on the steep slope of the ravine where the Lost Battalion was besieged. Much of the front is now farmland, but there are wooded areas cordoned off as unsafe because of unexploded shells and one can occasionally see traces of trenches. On top of Blanc Mont, I even slipped and fell into one. We also visited the American cemeteries at Bony, Belleau Wood, Fere En Tardenois, St. Mihiel, and Romagne. Among the more than 14,000 white crosses at Romagne, I located the grave of Frederick Trevenen Edwards, the only soldier whose death I describe in this book, and was moved to find a small bouquet at the base of his cross.

Over the last thirty years several books have appeared that I wish had been available when I researched this book. While this more recent scholarship would certainly change some minor points, I do not believe that major alterations are necessary. Aside from correcting some typographical errors, I have therefore made no revisions. Nevertheless, I want to mention at least a few of these newer books.

Donald Smythe's *Pershing, General of the Armies* and Frank E. Vandiver's *Black Jack: The Life and Times of John J. Pershing* give the AEF commander biographies that he deserves. Allan R. Millett's *The General: Robert L. Bullard and Officership in the United States Army, 1881-1925*, Heath Twitchell's *Allen: The Biography of an Army Officer, 1859-1930*, and Merrill L. Bartlett's *Lejeune: A Marine's Life* are other biographies that anyone interested in the AEF would find useful. Several soldier memoirs have appeared during this period, but one stands out—*Memoirs of My Service in the World War, 1917-1918*, by George C. Marshall, Jr.

David F. Trask viewed Pershing from a different perspective than the general's biographers in *The AEF and Coalition Warmaking, 1917-1918*, while James A. Hallas' *Squandered Victory: The First American Army at St. Mihiel* and Paul Braim's *Test of Battle: The AEF in the Meuse-Argonne Campaign* provide studies of America's greatest battles. In 1984, Lonnie J. White published the first division history since the early post-war period, *Panthers to Arrowheads: The 36th (Texas-Oklahoma) Division in World War I*. James J. Hudson's detailed history of the Americans' air war, *Hostile Skies: A Combat History of the American Air Service in World War I*, appeared when the original edition of my book was in press; hence I was unable to use it. Since then, Dale E. Wilson has brought out a study of American armor in the war, *Treat 'em Rough: The Birth of American Armor, 1917-1920*. In her *The Neck of the Bottle: George W. Goethals and the Reorganization of the U.S. Army Supply System, 1917-1918*, Phyllis A. Zimmerman examined the complex area of wartime logistics.

Other scholars have explored social aspects that relate to my topic. David M. Kennedy's *Over Here: The First World War and American Society* is a comprehensive approach, while John W. Chambers II has produced the definitive study of the draft of that period in his *To Raise an Army: The Draft Comes to Modern America*. Arthur E. Barbeau and Florette Henri answer the questions any of us might have about African American involvement in *The Unknown Soldiers: Black American Troops in World War I*, and Dorothy and Carl Schneider cover women's roles in *Into the Breach: American Women Overseas*.

It is appropriate that I should first acknowledge the significance of my father and those friends (O.C. DeCoursey, Arthur Gross, Hiley Cobb, and E.B. Bassett) whose conversations initially stirred my interest in the World War. As previously indicated, Phil LaFollette played a key role in bringing this interest to fruition.

During my research, I benefitted from discussions of various aspects of World War I with several friends: Forrest C. Pogue, Rexmond C. Cochrane, Daniel R. Beaver, Mrs. Charlotte Davis, and Guy Goodfellow. I also incurred debts to friends at the University of Wisconsin who advised and, in some cases, provided evidence from their own research. They are Richard H. Kohn, Richard Resh, Timothy K. Nenninger, Mrs. Francine Cary, John Thomas Crouch, and Richard Campbell. Marvin E. Fletcher also helped with proofreading and indexing. John D. Stevens took time from his own work on suppression of civil liberties in Wisconsin during World War I to read and comment on all but the last three and a half chapters of my manuscript. He also found in the Milwaukee *Sentinel* the quotation about Negro soldiers which I used in Chapter X.

A navy veteran of World War I and an authority on the history of the National Guard, Major General Jim Dan Hill, read Chapter III and advised me on National Guard statistics.

General Charles L. Bolté helped me in numerous ways. He, Mrs. Bolté, Colonel John L. Hines, Jr., and Mrs. Alice Hines Cleland were all generous with their time and brought to my attention valuable research material which they permitted me to use. General John L. Hines was also agreeable to my using his papers.

Colonel George W. Hinman, Jr., of the Army and Navy Club in Washington, D.C., time and again responded to requests for the names of survivors who had served in various capacities in the war. Colonel James S. Moncrief, Jr., has also earned my appreciation.

Librarians, archivists, and curators were always helpful at the State Historical Society of Wisconsin, the Memorial Library of the University of Wisconsin, the National Archives, the Manuscripts Division of the Library of Congress, the Margaret I. King Library of the University of Kentucky, the Oral History Research Collection at Columbia University, the Sterling Memorial Library of Yale University, the George C. Marshall Research Library, and the Cantigny War Memorial and Museum. I should give particular acknowledgment to Garry Ryan, Mrs. Sara Jackson, J.E. Taylor, Dr. Jacqueline Bull, Miss Eugenia Lejeune, Miss Ruth Davis, Miss Ellen Burke, Captain Henry J. Kelty, and Clinton Lokey. Miss Willie Rust and Miss Kate Ezell of the Hopkinsville [Kentucky] Public Library also helped.

I want to express my appreciation also to those persons whom I interviewed and to those who granted me permission to use quotations from unpublished papers and memoirs. The latter group includes Miss Elizabeth R. Satterthwait (for the published letters of her half-brother, Frederick T. Edwards), Mrs. Ben H. Bernheisel (for the memoir of her husband), Warren Pershing (Pershing Papers), Ralph Hayes (Baker Papers), Rear Admiral William H. Leahy (Leahy Papers), Henry T. Duncan (Duncan memoir), and Hugh Drum Johnson and John Dolan Harrington (Drum Papers).

At the University of Wisconsin, the Department of History gave me leaves in order to take advantage of support provided by the National Security Studies Group and the Research Committee of the Graduate School from funds supplied by the Wisconsin Alumni Research Foundation.

Emerson Beauchamp has been a friend in need throughout the research for this book, and Sheldon Meyer has been a patient editor who gave good advice. Mrs. Richard A. Whelan deciphered my manuscript and was a constructive critic as well as typist. Mr. Whelan secured the figure of World War I survivors from the Veteran's Administration for me. Louise Arnold-Friend and Muriel Sue Parkhurst provided the more recent veterans' data.

Finally, my wife Anne has heard much more about World War I than she really cared to hear, but she still listened and gave sound criticism.

Contents

Preface   vi

List of Illustrations   xiii

List of Maps   xv

Prologue   3

I   The Coming of the War   5

II   The Army Girds for Action   20

III   "War Isn't All Brass Buttons and Cheering"   54

IV   The Navy Does Its Share   86

V   Pershing Builds an Army   121

VI   A Divided Effort: War Department and GHQ   159

VII   The Romance and Reality of the Air War   187

VIII   "They Are Putting New Life into the Game"   212

IX   The AEF Comes of Age   262

X   The Final Blow   299

XI   The Stacking of the Arms   357

Essay on Sources   365

Index   397

Illustrations

BETWEEN PAGES 208 AND 209

Recruits in the fall of 1917.
"Juggy" Nelson at Corfu in the fall of 1918.
William S. Sims introduces King George V to an American baseball player.
The Secretary of the Navy, Josephus Daniels.

Issoudun.
Enroute to France and the war: Pershing, Harbord, and Alvord.
Hunter Liggett and Clarence Edwards in May, 1918.
Engineers cleaning up Cierges.

A quiet moment for the Rainbow Division in March, 1918.
Soldiers of the 92nd Division in August, 1918.

Robert L. Bullard with Philippe Pétain before the Meuse-Argonne attack.

A dangerous moment for First Division infantrymen
in Exermont, October, 1918.

Traffic jam at Esnes during the Meuse-Argonne offensive.
A gathering of the generals.

Charles P. Summerall with Frank Parker on Octo-
ber 31, 1918, before Sedan.
Hines, King, and Marshall of the First Division in
the summer of 1918.
Hugh Drum in his office at Souilly at the end of the
war.
Secretary of War Newton D. Baker and Peyton C.
March welcome Omar Bundy.

The aces are glad to be going home.
Men who fought at Belleau Wood in the 96th Company, Sixth Marines.

Frederick Trevenen Edwards.
Clayton K. Slack.
Sidney C. Graves.
Ben H. Bernheisel.
Frederick A. Pottle.

Maps

1 Western Front   xvi
2 U.S. Naval Operations in Europe   98
3 The Battles of Belleau Wood and Château-Thierry   218
4 The Battle of Soissons   238
5 The Aisne-Marne Offensive   254
6 The St. Mihiel Offensive   274
7 The Battle for the St. Quentin Tunnel   294
8 The Meuse-Argonne Offensive   302

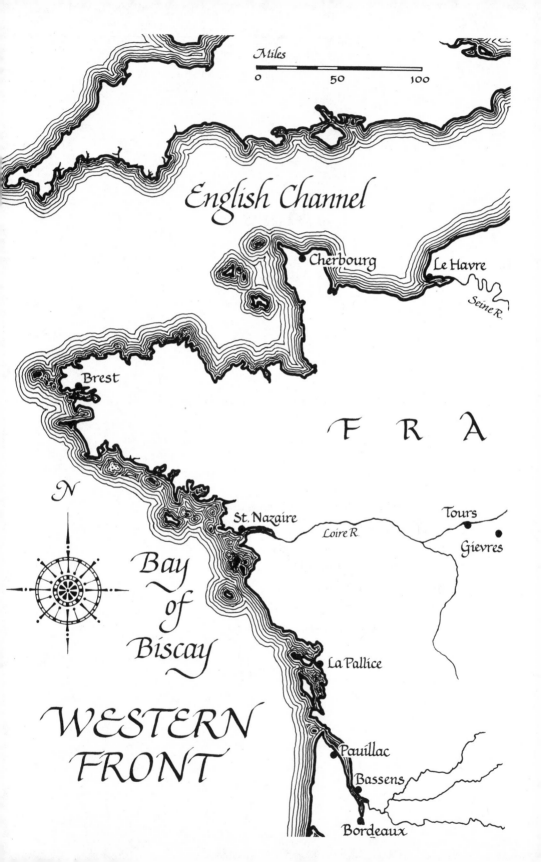

Miles

0   50   100

English Channel

Cherbourg

Le Havre

Seine R.

Brest

F R A

N

St. Nazaire

Loire R.

Tours

Gievres

Bay
of
Biscay

La Pallice

WESTERN
FRONT

Pauillac

Bassens

Bordeaux

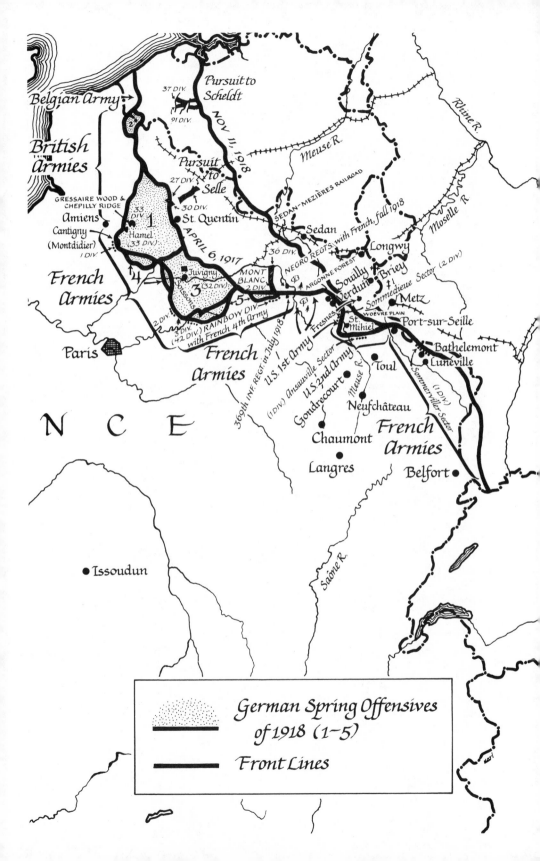

Belgian Army

British Armies

French Armies

French Armies

Paris

N   C   E

• Issoudun

37 DIV.

Pursuit to Scheldt

91 DIV.

NOV. 11, 1918

Pursuit to Selle

27 DIV.

GRESSAIRE WOOD & CHEPILLY RIDGE

33 DIV.

Amiens

Cantigny (Montdidier)

1 DIV.

Hamel (33 DIV.)

30 DIV.

St. Quentin

APRIL 6 1917

1

4

Juvigny

SOISSONS

3 (32 DIV.)

2 DIV.

3 DIV. (42 DIV.) RAINBOW DIV. with French 4th Army

5

MONT BLANC 2 DIV.

36 DIV.

NEGRO REGTS. with French, fall 1918

SEDAN–MEZIÈRES RAILROAD

Meuse R.

Rhine R.

Moselle R.

Sedan

Longwy

Briey

Souilly

Verdun

Metz

Sommedieue Sector (2 DIV.)

WOEVRE PLAIN

Port-sur-Seille

Fresnes

St. Mihiel

Bathelemont

Luneville

360th INF. REGT. in July 1918

U.S. 1st Army

Ansauville Sector

(1 DIV.)

U.S. 2nd Army

Meuse R.

Gondrecourt

Neufchâteau

Toul

Sommerviller Sector

(1 DIV.)

Chaumont

French Armies

Langres

Belfort •

Saône R.

German Spring Offensives of 1918 (1–5)

Front Lines

THE WAR TO END ALL WARS

Prologue

"Vive les Americains!" The shouts rang out in competition with the marching airs of an army band. Parisians, perhaps a million in all, crowded the streets and pressed against the gendarme lines. Many of the women wore black and, except for some soldiers on leave, there was a notable absence of young men in the throng.

The focus of this enthusiasm on July 4, 1917, was the first contingent of the American Expeditionary Forces to appear in Paris. The Sixteenth Infantry's second battalion had arrived the day before from the port of St. Nazaire, and now they were showing the flag. From Napoleon's tomb at the Invalides to Lafayette's grave at Picpus Cemetery, they attempted to march, while flowers showered on them and emotional men and women embraced and kissed them.

Most soldiers in their peaked campaign hats were regulars by name but not by training. The commander of Company F, Sidney C. Graves, recalled: "The officers were afraid of the showing we might make since we had so many recruits. . . . These men couldn't even slope arms. They were even more dangerous with a loaded rifle." But they were tall, bronzed and, above all, uncontaminated by life in the trenches. A French veteran looked them over and commented to an American reporter: "As human beings and raw material, they're the very best. . . . But they need a deal of training. The hardest thing to teach them is not to be too brave. They must learn first to hide. That's the first essential in this war." Later, John J. Pershing, their commander, who knew that some two-thirds of this unit were recruits, told a diplomat, "Yes, the boys looked and marched all right, but I cannot tell what would have happened if more had been required of them."

At their destination in Picpus Cemetery, there was some old-fashioned Fourth of July oratory with a Quartermaster lieutenant colonel, C. E. Stanton, hitting the keynote, "Lafayette, we are here!" Across the Atlantic the *New York Times* summed up the occasion—"The old debt is being paid. . . ."

·I·

The Coming of the War

The war that these Americans were entering amidst so much celebration was the disastrous culmination of a century of diplomatic maneuvering. European nations in playing the game of power had worked themselves into increasingly inflexible positions. Threats and counterthreats, advances and retreats in diplomacy and propaganda, had sustained the combustible situation during the first years of the twentieth century. The assassination of the Hapsburg heir in Sarajevo in 1914 broke the suspense and supplied the necessary momentum for catastrophe.

By the spring of 1917, the belligerents had settled into a pattern of war that was quite rigid in nature and unimaginative in practice. The initial campaigns had sputtered out and so ended the hopes of quick victory. On the Western Front, which stretched through northern France and Belgium from Switzerland to the English Channel some 470 miles away, a trench stalemate entrapped two large armies. Lengthy artillery barrages initiated attacks and churned ground into an almost impassable barrenness; then men charged against machine guns with predictable results. On other fronts—in the East and in Asia Minor—battles raged in a more fluid manner, but the Western Front, the focus of French and British activity on the Allied side, was a destructive deadlock. When the American battalion paraded in Paris, the statemate on the Western Front was well into its third year.

For years, Americans had watched warily as the European leaders constructed their alliances and fenced diplomatically. True, Theodore Roosevelt had barged into European affairs on occasion, but then TR was unique. Yet despite the ocean barrier, the United States was deeply involved, economically and culturally, with Western Europe. Then, too, with its bid for colonies, this nation had become entangled on the periphery of the power struggle. Indeed, in 1898 the friendliness of the British naval contingent toward the American fleet in contrast with the attitude of the Germans in Manila Bay was more than a casual illustration of national relationships.

When it became apparent that there would be no quick victory in 1914, American resources were a strategic factor which belligerent planners had to consider. In any consideration, the degree of American neutrality and the interpretation of neutrality itself were crucial. Almost from the first, the United States demonstrated a predominantly pro-Ally bias.

The ruthless German invasion of Belgium, which callously disregarded not only neutral rights but existing treaties; British control of the seas, which funneled American trade to the Allies; the huge loans which Americans had extended to the Allies; a skillful British propaganda campaign, enhanced by control of the transatlantic cable (they had cut the German cable); the bungling of various Central Powers' agents and the brutality of submarine warfare, which seemed to vivify Allied progaganda; and the prejudiced viewpoint of the President and the majority of influential American citizens—all helped make the United States pro-Ally. This is not to say that at any time between August 1914 and December 1916 most Americans wanted to go to war against Germany. A substantial majority of American citizens would have opposed such action. But it was equally evident that if America went to war, it would throw its weight to the Allied side.

During the first weeks of 1917, events triggered the American entrance into the war. The German High Command, in complete awareness of the probable effect of their move on American policy, authorized a resumption of unrestricted submarine warfare. Since the German government had promised not to stage such a campaign, this decision meant a break in German-American relations with the strong possibility of the United States entering the war. Woodrow Wilson reacted by breaking relations in early February. Later in the month, he asked Congress to authorize the arming of merchant ships and to grant him the power to use any other means he deemed necessary to protect American shipping and citizens. When Congress hesitated to give him such freedom of action, he released for publication the extraordinary Zimmermann note—a German message, intercepted by the British, which outlined a plan to entice Mexico and possibly Japan into war against the United States. Although this outraged people throughout the nation, Congress still did not act because of the stubborn opposition of a few Senators who disliked Wilson's tactics and who feared the consequences of giving the President such broad powers.

After Congress adjourned without acting on his request, Wilson, in early March, decided that he could place naval gun crews and guns on merchant ships by executive authority. In the middle of the month German submarines sank three American ships. The President called for a special session of Congress.

War was imminent.

On the warm, rainy night of April 2, Woodrow Wilson, guarded by a troop of cavalry, made the journey from the White House to Capitol Hill. When he entered the House of Representatives, an unusual scene met his eye—many Congressmen were wearing or carrying tiny American flags.

Shortly after eight-thirty, he began his address. As he spoke, his pointed lack of oratorical flourish enhanced the powerful emotion of the message. After briefly describing the situation, he asked the nation to "accept the status of belligerent which has . . . been thrust upon it . . . [and] to exert all its power and employ all its resources to bring the Government of the German Empire to terms and end the war." Then the President established the idealistic aims which he hoped his nation would attain. He concluded: "To such a task we can dedicate our lives and our fortunes, everything that we are and everything that we have, with the pride of those who know that the day has come when America is privileged to spend her blood and her might for the principles that gave her birth and happiness and the peace which she has treasured. God helping her, she can do no other."

Congress gave him a standing ovation and, four days later, its declaration of war.

The United States was at war on April 6, 1917. What this meant, no one knew. Before the American government could answer the inevitable question of the extent of its contribution to the Allied effort, it had to determine its military capacity as well as the actual situation and the needs of its co-belligerents. With a revolution in progress, Russia's future was uncertain. Closer to home, the German submarine campaign was hurting the British. Certainly, the Americans expected to extend credits and to provide matériel, but how much and what else would be required? A few days after Congress endorsed Wilson's appeal, the chairman of the Senate Appropriations Committee, Thomas S. Martin, had stated flatly, "Congress will not permit American soldiers to be sent to Europe." Indeed, would they be necessary?

During the latter part of April, the men with the answers arrived in Washington. The British mission came first. With the distinguished philosopher-statesman, former Prime Minister and current Foreign Secretary, Arthur J. Balfour, at its head, this group of experts commanded respect. Three days later, on April 25, the French arrived. Although a former Premier, René Viviani, led the delegation, American eyes and hearts focused on the massive figure of Marshal Joseph Joffre. Throughout his stay the nation gave the Hero of the Marne the enthusiastic welcome usually reserved for its own heroes. Later, the Italians, Japanese, Russians, Belgians, Rumanians, and, finally in December, the Serbians would come, but their visits were anticlimactic.

In their conferences with American officials, the British and French dignitaries described the disheartening war situation and pled for ships and money. From the first, one official asked for more. While the French mission was en route, the news of the disastrous failure of the spring offensive had confirmed "Papa" Joffre's blunt appeal, "We want men, men, men."

In public speeches Joffre was brief and bland, but in private conversations he made his points forcefully. After a disappointing, vague speech to the students of the Army War College on April 27, Joffre retired to the college president's office where he spelled out his advice to the nation's key military leaders. Newton D. Baker, the Secretary of War, Major Generals Hugh L. Scott and Tasker H. Bliss, the Chief of Staff and Assistant Chief of Staff respectively, listened attentively as Joffre talked through an interpreter. First, he advised them to send a division to France as soon as possible. Then, the Allies needed immediately technical forces such as transportation troops. He also impressed upon them the necessity for beginning at once to organize and train a large army which should be maintained as an independent American army. Five days later, on the afternoon of May 2, he followed this up with a personal appeal to President Wilson that a division be sent within a month. When he left the White House, he had Wilson's approval.

The British joined their ally in advocating a "show the flag" contingent and in requesting technical troops. But Major General G. T. M. "Tom" Bridges, a former combat division commander, struck a discordant note when he suggested that his army be allowed to recruit Americans into its units. Although Joffre had been more diplomatic in his counsel of an independent force, other French officers agreed basically with Bridges. This idea had occurred previously to Herbert Hoover, whose activities as a war relief administrator had brought him renown. In mid-February, more than six weeks before the American entry, he had outlined such a plan to Colonel Edward M. House, the President's intimate adviser, as the most effective method of rapidly adding American manpower to the Allied balance. Within three days, after passing through Wilson's hands, the proposal reached the War Department.

The basic advantage in this scheme was that it would mean the expansion of an existing military system rather than the establishment of a completely new organization. If the United States insisted on a separate force, it would have to start on the ground level and provide the administrative machinery and the great numbers of noncombatants necessary. To accomplish this would take more time, ships, and men. Throughout 1917 and 1918, the

Allies were acutely pinched by the shortage of all three. The French and British also knew that a large, separate American army would require leaders and staffs. Since they believed the Americans were incapable of providing such skilled personnel in the time available, they considered an independent American army in the field a gamble. In the face of German skill, bungling on the part of inexperienced leaders and staffs could be disastrous.

There were disadvantages. Employing perhaps a million Americans in battle under foreign flags might affront national pride. In particular, the slur on the capability of American military professionals was not taken lightly by these officers. Other considerations included the difficulty of getting Irish-Americans to serve in British ranks and the complications of placing Americans in French units where few would understand the language. From the standpoint of power diplomacy, this integration or, as it was called, amalgamation of American manpower into Allied armies might dissipate the appearance of the American effort and so decrease the American leaders' role in the war and in the peace negotiations. Finally, after almost three years of war, Allied high commands could display only a stalemate, long casualty lists, and war-weary troops. The fact that Sir Douglas Haig, the British commander in France, referred to casualties as "wastage" reflected the attitude of these leaders. One might question the effect of providing such generals with more cannon fodder. From this beginning to the climax of the amalgamation controversy in the spring of 1918, American military leaders adamantly opposed turning over their men to Allied command.

Amalgamation was only one of many suggestions made by the officers in the missions as they surveyed the American situation. One possibility, which they promptly dismissed, was that of sending American troops to Russia to skirt the German submarines and to bolster the Eastern Front. Both the French and the English made it clear that the Western Front was the most important theater. They also discussed organizational problems and found General Bliss particularly sympathetic to their criticisms. The British thought the strength of the American rifle company too small, while the French considered the division too large and unwieldy. In regard to equipment, Bridges pointed out the advantages of arming the Americans with the British rifle until the United States could produce enough of its Springfields. As they talked with their new comrades, the visiting officers became aware of one cardinal fact about the American military. One of the Englishmen summed it up in a cabled report, "They are quite unprepared."

This disgruntled comment explains European indifference to the American military establishment prior to the spring of 1917. Five years earlier, the War Department asked its attachés to sound out Europeans on what they thought of the American army, based on recent maneuvers. A captain on duty in Russia expressed the standard report, ". . . there is a universal belief that our army is not worthy [of] serious consideration. . . ." The Germans were more interested but not much more impressed. In 1911, a German newspaper published the views of an officer who had observed an American troop concentration in Texas. This soldier was struck by the failure of the volunteer system as evidenced by the division's being one-third under strength. More astounding to him was the low status of military professionals in this country and the large number of immigrants in the army. He thought that he was justified in referring to the infantry as the "American Foreign Legion."

Although the American army was not impressive by European standards, it had undergone basic reforms during the first decade of the century. In a period bridging the McKinley and Roosevelt administrations, Secretary of War Elihu Root, a New York corporation lawyer, laid the foundation for a modern army. As late as 1917, however, young, progressive officers and some of their elders recognized that they had to struggle to maintain advances in the areas of professional education, the general staff concept, and the relationship between the National Guard and the regular army.

As the nucleus of his reforms, Root emphasized increased training for officers. With the establishment of the Army War College and the revitalization of various other schools, he provided the necessary educational advantages. In particular the courses at Fort Leavenworth's School of the Line and Staff College stimulated a generation of professionals. Here young officers and, by correspondence, some older ones such as Brigadier General

John J. Pershing solved tactical problems with the help of German textbooks and topographical maps. At the time it appeared
ridiculous to pore over maps of the Metz area. A few years later
when some of these officers were routing troops into that area, it
seemed ironical.

To supplement their training, a few officers had the opportunity of visiting and observing foreign armies. During the Russo-
Japanese War, American military observers included Pershing
and the future Chief of Staff, Peyton C. March, as well as the man
who would head the wartime draft, Enoch H. Crowder, and a junior lieutenant, Douglas MacArthur. In 1912, a group of Leavenworth graduates, including George Van Horn Moseley and John
McAuley Palmer, saw first-hand the German, French, and English armies. Others, among them Captain Fox Conner, served in
French units. On their next visit to Europe, most of these men
would occupy key positions on the American Expeditionary
Forces staffs. These officers in 1918 represented the harvest of the
Root education system.

Yet, more was needed than well-trained officers. Throughout
the army's existence the lack of a coordinating agency had hindered it. Although a commanding general existed in name, he
was limited in fact by the chiefs of the various service bureaus in
the War Department. These bureaucrats—the Adjutant General,
the Inspector General, the Chief of Ordnance, and others—skillfully fought for and gained power, often with little regard for the
army as a whole. The Secretary of War thus was pushed and
pulled by parochial interests to the detriment of the army. There
needed to be established a general staff, composed of officers from
all branches of the service, which would study army problems as
a whole and make recommendations to a Chief of Staff who then
would pass them on to the Secretary. Root persuaded Congress to
create such an organization, but the influential bureau chiefs
fought desperately to retain their power. As late as 1916, they and
their friends in Congress almost succeeded in emasculating the
general staff principle.

The general staff system presupposed an understanding of its
functions and professional training. Many of the officers in the
prewar period lacked both. A Leavenworth graduate sadly noted
that he found in the War Department in 1912 cavalry officers con-

cerned with a new style of saber, while their infantry peers pondered the color of stripe on the dress-blue trouser. Nevertheless, that same year, Captain John McAuley Palmer demonstrated the value of the reform by producing with the aid of some fellow general staff officers a treatise on national military policy, "The Organization of the Land Forces of the United States."

The final reform dealt with the touchy area of militia-army relations. Since colonial times, the American military system had been based on the availability and adequacy of civilians to meet any defense need. Over the years, the militia had demonstrated repeatedly its vulnerability on both counts. Root attempted to make this legendary bulwark of defense more effective by introducing a much closer relationship between the militiamen and the regulars in the form of joint maneuvers and federal inspections as well as by increased standardization of the state-controlled units. This program worked to the mutual advantage of the militia and the army. Such officers on National Guard detail as Lieutenant George C. Marshall observed the capabilities and limitations of the citizen soldiers—a type who would make up the bulk of any wartime army—while the civilians learned the art and practice of war from the professionals.

The National Guard had its dress rehearsal on the Mexican border during 1916. The raid across the border by a Mexican leader, "Pancho" Villa, and the dispatch of an American punitive expedition into Mexico early in March, had led to a tense situation which could have developed into an unwanted war. In May President Wilson mobilized the Guard in three southwestern states. A month later, he called on the troops of the other states in a show of force against the Mexican government. When the units answered the executive appeal, they were not prepared in strength, equipment, or training. Most had difficulty in finding recruits to replace those who failed the physical examinations or who refused to enter federal service. Shortages in weapons and ammunition were matched by shortages in such comforts as cots and blankets. Regular army observers considered the state of training of nearly all of the units entering active service as little more than rudimentary.

During June and July, many Guardsmen came in wool uniforms complete with overcoats to drill in the 120° Texas temperature. They griped about the long train trips in the day coaches, but a few high spirits had chalked "Get Villa," "The only good Mexican is a dead one," and similar slogans on some of the coaches' sides. By December, the enthusiasm was gone, and the desire to go home, compounded by the months of monotonous training, brought about protest parades and demands for discharges. Before then, there were mutual recriminations between the Guardsmen and the War Department. Each blamed the other for the mistakes, rightly in part on both sides. Yet the three months or more service which these citizens had had on border duty provided them with much more training and experience than they ever would have received in their annual two-week encampments. When these men—more than 110,000 of them—returned to their homes, they were comparative veterans, though disgruntled ones.

Before the Guardsmen made their long training marches along the Mexican border, many other Americans paraded in preparedness demonstrations at home. The war in Europe gave impetus to the movement, but the predominantly pro-Ally leaders in America talked of inspiring patriotic spirit, maintaining national virility, and building up the military establishment. In addition to its parades, the movement embraced various formal organizations (National Security League, Association for National Service, Navy League, and others), semi-official committees (Naval Consulting Board and National Research Council among them), and civilian training camps.

Major General Leonard Wood referred to the archetype of the camps—Plattsburg—as "a voice to the slumbering people of the country." To most people, slumbering or awake, this voice had the dynamic timbre of Theodore Roosevelt. Since the vigorous ex-President and his politically oriented friend Wood were the outstanding figures in the preparedness movement, the drive for national defense tended to fuse with criticism of the Wilson administration. Certainly, in the presidential election year of 1916, TR and Wood often used the preparedness issue as a means to attack Wilson.

The training camps lent color to preparedness. Reporters delighted in seeing the mayor of New York City, John P. Mitchel, cleaning his rifle and the appearance of an ex-Secretary of State,

Robert Bacon, stiffening to attention. In July 1913 Wood, then Army Chief of Staff, inaugurated the program with two camps and some 200 college boys who paid for the experience of five weeks of military life. After the sinking of the *Lusitania* in May 1915 by a German submarine, young professionals and businessmen flocked to summer camps to learn soldiering. During the summer of 1916, regular army officers in twelve camps gave more than 16,000 some rudimentary training. Although Congress did pay their expenses that year, the trainees were mostly from the middle class. The "old college try" atmosphere and the evening gatherings about large campfires to listen to Wood and others give their views were in marked contrast to the war in the trenches 3000 miles away, but they were not irrelevant. These men were consciously setting an example, besides obtaining training which many presumed would qualify them for commissions in an emergency.

Although learning how to shoot a rifle the army way was a more compelling, personal expression of interest in national defense, some businessmen chose to approach the problem in a different manner. A Hudson Motor Car Company vice-president, Howard E. Coffin, established the framework of their efforts in his remark, "Twentieth century warfare demands that the blood of the soldier must be mingled with from three to five parts of the sweat of the man in the factories, mills, mines, and fields of the nation in arms." Financed almost entirely by private contributions, Coffin's Industrial Preparedness Committee surveyed the nation's industries. By September 1916 some 20,000 plants had reported on their wartime capabilities. Then, the dynamic executive and his fellow enthusiasts acquainted the nation, in a large-scale public relations campaign, with the role industry had in modern war.

To some who were aware of the United States economic involvement with the Allies, this aspect of preparedness seemed to be proof of big business' desire to profit from warmaking. To others, it appeared to be a realistic appreciation of the war situation. Among those was Dr. Hollis Godfrey, president of the Drexel Institute in Philadelphia. In the spring of 1916, he and Dr. Harry E. Crampton planned an organization which would integrate economic and military power. The culmination of their hopes was the Council of National Defense, in which six cabinet members and an advisory commission of economic and labor experts could coordinate national power.

Congress created this Council in August 1916 as one of its several preparedness acts that year. Both service secretaries supported such legislation, which also had Woodrow Wilson's approval. After the sinking of the *Lusitania*, the President began to realize the necessity for bolstering the nation's defenses. Although his critics accused him of being too late and then asking for too little, he had advocated a key economic preparation in 1914 only to be thwarted by Congress. When the war broke out, Wilson recognized the inadequacy of the Merchant Marine and requested congressional sanction to buy foreign ships in order to develop an adequate carrier fleet for American international commerce. Despite its possibilities he did not support the measure as a preparedness move, nor did opposition form on that issue. The opponents were against government intervention in private business and feared that the government operation of merchant ships would lead to friction with the British, who might seize former German vessels. Finally, in September 1916, when Wilson backed a much better bill, which included authorization of a Shipping Board, the wartime military use of the ships, and the right to construct as well as to purchase vessels, he won a legislative victory. With this, the foundation for the great transport effort of 1918 was in place.

Before the shipping bill became law, Wilson signed the more comprehensive National Defense Act. This controversial measure caused a split within the administration and the resignation of the Secretary of War and his assistant. For some time, the President had been irritated by the argumentative and intelligent former New Jersey judge, Lindley M. Garrison—the only cabinet member who dared interrupt him in cabinet meetings. In the period when Wilson was discouraging preparedness, Garrison and his genial young assistant, Henry Breckinridge, who had been one of Wilson's students at Princeton, had sought to do all they could to encourage just such moves without embarrassing the White House. During the spring and summer of 1915, they met with their military advisers at the Shoreham and the Army-Navy Club and attempted to mold General Staff plans into practical legislation. Thus in July when Wilson asked his service secretaries for defense programs, they had one almost ready.

At these sessions, they debated asking Congress for an endorsement of conscription but decided against it in favor of a large volunteer federal reserve. By building up this Continental Army over a three-year period, Garrison hoped to expand the existing reserve of seventeen men, the bulk of whom (13) were in New York City, to 400,000 men in territorial units throughout the nation. This blunt proposal to supplant the militia's role in national defense led to a bitter fight in Congress. A deadlock resulted because the inflexible Secretary refused to yield to the opposition in the House. When forced to intervene, Wilson withdrew his support of the Continental Army plan. This killed the idea and brought about the resignation of the civilian heads of the War Department. Several years later, Garrison bitterly recalled the President as "a man of high ideals but no principles."

Yet, Wilson's sacrifice of Garrison cleared the air between the White House and Capitol Hill and made possible the passage of the National Defense Act in June 1916. This measure permitted the regular army to increase its actual strength more than double its current total in five annual increments to approximately 11,450 officers and 223,580 men. The controversial militia also won an increase in strength to a possible 17,000 officers and 440,000 men. By virtue of this law the militia could be aptly termed National Guard, since the federal government increased its control particularly by requiring recruits to take a double oath to the federal as well as to the state government. It was under this provision that the President sent the Guard to the Mexican border. In the field of economic preparedness, the Act authorized the President to commandeer factories and provided for a government-owned nitrate plant. Finally, the Act furnished the means of training new officers by establishing a Reserve Officers' Training Corps in the colleges, augmenting the size of the cadet corps at West Point, and endorsing the Plattsburg summer camp program. The army appropriations bill supplemented the National Defense Act by more than doubling the current budget and by creating the Council of National Defense.

Despite the authority granted by the Act, the regular army

failed to recruit to the full strength allowed. On April 1, 1917, there were only 5791 officers and 121,797 enlisted men in the regulars, supplemented by 80,446 National Guard officers and men on federal service. The bulk of this force still remained on the Mexican border. As a second line, the army looked to another 101,174 guardsmen who were under state control. The active force of regulars and guardsmen were prepared neither in organization nor in equipment for service in Europe. The shortage of machine guns, the dominant battlefield weapon, particularly weakened the army. Although the War Department was well aware of the need for machine guns, it was still debating which model to adopt for standard issue when war was declared.

In some respects the army had failed to shake off the stagnation of the late nineteenth century. Although the Root reforms had provided the impetus, implementation was difficult when so many officers were lethargic. It was, in the words of Secretary of War Henry L. Stimson in 1911, "a profoundly peaceful army." After all, most of the officers above the rank of captain had entered the pre-Spanish-American War army, where aging Civil War veterans had dominated. As late as 1900, these old soldiers commanded all the infantry, cavalry, and artillery regiments, and some of their comrades held captains' rank. It was not until August 1915 that the last such veteran, Colonel John Clem, the famed drummer boy of Shiloh, retired; incidentally, only a few weeks after Dwight D. Eisenhower and Omar N. Bradley entered the army.

For the ambitious young officers, even though war raged in Europe, army life in 1915–16 was apt to be dull and uninspiring. Since the duty routine was usually over by noon, they had much of their time free. Some collected in informal study groups, taught themselves tactics, and attempted to keep up with the professional literature. Others spent their spare time at the card tables of the officers' clubs.

Life was harder but more rewarding for those attending the army schools, where the army's hopes rested. Although many older officers had taken advantage of the schools, their most common preparation for war was their experiences in the Philippines. Only a few brushed against the enemy in the brief Spanish War, but many fought and governed in the turbulent Philippines. Guerrilla war might not have provided the best training for the Western Front, but for the Americans who would hold high command in France it had to serve. In crushing the insurrection, pacifying the Moros, and handling the various tasks of a village or provincial administrator, these officers learned in a hard school how to deal with men. One of them who later commanded the air arm in France, Benjamin D. Foulois, summed up this experience: "Anyone who lived through the fighting in the Philippines could live through anything."

When war came, the United States possessed two great military advantages, manpower and industrial might. During the first year of the American participation, the French Army mutinied, the British squandered an army in Flanders, the Italians suffered a severe defeat at Caporetto, and Russia left the war. While Americans hastily prepared, their aid loomed as an increasingly important factor. How much help could they provide? How soon could this help reach the theater of war? And finally—would the American contribution be enough to turn the balance?

·II·

The Army Girds for Action

Before the United States could wage war on the scale demanded by the belligerents on the Western Front, it would have to expand greatly its military force and reorganize its military structure. During the formative period, which continued into the early months of 1918, delays, mistakes, and confusion hampered the developing war effort; yet, progress was made. Less than three months after the President made his appeal for war, the Secretary of War commented on the early stages of this progress: "Our preparations here in the United States seem to be getting forward fairly well although, of course, the size of the task is stupendous. There are many who are criticizing; but most of them have . . . no real comprehension of how hard it is to expand industrially an unmilitary country into any sort of adequate response to such an emergency as we are now facing."

Since Woodrow Wilson had little interest in military matters, his Secretary of War assumed unusually great responsibilities in the spring of 1917. A small man, unimpressive in appearance, and a known pacifist, Newton D. Baker had failed to talk the President out of appointing him to this cabinet post in March 1916. Although his knowledge of military affairs was limited largely to his reading about the Civil War, this Cleveland lawyer, then in his mid-forties, had several assets which would enable him to handle those responsibilities.

Above all, Baker had a sharp mind, which his friend Raymond B. Fosdick described as "one of those rare combinations in which swift perception is balanced by judgment, and clarity and sanity run hand in hand." An extraordinarily well-read man, Baker was not in the least pretentious, and his gentle sense of humor gave his brilliance a softening, whimsical touch.

Although he might seem more suited to an academic environment, Baker had devoted much of his adult life to politics. As city solicitor and, for four years, as mayor of Cleveland, he was caught up in the spirit of the Progressive Era and not only helped to create an efficient city government but also succeeded in making Cleveland a more pleasant place in which to live. In the process Baker became an effective administrator and mastered such subjects as sewage disposal and public transit problems. As a politician, he also developed his oratorical skill and gained experience in persuading others to follow his course.

A quarter of a century before he became a member of Woodrow Wilson's cabinet, Baker had studied under Wilson at Johns Hopkins University. Because of the coincidence of their living at the same boarding house, the professor and the younger man became well acquainted. Twenty years later, Baker's strong supporting role in the 1912 campaign served to cement this relationship. After his victory Wilson had offered his former student the position of Secretary of Interior, but Baker, immersed in his reform program in Cleveland, had declined. When he did come to Washington, Baker had the reputation of being very close to the President. His private secretary, Ralph Hayes, believed that this rapport resulted from the fact that "their mental processes were either so much alike or so harmonious."

A man who maintained in the most hectic periods an unruffled composure, Baker acted deliberately and unostentatiously but effectively. His quiet manner could be misleading to observers, and his method "of watching and waiting and listening when the situation," as one of his aides, Assistant Secretary of War Frederick P. Keppel, recalled, "in our judgment demanded a prompt and brilliant decision" was, at times, irritating. This cautious, moderate course made him vulnerable to legitimate criticism. Particularly, in the realm of economic mobilization, Baker's delay in reorganizing the army's supply agencies and his opposition to a strong centralized control of the wartime economy impeded an effective solution of the complex problems. But he was flexible and did reorganize the War Department and adjust to the new system in the spring of 1918.

When Baker entered his office with its high ceiling and dark woodwork in the sprawling State, War, and Navy Building, he found that two major generals, Hugh L. Scott and Tasker H. Bliss, would be his principal advisers. These two old soldiers— both reached the age of sixty-three in 1916—had been classmates at West Point when the new Secretary was a baby. Scott was the Chief of Staff and the elder by a few months, but evidently Bliss, as his Assistant, did much of the work. Baker came to admire and to have great affection for these two generals who taught him so much about the ways of the Service.

Scott, a personal friend of the President, had won his reputation on the Western Plains and in the jungles of Mindanao. He was, according to a young General Staff officer of that time, Douglas MacArthur, "a frontier-type officer." He had begun his army service in the Seventh Cavalry as a replacement for one of the lieutenants who died with Custer at the Little Big Horn. Throughout his years in the West and in the Philippines he not only fought the Indians and the Moros but also developed an unparalleled talent for dealing with them. They respected his firmness and reciprocated his trust. While he was in the War Department, it was not unusual to find him entertaining Indian visitors in their full regalia in his office and conversing with them in sign language which he had mastered as well as any white man. He was less articulate and probably less happy dealing with military routine. Indeed, on one occasion, he asked a junior officer to prepare a five-minute speech for him. Although he shocked the Secretary of Interior by falling asleep during a high level conference in February 1917, Scott was alert to the fact that modern war required conscription and a strong General Staff. His firm support of both would be of great benefit to the Secretary of War.

Bliss, who was much more at home behind a desk, acted as a complement to Scott. While Scott was pacifying Indians, Bliss had been teaching at West Point and the Naval War College and touring Europe to study military systems. For four decades, he had spent his off-duty hours in acquiring an immense learning. The Latin and Greek classics in the original were as familiar to him as the Infantry Drill Regulations were to a young lieutenant. As a staff officer, he had the valuable ability of being able to assimilate a great quantity of information and to present it in all aspects in a careful, reasoned analysis. The lengthy memos and letters, with the large signature scrawled across the bottom of the last page, corroborate the comment Baker made, "Bliss had in a higher degree than anybody else with whom I have ever been in contact the habit of deliberate and consecutive thinking . . . [his] mind was a comprehensive card index. . . ." Since Scott was absent on a mission to Russia from mid-May to August and retired in September, Bliss carried out the duties of Chief of Staff throughout most of the early period of the war.

A week before the President asked Congress for a declaration of war, Bliss wrote a friend, "just now we are swamped with work." This condition was standard for the handful of General Staff officers throughout 1917. Less than twenty General Staff officers were available in Washington to assist Scott and Bliss in analyzing the military situation and in preparing suitable plans. Since Germany and England went to war with staffs numbering 650 and 232 respectively, it is obvious that the Americans did not even have a suitable cadre for a wartime General Staff. Then, this staff was not accepted as yet by the bureaus which had opposed it throughout its existence. In 1916, the powerful bureau chiefs, through their influence in Congress, had been able to limit the staff in power as well as immediate strength in the National Defense Act.

Within this tiny staff, the eleven officers who made up the War College Division carried much of the planning load. When emergency legislation in May increased the General Staff to ninety-one and authorized even greater expansion, if necessary, this division grew to a total of forty-seven. But many of the members naturally were anxious for duty in the new units, so the Chief, Brigadier General Joseph E. Kuhn, took command of an infantry division, and various others, including Lieutenant Colonel John M. Palmer, a key planner, who went to France with Pershing as his chief of operations, left Washington as soon as they could. By mid-September, the War College Division was down to twenty-four officers. In contrast, at the end of the war, the three divisions of the reorganized General Staff (Operations, War Plans, and Military Intelligence) which had their nucleus in the War College Division consisted of 796 officers out of a total on the staff of 1073.

Despite its limitations, the small General Staff had made one particularly significant preparation for the war. In mid-February 1917, the War College Division submitted to Scott a detailed plan for raising and training a force of four million men—a "National Army." Although the basis for this project was peacetime universal military training, the planners also worked on a modified version which was adapted, in their term, "to emergency conditions." The major element of this plan, aside from the general idea of conscription, which the War Department would use, was the organization of sixteen divisional training areas. As one of the planners, John M. Palmer, later wrote, "Here, with little modification, was a nationwide war structure all ready for the selective draft to fill."

The Chief of Staff and the other General Staff officers assumed that conscription, selective service, universal military training, the draft—by whatever name one called it—would be the basis for a large wartime army. In a memorandum written in December 1916 the War College Division gave the reasons for rejecting the traditional volunteer system. "It cannot under the most favorable circumstances produce anything like the number of men required for the national defense. It is undemocratic, unreliable, inefficient and extravagant."

After the break in diplomatic relations with Germany in February 1917 Scott went to the Secretary of War with the argument that the United States should adopt conscription immediately if war came. In this conference, he effectively used the example of the British who waited to resort to the draft until 1916. Baker accepted Scott's advice and passed the recommendation on to the President. Wilson prompty approved and gave this order: "Have the law drawn at once so that, if I should be obliged to go to the Congress, I can refer to it in my message as a law ready to be presented for their consideration."

In a letter written long after, in 1932, Baker recalled his next step after securing the President's assent: "I then returned to the War Department, called General Scott, General Bliss, General [Henry P.] McCain [The Adjutant General] and General [Enoch H.] Crowder [Judge Advocate General] into conference and told them we were going to have a draft law if we went into the war and asked General Crowder to undertake its preparation. Crowder's remark as I recall it was, 'Mr. Secretary, a military draft is not in harmony with the spirit of our people. All of our previous experience has been that it causes trouble and that our people prefer the volunteering method.' I remember saying, 'That question is decided, General Crowder, as the President has approved a draft.'"

Paradoxically, it fell to the gruff bachelor, Crowder, not only to prepare the bill but also to be, as Provost Marshal General, the chief administrator of the draft when it came into being. And in both fields he lived up to his reputation as a prodigious and efficient worker. Upon his return from the Secretary's office, he called upon some of his assistants, among them a young cavalry captain who recently had obtained a law degree, Hugh S. Johnson, and put them to work on various sections of the bill. Within twenty-four hours, he was able to pull together these efforts, write a bill and present it to Baker.

In the preparation of the bill and in its later passage through the halls of Congress, the example of the Civil War draft was a specter. Conscription in that war not only was ineffective but also was the cause of various disorders throughout the Union and four days of bloody rioting in New York City. Many thousands of American citizens in 1917, including several Civil War veterans in Congress, well remembered the failure of the earlier draft as well as the stigma of being known as a conscript.

The most significant difference in the draft of 1917–18 and that of the earlier war was that local civilians rather than army officers administered it. The War College Division and apparently

Crowder had assumed originally that federal officials would again have to move into the multitude of communities to register and select the men. Baker, however, told Crowder to provide for civilian administration at the local level, and a Republican Congressman, Burnett M. Chiperfield, suggested the use of voting precincts for this purpose. Thus "friends and neighbors" rather than uniformed officers represented the army at the community level.

While the selective service plan was in its formative stage, Theodore Roosevelt made a proposal which, if adopted, could ruin a draft system and disrupt the military hierarchy. The ex-President wanted to raise a volunteer division, which he would personally lead to France in a matter of weeks. Although the foundation of a modern American army had been established during his administration, the "Colonel" considered his few glorious months as a Rough Rider as the benchmark for his approach to military affairs. In his special pleading, he repeated in detail his experiences in Cuba and provided a list of the regular army officers he would need for his unit. These regulars were among the best. His candidates for brigade command were Henry T. Allen, Robert L. Howze, and James G. Harbord, all of whom would win two stars and lead divisions in 1918, and his choice for division chief of staff was George Van Horn Moseley, who would become one of the most valuable staff officers and a brigadier general in the AEF. From early February until the middle of May, Roosevelt corresponded with Baker (two of his letters, April 22 and May 8, had a combined total of almost 30 pages in double-spaced typescript) and personally conferred with the President as well as the Secretary of War—to no avail. In advancing his cause, TR apparently influenced a delay of the draft bill in its course through Congress.

Although Republicans would naturally accuse the Democratic administration of political bias in thwarting Roosevelt's dream, Wilson and Baker had solid military reasons for denying the "Colonel" his division. They were well aware of his adventures in Cuba. On the basis of his known insubordination in 1898 as well as his position as an international figure, they felt that it would be impossible to fit Roosevelt into a large wartime army simply as another major general. They also recognized another danger in permitting him to raise a separate unit. Congress had reached a compromise by authorizing the President to raise four volunteer divisions. If Wilson took advantage of this provision to allow Roosevelt and two or three others to create their own units, he might place the divisions composed of draftees in a shadow. These colorful volunteer units would probably capture the imagination of people, just as the Rough Riders did in 1898, to the detriment of recruiting for the regular army and the National Guard and to the draft system.

When Baker asked Scott for advice, the Chief of Staff told him: "Our army, Mr. Secretary, must be commanded by a trained soldier, the best you have got. . . . This proposition goes directly athwart our plans for raising a real army." A dilettante at war with a political reputation and political ambitions was out of place in the American army of 1917–18.

Roosevelt was not the only obstacle to an easy passage of the draft legislation. Senators and Congressmen from both parties presented arguments against it. Some objected to the authority over personal freedom which the draft would give the federal government while others believed that it would take longer to raise a draft army than a volunteer force. One of the ironies of the time was that the Democrat President had to depend on a Republican Congressman, Julius Kahn, to maneuver the bill through the lower House, since the key Democrats—the Speaker, floor leader, and the chairman of the Military Affairs Committee—refused their support. Yet, both houses gave the draft their approval with large majorities, and the President was able to sign the bill on May 18.

The work of devising regulations and the necessary forms and of printing and mailing them to local officials was virtually complete before Congress passed the draft bill. Hugh Johnson and Captain Cassius M. Dowell managed these tasks with the cooperation of the Government Printing Office and the Post Office Department as well as the thousands of mayors and sheriffs. Aware of the possible cost of delay, Secretary Baker was delighted by the initiative of these two energetic officers. In late April, Baker also informed the state governors of the requirements of the selective service system and asked them to begin readying local machinery for the program.

After he signed the draft bill, Woodrow Wilson issued a procla-

mation designating June 5 as registration day. In this document,
which Hugh Johnson prepared, the President explained briefly
the reasons for selective service, which he called "a selection from
a nation which has volunteered in mass." On the appointed day
over nine and a half million men in the age group of 21–30 signed
up for "the great national lottery." Although the Secretary of War
and others were pleased with the general acceptance of the draft,
opposition appeared in some isolated areas. In a few rural counties in Texas, Oklahoma, and Montana, organized resistance led
by so-called "radicals" slightly hampered the system. Then many
Indians throughout the West and some mountaineers in Appala-
chia as well as Arkansas refused to cooperate, according to authorities, because of their ignorance. After the war, Crowder reported that in the entire war period "possibly 15 or 20 persons
were killed" in what he termed "pitched battles between resisters
and county and State forces." In the face of such overwhelming
acceptance by the nation at large, this opposition was relatively
small.

The selection process began dramatically on July 20 when
Newton D. Baker donned a blindfold, reached in a large glass jar,
and pulled out the number 258 that called up a man holding that
number in each local board area. For the next 16 hours and 46
minutes the drawing continued in the Senate Office Building
hearing room until 10,500 numbers (the highest number of men
registered anywhere) were recorded. The local boards then chose
out of this group men the army required. In early September, the
first large groups of these selectees began arriving at the cantonments. By the end of 1917, it was apparent that the local boards
could furnish more men than the army could equip. Although the
War Department had requested 687,000 men, it had been able to
handle only 516,000.

Despite the coercion of public opinion and the great propaganda effort, there were, during the entire war period, 337,649
draft deserters, men who did not report for military duty when
ordered, of whom over 170,000 were still at large in 1920. In an
effort to trap those who had failed to register for the draft, the
Department of Justice threatened the civil liberties of many citizens in 1918 by sending its agents, local police, and assorted vigi-
lantes on raids to apprehend the "slackers."

During 1918, the draft expanded to meet the demands of the war. At the request of the War Department in August, Congress broadened the age limits to 18–45 and halted volunteering for all services. In the end, the 4648 local boards registered some 24,000,000 men and furnished 2,758,542 to the armed forces— all but some 8000 to the army. With the aid of industrial defer-ments and Crowder's "Work or Fight" threat, the system also forced other men into war industries. The results of the selective service in this war erased the stigma of the Civil War attempt. In 1917–18, the draft not only worked, but, when one considers the magnitude of the operation, it worked very well.

Since the army only had facilities for housing the regulars, the prospect of a large wartime increase meant providing shelter for hundreds of thousands of new soldiers. In mid-March, Quarter-master General Henry G. Sharpe asked his Construction and Re-pair Division to give him estimates for camps for an army of one million men. The three officers in this division could do this plan-ning and, when war came, they could provide in addition housing for 40,000 officer candidates by mid-May. But Secretary Baker did not think that this small segment of the Quartermaster Depart-ment could handle the construction of the camps for the burgeon-ing army, so in May he created a semi-independent (from the Quartermaster Department) Cantonment Division, with the for-mer head of the Construction and Repair Division, Colonel Isaac W. Littell, as its director. Since there were so few experienced officers, the civilian architects, town planners, and businessmen of the Emergency Construction Committee under W. A. Starrett, a New York architect, played an important role throughout this early period.

In May, after an unexplained delay of a month, Secretary Baker told his six territorial department commanders to select sites for the new army posts. Although local delegations took up much of Baker's time and even reached the President with their "pork barrel" pleas for special considerations in locating the camps, the Secretary refused to interfere with the departmental commanders. By the end of that month, he had approved the rec-ommendation that the army provide wooden barracks for the 16 National Army cantonments and equip an equal number of National Guard camps with tents. During June, Baker approved the sites and saw that contracts were made, with the result that, before the month was out, the contractors were already at work on all but two of the cantonments.

The problems were myriad throughout the summer of 1917 as 200,000 workers rushed to build 32 cities—each for 40,000 inhabitants—by September 1. Because the tent camps required "only" a few wooden buildings and such basic necessities as roads and sewers, the main effort was to construct the 1500 or so buildings in each of the draft army cantonments.

Since the cantonments had to be ready to receive the first contingents of the National Army in September, this meant special provisions for labor, management, and raw materials. In order to ensure a continuous supply of labor, Baker made an agreement on wages, hours, and working conditions with the union leader Samuel Gompers and left complaints to a commission which included the young journalist Walter Lippmann. Since there was time neither for accurate and detailed estimates nor for a leisurely study of competitive bids, the War Department let contracts to well-known construction firms on the basis of a cost plus a fixed profit policy. Admittedly, this encouraged inefficiency and caused a difficult accounting problem, but it saved time. When a congressional committee questioned Littell about this, he answered, "The cost in most cases could not be considered. The work had to be done, and the only function we could exercise was to do what we could to keep it down as low as possible."

During the hectic summer of 1917, the Cantonment Division had to compete for raw materials with the other army and navy bureaus. The figures are overwhelming—two billion nails, 12 million square feet of window glass—as the builders used 30,000 tons of material each day. After the war, a statistician, apparently with nothing better to do, computed that the army had used in this construction project enough lumber to build a boardwalk twelve inches wide and one inch thick to the moon and halfway back. Because of the metal shortage in some places, the contractors even used wooden water pipes.

As the work progressed, new problems appeared. At several sites, there were not enough good foremen. Then, when the work crews started clearing ground at Yaphank, Long Island, for Camp

Upton, they found the remains of an oak forest. Getting those stumps out cost $200 per acre on land the army had secured at an average rental of 88 cents per acre. After the Cantonment Division had given the builders the model of a barracks to contain a company (150 men), the planners learned that Pershing had recommended a much larger division with rifle companies of 250 men. As Littell recalled, "we had to build a lot more barracks."

When September came, the cantonments were two-thirds done and had space available for over 400,000 draftees. By the end of the fall the National Guard and the first half-million men of the National Army were under canvas and roofs—respectively. There would be other construction projects—camps, munition factories, hospitals, airfields. In the final computation the $199,000,000 which the government spent in erecting the cantonments was just 24 per cent of the total expenditure on wartime construction. In the development of this work, Secretary Baker eventually gave all construction and maintenance responsibility to an outgrowth of the Cantonment Division—the Construction Division with Brigadier General Richard C. Marshall, Jr., at its head. Less than a month after the Armistice, Baker commented on the construction program, "In spite of the stupendous difficulties involved, the entire housing enterprise was completed practically on schedule, constituting one of the most remarkable accomplishments of the war."

In addition to raising and housing the army, there was the problem of supplying it. And, in the words of Hugh Johnson, "The supply situation was as nearly a perfect mess as can be imagined."

The army entered the war with five semi-independent supply bureaus. The Medical Department had the responsibility of procuring medical and dental supplies. For pontoon boats, survey and optical instruments, searchlights, and sound ranging equipment, combat troops had to rely on the Engineer Corps. The Signal Corps provided communications equipment from radios to pigeons (more than 15,000 birds would be trained for use in France), photographic supplies and odds and ends such as wrist watches and field glasses. Within the first year of the war, the aviation program would virtually overwhelm this bureau. The two major supply organizations, however, were the Quartermaster Corps and the Ordnance Department.

The army depended heavily on the Quartermaster Corps. Clothing, subsistence, and pay as well as construction, transportation, and the supply of horses and mules were under its jurisdiction. Seven months before the war Henry G. Sharpe took over this vital support agency as Quartermaster General. Although the Secretary of War would remove construction and transportation from quartermaster authority, the Corps still underwent tremendous expansion. Before the end of 1917, there were 5080 officers and 134,000 enlisted men wearing QMC insignia, in contrast so the approximately 8100 officers and men in the Corps when the war began. By the end of the year also there was a more forceful Quartermaster General—George W. Goethals.

The Ordnance Department furnished the army with its arms, large and small, and ammunition. In addition it provided the soldier with a cartridge belt and mess kit and the cavalry and artillery with harness and other equipment for their horses. As was the case of the other supply bureaus, this department expanded greatly. In April 1917 there were ten Ordnance officers on duty in the War Department. By December of the same year there were 950.

Since 1901 the Chief of Ordnance had been William Crozier, an officer who firmly believed that his technicians should dictate to the combat troops what weapons they should use. A controversial figure, Crozier would not finish the war as a bureau chief. At the time of the Armistice, there was a Chief of Ordnance, Clarence C. Williams, who had the opposite view of the relationship between the bureaus and the combat arms, as evidenced by a statement he supposedly made, "If the fighting men want elephants, we get them elephants."

Under any circumstances, the supply bureaus had an awesome task in equipping and maintaining a large force, but in 1917 several factors complicated the problem. Because Congress had not provided funds to build up large reserve stores and the Mexican border mobilization in 1916 had used up much of the existing reserve, supply officers faced the war crisis in the early spring of 1917 with little or no surplus stock. When war came, they had to provide for an army which was expanding rapidly to a then unknown ultimate strength. To carry out their respective missions, they had to compete with each other for raw materials and industrial facilities, synchronize transportation with their production and requirement schedules, secure storage space, and make certain that they were not interrupting the flow of raw materials and manufactured munitions to the Allies. At the same time the various supply organizations were undergoing the confusion of a vast increase in their own personnel. Finally, the bureaus had to act on faith during the first three months of war, since Congress did not appropriate enough to make the necessary great purchases until June 15.

In late February 1917 Joseph E. Kuhn, Chief of the War College Division, queried the supply bureau chiefs as to how long it would take them to equip an army of a million men. The answers generally ranged between six months and a year for the various articles, although Crozier replied that it would take about eighteen months to furnish such a force with machine guns and up to two and a half years for some other Ordnance items.

Two weeks before General Kuhn wrote his letters to the bureau chiefs, Bliss complained to Scott about the Ordnance situation: "Unless Congress will make the necessary appropriations there is little use in talking about speeding up delivery of material. We can speed up to the extent of the appropriations and no more."

The nation was still at peace, and Americans were notoriously uninterested in providing for a large military force in peacetime. From 1909 to 1916 inclusive, the Quartermaster General had requested funds to establish a reserve stock of clothing, but Congress had granted only one-third of the total requests. During the same period Crozier warned that large-scale arms production required prior notice of eighteen months or so to allow for the necessary retooling in the factories. In 1916, he had asked for enough money to begin a program to supply a million men with the necessary Ordnance equipment in three years. On that occasion Congressmen had cut his request by 35 per cent before it left the committee chamber.

When the war was two days old, April 8, Secretary of War Baker conferred with the bureau chiefs and the various civilian representatives of the General Munitions Board and other advisory groups about the equipment the wartime army would require. In the end it was decided, and Baker made the decision a formal order on April 12, that the bureaus would discard their traditional advertising for bids and that they would obtain their supplies on the open market with the aid of the civilian advisers.

Because of their business experience these civilians were invaluable to the army. After the war, Crozier indicated why they were so necessary. In reference to the officers in the army and navy ordnance departments, he wrote that they "had no experience in searching out manufacturing facilities, in bargaining for just prices, or in allocating to one another, in accordance with the pressure of their respective needs, a limited capacity for production. For these purposes, therefore, they had need of a general coordinating and supporting agency outside themselves." Nor were the ordnance departments isolated examples. In this early period apparently the Committee on Supplies, headed by the president of Sears, Roebuck, Julius Rosenwald, practically took over the purchasing function of the Quartermaster Corps.

Although the businessmen committees made a significant contribution in 1917, they lacked the necessary authority to control the supply situation. The Chief of Staff also did not have the power to overcome the independence of the several bureaus and to coordinate their efforts. In March, Bliss had urged that the bureau chiefs form a " 'steering committee' among themselves to ensure an orderly and uniform acquisition of supplies." But this was not done, and the bureaus entered the war with independent purchasing systems. The supply bureaus were particularly sensitive about their independence and they were, as Hugh Johnson asserted, "as jealous as the diplomatic corps of their protocol, prerogatives, and functions." This attitude led to such action as that taken by the commanding officer of the Rock Island Arsenal, George W. Burr, who, without regard for the needs of other supply organizations, gained control of the nation's leather market in the early days of the war. Later, he admitted that this was wrong, "but I went on the proposition that it was up to me to look after my particular job."

The tremendous demands of the war almost overwhelmed the bureaus, accustomed to peacetime procedures. Even when broken down into the various segments, the supply of the army presented huge statistics. For example, before the war ended, the Quartermaster Corps would procure some 17,000,000 woolen trousers and breeches, 22,198,000 flannel shirts, and 26,423,000 shoes.

In answer to the War College Division request a few weeks before the war, Sharpe replied that his bureau could clothe a million men in nine to twelve months. As the war approached, he gave the date of December 31, although he lacked a reserve stock. Throughout March, Quartermaster officers bought uniforms for the projected force, but, with the advent of war, their task became more complicated. They soon discovered that some factories had agreed to contracts which they could not fill. Within a few weeks, the introduction of 130,000 additional technical troops into mobilization plans called for more uniforms than the Quartermaster Corps had planned to provide. Then, Sharpe did not think that the army would send an expedition abroad until 1918. When the first elements of the AEF departed in the early summer, they needed clothing that was not included in the original Quartermaster estimates.

As the War Department contemplated calling out the first draft, Sharpe warned that unless he was given more time he would not be able to uniform all of the National Army contingent. The supply officers were trying desperately to keep up with the increasing demands. By mid-July, the Quartermaster Department had placed or was in the process of placing orders for clothing and equipment for one and a half million men, and Sharpe knew that he might have to begin considering an additional half-million. In this situation faulty liaison on the part of the General Staff did not help matters. Later that summer Sharpe was justifiably disgruntled because the General Staff had failed to consult with him or to inform him promptly about the overseas program.

Despite Sharpe's protests the army called out the first large elements of the draft army in September. When these men reached the cantonments, the Quartermasters discovered another complication. For years, they had purchased and issued uniforms on the basis of standard tables which indicated the number of each size required for a thousand soldiers. However, the draft brought in a higher percentage of very large and very small men than the peacetime regular army had in its ranks, so the Quartermaster Corps had to adapt its tables to the new situation.

Finally, Secretary Baker did heed Sharpe's appeals to the extent of delaying until 1918 the induction of 170,000 men, approximately one-fourth of the original draft. Nevertheless, there were shortages. Heavy clothing was so short in the severe winter of 1917–18 that it helped prod the Senate to investigate the supply problem at the turn of the year.

Before the winter made the situation serious, Bliss confided to Major General Henry C. Hodges, Jr., "As a matter of fact, calling them out and putting the Quartermaster Department on its mettle has forced them to do a great deal better than they believed possible." Bliss was right. By the time public criticism of the Quartermaster Corps was at its peak, the Corps had succeeded in overcoming most of its problems and was clothing the army quite efficiently.

Feeding the army was also a Quartermaster responsibility. In this field Sharpe excelled. For seven years before 1912 when the Subsistence Department became a part of the Quartermaster Corps, Sharpe had been the Commissary General. During this period he had worked hard to improve the ration and the preparation of food, in one way by establishing schools for cooks and bakers.

With the assistance of the civilian Food Administration, the Quartermaster officers purchased foodstuffs with relatively little difficulty. Once the food was available, however, the question remained—who would prepare it for the draft army? No such problem existed in the regular army and National Guard units since they had their own mess organizations. But Sharpe could provide only a few mess officers and sergeants to each cantonment. His solution was to call upon the hotel keepers and the chefs associations for aid. These men formed a committee which secured 4000 civilian cooks to prepare the food temporarily for the National Army. By November 1, the soldier graduates of the cooks and bakers schools at various cantonments had replaced almost all of the supplementary civilian cooks.

Theoretically, the Quartermaster Corps was responsible for transportation, but, under the pressure of wartime emergency, the other supply bureaus operated their own transport services. One result was highly inefficient use of rail facilities. Although during the Mexican border trouble the Quartermaster General had worked out plans with railway executives, after our entry into the war the competition among bureaus for rail facilities upset orderly procedures. As the Chief of Staff noted, "The result was a great congestion of freight at all important centers of traffic, great shortage of cars due to the fact that so large a number were standing to be unloaded, and at the very time when prompt unloading was so necessary, a great congestion of the unloading facilities." In December 1917, at the height of the transportation crisis, the federal government assumed control of the railroads. As a result, from then on in the war the Railroad Administration and the General Staff ended the chaos by not permitting carriers to accept shipments to congested areas without their approval.

Once the War Department decided on an overseas expedition, troop ships were needed as well as vehicles for animals to haul and motor-drawn vehicles. During the mobilization on the Mexican border, the army had increased its less than a hundred trucks to slightly more than 3000. In the course of the war the supply bureaus would buy some 85,000 trucks of various designs, in addition to thousands more of automobiles and motorcycles. Although the General Staff also took over motor transportation and worked toward a standardization program in 1918, the competitive buying of the bureaus in 1917 had placed such a hodge-podge of vehicles in service that providing spare parts became a nightmare for supply officers.

Horses and mules still had a basic role in army transportation, and Quartermaster officers had to purchase more than 300,000 animals. In addition, purchasing officers had to push wagon factories to the limit, as well as call on the furniture industry to provide spare parts.

In the early months of the war the Ordnance Department became a major competitor of the Quartermaster Corps over transportation facilities and for the purchase of many items of supply. But the Ordnance Department had complete control over providing weapons. As they contemplated their predicament, however, some Ordnance officers may have wished that they could share this responsibility and the criticism with other bureaus.

Soldiers were proud of their service rifle. The Model 1903 Springfield was a very accurate shoulder arm. Indeed, as late as the Korean War, rifle companies would still have a few "03s" on hand for use as sniper weapons. Yet, despite the superiority of this rifle, the 600,000 on hand in 1917 were an insufficient number to equip the infantry of the rapidly burgeoning army.

There were three possible solutions. The army could wait until private plants retooled to supplement the two government arsenals in quantity production of the Springfield, but this would mean a long delay. On the other hand, the army could take advantage of two Remington and one Winchester factories which were manufacturing great numbers of Enfield rifles for Great Britain. Although the small arms specialists of the Ordnance Department considered the Enfield to be inferior to the Springfield and its ammunition practically obsolete, this choice would save time. Instead, however, Baker made a compromise decision. Meeting late one night in May with Scott, Bliss, the Chief of Ordnance, the newly chosen expeditionary force commander, and other advisers, Baker decided to modify the Enfield so that it could use American ammunition. Thus, the major complaint against the Enfield was solved, and factories already in production could begin turning out weapons for the army.

When the Ordnance people began to remodel the Enfield, they discovered that the various parts in the rifle were not interchangeable. This meant not only that the weapons would be difficult to repair in battle but also that the rate of production would be slower. As a result the Ordnance Department experts decided to tolerate the immediate delay necessary to standardize key parts of the rifle in order to avoid later combat difficulties and to speed up mass production. By fall the modified Enfields were in production, but not until early 1918 were there enough rifles to arm the men in training. By the end of the war, though, American industry had more than met the demand. Over two and a half million rifles had been manufactured. The Springfield and Rock Island arsenals contributed almost 313,000 Springfields to this total, but the rest were remodeled Enfields.

Less than five months before the United States entered the war, Secretary Baker wrote, "Perhaps no invention has more profoundly modified the art of war than the machine gun." Despite this recognition of the value of this weapon, at the time the United States entered the war, only four machine guns were assigned to each infantry regiment, and the army as a whole had less than 1500 machine guns on hand. Indeed the War Department was still in the process of choosing a suitable machine gun, with tests scheduled for May 1917.

When the war came, the army carried out the planned tests but also, on Crozier's recommendation, purchased some 8000 of available models from plants which were producing machine guns for the Allies. In the May trials, the heavy machine gun developed by the civilian inventor, John M. Browning, made the most remarkable record. This gun fired 39,500 rounds before it stopped because of a broken part. The dependability and the simplicity of design both of Browning's machine gun and his automatic rifle particularly impressed the testing board. After they completed their analysis, they recommended the adoption of these two weapons as well as the Lewis and Vickers guns. Since the immediate need was so great, the Ordnance Department continued to order the guns (Lewis, Vickers, and Colt-Marlin) then in production and searched for additional factories to manufacture the Browning guns.

The infantry (which by 1918 had about 250 machine guns and automatic rifles in each regiment), the Tank Corps, and the Air Service would use thirteen different designs of these basic models during the war. In order to keep up with this demand, American industry was producing, at its peak in 1918, more such guns in one day than the entire army had on hand when the war began. Nevertheless, as a stop-gap measure, the French had to issue Hotchkiss machine guns and Chauchat automatic rifles to the American divisions until the summer of 1918.

Although there were enough Browning machine guns and automatic rifles in France before the Armistice to equip the American combat divisions, many American units at the front during the Argonne offensive did not have them because there was a breakdown in transportation. Those men who did fire them in combat liked them as well as their sons did in World War II and the Korean War. From the occasion of their first use in combat in the St. Mihiel offensive, as one report of that action stated, "the guns came up to the fullest expectations and, even though covered with rust and using muddy ammunition, they functioned whenever called upon to do so."

Rifles, machine guns, pistols, steel helmets, trench mortars, tanks (American industry built seventy-nine during the war), various kinds of artillery shells, assorted sizes of ammunition, as well as light, medium, and heavy guns—all these were items which the enlarged army expected the Ordnance Department to provide in great number. Before the war ended, Ordnance had succeeded either in meeting the demand for this war material or in developing facilities capable of doing so. Yet, the AEF had to lean heavily on the Allies, in particular the French, for its munitions. This should not be surprising, since industry needed twelve to eighteen months to progress from the intitial order to quantity production of artillery pieces, and the war lasted 19 months for the Americans. In France the munitions makers had been unable to provide an adequate supply of field guns until the end of 1916.

By the time the United States entered the war, the French and the British had reached a stage of gun production which permitted them to furnish some artillery to the Americans. In July 1917 the French agreed to equip the AEF with the famous 75 millimeter and the 155 millimeter guns in return for raw materials. The British later promised similar aid with different caliber guns.

These Allied commitments gave the Ordnance planners the time to develop their artillery program. Since almost half of all the artillery the army required would be a light gun of the caliber of the 75 millimeter or its slightly larger equivalent, the three-inch gun, the Ordnance Department concentrated on putting such a weapon into large scale production. In this attempt Crozier and his subordinates drew fire from an understandably anonymous Ordnance officer, who said, "Someone should get worse than hell for it, because it is a stupid mistake in judgment." While not as blunt, the Chief of Field Artillery, Major General William J. Snow and the chairman of the Senate Military Affairs Committee, James W. Wadsworth, agreed in principle with this comment. Two factors were mainly responsible for the error. For one, Ordnance policy makers characteristically ignored the opinions of the men who actually used the weapons. And there was also the point called by a French military adviser, Edouard J. Réquin, "the desire to construct ordnance that might still bear the stamp 'made in America'. . . ."

In April 1917 the army had 544 Model 1902 three-inch guns. Since the experience of the Allies indicated that a field piece of approximately this caliber (the French 75 and the British 18-

pounder) would be the mainstay of the Field Artillery, American planners realized the importance of mass-producing such a weapon. At this point, however, the Ordnance Department decided to concentrate on the Model 1916 three-inch gun and carriage which was still in the experimental stage rather than on the older model. By recalibrating the gun to conform in bore-size with the French 75 and by introducing other new features, Crozier and his officers hoped to have a much better gun. They overlooked, in the process, a major flaw in this "American 75." Within a few months manufacturers reported that the gun was difficult to build because it was so complicated, and, for the same reason, field artillerymen complained that it was not suitable for field service. "What was really needed in the Ordnance Department," Major General Snow later wrote, "was a realization of the fact that the Model 1916 was still in the experimental and development stage and that it had not yet reached the production stage."

After the Secretary of War had appointed Crozier to the War Council, thereby relieving him of his duties as Chief of Ordnance, the Ordnance Department, in early February 1918, decided to shift its emphasis from the "American 75" to manufacturing copies of the French 75. Although this was a proven gun without the faults which stymied mass production of the so-called "Crime of 1916" model, Ordnance officers had to deal with another set of problems. The French were extremely secretive about their famous gun. The restrictions resulting from this attitude hampered the manufacture of the gun and caused one exasperated American officer to exclaim that "the French would rather lose the war than make public the secret of the *soixante quinze*." Since the French depended on artisans for precision work rather than on assembly lines, American draftsmen had to take the time to put into the detailed drawings rigid tolerances and exact measurements which the plans had lacked before. Despite the efforts of the new Chief of Ordnance, Major General Clarence C. Williams, the war ended before the munitions industry could deliver one complete gun and carriage of the French 75 model to the Field Artillery.

The irony of the light gun program was that the Model 1902 three-inch gun would have served the purpose without modification. While Ordnance officers were impressed with their own experimental Model 1916 gun and their Field Artillery comrades were awed by the reputation of the French 75, a practical comparison of the French gun and the Model 1902 three-incher astonished officers in both branches. In the spring of 1918, upon completion of nearly four months of firing the French 75 and the three-inch gun, the officers of the School of Fire at Fort Sill reported on both guns. Much to their surprise, they found the American field piece to be as accurate, sturdier, and simpler to put in position for firing than its French counterpart. After the war even Crozier agreed with Snow that the abandonment of the standard issue Model 1902 gun had been a mistake. However, the French could and did provide enough 75s (1828 in all) to equip the AEF.

Fortunately, the light gun program did not give an accurate indication of the over-all accomplishment of the Ordnance Department. The American munitions makers could take pride, for example, in the production of over a billion pounds of powder and high explosives. They also completed 2008 guns of various calibers during the war. Such achievements in a dangerous trade, however, did cause the deaths of some 140 civilian workers because of explosions at two shell loading plants.

The focal point of the developing American military effort was the expeditionary force in France. In April 1917 army planners had to face a disturbing number of serious problems. The most crucial was whether or not the United States would send an expedition to the front. Before the planners could chart mobilization policy, they had to have a decision on this point.

If there was to be an expedition, available war plans were not particularly helpful. Although the War College Division had prepared two plans regarding Germany in 1915 and 1916, the earlier one was based on the premise of a German invasion of the east coast and the other was more concerned with internal security. Apparently the army's leaders did not think that war with Germany would require anything more than an increased defense force. Finally, on March 27, 1917, Bliss called for an estimate of how long it would take to transport 500,000 men to France. Four days later he summed up the reply of the War College Division:

"The war must last practically two years longer before we can have other than naval and economic participation."

Less than five weeks later, President Wilson promised to send an expedition to France. In the interim the nation had gone to war, and the Allied missions had arrived with their pleas for men. On the same day, May 2, that Wilson made his momentous pledge to Joffre, General Scott telegraphed the Commander of the Southern Department to select four infantry and one artillery regiments for duty in France. Scott added, "If plans are carried out, you will be in command of the entire force."

Major General John J. Pershing was the obvious choice for this assignment. Before he made his selection, Secretary Baker had reviewed the dossiers of all general officers and had weighed carefully each man's capabilities for such a difficult mission. In this consideration Pershing's recent experience with the Punitive Expedition in Mexico stood out. No one knew exactly what would be required of the general who would command the American army in France, but certainly the same skills which the Punitive Expedition demanded would be essential in that position. Loyalty to administration policy and discretion were as necessary as the ability to command a large field force.

During Baker's tenure in office Pershing was the only officer who had had the opportunity to exhibit such abilities. Throughout this period, the ranking major general and the most likely competitor for an important command, Leonard Wood, had occupied administrative posts and had been openly critical of Wilsonian policies. Although Pershing privately disagreed with Wilson's Mexican policy, he carried it out and, as a soldier should, refrained from public comment. Baker also discounted Wood because he had observed Wood's difficulty in walking up a hill at Plattsburg. He had never met Pershing but Baker had the general's dossier before him and, as he later wrote, "his record showed him to be a man of robust health and energy."

Baker saw Pershing for the first time on the morning of May 10th. At fifty-six, Pershing was an imposing figure, tanned, ramrod-straight, and meticulously groomed. This man had presence, and he was all soldier.

Thirty-five years had passed since Pershing had left the small

Missouri town of Laclede to enter West Point. For that span his military career can be divided into three periods. His four years at the Military Academy were the introductory phase. For the next fifteen years he excelled as a junior officer but nourished little hope of a future in the army. After the turn of the century, he seized his first great opportunity and gained an eminence which would make him available for the much greater opportunity Baker gave him in 1917.

When he became a cadet, Pershing, nearing his twenty-second birthday, was older than most of the other cadets. He was a man when they were on the verge of becoming men. In academic subjects he was in the middle of his class, but he was the acknowledged leader as class president and as First Captain, the highest military rank in the Cadet Corps. His classmates liked him, and above all they respected him.

In the 1880's the memory of the Civil War dominated West Point. During Pershing's cadet days, the two Superintendents, Oliver O. Howard and Wesley Merritt, were well-known generals in that war, and Grant, Sherman, and Sheridan were occasional visitors to the Academy. These old heroes impressed Pershing and his fellow cadets. Many years later, when he was a retired General of the Armies, Pershing recalled seeing Grant and commented, "I regarded him then and do now as the greatest general our country has produced."

When Pershing received his commission in 1886, the small army and the nation's military situation seemed to offer no hope of distinction such as the old soldiers had won in the Civil War. Despite his success at West Point, Pershing would not make a complete commitment to a military career. His ambition would not let him do so at this stage of his life. Later, he wrote, "From the day of my entrance into West Point up to middle age I had hoped the time would come when I could return to civil life while still young enough to take up law or go into business." With this course in view, he obtained a law degree at the University of Nebraska in 1893 while on duty. Yet, no one could accuse him of neglecting his duties. He was a strict but fair disciplinarian who carried out his tasks with an "unvarying impersonality." As a young cavalry officer he made an excellent record on the frontier and engaged in one of the last skirmishes with the Indians. For this reason he qualified his previous statement, "But successive assignments that offered chances for active duty and adventure had held me in the Army."

The Spanish-American War provided action, but it was over before the thirty-seven-year-old lieutenant could rise to prominence. He served in Cuba with the Tenth (Negro) Cavalry Regiment—a connection which gave him his nickname "Black Jack" —and won a commendation for gallantry at San Juan Hill. Because of wartime expansion, he also became a temporary major, but there were many other regular officers who had done as well in that brief conflict.

His chance came in the Philippines in 1902–03. Although only a captain, having reverted to his permanent rank, Pershing had the responsibility at times of a brigadier general in leading forces against the Moros on Mindanao. The departmental commander was so impressed by Pershing's skill in dealing with the natives that he shelved senior officers in order to give Pershing command of the troops in the field. By conquering and "pacifying" the Sultans of Bayan, Maciu, Taraca, Bacolod, and others, the cavalry captain gained national recognition.

Because of the restrictions of army promotion policy, which was based on seniority, the President could not reward Pershing with promotion unless he recommended him for a brigadier generalcy. This had been done in a few cases and, in 1906, Theodore Roosevelt, with the approval of Congress, gave such an unusual promotion to Pershing.

His next promotion came in September 1916, when Secretary Baker could recommend him on the basis of his efficient handling of the Punitive Expedition. Earlier that year Pershing, who was in El Paso and in command of the troops ordered into Mexico, had been the most logical choice to lead that expedition. He and his force of less than ten thousand men penetrated more than three hundred miles into Mexico and fragmented Villa's band. As the international crisis heightened, he withdrew his command to Colonia Dublan, about a hundred miles south of the border, and waited for the government to settle the situation. During the first week of February 1917, Pershing brought his troops back across the border. He had impressed both Baker and Wilson by his success in carrying out a difficult mission.

Pershing was well equipped for his greatest opportunity. He was tough, confident, experienced, and he possessed the ability, crucial to anyone in command, of matching the right man with the right job. He had, in the words of Douglas MacArthur, "strength and firmness of character"—the will to carry on under adverse conditions, to make and execute difficult decisions, and above all, the desire to fight and to win. His stoic acceptance of the tragic deaths of his wife and three children in 1915 and his service over three decades reflected this.

Finally, there was his ambition. "He was always a good courtier," as Robert L. Bullard observed. He made the right impression when he wrote President Wilson on April 10, 1917:

> As an officer of the army, may I not extend to you, as Commander in Chief of the armies, my sincere congratulations upon your soul-stirring patriotic address to Congress on April 2ᵈ. Your strong stand for the right will be an inspiration to the citizens of this Republic. It arouses in the breast of every soldier feelings of the deepest admiration for their leader.
>
> I am exultant that my life has been spent as a soldier, in camp and field, that I may now the more worthily and the more intelligently serve my country and you.

Once he had been chosen, Pershing, in turn, began selecting his staff. Because of his length of service and the small size of the officer corps, he knew a large number of the regular officers personally and many more by reputation. For the most important post of chief of staff, he picked his friend and fellow cavalryman, Major James G. Harbord, then a student at the Army War College. A large balding man, fifty-one years old, Harbord had entered the army as a private in 1889 and had worked his way up through the ranks. He had also made his reputation in the Moro country. Frank, and intensely loyal, Harbord became Pershing's closest adviser.

In less than three weeks, Pershing decided upon fifty-eight other officers to accompany him. A few had served with him in Mexico; others he had observed in various assignments. Some came on the recommendation of the bureau chiefs. Those who would head staff sections such as Quartermaster and Ordnance chose their own assistants. Several, including a former Ambassador to France, Robert H. Bacon, were reserve officers. Originally Secretary Baker had thought Pershing would take abroad only "one or two trustworthy aides"; yet this group of fifty-nine would be merely the beginning of the staff Pershing ultimately required.

By the time of Pershing's arrival in Washington, plans for the initial expedition were well under way. On the day, May 10, that Pershing reported to the Secretary of War, the War College Division submitted a five-page plan for "a possible expeditionary force to France," and Woodrow Wilson approved a general and "wholly flexible" plan which Baker had given him. The crux of both plans was that the United States would send a division of approximately 12,000 men to France. Although similar, the plan to which the President assented was not the War College plan. In the confusion of these early days of the war, there was a lack of coordination between the planners in the Secretary's office and those three miles away in the Army War College.

The three officers who prepared the War College Division plan —John McAuley Palmer, Briant H. Wells, and Dan T. Moore— did not know that Baker had designated a commander for the expedition; that Scott had ordered Pershing to select the regiments from his department for overseas service; nor that the Secretary had requested the President's approval of the selection of Pershing and the sending abroad of "about 12,000 men." Indeed, they recommended in conclusion "that the early dispatch of any expeditionary force to France is inadvisable because of lack of organization and training. . . ."

While they prepared their plan, Palmer and his colleagues, together with Major Fox Conner, conferred at length with Joffre's aides. Throughout this period the French influenced the Americans more than did the British because Joffre had a far greater reputation than General Bridges of the British mission, and the rotund Marshal of France made a better impression by asking for a combat division rather than replacements and service troops. Although American military observers in France had been sending back advice and information, it appeared to Major Edouard J. Réquin of Joffre's staff that this was "practically unutilized" by the American General Staff.

Since Joffre had asked specifically for a division, the Americans discussed the organization of this unit with their French advisers. In the course of these conferences, the French convinced their new comrades-in-arms that the American division, which consisted of three brigades of three infantry regiments each plus supporting troops—a total of 28,256 officers and men—was unusable in modern war. Réquin pointed out that there were too many infantry regiments, an "insufficient proportion of artillery and machine guns," and a general lack of subordinate units equipped to handle modern weapons such as trench mortars. At this time the United States did not have a single division in existence, so the Americans could afford to experiment, at least on paper, until they developed a division to their liking.

The French urged a smaller unit of 16,000 to 20,000 men. Palmer and his assistants responded by creating a "square" division—two infantry brigades of two regiments each—which with artillery and other auxiliary troops came to a division strength of some 12,000 men. Before Pershing sailed, the War Department version of this unit was a much larger "square" division of over 24,000. After he arrived in France, Pershing recommended personnel increases until he had raised the strength of the "square" division to about 28,500.

While in Washington, Pershing went over the organization of the expeditionary division and embarkation plans, discussed the munitions situation, and helped make the decision to use the Enfield rifle. The two and a half weeks he spent in Room 223 across the hall from the office of the Chief of Staff in the State, War, and Navy Building were busy ones. There were volunteers to reject and, in a few cases, to accept, formal calls to make on diplomats, and even an impromptu speech before an American Red Cross conference.

By the time Secretary Baker took him to the White House on the afternoon of May 24, Pershing knew that he would command all of the American troops in France and not just an expeditionary division. His first and only meeting with Wilson before sailing was brief and not particularly enlightening to the general. He expected the President to comment on the various Allied suggestions to feed American manpower into their ranks, but President

Wilson did not mention the question of amalgamation. Nevertheless, he did say, "you shall have my full support." They would not meet again until they shared the accolades of victory.

As their sailing date neared, Pershing and Harbord prepared to draft their own letter of instructions. Upon the completion of a rather general letter, they secured the signature of Bliss and assumed that this would serve as the official basis of Pershing's authority as commander of the expeditionary force. Thus, they were surprised when Secretary Baker handed Pershing another letter of instructions as they were leaving for New York. This Baker letter, which Brigadier General Francis J. Kernan, an assistant to the Chief of Staff, had prepared, was more precise than the Pershing-Harbord letter and specifically directed Pershing to keep the American army independent.

The fact that there were two such letters was slightly confusing but did not present a real problem to Pershing. The incident did reflect a situation, however, which worried Pershing and others who visited the War Department in the first months of the war. There was confusion and a lack of coordination under the great pressure of the emergency.

After his visits to Washington in August, Leonard Wood, a particularly bitter and hostile critic, observed, "If there ever was a concrete case of failure greater and more pronounced than the present administration of the War Department, I have never heard of it." In Wood's opinion, there was a lack of strong leadership. It also grieved him that the bureau chiefs were so powerful and that the General Staff, as he put it, "seems to have entirely petered out."

More objective commentators than the former Chief of Staff were also dejected by what they saw in the State, War, and Navy Building. Colonel Robert L. Bullard wrote in his diary in June, "Of my stay in Washington the great impression left is that *if we really have a great war, our War Department will quickly break down.*" Bullard, who passed through Washington on his way to France, also noted the inability of the General Staff officers to cope with the bureau chiefs and was discouraged by the fact that the Acting Chief of Staff, Bliss, was devoting so much of his time to minor details. Another colonel bound for France, Peyton C.

March, found Bliss spending "hours over things that ought to be handled in seconds." The backlog of paperwork—unfinished major and minor business—appalled March. To Pershing, "The War Department seemed to be suffering from a kind of inertia, for which perhaps it was not altogether responsible."

These officers were witnessing the spectacle of a peacetime organization in the throes of a wartime emergency. Men who had performed competently in 1916 were sometimes unable to deal with the problems of 1917. Methods which were effective in conducting the affairs of an army of 125,000 on a peacetime footing frequently were not applicable to the situation of sudden, overwhelming expansion. This was not only true in the War Department but also on Capitol Hill. On June 7, 1917, Secretary Baker expressed privately his irritation about the sluggishness of Congress in dealing with appropriations, "They are still apparently under the impression that they can make itemized and detailed appropriations, and that the War Department ought to be able to get along with the old routine way of doing unroutine things."

Throughout the first weeks of the war, uncertainty permeated the atmosphere and hampered the development of the war effort. Several basic policy questions remained unanswered: What would be the American contribution to the Allied cause? Would it be predominantly economic or naval aid or, perhaps, a large air armada? How large should the army be? On what basis, volunteer or draft, should the government mobilize an emergency army? Would the public accept the draft? Could a large army be fed, clothed, housed, armed, equipped, and trained within a reasonable period? Is an expeditionary force necessary? If so, how large will it be? Could a sizable force be transported to France? Although Americans might hesitate to ask this question, the Allies wondered if the American military professionals could staff and command a large, modern army.

As policy makers dealt with these questions, they also had to consider the position of the Allies. Later, before the Senate Military Affairs Committee, Secretary Baker described the situation: "It was not the problem of doing it our way and letting everybody else take care of himself, . . . but it was the problem of studying the then existing situation and bringing the financial, the industrial, and the military strength of the United States into cooperation with that of Great Britain and France in the most immediate and effective way."

In this period, when officials were considering and making these decisions, increased demands on their time gave them less time to spend studying the issues. The declaration of war brought to Washington not only the Allied missions, with their particular interests and somewhat conflicting advice, but also petitioners for favors, ranging from the location of camp sites to commissions for young men with no particular qualifications. The formalities of receptions and dinners in addition to the conferences with the missions, as General Scott lamented, used up "time by the bushel." And, as a friend of Secretary Baker's observed, "It seemed as if everyone having a moral, political, economic, military, or social fad had seized this time as the one within which the adoption of the fad could be most successfully urged." To control the stream of supplicants and, in effect, to serve as the custodian of his time, Baker relied on a dean from Columbia University, Frederick P. Keppel, who joined his office staff right after the war began.

Civilians such as Keppel (who became an Assistant Secretary of War in 1918) supplemented the military personnel and played a crucial role throughout the war. Particularly in the realm of logistics, the businessmen, lawyers, engineers, and manufacturers provided the skill and knowledge necessary to utilize as rapidly as possible the economic resources of the nation.

By merely supplementing the existing system, however, Secretary Baker ignored a basic problem—one which Wood, Bullard, and others had noted—the lack of an effective coordinating agency. Although the Secretary used his own office in an attempt to carry out this function, Baker was too cautious in dealing with the bureau chiefs, and, throughout 1917 he failed to force them to work together.

The most likely candidate for a coordinating agency within the army was the General Staff. Yet, the General Staff was small and divided, with the bulk of the officers isolated in the War College and out of close contact with the rest of the War Department, including apparently even the handful of General Staff officers in the Office of the Chief of Staff. During 1917, the General Staff neither supervised nor coordinated the bureaus or the other War

Department agencies; nor did the three generals—Scott, Bliss, and John Biddle, who acted briefly as Chief of Staff—increase the power of the General Staff.

George Soule commented on this situation in *The New Republic*:

> When General Pershing thinks of our Chief of Staff, he thinks of an individual who has no connection with any of the other war bodies. General Bliss never confers, for instance, with Mr. [Edward N.] Hurley of the Shipping Board, and none of his subordinates ever does. When Pershing wants to find out how many troops he can have by a certain date he has to refer to a program made up in the War Department. He cannot be sure whether anyone ever asked the Shipping Board upon what expectation of transports and supply ships that program is based. He cannot be sure whether the program for the requisite munitions has taken into account the steel that must be used for building those ships. He cannot be sure that either program has been checked up with the labor supply. If circumstances arise which must alter the program, the chances are that nobody knows it, or that nobody remembers to tell everybody concerned until the physical scarcity of ships or labor obtrudes itself. The remoteness of the General Staff from the conduct of the war naturally disinclines the army to regard it as other than an aloof and secret body which may be making perfect plans for some imaginative invasion of Baluchistan, but is not to be consulted about large, immediate problems.

In his last annual report, dated September 22, 1917, Hugh Scott indicated the solution when he strongly recommended; "There should be one and only one organ through which the Secretary of War commands the Army—the Chief of Staff. . . . [who] should be the medium of recommendation to the Secretary and of execution for his orders. He should have ample authority for securing the coordination of all the activities of the military establishment." To support the Chief of Staff, Scott advocated a powerful General Staff. The failure to give this power to the Chief of Staff and the General Staff, Scott believed, caused much of the delay and confusion throughout the spring and summer of 1917.

In the end, Baker accepted Scott's solution. Nevertheless, despite criticism justified and unjustified, the War Department accomplished much in 1917. The army inducted, fed, clothed, housed, armed, equipped, and began training a huge number of men (almost five times the strength of the regular army on April 1, 1917); and it managed to get some of these men to France. Yet, 1917 was predominantly a time of frustration and promise.

·III·

"...War Isn't All Brass Buttons and Cheering"

While it is impossible to reproduce the state of mind of the men who waged war in 1917 and 1918, perhaps a few specific details can provide a glimpse here and there of what it was like to be young and at war a half-century ago. Besides, there are concrete answers to some questions. How did the army secure officers? What was the state of training of the emergency army? What part did Negroes play in the war? How were conscientious objectors treated? Were welfare agencies important? How bad was the flu epidemic? And there is more to the answers than statistics.

When he reviewed the war experience, a few days after the Armistice, Secretary Baker wrote, "One of the most serious problems confronting the War Department in April 1917 was the procurement of sufficient officers. . . ." For senior commanders and crucial staff officers, the War Department would have to depend on the regulars with some help from the National Guardsmen. Many specialized duties could be performed by physicians, professional men, and ministers with little or no military training. But

Chapter title quoted from Frederick T. Edwards (June 9, 1917).

there still remained the task of developing a large corps of junior officers to fill the positions in the greatly enlarged army.

The wartime army, which reached an eventual strength of about four million, required some 200,000 officers. Since there were only 18,000 regular and National Guard officers, this meant that the War Department trained 182,000 officers within nineteen months. The Medical Department and other specialized branches gave commissions to 70,000 civilians. By commissioning qualified men from the ranks, the army picked up another 16,000 officers. The War Department also reduced the four-year course at West Point—finally to one year—but since there were so few cadets this step did not contribute very many officers.

Almost half—48 per cent—of the army officers who served in the war earned commissions in training camps which were patterned on the prewar Plattsburg idea. The first series of these camps of which there were sixteen located at thirteen Army posts went into operation on May 15. Reserve officers had to attend, and 30,000 other candidates took the first course. The candidates included in their number Spanish-American War veterans as well as college boys. Apparently the largest single group consisted of college upper classmen or recent graduates. For three months, regular, some reserve officers, and a few Allied army instructors trained the candidates. The training was at a basic level—close order drill, School of the Soldier, weapons and marksmanship, route marches, scouting, patrolling, elementary tactics, and, in the artillery and cavalry units, horsemanship. Primarily, it hardened the men physically and inured them to regimentation.

It was a hard summer for the men in the officers' training camps. During his first week at Fort Sheridan, Illinois, Frederick T. Edwards wrote home, "we get up at 5:15; and from then, until ten o'clock at night every hour is taken." Three weeks later Edwards, who had left General Theological Seminary to volunteer, commented to his half-sister, "getting ready for war isn't all brass buttons and cheering. It is like hoeing the garden on a rainy day and lying down every few minutes. Then, when you get tired, come in the house and sit on the edge of a bed and read a few columns of Webster's Dictionary (that's the nearest layman's book to a 'Drill Regulations'). Then go to bed and get up at five o'clock in the morning by bugle, and do it all over again."

At Plattsburg, a prominent Kentucky lawyer who managed to get in the camp although he was in his forty-sixth year (two years over the maximum age limit), Samuel M. Wilson, described one aspect of the training, "We drilled and fought dummies with bayonets until we couldn't see straight." At Fort Benjamin Harrison, Indiana, 700 miles away, Wilson's friend and fellow attorney, Clinton Harbison, wrote, "I wish I had studied military tactics all winter, and let everything else go hang. . . ."

Throughout the camps there was this sense of urgency, of making up for lost time under the pressure of being judged constantly. Shortly before the schools came to an end in August, Edwards described the tension, "Every minute we are able to read and are not studying drill regulations or something of the kind, we have that vague fear that somebody else is and getting ahead of us."

Training continued at a rapid pace despite some shortages of equipment: Harbison had to make an hour-and-a-half trip by trolley to Indianapolis to get oil and rags to clean his rifle, and Edwards started studying horses and horseshoeing without any horses available. The food, naturally, caused comment. Mark H. Ingraham, who graduated from Cornell University a few weeks early so that he could enter the camp at Madison Barracks, New York, recalled that the camp was well run except for the food. Ingraham's plight was relieved somewhat by the availability of Shredded Wheat with raspberries and cream on sale at the canteen. On the other hand, Harbison was surprised by the quality of the food, "They are feeding us here like lords," he wrote Wilson on July 4, 1917.

During the summer there were awkward moments. The most frequent occasion would be when friends had to part, as the instructors weeded out those they considered inadequate. But at Fort Oglethorpe, Georgia, on the battlefield of Chickamauga, the army officers created a painful situation when they asked a Union Army brevet general to speak to the candidates. John T. Wilder, who had led a brigade at Chickamauga in 1863, reminisced how he had killed Johnny Rebs and urged his listeners to go out and deal with the Germans in a similar fashion. The audience of young southerners was stunned. One of them, a poet from Vanderbilt University, Donald Davidson, expressed their attitude, "How could Lee, Stonewall Jackson, Jefferson Davis, or even

Braxton Bragg be equated, as enemies to be slaughtered, with Kaiser Wilhelm, Hindenburg, and *Les Boches?*"

Although the schedule was tight, a few literary officer-candidates managed to nourish their talents. At Fort Oglethorpe, John Crowe Ransom and Davidson, who would later lead the Vanderbilt Fugitive and Agrarian movements, would get together and talk of their art, and Ransom showed Davidson some of his poems in manuscript. In a later series of camps, at Fort Leavenworth, F. Scott Fitzgerald wrote his first novel. It is doubtful if his training unit commander, Captain Dwight D. Eisenhower, was aware of this activity of the handsome boy who slept through some lectures.

On the other side of what seemed to the candidates a large hurdle, the instructors had to work hard to prepare their charges for commissions. There was a shortage of training aids and equipment and, in some cases, of experience. A young reserve second lieutenant of 22 who graduated from Armour Institute of Technology in the spring of 1917, Charles L. Bolté, did have three summer camps to his credit, but at Fort Benjamin Harrison he had to work hard to stay ahead of his students. "When it came to teaching the 45 automatic pistol," he recalled, "I had to sit up all night long with a manual just learning how you took it apart and put it together again so the next day I could sit down as if I knew all about it and try to teach this company how to do this very complicated task. It was a case of the blind leading the blind."

Yet, the training camps did produce officers—27,341 in this first series alone. While a few received field grade rank upon completion of the course and over 3700 were given captaincies, the great majority became lieutenants in the Infantry and Artillery.

The army continued this training system with some variation through two more series and even set up camps in the Philippines, Puerto Rico, Hawaii, and Panama. The men who went through the second and third series had a severe winter to help toughen them. A Rhodes scholar, Chester V. Easum, who reached the United States in time to take part in the second training camp at Fort Sheridan, remembered: "We had to dig and live in trenches for a week near the end of the course. We couldn't drain them so we sloshed in the mud in the cold weather." Easum added, "For sheer hardship this surpassed the trenches in France."

Some military men believed that the officers' training program should do more than teach the fundamentals and toughen the students. Second Lieutenant Frederick T. Edwards indicated that a change was necessary. When he joined a Field Artillery battery after graduating from Fort Sheridan, Edwards wrote in his journal, "My duties are many; my ignorance beyond plumbing. I am quite lost. . . ." The Chief of Field Artillery, Major General William J. Snow, was aware of this situation and criticized the original training procedure for artillery officers, "The only uniformity among them [the officer training camps] was that each was distinguished for its wholly inadequate course of instruction, its incompetent instructors, and its insufficient equipment." What Snow wanted was a special school operated by regular Field Artillery officers. In the summer of 1918, such a school opened at Camp Zachary Taylor, Kentucky. At this time, War Department opened other schools or Central Officers' Training Camps for Infantry, Machine Gun, and later Cavalry officer candidates as well.

Initially, there was no provision for training Negro officers. Shortly after the first series of camps started, a group led by Dr. Joel E. Spingarn of the National Association for the Advancement of Colored People petitioned the army to give Negroes an opportunity to earn commissions. As a result, the War Department established in June 1917 a camp under Colonel Charles C. Ballou at Fort Des Moines, Iowa. Four months later, 639 Negroes received their commissions as Infantry captains and lieutenants. Later, a few Negroes, 140 in all, graduated from various other training camps. Altogether approximately 1200 Negroes held commissions. Those who did not attend the officer training camps entered the service as physicians, dentists, and chaplains, or as National Guard officers. A few others were former regular army NCOs.

During the last fall of the war, the War and Navy Departments cooperated in establishing a training program for some 150,000 students in over 500 colleges and universities. These members of the Student Army Training Corps or its Navy and Marine equivalent wore uniforms and were under military discipline as they took academic courses with some military instruction. Since the war ended within two months after this particular program began, neither service was able to assess its value in developing officers.

In thousands of family albums there is a photograph of a young man standing somewhat uncomfortably in uniform—broad-brimmed, peaked campaign hat, high-collar olive drab blouse and trousers with the unsightly and bothersome wrap leggings. He is saluting or awkwardly holding a rifle. Obviously he is a recruit.

During the year or two he spent in the army, this young man was examined physically and perhaps mentally, classified, counted, and included in many statistical computations and tables. The impersonal mass of statistics indicate certain characteristics about this "typical" recruit. He was in uniform only for the emergency, and chances were seven in ten that he was drafted. More than likely he was between the ages of 21 and 23 and a bachelor. According to the Medical Department of the army, he stood 5' 7½" tall and weighed 141½ pounds. And he probably did not like to be poked or punched in a physical examination or to answer the questions or fill out the forms in the strange, raw environment of a newly constructed army post.

As the army expanded so rapidly under the pressure of the emergency, the need was evident for what Secretary Baker called "a selective process by which we will get the round men for the round tasks, the strong men for the strong tasks and the delicate men for the delicate tasks." Because of the advances in psychology and in scientific personnel research, it seemed possible to develop a system which would make such a process scientific and more or less efficient. Yet on April 6, 1917, there was not a psychologist, as such, in the United States army.

Two university professors of psychology took the lead in rallying their associates to the task of classifying the men in the emergency army. Dr. Walter D. Scott, who not only taught at Northwestern University but also served as the Director of the Bureau of Salesmanship Research at the Carnegie Institute of Technology, was particularly interested in developing scientific personnel procedures, while the president of the American Psychological Association, Dr. Robert M. Yerkes of Harvard University, was fascinated by the possibility of testing and ascertaining the intelligence of such a large group. Although they met with some opposition and a considerable amount of misunderstanding within the army, they were able to obtain official support by the end of the summer of 1917. As an indication of this official sanction, the

War Department commissioned the two professors and a few
of their colleagues. Once in the service, Colonel Scott worked
through the Adjutant General's Department, and Major Yerkes
was affiliated with the Surgeon General's Office but was also a
member of Scott's Committee on Classification of Personnel in the
Army.

By the spring of 1918 the personnel program had gone beyond
the experimental basis. In May the Chief of Staff directed that all
soldiers fill out the 5″ × 8″ qualification cards and that officers
consider this information before making assignments. Despite
this support and the improved techniques, the personnel officers
recognized that there was one particularly obvious flaw in their
program. Unit commanders, hating to lose more intelligent men,
would not report these soldiers' real occupations or skills but list
them as laborers or farm hands. Nevertheless, with such a huge
group to choose from, the personnel people were able to locate
specialists for most tasks with a few exceptions—among them
truck drivers.

Within the army there was more opposition to the mental testing program than to the new personnel system. Major Yerkes at-
tributed this primarily to the misunderstanding and prejudice of
conservative officers. Despite this opposition, psychologists had
also passed through the experimental stage by the spring of 1918.
At that time, they began to administer on a large scale the alpha
and beta examinations for literates and illiterates respectively.
From May 1918 to the end of January 1919 they tested more than
a million and a half men.

The scientists could use the results of these tests in two ways:
to aid in assigning the individual soldier to an appropriate military occupation and to provide an enormous source of data for
analysis of a group as a whole. After the war they selected some
160,000 tests as a general sample, coded and transferred the data
to punch-cards to make possible mechanical sorting and started
examining their material. In addition to this large sample, Yerkes
and his colleagues used other smaller samples—at times limited
to several hundred tests from one camp—to answer their questions.

The results were somewhat surprising. Although the draft
boards had eliminated what the psychologists called "certain fee-

bleminded types," the scientists found that about 31 per cent of the soldiers tested were illiterate. They also declared that 47.3 per cent of the whites and 89 per cent of the Negroes were below the mental age of thirteen and, according to the standards of the day, morons. Either this pioneering testing venture was invalid or most American men in their twenties were very stupid.

The psycholologists had unwittingly directed their tests to a middle-class, fairly sophisticated, and educated group. Even the beta tests for the illiterates included a picture completion section in which the soldier was supposed to recognize that the horn was missing from a phonograph and a net was absent on a tennis court. The information portion of the alpha test was also more indicative of the social milieu of the university-trained men who prepared the test than of the background of the majority of soldiers who took the examination. There is not much doubt as to how Alvin C. York or thousands of his comrades would score on such questions as—

The Overland car is made in   Buffalo   Detroit   Flint   *Toledo.*
Mauve is the name of a   drink   *color*   fabric   food.
Scrooge appears in   Vanity Fair   *The Christmas Carol*   Romola   Henry IV.

Rather than intelligence the psychologists were ascertaining in such tests the soldier's social and educational background, to the disadvantage of the majority of men from rural areas and the urban slums.

The one predominant fact about the "typical" American soldier was that he was temporarily in uniform. He may have entered the regular army or the National Guard by volunteering or come into the National Army via the draft (and regulars looked down on Guardsmen, who in turn were contemptuous of draftees), but he and the great majority of his fellows did not intend to stay in the service. Although the War Department had set aside 1-25 for the regulars, 26-75 for the guardsmen, and 76 on up for the National Army, when it began numbering the divisions, it did not use all of those numbers. Besides, within a year the divisions regardless of designation contained a mixture of components. The army's Chief of Staff recognized this similarity in personnel in August

1918 by ordering the elimination of any distinction among the three components. This resulted in a symbolic removal of the "NG" and "NA" from the "US" collar ornament and in a simplification of officer promotion procedure.

There were professionals, of course, but many of the officers and "noncoms" were serving in the National Guard and National Army divisions while others acted as cadres for newly created regular units. Thus the bulk of the enlisted men and many of the junior officers (including Frederick T. Edwards and F. Scott Fitzgerald) who were in regular units in 1918 had donned uniforms since April 1917.

Entering the army was an unforgettable experience for these citizen soldiers. Almost half a century later, many could recall the exact date. The actual beginnings of their military careers would differ somewhat for those in the three components; yet once in camp their routines varied little.

For those who enlisted in the regular army it meant undergoing a physical examination and, if they passed, taking the oath of allegiance. In a few instances, the procedure was so rushed that men took the oath while still naked. Then there might be a boring wait at a recruit depot until enough men collected to go to one of the units in training.

When the war began, and in some cases before, the National Guard units began recruiting up to full strength. The primary appeal was that the volunteer would serve with his friends in a local unit. The New York "Fighting 69th" Infantry Regiment looked for young Irish Catholics and got them from the Irish County Societies and Catholic Athletic Clubs of New York City. Other units throughout the nation used the influence of their members, the proud traditions, and the stirring music of regimental bands to bring in recruits.

The particular Guard unit the volunteer chose to join might differ considerably in experience from another. A few regiments had remained on active duty since the days of the Mexican Border crisis of 1916. Others, the War Department had called to active service in late March or early April to guard utilities, railroad bridges, and other installations so that, when the war began, slightly more than 80,000 Guardsmen were already in the federal service. In July the President ordered out all of the other Guardsmen with the instructions that all would be in the federal service by August 5.

The volunteer might spend his first nights in the National Guard at home or in the local armory until his unit left for a general concentration area at the summer camp, the state fairgrounds, or at a park in one of the state's large cities. Up to this point he would have a uniform, but probably not much more, to indicate that he was a soldier. There was so much administrative work involved in the organizational process and in preparing for the federal muster that the officers and noncoms had little time to devote to training recruits. Physical examinations and the various inoculations would also hamper a training program; yet, there was enough "squads right" and "squads left" to keep the recruit busy. After a few weeks most of the 433,478 Guardsmen took a train trip to one of the newly established camps in the South or Southwest where serious training began.

While the new Guardsmen were becoming used to camp life, over half a million other young men were undergoing the scrutiny of their friends and neighbors on the Selective Service local boards and the physical examinations prior to their induction into the National Army.

There would be other drafts during the war, but in September 1917 the war was still young enough to permit a spontaneous holiday atmosphere at the departure of these first contingents. Sadness mingled with gaiety as the celebrations eased the pain of farewells. Some communities would give dinners for the selectees and perhaps furnish each man with a kit containing such necessities as a razor, blades, and toothbrush. Bands played—frequently, Civil War airs—as the crowds followed the draftees to the railroad stations throughout the nation.

Some draftees intensified their celebrating after they boarded the train. Three years after the war, Benedict Crowell, a former Assistant Secretary of War, noted one striking incident when a trainload of Arizona draftees were not just drunk "but extravagantly and supremely drunk." There were enough incidents of drunkenness on the trains to cause the Provost Marshal General to change mobilization regulations and to give armbands to the draftees so that technically they would be in uniform, hence subject to discipline.

The draft procedure must have been confusing for the large number of foreign-born (perhaps 18 per cent of those drafted during the war)—many of whom could neither speak nor understand much English. The jumble of new experiences, no doubt, also awed the many native-born Americans who were leaving their counties for the first time. As a draft train sped over the countryside fifty miles west of Danville, Virginia, one of the amazed mountaineers announced, "Bud, if this old world is as big the other way as she is this, she's a hell-buster for sartain."

Hughes Combs of Fairview, Kentucky, and most of his contemporaries dressed up in their Sunday-best suits and hats to go to war. John L. Barkley of Holden, Missouri, later admitted that "he felt like a fool" because he wore overalls on the train to Camp Funston, Kansas. He felt better, thirteen months later, when he won a Medal of Honor in the Argonne campaign.

Since the army did not have enough uniforms, many went for weeks about their military routines wearing some or all of their civilian clothes. Clayton K. Slack of Madison, Wisconsin, wore out his civilian shoes before he received his army issue footwear at Camp Grant, Illinois. He recalled: "It was about two months or so before I looked really like a soldier."

In the fall of 1917 the new soldiers found the partially completed camps and cantonments in rather raw condition. At Camp Wadsworth, South Carolina, New York Guardsmen of the 27th Division had to grub stumps in their company areas, while the Wisconsin and Michigan Guardsmen in the 32nd Division found the remnants of a cotton crop at Camp MacArthur, Texas. And regulars in the Fourth Division at Camp Greene, North Carolina, crowded ten to twelve men into pyramidal tents designed for eight. In the National Army cantonments, workmen were still driving nails when the draftees arrived. First Lieutenant Mark Ingraham, who joined the cadre of the 78th Division at Camp Dix, New Jersey, after completing the officers' training course, was amazed, "This was almost complete disorganization."

The concurrent reorganization of regular and National Guard units compounded the confusion caused by the influx of large numbers of recruits. The War Department used regular battalions as cadres for new regiments. The Fourth Infantry Regiment thus stayed in existence while it furnished cadres for the 58th and

59th Infantry Regiments. The Guardsmen, in turn, had to merge many of their units to conform to wartime strength requirements. In this painful manner, New York consolidated the men of nine regiments into four. At the same time, the War Department forced many Guardsmen to learn new tasks by changing cavalry regiments into artillery and machine gun units. At the camps, there were mock funerals as the citizen soldiers sadly buried their cavalry yellow cords and adapted to their new arms.

Such matters in the regular army and National Guard were of no concern to the draftee. He was too involved in adjusting to his new life. He took a bed ticking, filled it with straw or hay, and established his new home on a cot in the raw barracks. Then he stood in line: at the supply room, he picked up odds and ends of uniforms, blankets, and whatever else was available for issue; at the mess hall, he waited for his food. Like his forebears and successors, he learned that "hurry up and wait" was an army tradition.

While the atmosphere might leave something to be desired, the food was wholesome and plentiful. (The army's daily ration was 4761 calories.) Although the food varied from day to day, a menu from Fort Riley, in the summer of 1917, showed what a soldier might expect:

Breakfast:	Cantaloupes, corn flakes, sugar and milk.
	Fried liver and bacon, fried onions.
	Toast, bread, coffee.
Dinner:	Beef à la mode.
	Boiled potatoes, creamed cauliflower.
	Pickles.
	Tapioca pudding, Vanila [sic.] sauce.
	Iced tea, bread.
Supper:	Chili con carne, hot biscuits.
	Stewed peaches, iced tea.

Yet, soldiers always welcomed a supplement, as a regular recruit, Robert A. Scudder noted, "Oh, my, a box of cake from Mrs. Hazel Leroy Hulit. It sure will hit the spot!"

The new soldier was on the run throughout most of the seventeen-hour day from reveille to taps. A Wisconsin Guardsman, John C. Acker, wrote, "It was drill, drill, drill and then occasionally there were details more tiresome than drill." What time the calis-thenics, drills, training classes, and long marches did not take up, "policing the area" (picking up cigarette butts and assorted trash), helping out the cooks on kitchen police, and assorted other maintenance tasks did.

Several factors complicated the training of recruits—indeed, virtually the entire army—in the fall of 1917. Inexperienced offi-cers and noncoms found it difficult to follow training schedules. Although the French and British provided more than 700 officers and noncommissioned officers to give instruction in the new weapons and techniques of trench warfare, they could not take over the responsibility of training even if the War Department had permitted them to try.

A shortage of weapons also hampered the progress of the new divisions. The men in the Stokes mortar platoons of the 82nd Di-vision never saw a three-inch Stokes mortar until they reached France. In this same division, hand grenades were so scarce that only the officers and noncoms who attended a Grenade School got to throw them. The artillerymen in the 33rd Division had to train with dummy guns for the first weeks. In this entire artillery bri-gade the only officer with Field Artillery experience was the bri-gade commander, Brigadier General Henry D. Todd, Jr. Machine gunners in this Illinois National Guard division were not much better off. By November 1, 1917, after being at Camp Logan, Texas, almost two months, they had yet to shoot an actual ma-chine gun.

Traditonally, the American soldier was a rifle marksman, but in 1917–18 many who wore the crossed rifles insignia of the in-fantry had never been on a target range. Initially, the shortage of rifles forced some drilling with wooden sticks, but when the sup-ply of rifles increased, the rush call for divisions to report to em-barkation ports prevented recruits from using their weapons in practice firing. In June 1918 a staff officer surveyed eight divi-sions in France and found in two extreme cases that perhaps as many as 40 per cent of the men in the Fourth Division and 45 per cent of the total personnel of two infantry regiments in the 77th Division had not fired a rifle in training.

Many who did go through the marksmanship courses were handling a firearm for the first time. Alvin C. York was amazed by the performance of some of his urban comrades in the 82nd Division, "They missed everything but the sky." The mountaineer added, "Of course, it weren't no trouble nohow for me to hit them big army targets. They were so much bigger than turkeys' heads."

Frequent transfers of large numbers of men into and out of the divisions played hob with the training program. To a certain extent, the classification people contributed to the confusion by trying to place specialists in units where they could use their skills. The 82nd Division lost 3000 men this way after three months of training. The official historian of that division complained that the personnel experts had overlooked an important consideration. "Although the soldier might be a very good plumber, lumberman, blacksmith, or structural iron worker, a great deal of Government time and money had been expended in making him an even more valuable specialist in his present occupation: namely, that of a noncommissioned officer, bayonet instructor, hand-grenade expert or machine gunner." Any company officer resented losing his more intelligent men.

The War Department caused more consternation and confusion in National Army divisions by transferring thousands of men to regular, National Guard, and other National Army divisions higher up on the overseas priority list. Thus the 78th Division, which had companies consisting of some 175 men each in November, had less than fifty in those companies in January. On April 1, the division was still at less than half-strength; yet, within two months the 78th sailed with a full complement. In this transfer process the training of both old and new men suffered.

Theoretically, a depot brigade at each National Army cantonment was to provide replacements as well as specialists, but this system did not begin to function properly until the spring of 1918. At that time, the Chief of Staff, General Peyton C. March, decided that the depot brigades could not meet the demands of the increased manpower program, so he ordered the establishment of large training centers where infantrymen, artillerymen, machine gunners, and the various specialists could receive their training before they joined divisions. Earlier in the war, Secretary Baker had rejected the idea of forming centers specifically for training replacements because, as he later explained to March, "the country at the outset would have been shocked to discover how large we thought the losses were likely to be." The new system was more effective, but it came too late to solve the problem for the AEF. Under the pressure of the heavy losses in the Argonne campaign, General Pershing had to break up some divisions in order to obtain replacements for his combat units.

Nature also hindered the training of the wartime army. The severe winter of 1917–18 restricted the outdoors training in the northern camps but the barracks were warm enough to prevent hardship. In the southern tent cities, life was miserable as the soldiers had to cope with extreme cold and snow storms.

Lieutenant Kenneth Gow wrote home from Camp Wadsworth, South Carolina, on December 14, "Everything is frozen up, and we have to melt snow for water to wash in." Two days later he wrote that snow had been on the ground for six days, "Just think of that in South Carolina! The men are suffering a great deal. The thermometer has risen some, but still averaging between ten and fifteen degrees, which is some cold in a tent. My feet are frostbitten, and they are bothering me a good deal."

At Fort Oglethorpe, Georgia, Private Robert A. Scudder used a quilt his mother had sent him to help keep warm. On one morning after a snow-sleet-rain storm at Oglethorpe, Private Frederick A. Pottle and his tentmates found their clothing frozen as the temperature stood at four below zero.

The regulars in the Fourth Division at Camp Greene, North Carolina, had to cut down pine trees and attempt to burn the green wood in the hope of warming up their tents. When the temperature rose, the dirt roads thawed into strips of mud. Since trucks could not move in the morass, the division depended on mule trains to pack rations into the camp. Because of such weather, the men in this division trained only sixteen days between December 10, 1917, and March 4, 1918.

Despite all of the obstacles, men did receive training. The New York National Guardsmen in the 27th Division reached a very high level of training—to the point of engaging in live firing during tactical maneuvers; but others such as the regulars in the Fourth Division had the more common experience: relatively little training beyond physical conditioning and drill. Later, the chief of staff of the 81st Division, Colonel Charles D. Roberts, summed up the training period in a sentence, "We had to improvise."

During World War I, Negroes contributed their share to the American war effort. Often ignored when not maligned, the role of the Negro soldier is still difficult to assess, particularly since the contemporary observers and participants viewed affairs as if through a prism in which they saw themselves and their backgrounds as much as the subject.

Many southerners feared the prospect of training and arming large numbers of Negroes who might be stationed in southern camps. They believed that the uneasy and sometimes violent racial status quo which they maintained might not withstand the wartime upheaval. Conversely, Negro leaders welcomed the opportunity to serve in the hope that their people would discard their status as second-class citizens in the process. Those who attended a conference of the NAACP in mid-May 1917 resolved: "We, therefore, earnestly urge our colored fellow citizens to join heartily in this fight for eventual world liberty. . . ." The editor of the NAACP monthly magazine *The Crisis*, W. E. B. Du Bois, a Harvard doctor of philosophy, strongly endorsed this stand, "Our country is at war. . . . If this is OUR country, then this is OUR war. We must fight it with every ounce of blood and treasure."

The army needed manpower—of any color. For fifty years, four Negro regular regiments (9th and 10th Cavalry and 24th and 25th Infantry) had served and had compiled good records in the Indian wars, the Cuban campaign, and the Philippine Insurrection. In April 1917 there were some 10,000 Negroes including one infantry and two cavalry officers on active duty, among them a West Point trained lieutenant colonel, Charles Young. Another 10,000 Negroes were active at that time in National Guard units in seven states and the District of Columbia. Yet, white regular officers had definite views on how to employ Negroes. John J. Pershing, who had served in the 10th Cavalry in Cuba, expressed this opinion, "Under capable white officers and with sufficient training, negro soldiers have always acquitted themselves creditably."

Secretary Newton D. Baker and Frederick P. Keppel (an Assistant Secretary of War), who had general supervision of racial matters, were more liberal than the regular officers and earned the appreciation of Negro leaders. Later, in the 1930's, it was

Baker who suggested and Keppel, as president of the Carnegie Corporation, who instituted the landmark study of the American race problem of the Swedish scholar Gunnar Myrdal. In October 1917, to aid and advise on racial affairs, Baker appointed as his special assistant a Negro, Emmett J. Scott, the secretary of Tuskegee Institute and an associate of the late Booker T. Washington.

Since the War Department limited volunteering to existing Negro regular and National Guard units, the bulk of Negroes (367,710 of a total of approximately 400,000 in the wartime army) entered the service by conscription.* This restriction on volunteering is a practical explanation of the overdraft of the Negroes, who made up some 10 per cent of the registrants yet 13.08 per cent of the draft army. Another explanation is that Selective Service medical examiners found a higher percentage (almost 5 per cent more) of Negroes physically fit for service than whites who did not volunteer. Then, undoubtedly, some draft boards discriminated against Negroes. Because of such unjust proceedings, Secretary Baker removed the men on three draft boards from office.

In the fall of 1917 the first Negro drafts went to camp under the shadow of two notorious race riots in East St. Louis and Houston in the summer. The Houston riot, which occurred in August, was a clash between Negro soldiers of the 24th Regulars and native whites. The resulting courts-martial of more than a hundred Negroes and the execution of thirteen of the soldiers without benefit of an appeal to the War Department shocked many Negroes, while the incident of the riot stimulated southern protests against quartering Negro troops in the South. Despite the arguments of southern political leaders, the army scattered the Negroes throughout the entire country. Nevertheless, as a nod to existing prejudice, the army tried to preserve a numerical ratio of two to one in favor of the whites in each camp.

Those Negroes who entered the service with expectations of a radical change in white mores were promptly disappointed. Their assignment to separate sections of the camps was no surprise, but some other situations caused comment. Charles H. Williams, a

---

* There were 5,328 Negroes in the Navy and apparently none in the Marine Corps. John W. Davis, "The Negro in the United States Navy, Marine Corps and Coast Guard," *Journal of Negro Education*, XII, 3 (Summer 1943), 345.

Negro who investigated camp conditions for the Federal Council of Churches of Christ, told of one such incident: "In Camp Lee, Petersburg, Virginia, a prayer meeting was conducted in an area where Negro soldiers were located, but a soldier with a rifle on his shoulder was doing guard duty, pacing in a circle around the group to see that no Negroes attended. The comments made by the Negro soldiers under the circumstances were interesting."

Throughout the army, white officers admonished Negroes to avoid trouble off-post by obeying local segregation restrictions while signs—"This building is for white men only"—went up on army posts. Later, Negro soldiers complained that they were more closely confined to camps and punished more severely than whites. Williams summed up their relative status as wartime soldiers, "When there was a shortage they were the ones to suffer."

The most extreme case of discrimination during the war probably took place at Camp Hill, Newport News, Virginia, where stevedore units organized for overseas shipment. In the bitter winter of 1917–18, according to Williams, the Negroes, some of whom had no blankets, lived here in tents without floors or stoves. For four months, the army did not provide these men with changes of clothing or even bathing facilities. Because of these conditions, together with a lack of adequate medical facilities, the death rate at this camp was abnormally high. Before the end of the war, however, the army improved conditions at Camp Hill and even renamed the post Alexander in honor of a deceased Negro West Pointer.

Morale was particularly low in the labor units in which about three of every four Negroes served. These men who loaded and unloaded the cargo ships, built roads, cut wood, and, after the war, reburied the battle dead, were often culls from the Negro combat units. As Williams reported, "In such organizations it was not unusual to find that 75 per cent of the men were illiterate." He added that many had never heard of Germany, much less the Kaiser. Usually under white officers and sergeants who were frequently southerners, they worked hard and received little or no military training. One veteran recalled, "Our drilling consisted in marching to and from work with hoes, shovels, and picks on our shoulders."

The Negro combat units naturally attracted more attention than did the labor battalions. Although the War Department originally considered placing Negroes in separate units within white infantry divisions, it finally created a single Negro division and permitted four other infantry regiments to go to France.

As far as the army was concerned, the 92nd Division was an experiment. Not only were Negroes going to serve in the artillery and various technical branches but also, initially, a large majority (82 per cent) of the officers were to be Negroes. Nevertheless, it was a controlled experiment, since whites held all key positions including all those calling for officers of general and field rank. Since some Negroes had hoped that Colonel Charles Young would command a regiment or perhaps the division, his retirement because of high blood pressure in June 1917 was a great disappointment.

Like the other divisions, the 92nd suffered from fluctuations of personnel, transferring in and out of its units. Over one-fourth of its enlisted men—7511, most of whom had not had any training —joined during the month before it sailed for France. The severe winter also restricted its field training. But the most crucial defect in the preparation of the unit was that it did not train as a complete division in one place in this country. Since elements of the division were scattered in seven cantonments across the country from Camp Funston, Kansas, to Camp Upton, New York, the unfortunate result was that seven different local commanders organized and trained the various units without coordination.

The commanding general of the division, Major General Charles C. Ballou, a West Point classmate of Pershing's, was apparently popular at first with the Negroes. He had served in the 24th Infantry prior to the war, and during the summer of 1917 had commanded the Negro officers' training camp. Although he was the division commander, he had only his headquarters, division trains, and some machine gun troops under his personal command at Camp Funston. Before he took the division to France, he damaged his prestige with Negroes by issuing Bulletin #35 which his chief of staff, Lieutenant Colonel Allen J. Greer, a Tennessean who had a strong bias against the Negroes, signed. This bulletin instructed the soldiers to respect local segregation restrictions in Kansas and tactlessly warned, "White men made the Division, and they can break it just as easily if it becomes a trouble maker."

Since they trained in southern camps, the men in the four separate Negro infantry regiments were in potentially more explosive situations than were the soldiers of the 92nd. Shortly after the Houston riot, the War Department sent the Eighth Illinois National Guard regiment, which consisted of all Negroes from colonel to private, to the camp just outside of Houston. Although their journey from Illinois to Texas was, in part, through a gauntlet of jeering and, on one occasion, stone-throwing whites, these Guardsmen endured the abuse and stayed at Camp Logan without a major racial incident until the following spring, when they moved to a port of embarkation.

The Negroes in the 15th New York regiment had a much briefer stay at Camp Wadsworth, South Carolina. After a few days, the white colonel considered the situation so tense that he asked the War Department to move his regiment. Thus, the 15th "Heavy Foot," as its white officers called it, spent only two weeks in Dixie. In contrast, another Negro regiment, the 371st, consisting of drafted men and white officers, remained at Camp Jackson near Columbia, South Carolina, throughout its training. Nor did the men of the 372nd which consisted of the various Negro National Guard battalions and companies have any unusual trouble at Camp Stuart, Virginia.

During the war there was a change in the attitude of some southern whites as their worst fears did not materialize. The governor of South Carolina, who had gone to Washington in 1917 to argue against stationing Negroes in the South, commended the behavior of the Negro troops in March 1918. And an editorial writer of the Columbia [South Carolina] Record [April 2, 1918] commented, "we have yet to hear of the first unfavorable criticism of the conduct of Negro soldiers in Columbia."

The general white attitude perhaps was best expressed by the chief of police of Rockford, Illinois, who had to deal with off-duty troops from units of the 92nd Division stationed at Camp Grant. He praised the conduct of the Negroes and added that they did "much better than was expected." Apparently, the discipline of the combat units was good, but the question remained of how well the men would do in battle, particularly those in units with Negro officers. Both whites and Negroes assumed that the answer would be determined on the Western Front.

When the Secretary of War reviewed the war experience, in 1919, he declared, "Perhaps the most vexatious problem of military discipline was that affecting the so-called 'conscientious objectors.'" While it was difficult for the wartime generation to understand the position of men whose conscience would not allow them to take up arms, it was virtually impossible for most Americans in 1917 and 1918 to recognize the rights of those who flatly refused to serve in any capacity.

There seemed to be two predominant attitudes toward the objectors. Theodore Roosevelt bluntly expressed what was probably the most prevalent point of view. "The bulk are slackers, pure and simple, or else traitorous pro-Germans." Newton D. Baker represented the other attitude in a letter to President Wilson. The Secretary had just talked with several objectors at Camp Meade, Maryland, when he wrote, "Only two of those with whom I talked seemed quite normal mentally."

There were not very many conscientious objectors. Originally, the Selective Service Act provided only for those members of "any well recognized religious sect . . . whose existing creed or principles forbid its members to participate in war in any form." Later, in December 1917, Secretary Baker stretched the law to permit anyone who had "personal scruples against war" to be considered a conscientious objector. Yet, in all cases, objectors were expected to accept alternative service. In the course of the war, many who registered their objection at one time or the other changed their minds; some, including Alvin C. York, saw combat.

After passing through various stages of persuasion, only 3989 men persisted in their objections. Of this number, 2599 accepted the alternative of noncombatant service, furloughs to work on farms, or assignments to the Friends Reconstruction Unit in France. This left fewer than 1400 men who refused to serve in any capacity. It was this small group which vexed the army. Contrary to public opinion, most of these men were native-born Americans, and, according to the army psychological tests, they were above average in intelligence. The most intelligent, apparently, were the political objectors, many of them socialists, who refused to fight in a capitalistic war. One of these men, Carl Haessler, was a former Rhodes scholar and a professor of philosophy.

When the problem of conscientious objectors arose in the fall of 1917 as the men of the first draft reported to the army, Secretary Baker assigned the task of handling it to his assistant, Frederick P. Keppel. A well-informed, witty man, Keppel had the sensitivity and persuasive ability so necessary in the performance of his delicate assignments. Later, Baker praised him for his accomplishments as the man "standing between the vast impersonal machine of the war-making department and the human beings who were caught, amazed and uncomprehending, by its movements."

Both Baker and Keppel recognized the difficulty inherent in dealing with conscientious objectors within the framework of military discipline. In October 1917, Baker attempted to alleviate the situation by ordering post commanders to segregate the objectors and to treat them with "kindly consideration." Despite the best intentions of the Secretary and his assistant, the objector was virtually at the mercy of his fellow recruits, noncoms, and officers. Much depended on the attitude of the post commander. Major General J. Franklin Bell gave little cause for complaint to objectors at Camp Upton, New York, while conditions at Fort Riley and Camp Funston, Kansas, where Leonard Wood ruled, were particularly bad.

Uncooperative conscientious objectors obviously were not conducive to good discipline and caused, at times, harsh reactions from officers and noncoms. At Camp Sheridan, Alabama, Lieutenant Scott Fitzgerald pulled out his pistol and forced one in his company to drill at gun point. Others who fell into the hands of sadists were beaten, jabbed with bayonets, and abused in various ways.

In the face of the continued refusal of some objectors to serve in any branch of the army, Baker gave in to the advice of his Chief of Staff, General Peyton C. March, and authorized courts-martial for those who were "sullen and defiant," insincere, or active propagandists. In order to determine whether or not a man was sincere or insincere, a Board of Inquiry, consisting of an army officer and two civilians (one was Dean Harlan F. Stone of Columbia University Law School, later Chief Justice of the Supreme Court), visited camps and interviewed objectors. A major criterion for sincerity was whether or not the man objected only to this particular war.

In the end, 504 objectors wound up in front of court-martial boards. According to Norman Thomas in *The Conscientious Objector in America*, the army avoided the legal questions involved in conscientious objection and tried the men for disobedience of a direct order. The trials were swift and decisive: reportedly, one man was tried and convicted in eighteen minutes. And they were unusually harsh, as officers sentenced seventeen to death, 142 to life imprisonment, 299 to terms from 10 to 99 years, and the remainder to lesser prison terms. Only one was acquitted, although higher authorities disapproved 53 of the convictions. Yet, the army did not carry out the death sentences, and within three months after the Armistice it began releasing the objectors from prison. By the end of November 1920 all were free.

The federal government erred in leaving objectors to the jurisdiction of the army. Although Baker and Keppel tempered the army's approach to the problem, in the end, officers treated the objectors as recalcitrant soldiers. There were a few who, by refusing to report when drafted, did become civilian rather than military offenders. Had the government handled all objectors within civilian courts, this confrontation between military discipline and a man's absolute opposition to this war would have been avoided.

Professional soldiers bored Woodrow Wilson, but the hundreds of thousands of young men who became temporary soldiers in 1917–18 were another matter. Although the President could never become very interested in technical military affairs, he was very much interested in the well-being of those young men. He and Secretary Baker were determined that this great draft army would be different, better than armies of the past: this army would not be contaminated by the traditional vices—liquor and prostitutes. As the President wrote in April 1918, "I do not believe it an exaggeration to say that no army ever before assembled has had more conscientious and painstaking thought given to the protection and stimulation of its mental, moral, and physical manhood."

For several months before the war, Baker had considered ways to protect soldiers from vice. As a former Progressive mayor, he was not only aware of the problem but also equipped to deal with it. During the mobilization on the Mexican border, in the summer of 1916, conditions became so bad that complaints reached the War Department. The Secretary asked Raymond B. Fosdick, an energetic young lawyer, social worker, and experienced city official, to investigate the situation. When he returned from a five-week tour of the area, Fosdick corroborated the reports—wherever soldiers were, saloons and brothels had mushroomed and were flourishing. Although a few commanders, notably Major General John F. O'Ryan of the New York National Guard Division, had attempted to do something to remedy the conditions, most officers were apathetic. Baker put an end to this apathy by ordering the commander of the border force to bring vice under control by threatening to move troops away from vice-ridden towns.

In the fall and winter of 1916–17, Baker and Fosdick continued to confer about the vice problem. On April 2, 1917, Baker summarized their conclusion for the President: the army must provide wholesome, organized recreation to counter the temptations of whiskey and women. Within the month, Baker created the Commission on Training Camp Activities and appointed Fosdick its chairman to supervise recreational facilities on army posts. Secretary of the Navy Josephus Daniels soon turned over similar authority on naval bases to the Commission. Later, the secretaries also gave the Commission the responsibility of enforcing sections 12 and 13 of the Selective Service Act which prescribed vice-free zones around the camps and prohibited the sale of liquor to service men in uniform.

Countless soldiers who enjoyed the benefits of Fosdick's organization never heard of him, for the Commission was a coordinating body which supervised the YMCA, YWCA, Knights of Columbus, Jewish Welfare Board, American Library Association, American Social Hygiene Association, War Camp Community Service, Red Cross, Salvation Army—all such agencies which had direct contact with the soldier, as well as the athletic directors, song leaders, and even the post exchanges.

The YMCA, supplemented by the Knights of Columbus and the Jewish Welfare Board, played a key role in the effort, as

Newton D. Baker described it, "to rationalize, as far as it can be done, the bewildering environments of a war camp." At the Y hut with its Red Triangle insignia, the soldier could find stationery and stamps or he might use the long-distance telephone service. At night he could forget army routine by attending a movie or watching the antics of his buddies at the weekly stunt night. Or he might just want to get away from the barracks, sit in a comfortable chair, and read a magazine or a book. There were also educational classes with emphasis on reading and writing for illiterates and, naturally, conversational French for others. One private expressed a view many shared when he wrote, "Here is light, warmth, decency, civilization."

There were complaints. Negroes were not mollified entirely by "separate but equal" huts. Then, in the AEF, the term "that damn Y" was prevalent. The soldier who purchased cigarettes from a Y man found inside the pack a card stating that the cigarettes were a gift, perhaps used stronger language. The basis for such incidents and for much of the criticism was that, at Pershing's request, the YMCA operated the post exchanges in France. The soldier thus saw the Y field secretary as a businessman as well as a social worker and was confused. Overseas, the Salvation Army was the doughboys' favorite organization.

Wooden barracks or pyramidal tents—hundreds of them where only months before there had been fields—offered few amenities, but the Commission on Training Camp Activities generally could take credit for those few. The YWCA operated Hostess Houses where soldiers could entertain their guests in comfort. The K of C and the JWB maintained huts similar to those of the YMCA. The American Library Association serviced well-stocked libraries. Liberty theaters made available movies, vaudeville, and plays to large audiences. If the soldier wanted to buy cigarettes, candy, razor blades, or a magazine, he went to a PX operated by the Commission. When he visited the nearest town, the War Camp Community Service provided service clubs and introductions to the townspeople. In short, the Commission did all it could to ameliorate camp life.

The Commission also set up sports programs at each training camp. Athletic directors, frequently college coaches, supervised instruction and developed intramural teams. Organized athletics was a novelty to most of the men; as a result, the coaches had to begin by getting across the idea of organized play. Football, baseball, soccer, tennis, all the sports, were on the agenda. Boxing was particularly popular. At Camp Devens, Massachusetts, one could see a former Greek instructor from Amherst, Walter R. Agard, sparring with the world champion light heavyweight, "Battling" Levinsky. This was, indeed, a different army.

Old soldiers needed little convincing to support an athletic program, but another Commission project initially provoked grumbling and wry comments. Prior to the war, the singing of some German troops on the march had impressed Fosdick, so when his opportunity came in 1917 he tried to make the American army a singing army by appointing song leaders. According to those who supported the "sings," generals became as enthusiastic as privates about group singing. All over the nation, soldiers and sailors roared out—"Where do we go from here, boys," "Over There," and "We'll hang Kaiser Bill to a sour-apple tree," as well as "Old Black Joe," "Swanee River," and spirituals. Music made tasks easier, song leaders argued. At one camp where a work detail struggled with the onerous chore of pulling stumps, a song leader passing by stopped and led the group in a rousing chorus of "Yaaka Hula, Hickey Dula." After a few more songs, he left them as they continued singing and pulling stumps. A singing army might not be invincible, as one writer vowed, nor did a singing nation emerge from the war as Secretary Baker predicted, but at least music was an improvement over some of the other sounds one usually heard on army posts and naval bases.

Although they were not under the aegis of the Commission, the chaplains played an important role as ex-officio morale officers. Since there was no organized Chaplains' Corps in 1917 and 1918 nor funds to build or to furnish chapels, the function of the 2300-plus army chaplains who served in the war was largely dependent upon their personalities and the will of their unit commanders. Frequently the commanders used them as extra-duty officers to handle mail, the post exchange, or to serve as mess, recreation, and club officers or even as defense counsels in courts-martial. As first lieutenants, the rank held by most, some of the chaplains had to demonstrate their proficiency with pistols on the marksmanship range. Finally, most worked closely with the various welfare agencies to make life more bearable for the soldiers. All of this in addition to visiting the sick, counseling, and holding religious services. As Father William P. O'Connor, First Lieutenant and Chaplain of the 120th Field Artillery Regiment and later Captain and Senior Chaplain of the 32nd Division, commented, "I didn't have any trouble in using my time."

In units, such as the 120th, which had only one chaplain, the priest, in this case, held two services—one for Catholics and one for all others. At Camp MacArthur, Texas, Father O'Connor, who later became a bishop, used the Y hut for masses and then preached atop a boxing stand behind the Y for the general service. Attendance was large for, as Chaplain O'Connor said, "These were very good boys."

The Commission on Training Camp Activities did all it could to keep them "good." The services under Baker and Daniels had one policy as far as liquor and prostitutes were concerned—absolute repression. Under the authority of the Selective Service Act (Sections 12 and 13), Fosdick proceeded to effect this policy. Prohibition was the order of the day for all men in uniform; however, the major goal was to hold down venereal disease, for this was a matter of manpower as well as Progressive morality. In the summer of 1917 the British Expeditionary Force in France had 23,000 men (the equivalent of two of their infantry divisions) in hospitals as venereal cases, and up to that time the French Army had reported a million cases of syphilis and gonorrhea since the beginning of the war. The Americans were determined to avoid such a waste of manpower. As Fosdick later wrote, "Our argument had been not primarily one of morals, but of military necessity, for in those pre-penicillin days venereal disease was a far more crippling disability than it is now."

To the astonishment of many and the outright disbelief of others, Fosdick set out to close the red light districts in the United States. Despite the protest of some politicians—the mayor of New Orleans made two trips to Washington—the Law Enforcement Division of the Commission shut down 116 such districts and attempted to eliminate the streetwalkers from towns near the camps.

Within the camps, the army and the Commission carried on an extensive educational program with movies, lectures, pamphlets,

and posters—all with blunt messages. The army made prophylaxis available. If a soldier turned up with venereal disease, the
army punished him for his carelessness. Under these circumstances, relatively few soldiers contracted disease. While soldiers
might consider the so-called "short-arm inspections" degrading,
one enlisted man recalled—"It got to be so much a matter of
habit that we thought little about it." A study of venereal disease
in five camps during the year ending May 21, 1919 showed that
96 per cent of the men who were diseased were infected before
they entered the army.

Measles, mumps, diarrhea, tuberculosis, smallpox, chicken
pox, meningitis, typhoid, diphtheria, and other diseases, major
and minor, afflicted many and killed some of the men in uniform
in 1917–18. Yet, since the army doctors enforced the general
principles of camp sanitation and preventive medicine while the
Public Health Service cleaned up towns adjacent to the camps,
the disease rates were low. Until mid-September 1918 the Army
could be proud of its record in controlling the sickness of the millions of men in its ranks. Then came the flu epidemic.

"Had the Spanish 'flu' . . . ," wrote Sergeant John C. Acker of
the 107th Ammunition Train, 32nd Division, AEF, in July 1918.
"They started calling it the 'three-day' fever here but couldn't
camouflage it with a name when it runs its course in a week or
more. It hits suddenly and one's temperature nearly chases the
mercury out thru the top of the M.D.'s thermometer, face gets red,
every bone in the body aches and the head splits wide open. This
continues for three or four days and then disappears after considerable perspiration, but the 'hangover' clings for a week or two."

Sergeant Acker was lucky since his flu did not develop into
pneumonia. Those less fortunate, and almost all of the fatal cases
had pneumonia, began to turn blue or a "muddy, claylike pallor,"
coughed a great deal, had temperatures of 103° or above, were
restless and delirious, and frequently died within a week.

Many soldiers and sailors had influenza or another form of res-
piratory disease prior to September 1918. In fact, over a quarter
of the army had it at one time or the other during the war, while
the Surgeon General of the Navy estimated that 40 per cent of the
sailors had such a disease in 1918 alone. In the spring there was a

fairly large epidemic affecting some twenty-four camps in the United States, and in the spring and summer many in the AEF were ill with flu or pneumonia. But the disease emerged as a large-scale killer in September, peaked in mid-October, when one week four out of every 1000 soldiers in the United States died of it, and had almost subsided by the end of the war.

The first cases of the fall epidemic showed up in this country at the naval receiving ship at Commonwealth Pier in Boston during the last week of August. From there it spread over the nation so rapidly and with such deadly concentration on military installations that many people thought it was the work of German agents. Millions of civilians had it, and perhaps as many as a half million died. In Washington, D.C., the schools and churches closed and the government bureaus set staggered work hours to avoid crowding the streetcars. Many people wore gauze masks to evade infection.

At various camps, army doctors unsuccessfully tried to prevent the disease by vaccination or by compulsory daily throat spraying and gargling. Among many people, folk remedies had their sway. In the guard company at Walter Reed Hospital, the rumor circulated that chewing tobacco would ward off the flu, so soldiers manfully chewed tobacco.

On November 5, 1918, General March cabled General Pershing about the situation: "Influenza not only stopped all draft calls in October but practically stopped all training." Since those people in the age group 20–40 were particularly susceptible, military bases virtually became huge flu wards with the well nursing the sick. Recruits, particularly those from rural areas, were the most vulnerable, as over 60 percent of the men in the army who had the disease had been in uniform less than four months. At Camp Cody, New Mexico, one out of every two men in a draft group which reported before the draft calls stopped came down with flu in their first four days at the camp. The hardest hit camp was Camp Sherman, near Chillicothe, Ohio. Here, 46 per cent of the men were recruits. During a terrible period—September 27 to October 13—13,161 men (39.6 per cent of the men at the post) had flu or pneumonia, and 1101 (3.3 per cent) died. At most posts, the epidemic lasted longer—about five weeks on the average—but took a smaller toll. In camps where there were a large number of men who had gone through the milder spring epidemic the rates of incidence and death were much lower. The outstanding example of this was Camp Shelby, Mississippi, with only an 8 per cent incidence rate and 0.29 per cent death rate. Apparently those who had influenza in the spring had a degree of immunity. This is also a reason for the epidemic being less severe in the AEF.

Medical officers commandeered barracks as hospital annexes and tried to do all they could to prevent the spread of the disease. They quarantined the camps, held frequent inspections, ordered the men to put their windows down, tried to reduce crowding in the barracks, put up sheets between beds, and, at one camp, hung up sheets in the center of the tables in the mess halls. The men in tents at some camps furled the sides and put out their bedding to air every day. If a man still contracted the disease, about all the doctors could do was to put him to bed, give him aspirin, keep him warm, feed him a light, hot diet, and hope that he would not get pneumonia.

In the two months, September 14 to November 8, there were 316,089 cases of flu and 53,449 of pneumonia in the army in this country. Although the AEF did not suffer as much from the epidemic, the hospital admission rate in Europe was approximately 64 per cent of that of the soldiers in the United States, and 12,423 in the AEF died because of influenza and pneumonia during the year.

In addition to halting the draft calls and bringing training virtually to a standstill, the epidemic also affected the flow of men to France. At first, the War Department cut shipments by 10 per cent. Within a few days, the General Staff subtracted another 10 per cent. Although the President personally asked General March to eliminate troop shipments altogether during the epidemic, the Chief of Staff argued successfully against cutting off this lifeline to the AEF. Nevertheless, because of the flu March had to ship men who were available rather than follow the normal organizational shipment schedules.

At sea, on the transports, the dreaded symptoms developed despite the careful screening before embarkation and man after man went on sick call. When the flu had run its course, the navy reported that 8.8 per cent of the soldiers who made the crossing during the epidemic caught the disease and over 6 per cent (733 men) of those who had it died. But these proportions compared favorably with the incidence and fatality rates of the disease on land.

After the war, the navy reported 5027 deaths among its ranks from influenza and pneumonia in 1918—more than twice as many as those who died as a result of enemy action—while the army gave out a total of 46,992 deaths (some 3500 less than the total of battle deaths for the entire war period).

For the generation which lived through the war, the world-wide influenza epidemic was a common denominator. Whether at home, in the camps, at sea, or in France, all—soldiers, sailors, civilians—remembered the uncertainty and the fear; and some— the loss.

In the United States in 1917 and 1918, a large army material- ized from a small professional force and hundreds of thousands of civilians. Because of the press of time, the men did not jell into a fighting force until they reached the Western Front. Indeed, many virtually untrained men made the transatlantic crossing.

There were differences in the training camps as men of varied backgrounds met on a common ground. Regulars did not think Guardsmen were professional enough. Some National Guard units were hypersensitive about state pride—who in the 42nd Di- vision could forget the fights between the men of the Fourth Ala- bama and the 69th New York at Camp Mills. Then volunteers despised draftees, and whites kept Negroes "in their place."

There were hardships as men had to adjust hastily to the rigors of military life, and many had to endure the severe winter of 1917–18 with inadequate clothing and tents. And there were deaths: 31 per cent of the men who died in the army during the war died in the training camps.

For many, the war was an adventure with the goal of going "Over There." Yet, others probably shared the mood of a serious young artillery officer. Just before Christmas 1917, Lieutenant Frederick T. Edwards wrote to his family: "How I wish the whole business was over, and that we could pick up the things we did and dropped last Spring. . . . for the war is like a Winter, chill- ing and freezing the soul."

Another young soldier attempted to describe the atmosphere of

the camps in an article in *The New Republic* of December 8,
1917: "The prevailing attitude among the men on the roll of
honor of our new army I am very sure is stoicism, verging on
fatalism. . . . The troubles are being packed away honestly and
courageously in the old kit bag, however wan the smile may be."
But Private Walter R. Agard, late of Amherst, now of Camp Devens, was optimistic: "I am persuaded that this affair means clear
gain for democracy. Men are learning to work and feel together,
chiefly in a clean and vigorous fashion. . . . Oh, yes, in spite of
the popularity of sickening sentimentality in songs . . . and the
continuous and vacuous profanity, one feels that the future for
democracy is considerably brighter because of the community of
thought, feeling and action that these training camps are making
to be."

While the stuff of democracy was in those camps, the objective
was war. Ahead for some two million of these soldiers lay France
and for many, the trenches.

·IV·

The Navy Does Its Share

The extent of the American participation in World War I hinged on the control of the Atlantic Ocean. While the 3000 miles of sea that separated America from her Allies alone presented a logistical challenge in developing and maintaining a large transportation service, the German submarines in the spring of 1917 made the sea an apparently insurmountable obstacle. The thoughts of British naval officers who sadly plotted on their secret Admiralty charts the effects of the U-boat blockade confirmed the expectations of their German counterparts. Before the Americans could make a contribution large enough to gain the balance of victory, they, in concert with the Allies, had to overcome the Atlantic barrier.

Although the American navy had expanded greatly in the previous two decades, there was a legitimate question of its readiness to meet the immediate wartime situation. Traditionally, the navy's basic task had been defense of the continental United States, but the results of the quick war with Spain had enlarged the scope of its mission. The acquisition of the Philippines made it necessary for the navy to provide a guard against Japanese ambitions, while the nation's active involvement in Caribbean affairs required a strong naval posture in that area as well. In that so-called Age of Innocence, the measure of seapower was the dreadnought. These mighty battleships dominated the thinking of the professionals and the civilian enthusiasts. So strong was this almost unshakable confidence that the ominous submarine exploits in 1914 and 1915 failed to break the spell. The submarine had set a new course in warfare and, accordingly, made imperative adjustments in theories as well as in the tools of war. Despite this injunction, as late as November 1915 Admiral George Dewey, who represented the navy's senior advisory board, wrote, "the submarine is not an instrument fitted to dominate naval warfare. . . . the battleship is still the principal reliance of navies, as it has been in the past." When the nation entered the conflict some sixteen months and many U-boat sinkings later, the navy was just beginning to adjust to the demands of the war in progress.

After the war a controversy evolved over the placing of responsibility for the lack of naval preparation. In a congressional hearing in the spring of 1920, various admirals and senior captains heaped the blame on the Secretary of Navy, Josephus Daniels, who countered with the testimony of friendly naval officers and charges of his own. The heat of this dispute, however, obscured the major qualifying facts that, prior to 1917, the United States was neutral and was not preparing to fight a specific enemy. On February 3, 1916, President Wilson had called for "incomparably the greatest navy in the world," and Congress complied in August with appropriations for unprecedented naval expansion. War against Germany made this program seem irrelevant, but at the time the large naval program underlined the nation's neutral stance. At the end of the projected three year building program the navy would be ready to face Japan, Germany, or even Britain with a strong balanced force. Since seven months after Congress passed the great navy bill it was called upon to fight German submarines in cooperation with the Allies, virtually all of the projected large ships were unnecessary. What was needed were small craft—destroyers and patrol boats—which were particularly effective against submarines.

The man ultimately responsible to Woodrow Wilson for achievement or failure in the navy was Josephus Daniels. Intensely loyal to the President, Daniels received in return Wilson's support throughout his eight years in the cabinet. When he took over the large office, overlooking the White House, in the State, War, and Navy Building, Daniels had an established reputation as an influential editor and a powerful politician in North Carolina. As Secretary of the Navy, Daniels never forgot the advice his predecessor gave him—"keep the power to direct the navy here" —and, in his hands, the power remained.

The navy represented a challenge to Daniels's Progressive ideals. In a series of orders which shattered traditions, he provided educational opportunities for enlisted men, barred liquor from ships and naval stations, and established promotion by selection rather than seniority. He maintained a strict vigil on profiteering in navy contracts and repeatedly in annual reports called for an international conference to halt the naval arms race. A friendly, courteous man, Daniels was determined to impose his will upon the navy, and he succeeded at the expense of incurring the wrath of a large part of the officers corps.

Although civilian control of the military is one of the basic principles of the American governmental system, few service secretaries have been strong enough to dominate their professional advisers. After all, the civilians stay for a few years and then return to their primary careers, while the officers remain long entrenched. Daniels was able to succeed because powerful southern Democrats on Capitol Hill supported him as strongly as did his friend in the White House. In addition, he handled his subordinates with shrewdness and toughness. Above all, he carefully protected his position as the only coordinating authority in the Navy Department.

While much of the service opposition to Daniels resulted from the pettiness of conservatives who lamented the loss of the amenities of a wine mess and what they considered the coddling of enlisted men, some of the navy's most brilliant officers, led by Rear Admiral Bradley A. Fiske, had more serious criticism. Their main point of contention with Daniels was his opposition to the establishment of a general staff system. While, as has been mentioned earlier, such a system was set up for the army, principally through the efforts of Theodore Roosevelt and Elihu Root, TR could not convince Congress to reorganize the Navy Department on the same basis. Under such a reorganization the power heretofore divided among the eight separate administrative bureaus would be concentrated into a single office, and the Secretary would receive his professional advice through that office. Since the bureau heads were particularly sensitive about maintaining their independence, even though their responsibilities overlapped considerably, the bureau system led to confusion. President Taft's Secretary, George von L. Meyer, had attempted a partial reform on his own by dividing the bureaus into four logical groups and placing a high-ranking officer over each section. These officers, who were designated as his aides, would then advise him on policy.

Daniels inherited Meyer's reform but clearly recognized that a general staff might lessen his power. Instead he held the coordinating authority at his desk. If Congress established the general staff, which it was considering again in 1915, coordination would center in a naval officer. This bill provided for a Chief of Naval Operations, "responsible for the readiness of the Navy for war and . . . charged with its general direction," with the assistance of fifteen officers. This was "Prussianism" as far as Daniels was concerned, and he used his influence to gain a modification of the plan. The bill which passed merely provided for one officer who was definitely responsible to the Secretary of the Navy. Daniels then bypassed the admirals and chose the cooperative commandant of the Philadelphia Navy Yard, Captain William S. Benson, as his Chief of Naval Operations. In 1916, as a part of its great navy bill, Congress strengthened the office under Daniels's careful watch, but the compromise solution did not please the general staff advocates. It would take almost thirty years and the influence of Fleet Admiral Ernest J. King to bring about full realization of the power of the Chief of Naval Operations in World War II.

The struggle over the general staff emphasized the gulf of understanding and the difference in viewpoint between Daniels and many of his officers. Rear Admiral William F. Fullam, the wartime commander in the Pacific, later testified, "he did not want to give admirals much authority, and I cannot tell you how it hurt us. He did not trust us. He did not take our advice. . . ." A younger officer who served from 1913 to 1915 in the Navy Department and during World War II as Chief of Staff to the President, Fleet Admiral William D. Leahy, commented, "I had always a feeling that he did not like naval officers as such and had little sympathy with or understanding of their troubles." In turn, naval officers demonstrated little appreciation of Daniels's progressive beliefs and his attitude toward civil-military relations. The young Assistant Secretary, Franklin D. Roosevelt, a navy enthusiast and admirer of some of Daniels's most bitter naval critics, was able to alleviate the situation somewhat, yet mutual distrust remained. During the war the Secretary did not delegate authority as freely or fully as did the Secretary of War. His attempt to maintain a tight rein on his leading representative in Europe, Admiral William S. Sims, even to the point of picking his key subordinates, caused more bitterness and problems. The resulting hierarchy of command, which would give the impression that Daniels was dividing his admirals in order to master them, tended to impede decisions and to create confusing situations. A more understanding or diplomatic man should have been able to retain civilian control without the bitterness and without sacrificing maximum efficiency.

Whether he liked the officers or not, and he did have a small coterie of favorites, Daniels had to depend on them to carry out his policies. On the eve of the war in 1917, there were 4376 commissioned and warrant officers in the regular service. The seniors in rank and age had begun their careers on sailing ships in the 1870's and 1880's. Now they were forced to deal with the complexities of oil-powered warships which dwarfed the mightiest sea craft of their youth, and they also had to assimilate the impact of such recent innovations as the submarine, airplane, and radio. Some had the advantage of higher professional training at the Naval War College, which, incidentally, Secretary Daniels encouraged, but most measured their professional ability by the years of sea duty in the days of sail, coal, and, now, oil. Naturally, they were cosmopolitan, and a few such as Hugh Rodman, who would be one of the more important admirals in World War I, had an inexhaustible supply of yarns about experiences which spanned the world. As a group, the officers were conservative.

Throughout their careers, the system of promotion by seniority, which Daniels recently had abolished, nourished such an attitude. Only a few had risked unpopularity by rising above its confines, among them the lowest ranking rear admiral in March 1917, William S. Sims. Tough and ambitious, the officer corps would demonstrate its competence in wartime.

During the war, the Navy Department had to take some special steps to obtain officers to supplement the total of 5100 regulars and reservists who held commissions in the navy and to expand the Marine Corps officer corps from just over 400 to almost 2400. The navy needed 26,000 officers within a matter of months. Secretary Daniels encouraged giving enlisted men opportunity to obtain commissions and developed emergency officer programs in both the navy and Marine Corps for that purpose. But some civilians were still required. Merchant marine officers and professional men with special skills helped out, but Daniels had to order the commandants of the various naval districts to select qualified recruits as well as other enlisted men for training in "Officer Material" schools to fill the quota. The navy also trained 2300 reserve officers in a special course at Annapolis and shortened the regular course at the Academy to three years, while the Marines put about 400 candidates through officers' training at their new base at Quantico, Virginia. Toward the end of the war, the navy also cooperated with the army in the college-student training program, but the war ended before this could be of much help.

In early 1917, the regular officers and the force of some 60,000 men who manned the 300 ships and 130 shore stations went about their normal peacetime chores. The element of the navy most likely to be affected by any changes in the European war was the Atlantic Fleet, which was at its winter base in Guantanamo, Cuba. On February 3, however, the break with Germany provoked emergency action. Prior to this there were preparatory moves at a higher level, but they had little impact on the routine. The creation, in 1915, of a consulting board, chaired by Thomas A. Edison, had carried out a survey of the nation's industrial preparedness. Later, emphasis on reserve and militia affairs, including the development of an "Ocean Plattsburg," had increased the potential of civilian components. Then, the congressional enactment of the large navy program in 1916 had stimulated per-

sonnel increases as well as the laying of keels. But these steps had
little immediate effect on the officer on watch or the seaman
checking a pressure gauge on one of the Atlantic Fleet's warships.
The break with Germany, however, meant that these officers and
men had to be ready for combat at short notice.

Two months remained before the actual declaration of war.
During that period the Secretary and his Chief of Naval Operations acted deliberately and carefully to avoid stepping beyond the
bounds of neutrality. In the previous October, the Germans had
made the point that the United States was within range of their
submarines when the U-53 called at Newport, Rhode Island.
Without taking on fuel or supplies, the U-boat went back to sea
after a few hours. The visit encouraged the fear of a large-scale
German submarine raid so the navy primarily took precautions
against submarine attack. Now the Atlantic Fleet left Guantanamo for a safer Cuban harbor and, in March, steamed north without lights under wartime conditions. The Navy Department began
a recruiting drive, which was stepped up again in late March
when the President authorized an emergency expansion in personnel. The ships were still short of officers and men, and the
decision to requisition regulars from warships for the gun crews
on merchant ships increased this shortage. For war service, approximately two-thirds of the battleships, cruisers, and destroyers
required material repairs. In Washington the group of senior advisers—the General Board—together with younger officers, drew
up various plans. Antisubmarine warfare was the keynote, but in
a neutral, defense-only vein. On March 24, Secretary Daniels conferred with shipbuilders, placed an order for 24 destroyers, and
commented in his diary, "Did so only because of emergency." In
those last days of neutrality some naval officers perhaps could
draw consolation from the prevalent idea that, if war came, the
American contribution would be moral and financial. This
seemed realistic on the basis of an appraisal of the nation's military and naval preparations.

During the last week of March, Woodrow Wilson made the decision to begin active collaboration with the British navy. As war
became inevitable, he wrote Daniels, "The main thing, no doubt,
is to get into immediate communication with the Admiralty on
the other side (through confidential channels until Congress has

acted) and work out the scheme of cooperation." A cable from the ambassador in London prompted this action—the dispatch of an admiral to confer with the British. After choosing and then rejecting Captain Henry B. Wilson for this secret mission, Daniels consulted with Assistant Secretary Roosevelt and chose the President of the Naval War College, Rear Admiral William S. Sims. Sims was called to Washington and, in brief interviews with Daniels and others, given oral instructions. Although there would later be some confusion over the exact nature of his instructions, Sims assumed that he was to determine how "America could best cooperate with the Allies in the event of war." He was also impressed by Admiral Benson's admonition. The Chief of Naval Operations, who was well acquainted with Sims's strong pro-British attitude, warned, "Don't let the British pull the wool over your eyes. It is none of our business pulling their chestnuts out of the fire." When Congress declared war a few days later, Sims and an aide, traveling incognito in civilian clothes, were at sea on the passenger steamer *New York*.

Daniels made one of his wisest decisions in selecting Sims for the task which would make him the most prominent American admiral in the First World War. At fifty-eight, the tall and handsome admiral with a precisely clipped beard was in his forty-first year of service. After the war, he wrote, "Verily, we must be on our guard against the dangers of a lack of vision and of a lack of confidence in the conclusions derived from a candid and logical examination of the significance of established military facts." Throughout his career, Sims had provoked many of his superiors or "P.D.s," "Principal Dignitaries" as he referred to them, in his forceful pursuit of that policy. One of his subordinates, Fleet Admiral William F. Halsey of World War II fame, later commented, "He seemed to exult in affronting authority." Another World War II leader who served under Sims, Fleet Admiral Ernest J. King, added, "To him all matters were clear white or dead black." As a lieutenant, Sims had jumped over his senior officers in an unorthodox direct appeal to President Theodore Roosevelt to improve the navy's poor marksmanship. And he drastically improved gunnery as a result. When he commanded the Destroyer Flotilla of the Atlantic Fleet, he had established by training a general standard approach to situations so that detailed instructions became unnecessary in most cases—a doctrine for destroyers. A graduate of the Naval War College, Sims deplored the tradition-minded "old-salt" type of officer who never rose above routine thought. In his unending assault on inefficiency, Sims made a multitude of enemies. His biographer wrote, "The cheerful crusader rode off in many directions and if he did not always deliver Jerusalem, he killed a gratifyingly large number of infidels on the way." Brilliant, supremely confident, and right most of the time, Sims kept up his crusades through his retirement years until death stilled his acid comments.

In 1917, probably no other American officer was as welcome in British naval circles as was Sims. Since 1900, he had developed close relationships with various British officers including the First Sea Lord of the Admiralty, Sir John Jellicoe. Through his gunnery interests, Sims had cultivated these men on annual visits to England, had exchanged information with them, and had established close friendships. Born in Canada of American parentage he enjoyed his daily tea and admired the code of manners of the English cultivated gentleman. In one celebrated incident, he had stated indiscreetly his views on British-American relations. During a good-will cruise in 1910, Sims, then in command of a battleship, had given an informal speech at Guildhall in London. He struck the keynote in these words, "If the time ever comes when the British Empire is seriously menaced by an external enemy, it is my opinion that you may count upon every man, every dollar, every drop of blood, of your kindred across the sea." This, of course, greatly exceeded an officer's prerogative and infuriated President Taft, who publicly reprimanded him, but the British were delighted. With this background they immediately accepted Sims.

On April 10, Sims arrived in London and called on Admiral Jellicoe. After the two old friends exchanged greetings, Jellicoe handed him a record of shipping losses. In the past two months of unrestricted submarine war, the Germans had sunk over a million tons, and the figures for early April indicated that they would almost double that total by the end of the month. Since the British government had distorted this information in the press, Sims was not prepared for such astonishing news. He expressed his amazement to Jellicoe, who commented, "It is impossible for us to go on with the war if losses like this continue. . . . They will win, unless we can stop these losses—and stop them soon." When Sims asked, "Is there no solution for the problem?" Jellicoe replied without emotion, "Absolutely none that we can see now." In the next few days, as Sims met various other civil and naval officials, he learned that pessimism was general—the current estimate being that Britain could not hold out beyond November 1. The Prime Minister, David Lloyd George, seemed to be the only source of optimism, and Sims ascribed his attitude to "his irrepressible gaiety." Four days after his arrival, Sims cabled the Secretary of the Navy a description of the desperate situation and made the recommendation to send immediately the "maximum number of destroyers . . . accompanied by other antisubmarine craft. . . ."

While Sims was becoming acquainted with the situation in the Admiralty, Daniels and three naval advisers—Admirals Benson, Henry T. Mayo, and Captain Henry B. Wilson—conferred in Washington with a British vice admiral, Sir Montague E. Browning, and Rear Admiral R. A. Grasset of France. On the afternoon of April 11, these Allied representatives made their suggestions for the use of the American navy. In the main, they wanted the Americans to patrol their own Atlantic coast and to assume the responsibility of the Caribbean, Gulf of Mexico, and waters off the coasts of Canada and South America. Two weeks before, Daniels had decided to form such a patrol and had selected Captain Wilson as its commander. The rest of the policy seemed to be a logical cooperative move, so Daniels agreed. Before the afternoon session ended, Admiral Browning asked that the Americans send at least one destroyer to show the flag in European waters. Daniels responded by turning to Mayo, the commander of the Atlantic Fleet, and ordering him to prepare six destroyers for distant service. "O for more destroyers!" Daniels wrote in his diary that night, "I wish we could trade the money in dreadnaughts for destroyers already built." On April 24, the six destroyers left Boston Harbor for the war.

The most difficult problem in fighting submarines was finding them. Because of a destroyer's speed, maneuverability, and the newly developed depth charge (a large can of 300 pounds of TNT which could be hurled overboard to designated depths), the destroyer was more than a match for a U-boat if it could locate one.

However, the Allies had failed to come up with a tactic which would employ the destroyer effectively. As it was, the destroyers merely patrolled individually in allotted areas in the danger zone and hoped to find a submarine. When Sims talked with Jellicoe, he suggested grouping together several merchant ships and escorting them through the zone. Such a tactic would force the submarines to come to the destroyers. An element of chance was also involved. Under existing conditions, submarines could easily avoid destroyers and have twenty to thirty opportunities to attack single vessels, for example, while an escorted convoy of twenty to thirty vessels would afford only one target protected by several destroyers. President Wilson had thought of this possible solution in late February, and the Prime Minister was enthusiastic about it, but Jellicoe demurred. He told Sims that the Admiralty had debated adopting the convoy in February but had decided against it. "The merchantmen themselves are the chief obstacle to the convoy," he said, because they did not believe that they could steam in such close formation and carry out the protective zig-zag maneuvers.

Desperation forced a trial of the convoy in May. The British formed a convoy and routed it from Gibraltar to England. On the day after these ships arrived safely the Admiralty voted to adopt this tactic. There was grumbling among merchant captains, and some merchant ships always straggled in the formations, but by the end of the summer the convoy operation was working smoothly. In time the system resembled, as Sims described it, "the method of handling freight cars on the American . . . transcontinental lines." Railroad terminology was even used as convoying became routine.

The nerve center of this great transportation organism was an office in the Admiralty. Here representatives of all nations involved in the operation gathered about the huge chart which showed not only the convoys at sea but also their submarine enemies. Since the U-boats were notorious for their chattering radios, British Intelligence usually knew their courses. On the basis of this information, Allied officers scheduled departure and arrival times and routes for the convoys.

The American contribution to the convoy operation was an integral part of the Allied system. Many of the cargo and transport vessels were American, and the United States provided also a large share of the escort ships. On May 4, 1917, the first six destroyers took station at Queenstown, in southern Ireland. Four months later, the navy had strengthened this detachment to thirty-five and had sent converted yachts (including J. P. Morgan's pleasure craft *Corsair*), older, smaller destroyers, coast-guard cutters, and minesweepers to Brest and Gibraltar. As the Atlantic Ferry reached its peak in 1918, the Americans opened up new bases and increased the size of their early ones. When the war ended, a large majority of the 373 ships plus many of the airplanes operating off the European coast were directly involved in protecting convoys, while another twenty-four cruisers were running out of American ports to conduct the transports across the Atlantic to the rendezvous with the destroyers or other patrol craft. Sinkings continued but at a drastically reduced rate. In November 1917, the date which prior to the adoption of the convoy the English thought would mark the end of their endurance, the losses were down to about one-third of the April total. Shipbuilding soon surpassed losses, and, during the last months of the war, convoys lost only one per cent. After an analysis of the panorama of the war effort, Sims later concluded, "The most important agency in frustrating the submarines was the convoy system." Admiral Jellicoe agreed and in his book *The Submarine Peril* added, "this was only made possible at the date adopted, by the entry of the United States into the war." So impressed were American naval officers that in World War II they were unwilling to dispense with the convoy system when scientific advances made new methods more feasible.

Generally, Woodrow Wilson was not interested in military affairs, but the pressure of the submarine war forced him to think about naval strategy. In February 1917 he had discussed the possibilities of convoying with Secretary Daniels, and throughout the ensuing summer he repeatedly urged an offensive against the submarines. "We are hunting hornets all over the farm and letting the nest alone," he protested in an impromptu speech to the officers of the Atlantic Fleet in August. Wilson's homely metaphor was undoubtedly logical. At the peak of their strength in October 1917 there were 127 German submarines. If the Allies could find a way to keep those submarines from reaching the open sea, the

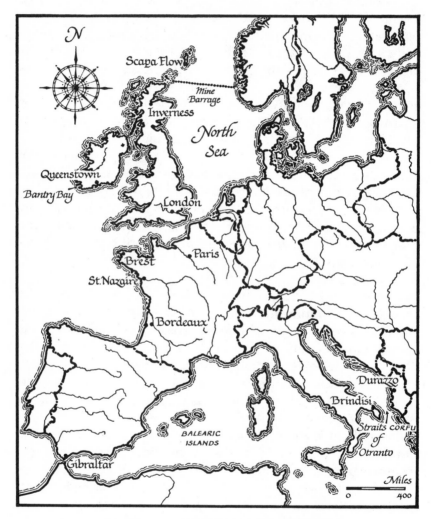

N

Scapa Flow

Mine
Barrage

Inverness

North
Sea

Queenstown

Bantry Bay

London

Paris

Brest

St.Nazaire

Bordeaux

Durazzo

Brindisi

Straits CORFU
of
Otranto

BALEARIC
ISLANDS

Gibraltar

Miles

0   400

U.S. NAVAL OPERATIONS IN EUROPE

submarine war would be over. Two American inventions would help make Wilson's proposal realistic.

The first was a listening device which not only could detect submarines up to twenty miles away but also could determine the direction of the sound. Since the Americans were building a small patrol craft—the 110-foot wooden subchaser modeled on the sturdy New England fishing boat—they had an excellent vehicle for the detection instrument. Equipped with radios, these small boats, operating in groups of three, would drift with their long tubes suspended in the water. When they got a fix on a U-boat, they could converge on it and drop depth charges or call for help from destroyers. Eventually, 120 American subchasers were operating out of four European bases. Manned and officered largely by young reservists, these small boats made life uncomfortable for submarines and helped to seal off egress from the Austrian Adriatic ports and from the English Channel.

The second invention, the result of a collaboration between a civilian, Ralph Browne, and a naval officer, Commander S. P. Fullinwider, made possible the mining of the 250 mile North Sea strait between Scotland and Norway. A glance at the map had caused many civilians, including Assistant Secretary Roosevelt, to consider the feasibility of such an operation. But navy men knew that with the mines then available (which required actual contact to explode) the mine barrage would require a logistical investment far beyond its return. Besides in 1917 the ships required for laying and patrolling the field were needed to conduct the convoys. By July, however, Browne and Fullinwider had a mine, with an electrical antennae firing device, which could reduce the original estimate of 400,000 old-type mines to 100,000 of their version. In November the British and Americans agreed to try the scheme. Seven months later the mining force arrived in Scotland to begin the dangerous task. With the American Rear Admiral Joseph Strauss in general command and another Yankee, Captain Reginald R. Belknap, a stern disciplinarian and experienced mine-force commander, in charge of the actual sea work, the ten mine-layers were ready for their mission. During the five months remaining, the Americans planted 56,571 of the 70,117 mines in the North Sea Barrage. Although the British and American mine-layers did not complete the planned minefield, they struck a hard blow at the submarine. The tally of actual destruction of submarines was always difficult, so the miners could only claim four certain kills and four possibles; but the impact on the morale of submarine crews was immeasurable.

New dimensions in war provided other antisubmarine weapons. Aircraft could reconnoiter near ports as well as bomb enemy bases. During the war the Americans operated twenty patrol bases in England, France, and Italy and contributed 112 planes to the Northern Bombing Group with the mission of striking the German bases. The nucleus of 129 pilots and mechanics who arrived in France in June 1917 expanded to some 19,400 officers and men overseas—an awesome total in comparison with the 278 in naval and marine aviation on the day the war began. Submarines and "Q" or mystery ships also fought the German menace. Twelve American submarines operated out of the Azores and Ireland during the war. The men who took these vessels under water had as much to fear from cases of mistaken identity as from the enemy. Although they did not receive credit for an actual sinking of a German U-boat, one, the A L-2, had the surprising experience of seeing a U-boat blow up accidentally in the summer of 1918. The "Q" ship was a pet project of the English. These disguised, heavily armed merchantmen attempted to decoy submarines to a surface attack and then destroy them with gunfire. The one American "Q" ship, *Santee,* had the disgusting misfortune of being torpedoed before getting a crack at its enemies.

The vaunted dreadnoughts and their smaller sisters, the cruisers, also played a role in the submarine war. Indeed, the British preponderance on the surface had forced Germany to seek victory through submarines. Although surface actions were few—no really great actions after Jutland in May 1916—the British Grand Fleet, running out of Scapa Flow and Rosyth, served as a crucial deterrent. As long as the Allies possessed that mighty instrument of war, German naval activity was limited to submarines and occasional sorties by surface raiders. The Grand Fleet also made possible the blockade which kept German merchant ships from the high seas and dampened the German war effort. In order to replace some of their battleships, the British asked for a division of American dreadnoughts. The five, coal-burning battleships joined the Grand Fleet as its Sixth Battle Squadron in December.

As far as operations were concerned, these American battleships became a unit of the British Navy under the orders of Admiral Sir David Beatty. The Americans and the British did more than work smoothly together in the Grand Fleet. As the American commander later wrote, "Our friendship ripened into a fellowship and comradeship, which, in turn, became a brotherhood. . . ." This commander, Rear Admiral Hugh Rodman, who was a Naval Academy classmate of Sims, did much to create this relationship. A colorful Kentuckian who loved the sea, Rodman, according to Fleet Admiral Ernest J. King, had "no sympathy for a theoretical approach to his profession"; but he quickly became a favorite with the British and with his earthy comments and yarns even made the King laugh. Another American contingent of three battleships, under the command of Rear Admiral Thomas S. Rodgers, made their base in Bantry Bay on the southwestern coast of Ireland in late August and early September 1918. Their mission, which fortunately proved unnecessary, was to be available if German surface raiders made a last attempt to break out and attack the shipping lanes.

In all, some 81,000 Americans operated 47 bases and more than 370 ships in the European theater. The commander of this force was Sims, who received promotion to Vice Admiral in May 1917 and, in early June the title of Commander, U. S. Naval Forces Operating in European Waters. Throughout the war, Sims maintained his headquarters in London. It was indicative of the increased complexity of war that his quarterdeck was a residence in Grosvenor Gardens instead of the traditional warship. Although he visited many of the bases and the ships located in Ireland, England, Scotland, France, and Italy, his primary duties called for his presence at conferences with his staff and with Allied naval leaders.

His headquarters, which consisted of 200 officers and approximately 1000 sailors in the fall of 1918, took up six residences near the American Embassy. It had begun with just two officers —Sims and his aide, Commander J. V. Babcock, who had to type out the early reports with his two-finger system. One of Sims's most telling criticisms of the Navy Department—that is, Daniels and Benson—was that he had to carry out his duties on this basis in a small room in the American Embassy during the first four months. Despite Sims's repeated requests for more help, the Navy Department pled a shortage of officers and did not decide to build up the London headquarters until November 1917. This was in marked contrast to the attitude of the War Department toward Pershing and his staff.

Once he got one, Sims knew how to use a staff. He avoided the greatest pitfall of a commander in that he refused to lose himself in details. After he obtained enough officers, he divided his staff into twelve sections,* named their chiefs, and then placed complete trust in them. A thirteenth section, Planning, which consisted of five Naval War College graduates, he used to keep constant watch on the efficiency of organizations and methods as well as to make plans.

Many old-time sailors such as Rodman never appreciated the change in warfare which caused Sims to build up a large staff and to hold command in a shore headquarters. The image of Dewey on the bridge at Manila Bay was still too strong. Sims stayed in the Carlton Hotel and daily walked to his headquarters, attended conferences, signed papers, and made decisions. To be sure it was less dramatic than lashing oneself to the rigging like Farragut at Mobile Bay, but Sims was fighting another kind of war.

The sea war also forced Sims to take a different approach to relations with the Allies from that of Pershing. Conditions on the Western Front allowed Pershing over a year to develop an organization and to collect a sizable force before the American infantrymen went into battle in large numbers. Although the Allies constantly protested that it was a luxury, the situation permitted Pershing to form an independent army. When Sims arrived in London, the naval situation was desperate. There was no time even to consider building a separate force. The Allies needed men and ships immediately. Sims's reaction was to accept the position of a junior partner both in experience and in material contribution. The American navy in European waters thus became in his words, "virtually a part of the Allied navies." The commander of the American force at Gibraltar, Rear Admiral Albert P. Niblack, explained the relationship in these terms, "We consolidated with

* Intelligence, Convoy Operations, Antisubmarine, Aviation, Personnel, Communication, Matériel, Repair, Ordnance, Medical, Legal, and Scientific. A civilian scientist headed the last section.

them." This did not mean that the Americans were replacements in the sense of one American vessel joining a British unit but that Rodman's battleship division retained its national identity while under orders of the British Grand Fleet commander. The result was impressive as the officer who took over the first division of destroyers, Commander Joseph K. Taussig, commented, "The unity of command at Queenstown resulted in an efficiency of operation throughout the war which was beyond anything I had dreamed possible. . . ."

This successful collaboration required tact and "a spirit of self-effacement" for which Lord Jellicoe later praised the Americans. It also demanded an overlapping command system. Sims fostered the cooperative attitude by personal example and by ordering his officers to refrain from criticism of the Allied "methods, manners, and customs."

The command problem was more complex. Sims met frequently with the Admiralty, worked out general problems with these officers, and approved or disapproved decisions involving his forces. He also attended the conferences of the Allied Naval Council and helped shape general policy and, accordingly, allocated resources as the American representative. Although he was the commander of the American forces, he delegated the operational command of the many units to the various Allied senior officers actually present while he retained administrative control. For example, at the large destroyer base at Queenstown, a British Vice Admiral, Sir Lewis Bayly, assigned the American destroyers to their particular tasks, while an American captain, J. R. P. Pringle, was responsible for the maintenance of the ships and administration of the American unit. The American naval forces in France, under Vice Admiral Henry B. Wilson, operated somewhat differently. At Brest, Wilson, who left the patrol force in the summer of 1917 for overseas duty, took the responsibility of handling the operations as well as the maintenance of the convoys and their escorts.

Between the London headquarters, *Simsadus* in code, and the key subordinate bases there was a steady reciprocal flow of information, with the former also sending instructions and receiving recommendations. If one of the subordinate commanders did not agree with the order of an Allied commander, he could protest to

Sims. In the North Sea mining project, British Admiral Beatty gave American Admiral Strauss an order not to mine an area in the vicinity of the Orkney Islands; Strauss thought that this decision was unwise and so informed Sims. In turn, Sims took the question up with the Admiralty and brought about the rescinding of Beatty's order.

In the period prior to almost instantaneous communication around the world, the problems of time and space seemed to dictate increased responsibility for a commander at great distance from his home base. The War Department granted Pershing almost complete independence, but the Navy Department took another approach to Sims's position. While of necessity Daniels and Admiral Benson delegated much of the authority and the responsibility to Sims, they never permitted him certain prerogatives or gave him the support which he deemed the task required. Naturally, Sims complained because the Secretary did not allow him to participate in the choice of the flag officers who held command under him. Then, he had the title of force commander for months before he was able to get the Department to send him a real staff. Sims also protested the delay at home in acting on his recommendations. For instance, he received the first general statement of policy on cooperation with the Allies in July—three months after his arrival in London. At times he was caused embarassment when the Department made decisions without informing him. For example, as Sims wrote Rear Admiral Mark L. Bristol on September 2, 1918, about the assignment of three battleships to Berehaven, Ireland, "I was, of course, not consulted about the ships that would come over here on the duty in which you are now engaged. I may also say that the sending of the ships over here was not a part of a plan made on this side." The phrase "of course" is indeed a comment on the Sims-Navy Department relationship.

While one might expect some friction and misunderstanding in a situation in which a commander is 3000 miles distant from his superiors, other factors helped promote difficulties between Sims and the Navy Department. In the first place, the men in Washington believed Sims to be pro-British. During the fall of 1917, the Secretary sent abroad Benson and Admiral Henry T. Mayo, commander of the Atlantic Fleet, in part to make sure that American interests were being represented properly at Allied conferences. While he was in London, Benson told Sims, "that there was a feeling that he was being influenced unduly by the British . . ." and urged him to be more careful. He repeated the advice in 1918. After the war, Daniels accused Sims of suffering from the "peculiar malady which affects a certain type of Americans who go abroad and become in many respects un-American." Thus, Daniels and Benson viewed Sims's recommendations with a degree of suspicion.

There was also an initial difference of interpretation between *Simsadus* and Washington over the role the American navy should play in the war. When the nation entered the war the reaction of the Navy Department was to defend its home waters. The conference with the British and French admirals in Washington on April 11 seemed to confirm this policy. Despite Sims's repeated recommendations, the Navy Department delayed in turning its major effort into the European theater. Sims was correct in his assumption that his superiors did not grasp immediately the seriousness of the situation in European waters. Benson later admitted that he did not accept Sims's estimate in the initial cable because he thought Sims had been in London too short a time to have a full understanding of conditions. Secretary Daniels and Benson measured Sims's recommendations against those of the Allied admirals—Browning and Grasset—and decided to carry out the policy the Allies recommended. As mentioned earlier, they suggested that the American navy's primary task should be to patrol the Atlantic coastal waters from Canada to South America. This they did for the first weeks of the war until they realized the accuracy of Sims's estimate. It is also indicative of the poor relationship that Sims learned accidentally of Daniels's agreement with these Allied admirals sometime later. Evidently the Secretary did not think it necessary to inform him immediately of these crucial decisions.

Finally, there was the matter of Sims's place in the navy's command structure. Neither Daniels nor Benson demonstrated in their postwar comments a clear understanding of staff and command duties or relationship. The hierarchy of command which they created reflected this confusion. In June 1917 they named Sims a force commander. Two weeks later, they notified him that he was subordinate to the commander in chief of the Atlantic Fleet, who was in Yorktown, but that Sims was to continue direct correspondence with the Navy Department and that his orders would come from Washington. The Atlantic Fleet commander, Admiral Mayo, who was already irritated because Benson had given orders direct to elements of his command without previous consultation, was understandably confused. In effect, Mayo had technical or "paper" command but neither the real authority nor the actual responsibility of the forces in Europe. Sims did not receive a single operational order from Mayo during the course of the war. When Mayo wanted to go to Europe to take actual command, the Secretary rebuffed him. Daniels gave the reasons in his diary on April 15, 1918, "Mayo would supersede Sims. I saw the President and he agreed not to send." Admiral Benson was in agreement on this decision.

In fact, Sims exercised command of American naval forces in Europe. His subordinates recognized his authority, and his superiors used him in that capacity. After the war Daniels initially praised Sims's accomplishments and recommended him for the permanent rank of Admiral. Later, in 1920, after the publication of Sims's criticism of the Navy Department, Daniels, Benson, and others attempted to denigrate his wartime responsibilities. Daniels referred to him as "a liaison officer," and Benson said that Sims "had an exaggerated idea of what his mission was." But the facts of 1917–18 do not substantiate the tenor of those comments.

There were attempts on both sides of the Atlantic to ease the friction. Cables and emissaries crisscrossed the ocean. Benson, Mayo, and Assistant Secretary Roosevelt made inspection trips to Europe, while Sims returned his aide, Babcock, for consultation and, by the summer of 1918 he kept liaison officers on trips back and forth to Washington, as he put it, "to keep the inevitable misunderstandings from arising." The force commander also supplemented his formal reports with personal letters to Daniels, Benson, various bureau chiefs, and, in particular, his former Chief of Staff in the Destroyer Flotilla, Captain William V. Pratt, who was assistant to the Chief of Naval Operations.

Although the postwar controversy would indicate an extremely difficult relationship, during the war Sims and his superiors managed to work together without the explosion one might expect from a combination of the three such personalities. Sims had a reputation for caustic criticism. Benson was a deliberate officer who, as Fleet Admiral King said, "had an obsession for meddling" and too much concern with details. The civilian in the triumvirate, Josephus Daniels, always conscious of civil control, was also cautious and too slow in making decisions early in the war. Then, neither Daniels nor Benson would permit Sims the independence which Secretary of War Baker gave Pershing from the beginning. There was friction and misunderstanding but the three were able to hold down their differences enough to make a sizable contribution to victory. However, this success might well have been facilitated if there had been closer coordination with a better command organization.

Soon after the United States entered the war, a group of destroyer officers were talking on a pier in the Boston Navy Yard. The subject of their discussion was the gangway on a recent model destroyer. As they studied the convenience (now one could walk sedately up the gangway rather than climb hand over hand on rungs), they concluded that it was a "grave mistake." One of the senior destroyer commanding officers, a junior lieutenant commander, summed up their apprehension, "Why, if we make it this easy for an officer to come aboard the destroyer, we may have commanders coming on board looking around. Who knows? There even may be a captain come on board." Youth was not just an advantage but virtually a necessity on the "four pipers" (a nickname based on the four smoke stacks).

Life on a destroyer was not pleasant even in peacetime. As Ensign Joseph Husband said, "There is no motion on land or sea comparable to that of a destroyer. Rolling often in five-second jerks at an angle sometimes over 50°, there is combined with the roll a quick and violent pitching. . . ." The oil burners provided a particular atmosphere as well, "Grimy with soot of fuel oil, reeking with oil gasses, they roll and plunge at express-train speeds."

During the war the destroyers were at sea up to eight days at a time, often in heavy seas. If the weather was bad, and the winter of 1917–18 was an unusually hard one, not only was it impossible to eat off tables but also it was difficult to sleep in bunks. Simply running the ship was physically wearing under such conditions, even without a dangerous mission. The watch constantly scanned the area for submarines. If one were sighted, the crew had to be ready for action, so most never took off their clothes throughout an entire tour. Yet, there was a "terrible monotony" in the routine of patrol and convoy duty. Once the crews had overcome their initial excitement and had stopped seeing imaginary submarines everywhere, they settled down to the dull hard work which was interrupted rarely by actual contact with the enemy.

The first American destroyers to go to war shoved off unostentatiously, as if for a drill, from Boston in the late afternoon of April 24, 1917. Commander Joseph K. Taussig, a thirty-nine-year-old Annapolis graduate whose brother officers thought "a hell of a fine fellow," commanded this contingent of six oil burners. After a ten-day voyage which included some heavy weather, the destroyers steamed into the harbor of Queenstown, Ireland, and found the shore filled with a welcoming crowd.

When Taussig went up the hill to greet the British commander at the Admiralty House, Vice Admiral Sir Lewis Bayly, a taciturn man with the reputation of a "tartar," promptly asked when the Americans would be ready for sea duty. Taussig made the right impression with his reply, "I shall be ready when fueled." Men and ships were ready, but these sailors had a lot to learn. Bayly could give them some advice, but a much younger officer, Commander E. R. G. R. Evans, a distinguished destroyer officer, had the assignment of filling in the details. Although the Americans were all regulars and many had been in destroyers for several years, most had never heard of a depth charge.

Four days after their arrival, they started out on their first patrol. At this stage they were rather excitable. The *McDougal* fired the first shot but found the target to be a buoy. On board the *Wadsworth*, Taussig's ship, the crew went to general quarters some twenty-four times during the first four-day patrol. Evans, who accompanied Taussig, merely commented, "Well, you certainly do keep a good lookout on this ship." Later, when the *Wadsworth* actually made its first sighting of a German sub, the watch mistook it for a fishing boat and did not get off a shot. The next submarine they were prepared for, and they opened fire but discovered before it was too late that it was British.

By mid-summer, twenty-nine other destroyers had joined the

original six on patrol duty out of Queenstown. At this time their schedule was five days at sea and three in port. At sea, each destroyer would cruise in a 900 square-mile zone. Although the destroyer would escort an occasional cargo ship passing through the area and, of course, be available to combat submarines or to pick up the survivors of their victims, the main purpose of the patrol was to keep the submarines from cruising on the surface. This deterred the Germans from using a favorite tactic of engaging a merchantman with a deck gun rather than firing the more expensive torpedo. Day after day, the four-pipers moved through water, often filled with debris, dead horses, boxes, barrels, and other vestiges of sinkings. One destroyer veteran recalled, "You'd almost be glad to see a ship sunk, anything to cheer up the monotony of the patrolling." Some destroyer men, among them Commander William F. Halsey, spent months in the war zone without ever definitely seeing a submarine. In port, the maintenance men worked night and day to get the ships ready for sea again. These destroyers were averaging over 6000 miles each month, and it is a tribute to the men of the *Melville* and the *Dixie*, the maintenance ships at Queenstown, that they kept on this schedule.

As the convoy system came into general use, the regular schedule of the destroyers as well as the loneliness came to an end. Now they traveled in groups of five (more or less, depending on the size of the convoy) and stayed out as long as it was necessary to bring in the convoy. Taussig reported that during his last thirty days as commander of the *Wadsworth* he spent twenty-two days at sea on three escort trips. The sea, incidentally, was so rough during this period (mid-October to mid-November 1917) that it was impossible to set the mess tables for eighteen of those twenty-two days.

On convoy duty, the destroyers would pick up their charges some forty-eight hours out of port, relieve the cruiser escort, and bring the ships into harbor. Then they would turn around and proceed to shepherd an outgoing convoy through the danger zone for another two days. At this time the convoyed ships would disperse for the homeward journey. Since the slowest ship set the speed of the convoy, the time would vary. It might take twice as long to escort a slow merchant convoy than the three days a fast troop convoy would require.

There were several advantages in escorting troop convoys rather than merchant ships. The transports were faster, hence the escorts had to spend less time at sea. As a rule, the troopers were better drilled and more prompt in their movements. Then, as Taussig recalled, "when we met a troop convoy, the whole atmosphere seemed to be surcharged with joy, emanating from the thousands of men on the ships." And the letters and diaries of the men on those ships reflect this sense of relief they had when they sighted the destroyers. The destroyer men sometimes had more somber thoughts as they looked up at the men on the decks of the transports. Bill Halsey described this in his diary after meeting the *Antigone* with a load of doughboys. "You look at them and pity them having to go in the trenches. Suppose they look at us and wonder why anyone is damn fool enough to roll and jump around on a destroyer."

As the great troop movement gained momentum in late spring 1918, Sims decided to make Brest the major escort base and shifted some of the destroyers from Queenstown 250 miles southeast to Brest. Before this the Queenstown destroyers frequently took convoys into the French port but would return without a convoy to Queenstown. This was inefficient but necessary because of the shortage of fuel oil storage facilities at Brest. After the Americans had almost quadrupled the storage capacity, the transfer was possible.

The escort force at Brest as well as at Gibraltar included a number of older, hence smaller and coal-burning, destroyers and twenty-five converted yachts. One group of the former, which at 420 tons were less than half the size of the recent model destroyers, made a 12,000 mile journey from the Philippines to Gibraltar. Although previously considered capable of limited service, these destroyers, under the command of Lieutenant Commander Harold R. Stark (who later became Chief of Naval Operations), completed the remarkable journey in good condition. The yachts, with a large number of reservists in their crews, also stood up well under the wartime demands. With the title of "Suicide Fleet," these former pleasure craft in the Bay of Biscay amazed Sims by staying at sea even during the stormy winter of 1917–18. One of them based at Gibraltar, the *Lydonia*, attained the rare distinction of sinking a submarine.

In addition to escorting troop and cargo convoys on the first or last laps of transatlantic voyages, the Brest detachment joined with the Gibraltar force in providing protection for merchant ships in the Bay of Biscay. This brought them into close coordination with the French. The French navy assigned pilots to those ships which escorted the coastal convoys. The thorough knowledge of these men, their ability to locate the position from a glance at the coast line impressed the American officers. There was no problem between allies here.

Convoy duty out of Brest was generally similar for both yachts and destroyers. As a rule, the convoy would leave just before dark so as to take advantage of the night and make as much of the journey as possible before dawn. A reserve lieutenant on the *Nokomis*, a yacht originally built for Horace E. Dodge of Detroit, left a description of one such trip. In a letter dated October 17, 1918, George E. Lawrence wrote,

> we took out 26 ships and left them at the western edge of the sub zone and then headed for the point where we were to meet the incoming convoy—six of us in a single column 800 yards apart steaming through a black night when driving rain and spray were mixed—a German sub talking with her wireless less than 50 miles from our new convoy and making for them but our fleet like a lot of hound dogs on the scent telling the Fritz that he would not get them—next morning at daylight we had come 150 miles through the night and found our convoy of 22 ships and took positions on the outskirts and brought them in safely.

For the *Nokomis* and other ships at sea the war did not end abruptly on November 11, as Lawrence told his friend about a week later, "We were informed last Monday that the armistice was signed at 5:00 a.m. and hostilities ceased at 11:00 a.m. same day but the same telegram told us that several German subs were still at sea in vicinity of Gibraltar which had not got word and to 'take measures to forestall attack by them'—I asked the capt what he considered that meant & he left no room for doubt in his reply —he said 'Shoot hell out of them.'" On November 13, the *Nokomis* did see something that looked like a periscope and fired thirty-six rounds at the object until it disappeared.

In their postwar attack, the men on the *Nokomis* did not know if they had sunk a submarine. Their experience had been the same many times in the war. Since a submarine would disappear, in all probability, when attacked, the pursuers remained ignorant of its condition. Was it sunk or damaged? Indeed, in some cases, there was a question as to whether or not it had been a submarine.

Four actions, including the two in which the Americans scored definite kills, indicate what could happen on a routine patrol or convoy mission.

A destroyer in the third group to arrive at Queenstown in the latter part of May became one of the first to make contact with the enemy. At 4:21 on the afternoon of June 16, the *O'Brien* was escorting a ship a few miles from the entrance of the Queenstown harbor when a lookout sighted a periscope about 800 yards off the starboard bow. The *O'Brien* immediately changed course, increased speed to 20 knots, and approached the spot, although the periscope was now out of sight. A minute later, the periscope reappeared dead ahead at a range of 100 yards. The lookout in the foretop shouted that he could see the bulk of the submarine close to the starboard side. It seemed to him that the destroyer was going to ram the submarine. The *O'Brien* dropped a depth charge but no one could see the submarine, which evidently had continued to dive. The TNT exploded and shook the destroyer. Less than three minutes had elapsed since the initial sighting. Lieutenant Commander C. A. Blakely, the captain of the *O'Brien*, reported, "The spot was circled immediately after the explosion, but no evidence of the submarine could be found." The *O'Brien* then resumed her escort duty. Three hours later a British destroyer passed through the area and saw large patches of oil. The men of the *Cushing* also reported seeing this oil when it steamed over the spot the next day. The British Admiralty eventually gave the *O'Brien* credit for possibly seriously damaging a submarine.

There was absolutely no doubt to the victory won by the Americans on November 17. On that day, a few miles outside of Queenstown harbor, six American destroyers and two British warships were forming an escort about a convoy when, at 4:10 p.m. Coxswain David D. Loomis, on the bridge of the *Fanning*, saw a periscope. The destroyer raced to the site and dropped a depth charge. The *Nicholson* noticed the excitement, cut through the convoy column, deposited another "ash can," and joined the

Fanning in a search for debris. The crews of the two ships were beginning to despair when, to their surprise, the submarine surfaced. Both destroyers opened fire with their guns, and the *Nicholson* hurled another depth charge at the Germans. A reserve ensign, H. W. Dwight Rudd, who had just joined the crew of the *Nicholson,* described the next scene. "Out came the first Hun I, or anybody present, had ever seen in the War. I shall never forget the sight of that man as he ran frantically up and down the deck, his hands over his head. He, anyway, had surrendered; there was little doubt of that. Bees from out a hive had nothing on the crew of that submarine. They simply poured out of those hatches, until the deck was black with them."

The Americans kept up their alert as they watched this amazing procedure. The *Fanning* pulled alongside and prepared to pick up the prisoners and to take the submarine in tow. Although the Germans seemed to be happy enough to surrender, they disappointed their captors by scuttling the submarine. Nevertheless, the *Fanning* did bring the thirty-nine prisoners into port. They reported that the *Fanning*'s depth charge had made the submarine unmanageable by wrecking its motors and diving rudders. Kapitan Leutnant Gustav Amberger was left with the choice of certain death in sinking or the uncertainty of surfacing (which he could still do by blowing the ballast tanks) in the face of the destroyers. He chose the latter course and was pleased with the hospitality of the *Fanning*. Time was usually in short quantity in these sea encounters. From the time Loomis first saw the submarine until the U-58 sank, only eighteen minutes elapsed.

Commander Frank D. Berrien of the *Nicholson* and Lieutenant A. S. Carpenter of the *Fanning* had good reason for pride in the rapid and proper reactions of their crews. Sims sent his congratulations and added, "Go out and do it again." The Admiralty was equally appreciative and gave the *Fanning* credit for the victory.

The only other American warship to receive credit from the Admiralty for the definite destruction of a U-boat was the 500-ton yacht *Lydonia*. The incident occurred south of the Balearic Islands in the western Mediterranean on May 8, 1918. The *Lydonia,* together with several British warships, was escorting a convoy when the executive officer of the yacht, Lieutenant Claud F. Reynaud, saw a submarine fire a torpedo. The missile went on its way and sank the British vessel *Ingleside*, but the *Lydonia* and the HMS *Basilisk* laid down a barrage of depth charges. Three months later the British were able to say with certainty that the UB-70 was their victim.

There were losses to counter the victories as the Germans could take credit for sinking three American warships: the yacht *Alcedo* in November 1917 off the coast of France, the destroyer *Jacob Jones* a month later near the southeastern tip of England, and the cruiser *San Diego*, which struck a German mine near Fire Island, New York, in July 1918. Of these three, the *Jacob Jones* suffered the most casualties, as sixty-four officers and men died.

In the afternoon of December 6, 1917, the *Jacob Jones* was returning to Queenstown after taking a convoy into Brest. Since it had been in the second group of six destroyers to arrive in Queenstown on the previous May, the ship was relatively a veteran among the American craft in the European theater. At this time, it was traveling alone because it had fallen behind its fellow destroyers to have target practice.

The first indication that a submarine was in the area occurred when someone saw a torpedo approaching at an estimated 40 knots an hour. The captain, Lieutenant Commander David W. Bagley, who was the brother-in-law of Secretary Daniels, took a look at the torpedo and concluded that he could not maneuver to avoid it. At 4:21, the torpedo struck about three feet below the water line. Although no ammunition exploded and the fuel oil did not ignite, the blast cleared about twenty feet of the deck, carried away the mainmast, and terminated the electric power. Since he could not send an SOS on the radio, Bagley ordered a gun fired in the hope that he might attract attention. Then, all of the surviving officers and men attempted to launch the rafts and to clear the ship. In the brief time remaining, Bagley remembered to destroy the confidential publications. Altogether, there was not much time. Eight minutes after the impact, the ship twisted stern down, as the depth charges exploded, to an almost vertical position and sank.

The survivors collected in a motor dory, with the motor out of commission, and three rafts. In the distance they saw the U-53 surface and pick up two prisoners. Ironically, this was the same submarine which had paid a call on Newport, Rhode Island, in the fall of 1916. The submarine had hit the *Jacob Jones* with a lucky shot at a range of about two miles. Later, the survivors learned that Hans Rose, the captain, had sent an SOS and given their location to Queenstown. At the time, they merely watched the U-boat disappear.

Bagley knew the exact location since Lieutenant Norman Scott, his executive officer, had fixed the position only a few minutes before the disaster. He decided that he and Scott, who later as a rear admiral was killed in action off Guadalcanal in November 1942, would take the dory and attempt to reach the Scilly Islands, some forty miles away. Within four hours, the men on one of the rafts which had become separated were rescued. The next morning, the HMS *Camellia* found the other two rafts, and at about one p.m., a patrol boat picked up Bagley and his men on the dory as they neared their goal. Several of the men had died from exposure in the cold winter night before the craft were rescued. In all, forty-six survived out of the 110 men on the destroyer.

By the summer of 1918 the destroyers had a new ally in their campaign against the submarines—the so-called "Splinter Fleet" of subchasers. At less than 100 tons, these wooden ships did not look impressive beside the new 1200-ton destroyers, but with their listening devices and a supply of depth charges they could be just as deadly.

The men who operated the subchasers considered themselves a group apart from those in the "Iron Navy." The great majority of them were reservists or regulars who had enlisted merely for the duration of the war. There was not much of a social line in this branch since ninety days of intensive training and a gold stripe did not make that much difference between the officers and many of their men who had attended the same colleges. Not all were college graduates, of course. Ray Milholland, in a résumé of his shipmates, accounted for a Chicago cabbie, a tractor mechanic, a deserter who had re-enlisted under an assumed name, and a former lemonade salesman from a circus, as well as the sailor who spoke five languages and another who amused himself by reading Greek.

Whatever their backgrounds, these men had to be sturdy in order to go to war in subchasers. Living on a subchaser was a strenuous effort. Milholland explained why in his book, *The Splinter Fleet,* "Water and dampness are everywhere. Combined with the nerve-racking roll and pitch is the constant vapor of salt spray and spent exhaust gases belching from the engine ports. . . . At no time at sea—and we spent most of our time there—was the reek of gasoline and salt spray any better than just endurable." Yet these temporary sailors took their 110-foot-long ships across the Atlantic Ocean.

The English Channel and the Strait of Otranto between Italy and Greece were the areas where American subchasers initially would help most. Accordingly, of the first seventy-two to make the ocean voyage, half went to Plymouth, England, and the other half to the beautiful island of Corfu. Later, in September, thirty began operations out of Queenstown, and, during the last week of the war, eighteen joined the force at Gibraltar. Wherever located, the subchasers presented another barrier to submarines. At Corfu, the detachment even took part in a raid on an enemy naval base.

Because of the success of the German and Austrian submarines in the Mediterranean, the Allies decided to attempt to close off the exit from the Adriatic. In the forty-mile-wide gap of the Otranto Strait, the British, French, and Italians placed warships, motor launches, trawlers, balloons, and airplanes, while the Americans contributed thirty-six subchasers.

Duty on the Otranto Barrage consisted of picking one's way through minefields, finding the proper position, and then settling down for days of drifting and listening—always on the alert. Since twelve subchasers were constantly on duty, this meant that a subchaser crew was at sea a third of the time. Out there, during a summer day, the heat could be almost unbearable. Hilary R. Chambers, Jr., who commanded one of the subchasers, claimed that the temperature in early August reached 140° on the deck of his ship. To add to the discomfort there was a food shortage. Nor did Corfu, despite its natural beauty and historic traditions, have much to offer to these young American sailors.

They did not need a morale officer, however, since they had "Juggy" Nelson. The mention of Captain Charles P. Nelson, the rotund regular officer in command of the two subchaser squadrons at Corfu, brought a smile to the face of one of his subordinates almost a half century later. Admiral Sims shared this appreciation, as he indicated, "the American navy possessed few officers more energetic, more efficient, more lovable, or more personally engaging than Captain Nelson." And a temporary sailor, an enlisted man, summed up his admiration for his commander by citing Nelson's "unusually magnetic powers of leadership." "But always," Milholland continued, "whether he was giving carefully measured praise for work well done, or thundering his Jovian anger, there was a human twinkle in Captain Nelson's keen eyes that never quite let a man believe himself to be altogether the hero or the hopeless fool."

The idea of serving as a deterrent with the hope of catching a submarine in the barrage were not enough for Nelson. He wanted to strike at the enemy base. When near the end of September he received orders to report with twelve subchasers to the Italian side of the Strait for special service, he thought that the time had come. After conferring with the Allied commander at Brindisi, he returned to his flagship, Subchaser # 95, and told his officers, "It's going to be a real party, boys." The plan was for the subchasers to protect six cruisers, the accompanying destroyers, and Italian torpedo boats as they attacked the ships and installations at the Austrian base of Durazzo.

Eleven of the subchasers—the twelfth was left behind because it fouled its propellor at Brindisi—cast off in the early morning darkness of October 2 for Durazzo. When they arrived in advance of the main force, they began to take up their positions. Two units of three each, under Nelson's personal command, stayed out at a range of several thousand yards in order to provide a protective screen for the bombarding warships. The other subchasers moved in closer to patrol the capes on either side of the harbor. There was enough excitement for all, with the cruisers and destroyers shelling, a large flight of airplanes bombing, and the tiny Italian torpedo boats darting in and out of the harbor. The Austrians returned the fire, but fortunately, were inaccurate.

Unit B, which had the assignment of guarding the northern cape, found submarines before it reached its post. The subchaser in the rear, # 129, sighted a periscope at 1600 yards and signaled to Lieutenant Commander Paul H. Bastedo, the unit commander. As Bastedo turned in # 215 to look, another periscope appeared on the port side about 750 yards away. The two subchasers # 215 and # 128 left their companion and went after the nearer enemy. The lead subchaser (# 215) opened fire with its three-inch deck gun and port machine gun and hit the periscope with the second shot. Then Bastedo and Ensign Hilary R. Chambers, Jr. of # 128 moved in for the kill with depth charges. They saw wreckage and oil but did not delay to examine the debris, since # 129 seemed in trouble. Ensign Maclear Jacoby and his men on the # 129 had hurled eight depth charges at their sub. The explosions had damaged temporarily the engine but evidently had sunk the submarine. At least the crew had seen oil, wreckage, and bubbles. In the melee, another submarine appeared, but the subchasers left this one for the British destroyers which were firing at it. Despite the energetic defense, one of the enemy had managed to get off a torpedo which damaged the British cruiser *Weymouth*.

That night there was a celebration at Brindisi. The Splinter Fleet had come through the raid without suffering a single casualty. And the men of Unit B could now hoist gold stars above the crow's nests of their subchasers. Later, commendations came from high sources. "Their conduct was beyond praise," was the written opinion of the commander of the British Adriatic Force. Nelson was ready to repeat the raid with another group of his subchasers, but before he had his chance the war in the Adriatic ended.

While "Juggy" Nelson and his men were patrolling the Otranto Strait, another group of Americans were dealing with the submarines in a different manner. The men who planted the North Sea mine barrage were, as a member of Sims's staff said, "living on the edge of eternity," for they went to sea in ships packed with high explosives. As their commander, Captain Reginald R. Belknap, recalled, "mines were constantly at one's elbow. . . ." In a fifty-hour period, the makeshift minelayers (two former cruisers, relics of the 1880's, and eight converted merchantmen and passenger boats) would steam out to position, form three to five abreast at 500 yard intervals, drop their one yard in diameter mines, containing 300 pounds of TNT overboard, and return to base. "Precision and quickness of action while at sea were imperative, from start to finish," Captain Belknap noted. To ensure efficiency, Belknap was strict, very strict, but he was fair and apparently well liked.

Throughout the thirteen regular excursions, there could be no relaxation from tension. The actual discharging of mines might last from just under four to seven hours, but cruising in darkness or in bad weather with such cargo kept everyone alert. As Belknap wrote his wife in August, "Interesting as these trips are, no sane person would take two for pleasure." Even after a safe return to Inverness or Invergordon, it took time to unwind from the tension. Yet, the men evidently maintained high spirits, and there was no friction among their leaders. "A more congenial, cordially friendly lot I never saw," was Belknap's description of his captains.

By the end of the war, the British and Americans had laid a belt 230 miles long and 15 to 35 miles wide. The Americans contributed four-fifths of this vast minefield. Although as many as 5 per cent of the mines laid in the early expeditions blew up at the time or soon thereafter, enough remained to deter the stoutesthearted German. The results of this effort were at least four certain victims—a figure which matched the total number of submarines accounted for by American destroyers, yachts, and subchasers.

The eight submarines, and perhaps a few more, which the American navy destroyed were only a fraction of the 130 or so submarines which the Germans lost in the last two years of the war. Later, Admiral Sims said, "we did not get many submarines, because our business was not to hunt submarines but to protect the convoys and troops." Besides, as Sims freely admitted, the American contribution was a fraction of the Allied effort. In contrast with Britain's 5000 vessels ranging from battleships to trawlers, the United States had 373 ships in European water. Yet, this aid came at a desperate time and, as Lord Jellicoe concluded, it made possible the adoption of the convoy system. The transportation of two million men and a large part of their supplies across the Atlantic resulted from the effectiveness of this system.

During the war the navy expanded to almost a half-million men and women (for it did enlist 11,000 of the latter). It put gun crews on merchantmen, regulars and reservists on transports, and even sent sailors to the Western Front to man the five 14-inch gun batteries which the Navy Department mounted on railroad cars. All of these were in addition to those on the warships and in the aircraft and the thousands of others in warehouses and at desks.

At this time naval officers and their civilian superiors learned to deal with numbers and problems which a few years before they would have considered unbelievable. They also mastered the art of allied warfare. These achievements contributed to victory in 1918 and were a part of the foundation of an even greater victory which many of the same men would help win in 1945.

·V·

Pershing Builds
an Army

By June 1918 the Americans had laid the foundation of a great army in France and had won their first battle. It was an arduous, complex task for General Pershing and his staff to delineate strategy and to develop the logistical base. Meantime, the men who would carry out these plans were arriving, becoming acquainted with the French, and learning the techniques of war. By April 1, 1918, four of the American divisions were ready for combat. When one considers the state of military affairs in the United States in April 1917, the achievements of the year represent an impressive effort. But this was no time for pondering past achievements as German offensives spurred the Americans to even greater efforts.

German and Allied strategists agreed on one issue in early 1918: the decision depended on how fast a large number of Americans could reach the front. Accordingly, the Allies projected a defensive strategy throughout 1918 and looked toward victory in 1919, while German leaders hoped to strike the decisive

blow against weakened and war-weary Allied troops prior to significant American reinforcement. In later years, when, out of ignorance or for propaganda purposes, some soldiers, politicians,
and historians negated the crucial American role, they overlooked
this cardinal fact which the strategists understood in 1918—with
enough Americans, the Allies would win; without, they would lose.

On Monday, May 28, 1917, a gloomy foggy day, General Pershing and his staff boarded a launch at Governor's Island in New
York harbor and made the rough, choppy trip to the White Star
liner *Baltic* out in the channel. The only uniforms in evidence
were worn rather awkwardly by four newly commissioned doctors. Pershing was annoyed. Not only the show of uniforms but
also the artillery salute by the garrison at Governor's Island and,
even more irritating to one concerned with secrecy, the boxes
labeled "General Pershing's Headquarters" which had been in
plain view on Pier 60 for two days, were more than enough to
raise his temper.

Shortly after five o'clock that afternoon, the *Baltic* and the nucleus of the American Expeditionary Force were under way.

During the ten days at sea, Pershing put his staff to work on
logistical plans for the ambiguous future. As Harbord, his chief of
staff, noted in his diary: "Officers whose lives have been spent in
trying to avoid spending fifteen cents of Government money now
confront the necessity of expending fifteen millions of dollars—
and on their intellectual and professional expansion depends
their avoidance of the scrap heap." At the same time, Pershing
and Harbord considered and outlined the organization of a General Staff, and Pershing tentatively decided that he should base
initially all plans on an AEF of a million men.

It was a busy crossing and not an unpleasant one. A Colonel
Puckle of the British Army Service Corps gave lectures on the
British Army and logistical problems. There were other lectures
and French lessons twice daily for the officers: they were determined to learn to read "La Marseillaise" even if they could not
sing it. In the evenings while a few studied, others formed four-
somes for bridge and had entertainments by opera singers and
members of an English theatrical company. Then, for the Pershing party—some 190 altogether, a group which included Cap-

tain George S. Patton, Jr., and a chauffeur, Sergeant First Class Edward V. Rickenbacker—there were the inevitable typhoid inoculations. As they steamed into the danger zone, all took increased interest in the regular boat drills. Within the next year and a half, two million American soldiers would undergo the same tension, followed by enthusiasm and relief when the escorting destroyers came into sight for the last leg of the journey.

At nine-thirty on the morning of June 8, the local dignitaries and an honor guard, complete with the regimental mascot, a formidable-looking goat, of the Royal Welsh Fusiliers turned out to welcome Pershing to Liverpool. After the ceremonies, the Americans went by train to London, where they spent a hectic four days. At luncheons and dinners and the conferences in between, Pershing and his staff met personages whose names and faces they heretofore had seen only in newspapers: King George V, David Lloyd George, Field Marshal Viscount French, Generals Sir William Robertson, Jan Christian Smuts, and many others, including the Minister of Munitions, Winston Churchill, who impressed Pershing as being "unusually well informed on American affairs." Admiral Sir John Jellicoe and the American Admiral William S. Sims told the doleful story of German U-boat successes, and all talked of hopes for the future. The British took them to tea, a play, and even church services at Westminster Abbey, and the lower-ranking staff officers had some time for sightseeing. Major John L. Hines wrote his wife: "It has been so fine to go to see all the old places we have so often read about." Most of all the two groups of men who would have to work together in war looked each other over and tried to determine who knew what, who could be trusted and how far one could extend that trust.

Early in the morning of June 13, Pershing and his officers left the Savoy Hotel for the last lap of their trip to France. A few hours later they landed in Boulogne. Again there were ceremonies, followed by a train trip to Paris. That afternoon was the climax. Parisians thronged the streets shouting "Vive l' Amerique," pelted the completely surprised Americans with flowers, and surged toward them to shake or just touch hands.

For the next few days the ceremonies continued as the French showed their gratitude to this small group of men from whom they expected so much. Pershing made the right gesture when he kissed the sword of Napoleon at Les Invalides and withal was equal to the role the situation demanded: lunch with President Raymond Poincaré, dinner with Paul Painlevé, the Minister of War, visits to the Chamber of Deputies, the Senate, and, of course, to the tomb of Lafayette. The American general and the hope of great reinforcements captivated Paris. For the French it was a joyous break in a melancholy period. As one of the American staff officers noted, "This is a beautiful country but a very sad one. War is evident by the mourning worn by the great majority of people."

Would Pershing's popularity last until the hope materialized? Harbord was perhaps thinking of that when he described his chief: "But whatever the future holds for him, General Pershing certainly looks his part since he came here. He is a fine figure of a man; carries himself well, holds himself on every occasion with proper dignity; is easy in manner, knows how to enter a crowded room, and is fast developing into a world figure."

French enthusiasm was still mounting, however, when on June 16 Pershing and his staff paid their first visit to the French General Headquarters at Compiégne. Here the Americans met a Frenchman who was famed neither for enthusiasm nor optimism —Henri Philippe Pétain. In the midst of his task of bringing an entire army to order after seeing it almost disintegrate in mutinies since mid-May, Pétain was not in the mood for celebration. A tall, brusque man, the French commander in chief did not talk much but he looked one in the eye when he did. And he was very serious when, after acknowledging the expectation of American aid, he told Pershing, "I hope it is not too late."

Before Pershing returned to Paris that day, he got his first glimpse of the Western Front. From an artillery observation point two miles behind the line opposite St. Quentin, he studied the scene through a telescope. In the coming weeks, others of his staff would visit various sectors of the front. One of them, the assistant adjutant general, John L. Hines, could not describe the awesome place to his wife but could only write, "You can't conceive of the absolute destruction without seeing it." On this occasion, however, John J. Pershing made no comment.

The next day, a Sunday, Pershing and his staff settled down to the task of laying the foundation for what they assumed would be a huge expeditionary force. They had begun studying the various problems while en route on the *Baltic* and, when they arrived in Paris, they found that a small mission headed by Major James A. Logan had already consulted with the French about possible ports and training areas. Logan had also rented a temporary headquarters for them at 31 rue Constantine—a small private house opposite the Invalides. Here the American officers, divided into tiny groups, began developing the various segments of the over-all plan. This is where the army's investment in the School of the Line and the Staff College at Fort Leavenworth paid dividends. As one of the key planners, Hugh A. Drum, wrote his wife, "my Leavenworth training is standing me in good stead these days." He was in the operations section which in September consisted, he added, of "all Leavenworth men who were at the school as instructors or students with me."

Since the AEF was to be an independent army, according to the intent and the letter of Pershing's instructions, the question immediately arose as to which sector of the front the Americans would occupy. Before the planners could make a recommendation, they would have to make interrelated decisions on which ports, railroads, and training areas to use. To a great extent, the availability of those facilities would dictate the choice of sector. Since the British desired to guard channel ports and the French wanted to be in position to protect Paris, the alternatives narrowed to the eastern segment of the front.

By June 26, when he made a second trip to Pétain's headquarters, Pershing had decided to ask for the Lorraine sector between the Argonne Forest and the Vosges Mountains. This would permit the AEF to make the most effective use of available facilities—the ports of St. Nazaire, La Pallice, and Bassens and the linking railways which crossed France on a northeast diagonal to Lorraine. As the generals discussed the question they turned to the specific point of the first American offensive. A study of the map convinced Pershing that the AEF should eliminate the German salient at St. Mihiel. This sector also held out the possibility of striking a decisive blow. If the AEF could break the lines and penetrate deeply into German territory, it could cut off the rail center at

Metz and block German use of the iron ore deposits in the Longwy-Briey area and the coal fields of the Saar. Pershing left Com-piégne with Pétain's tentative agreement to his plans.

It would be months before there would be enough troops in the AEF to mount the offensive which Pershing envisaged. At the time he hoped that it would be possible to carry it out in the spring or summer of 1918. Nevertheless, Lieutenant Colonels John M. Palmer and Fox Conner and Major Drum reconnoitered the front and began planning for the reduction of the St. Mihiel salient. When they were students at the Army Staff College some years before at Fort Leavenworth, all three had worked out war games on maps of the terrain they now examined with more serious intent.

Palmer and his assistants were merely doing their job as the Operations Section of Pershing's general staff. While they worked up operational plans, other officers under the quartermaster Major James A. Logan, who was virtually indispensable at this stage because of his knowledge of French affairs, were handling a wide variety of problems under the general heading of administrative policy; Major Dennis E. Nolan was collecting a few other officers and trying to learn the intricacies of a military intelligence service; and Lieutenant Colonels William D. Connor and Paul B. Malone were finding that their tasks as chiefs of the Coordination and Training sections were rapidly growing larger. Although General Order # 8 (July 5, 1917) outlined the specific responsibilities of each of the five general staff sections, the particular functions changed somewhat as the AEF evolved. In the case of the Coordination section, for example, its officers became almost entirely involved in supply matters in 1918.

Nolan was the only staff section chief to hold office throughout the war. Colonel Fox Conner took over as Chief of Operations, or G-3, when Palmer became ill, while two officers who came over with the First Division, Colonels George Van Horn Moseley and Harold B. Fiske, became Chiefs of Coordination (G-4) and Training (G-5) sections. Pershing also brought in his Academy classmate Colonel Avery D. Andrews, to succeed Logan as G-1 in the summer of 1918. In the rotation process from staff to line, the redoubtable Harbord gave up the crucial post of chief of staff to the less formidable but no less effectual Major General James W.

"Dad" McAndrew. The importance of these men was explained by one of them, Moseley—the G-4: "The Chiefs of the General Staff Sections of the AEF were . . . a part of the great Commander-in-Chief himself and spoke for him."

Pershing picked good men and knew how to use them properly as staff officers. Yet, in the summer of 1917, when nearly every move was a precedent, he personally saw and edited staff papers and outgoing cables which would be considered routine a year later. As soon as the staff knew and understood what "J.J.P."—as they called him, but not to his face—wanted, there was no need for him to give such attention to details. As John M. Palmer recalled, "General Pershing was never swamped by his task. His mind was always free for the big problems and the big decisions." At the time, a visitor from the War Department, the future Supreme Court Justice Felix Frankfurter expressed a similar view in his report to the Secretary of War: "General Pershing impressed me as in the grip of a responsibility, the truly awful nature of which he thoroughly understands."

Since the President had delegated such broad authority to him, Pershing determined to a great extent the scope of his task. Within a month of his arrival in France, he cabled the War Department that he was planning to have a million men in the AEF by May 1918. A few days later, on July 11, he followed this up with a detailed plan delineating the organization of all combat elements from army level to the infantry company, which he wanted to increase to 250 men. In this "General Organization Project" Pershing spelled out his grand design: "It is evident that a force of about 1,000,000 is the smallest unit which in modern war will be a complete, well-balanced, and independent fighting organization. . . . Plans for the future should be based . . . on three times this force—i.e., at least 3,000,000 men."

Before he sent this plan home, Pershing had to deal with a War Department mission which had come independently to France to study the situation and make recommendations on organization and general policy. Well aware of the possible difficulties if dissimilar recommendations reached Washington, Pershing asked the head of this group of officers—a West Point classmate of his, Colonel Chauncey B. Baker—to confer with the AEF staff. For two days in early July Baker and his officers discussed the situation with Pershing's staff in the rather glamorous atmosphere of 73 rue de Varenne, the luxurious Paris townhouse with park-size grounds which Ogden Mills had turned over to Pershing for the duration of the war. The one crucial difference in recommmendations was over how much artillery the AEF required. Colonel Charles P. Summerall believed that the AEF would need guns in unprecedented quantity to break the trench deadlock. Pershing's staff disagreed and won the argument.

In mid-July, Pershing wrote the Chief of Staff, Hugh L. Scott, "We are all working very hard here in France, trying to get things in shape for the large part we are to play in this great war drama. The outline of our plan is now fairly well completed and we know exactly what we are working toward." And he continued to work toward his own goal, although later that month the War Department cabled that by using all available shipping it could send only 634,975 men to France by June 15, 1918. Together with the Americans already in the AEF, this meant in round numbers 650,000 men. Despite this disturbing information Pershing approved and forwarded to Washington in September and October the rest of his personnel program (support troops) and a priority schedule for the War Department to follow in shipping both the combat and support troops. When his staff completed their computations, they estimated that their program entailed 1,328,448 men—not the original million Pershing had mentioned in July.

Pershing was planning for a force twice as large as the War Department envisioned. This great disparity can be explained in part by the fact that Pershing and his staff based their plan on what they believed necessary to make a decisive contribution to the Allied effort, while the staff officers in Washington were apparently more aware of the critical questioning of shipping. In his letter of July 17, to Scott, Pershing had written: "The great problems of sea transportation must of course be handled at home. . . ." He asked for as many men as he thought he needed; the War Department thought in terms of the number possible to transport. These two approaches would never be entirely reconciled throughout the war; but then future developments in the war would cause many revisions in plans on both sides of the Atlantic.

Before troops arrived in large number, Pershing had to create a logistical framework for their support. On July 5 and August 13, he issued general orders which outlined in broad terms the Line of Communications. Although in subsequent months, the organization changed as did its name—Services of Supply—the mission remained constant: "to relieve the combatant field forces from every consideration except that of defeating the enemy." At its peak the Services of Supply would have almost 670,000 men involved in the many tasks necessary to maintain a large army in the field. These men handled construction projects, managed railroads and hospitals, operated communication systems, and kept supplies moving toward the front. After brief tenures by two generals in the formative period, Major General Francis J. Kernan, with an excellent reputation as a staff officer, developed the final organization, which in the final months of the war Harbord, by then a major general, would push to its maximum efficiency.

From the headquarters of the SOS in the old French regimental barracks at Tours in 1918, orders went out to detachments in ports in England as well as France where American soldiers passed supplies on toward the front. Hospitals, schools, repair shops, replacement centers, bakeries, salvage points, and storage depots including the huge one at Giévres which covered twelve square miles—all were part of the SOS.

As Pershing said, it was "a great business enterprise," and many of its officers were businessmen temporarily in uniform. Two civilians turned soldiers who played particularly important roles in the SOS were Charles G. Dawes and William W. Atterbury. A Chicago banker and close friend of Pershing's since the 1890's, Dawes neither looked nor acted much like a soldier, but as the General Purchasing Agent he obtained some ten million tons of supplies in Europe and thus saved that much valuable cargo space on the ships making the Atlantic crossing. Atterbury left his position as a vice president of the Pennsylvania Railroad in order to supervise the transportation empire of the AEF. Although he had some difficulty adjusting to military methods and requirements, Atterbury stayed on and kept the supplies moving.

Men, supplies, and even the SOS organization itself were still in the future in July 1917. Pershing steadfastly planned, but the condition of the French army and the lack of cooperative spirit among the Allies must have made him wonder whether his plans would ever materialize. "The fact is that France is very tired of this war," he wrote to Secretary Baker, on July 9, in a letter which also passed on news of the mutinies and Pétain's pessimistic comments. Three days later, Harbord noted in his diary, "Our Allies seem to hate one another."

Pershing had spent a sobering and busy five weeks in France by the time of his initial call on Field Marshal Sir Douglas Haig at British General Headquarters in Montreuil. For four days Pershing and three staff officers observed the British staff and command procedures. Already the preparatory bombardment for the Flanders offensive was in progress, and at Fifth Army Headquarters Pershing examined a miniature terrain reproduction of the German sector which the British hoped to penetrate.

The two former cavalry officers, Haig and Pershing, established a cordial relationship during this visit. The Field Marshal kept a diary in which he frequently recorded caustic remarks about his contemporaries; but, after his first conversation with the American commander, he was unusually pleasant, although patronizing, in his comments, "I was much struck with his quiet gentlemanly bearing—so unusual for an American. Most anxious to learn, and fully realises the greatness of the task before him. He has already begun to realize that the French are a broken reed." Pershing came away from the same conversation impressed by Haig's attitude toward the French, "His remarks entirely confirmed the belief that I had long since held that real teamwork between the two armies was almost totally absent."

When he returned to Paris, Pershing attended his first Allied conference. Except for the Italian commander, General Count Luigi Cadorna, he had met previously the other participants: General Sir William Robertson—the pragmatic "Wully"—the only man who ever rose from private to Chief of the Imperial General Staff, and eventually to Field Marshal; the charismatic French Chief of Staff Ferdinand Foch, of whom the British historian B. H. Liddell Hart wrote, "Faith was his greatest quality, and often blinded him to facts"; and Pétain, who was more concerned with the facts. Ostensibly the Allies met to discuss the Balkans, but the weakening situation in Russia caused the military leaders to ponder their strategy if Russia left the war. In his diary, Pershing commented, "All pessimistic and reserved." Then he cabled Washington that the Allies planned to withdraw troops from the secondary theaters in order to strengthen the Western Front, which they hoped to hold until enough Americans arrived "to gain ascendancy."

Although there were advantages in having his headquarters in Paris, Pershing decided to move GHQ to a location closer to the sector he had selected in Lorraine. On the first day of September his staff occupied their new offices in the four-story regimental barracks at Chaumont, a city of 15,000, in the scenic rolling countryside of the upper Marne. The center of activity of the hub of the AEF was on the second floor of the main barrack building in a room 18 by 12 feet, with a desk, a few chairs, a clock, and a large war map which virtually covered one wall. John J. Pershing never slouched behind the desk. Here he met visitors, questioned officers, and read the papers which came befor him for appraisal and decision. If he began to slump as he read, he would straighten, thrust out his chest, and always be the soldier.

At Chaumont the work schedule was heavy. But there was more room with only two or three officers in each office rather than five or six as there had been in Paris. Then Chaumont was a less expensive place to live for the junior officers. In October 1917 one of the staff officers, John L. Hines, wrote, "We are working pretty hard and the hours are pretty long—8:30 a.m. to about 7 p.m.—some times later with an hour for lunch." An occasional free Sunday broke the routine, as did long walks or early morning horseback rides, the camaraderie at mealtimes, and, for some, inspection or business trips. By the end of September, there were slightly more than 61,000 officers and men in the AEF responding to the plans and the orders pulsing from Chaumont.

While Pershing and his staff pored over statistics and planned hopefully for the future, the first combat elements of the AEF arrived. In the last week of June, the officers and men of the 16th, 18th, 26th, and 28th Infantry Regiments landed at St. Nazaire. After a brief stay at the port, and for some who took part in the Fourth of July ceremonies a pleasant side trip to Paris, the infantrymen crossed France in the uncomfortable 40 and 8 (40 men/8 horses) boxcars. Their destination was Lorraine. Here in the fertile valleys dotted by small hamlets within the sound of the guns at the front, the First Division embarked on its training program.

As they trained, these American soldiers, like their compatriots who would follow, had to adjust to the customs and conditions of a foreign country. "Sunny France" proved not to be sunny; indeed, almost constant rain, mud, and pervading dampness made the term a joke. Living quarters, European style, were billets—usually stables and barns. The soldiers ate out of their mess-kits in the streets. And one could not seem to escape the pervasive odor of the "fumier." This heap of manure in front of each house was, as one officer wrote, "a disagreeable thing, irritating and dangerous in the dark. . . ."

Neither Gondrecourt, a town of some 2000, nor the smaller satellite villages occupied by the First Division offered much opportunity for diversion. Visiting friends in other billets, reading old newspapers, playing a card game, or pitching a ball almost exhausted the range of possibilities. For those who had the inclination, the time, and the money as well as the opportunity, wine and women did represent alternatives.

Although prohibition was the rule for men in uniform in the United States, Secretary Baker relaxed the regulation in France out of deference to local custom. There was some drunkenness. In the 26th Infantry after the first payday, the regimental commander suspended training for two days to allow for a drinking and sobering up interlude. The commander of the Fifth Artillery Regiment, Colonel George Van Horn Moseley, who also had trouble initially with drinking in his regiment, commented, "They were afraid that the cheap wine wouldn't last." But the wine did last, and while doughboys drank their share, one could hardly say that the AEF was debauched.

Women represented a more serious problem.

Every morning as he looked over the papers on his desk, Pershing paused to examine carefully the venereal report. When he inspected he always demanded to see that particular unit's report of venereal cases. If the rate seemed too high or if there was an increase, he wanted an explanation. As Harbord said, "There was no subject on which more emphasis was laid, throughout the existence of the American Expeditionary Forces."

From the arrival of the first combat troops to his own departure from France, Pershing made it very clear that he intended to do all he could hold down the venereal rate. During his first six months in France, he issued three general orders on the subject. Through these orders and other publications as well as lectures, GHQ made the doughboy well aware that he was expected to be continent; that the AEF would try to provide recreation and to eliminate temptation and would, all else failing, provide prophylaxis. If a soldier still contracted a venereal disease, he could expect a court-martial and punishment. Finally, unit commanders learned that Pershing would hold them responsible for the venereal rates in their units.

The man who was directly in charge of the venereal disease program was the distinguished surgeon and urologist, Dr. Hugh Young of Johns Hopkins University. A witty southerner (the son of a Confederate general) who could joke about his work while still going about it very seriously, Young set up treatment for venereal cases at regimental level, thus avoiding the waste of transportation and hospital beds. He also inaugurated medical service for French civilians in areas where American troops were stationed. Young's efforts, strongly supported by Pershing, resulted in a venereal rate in September 1918, which was less than one case among each 1000 soldiers. In their fight against the social disease, Young and Pershing did have a great advantage over the military authorities in the United States, since infected soldiers were not permitted to board an AEF-bound transport; nevertheless, they made a remarkable record in holding down the number of ineffectives resulting from venereal disease.

The French initially did not consider the American approach to the venereal problem practical. In February 1918, Premier Clemenceau, in a letter to GHQ, criticized the repressive policy and suggested, as an alternative, licensed houses of prostitution, which he would help to establish. The American reply denied that Clemenceau's information was correct and called for a conference on the matter. Meanwhile Pershing gave Raymond Fosdick a copy of the letter to show to Secretary Baker. When Fosdick passed the letter on to the Secretary, Baker read it twice and then exclaimed, "For God's sake, Raymond, don't show this to the President or he'll stop the war." Despite the French protest, Pershing continued his policy, while Young and other medical officers argued the question at the conference. According to Young, the

Americans succeeded in convincing the French that the repressive approach was the better course. At least, the Premier wrote no more letters on the subject.

No one could expect the French and the Americans to get along perfectly with each other. The query—"Don't any of these people speak American?"—which many soldiers asked in exasperation explains part of the problem. But a more complete, yet succinct, explanation came from an officer, a Russian Jewish immigrant with years of regular service as a noncom. As adjutant of a medical unit, he lectured the men upon their arrival in France, "Their vays are not our vays."

The war placed an army of more or less provincial soldiers in the midst of an equally provincial citizenry. While the French might welcome the Americans as reinforcements, the fact was that in the Lorraine villages and later in various other sections of France the American army was virtually an occupying power. Medical officers in their quest for sanitation disrupted local habits, centuries old. The spendthrift ways of the doughboys met with an ambivalent response of jealousy and greed. The Americans seemed to have in abundance items long scarce in French civilian circles and apparently were reckless in their attitude toward private property. On the other hand, the American soldier believed that he was being overcharged consistently. Then, as a soldier (Private William P. Carson) who arrived in France in 1918 recounted, "We had the feeling that we were over there to help them. . . . Yet, all that concerned them was getting paid for damages." The language barrier heightened minor difficulties. When the commander of the First Division, Major General William L. Sibert, reported on the progress of his command on October 8, 1917, he complained, "Much trouble has been experienced with interpreters. It is particularly difficult to secure an interpreter who will convey the full meaning of one's remark to the person addressed."

Children provided a bridge. Soldiers like them, and the strange men in uniform fascinated the youngsters. Frederick Palmer, the famed war correspondent who served as chief censor on Pershing's staff, believed that the soldiers picked up the smattering of French that they had primarily from children. Certainly the little ones were much in evidence in the village streets. A welder turned infantryman, Ben H. Bernheisel, remembered, "The small French children about our quarters had learned our drill quite well. . . . Their leader would give the commands in fine English, not omitting the profane. It was really a show to watch them."

On Christmas Day 1917 the soldiers of the First Division entertained their young friends. After they quickly collected 35,000 francs from the doughboys, a committee went to Paris "to buy out the town." When the important day came, there was a decorated tree in every village within the division area. A soldier Santa Claus gave the children toys, fruit, nuts, and hard-to-get candy, and, to each of the three-hundred-odd Belgian and French orphans, a complete clothing outfit as well. Lieutenant Colonel Benjamin F. Cheatham, who initiated the idea, was pleased with the results, "I don't know who were the happiest—the men who gave, the children who received, or the parents who were looking on. . . ." Before the day was done, the grateful mayor of Gondrecourt expressed his appreciation in writing, "Never, perhaps, have such bonds been obtained between two nations. . . . It was, indeed, a feast of two great families. . . ."

Many overcame the prejudices, the distorted stereotypes, which separate nationalities. Some married French girls; others made lasting friendships with the French families with whom they were billeted. Following World War II, the then Secretary of State, George C. Marshall, who had lived in Gondrecourt as a young officer, stopped by with his wife and aides to visit his friends of 1917. In the intervening decades, countless other AEF veterans had kept up correspondence and had made similar visits.

When the first American troops arrived in Lorraine, they learned that the "Blue Devils" of the crack French 47th Division—Chasseurs Alpin—would be their tutors. But, before the French could start explaining the intricacies of trench warfare, the American officers decreed a heavy dose of physical conditioning and drilling with emphasis on, as General Sibert said, "development of a proper disciplinary spirit." After all, so many in the First Division were recent recruits.

The French wanted to make training as realistic as possible, so the Americans dug a large trench complex—"Washington Center"—near Gondrecourt and smaller ones in the other training areas. Thus the "Blue Devils" could demonstrate not only their

weapons which now the doughboys must use—Chauchat automatic rifle, Hotchkiss machine gun, 37 mm gun, and grenades—
but also the proper solutions of tactical problems in trench warfare. Despite differences in language and temperament, the
Americans respected and got along well with the "chasers."

Training was rigorous. Officially the training schedule took up
eight hours a day, five days a week, and Saturday morning, but
there were also unbroken forty-eight-hour stretches in the practice trenches before the departure for the front. It is not surprising that there were some heads nodding when the men paused in
their vigorous activities to watch the French give demonstrations.
The poilus did get undivided attention, however, when they
brought out flame-throwers and tried to explain how to defend
against gas attack. Private Bernheisel and his "buddies" in F Company, 16th Infantry, thought the use of gas "cowardly and inhu-
man," and they were, in his words, "terribly embittered" that gas
and flame were now being used in warfare. Apparently this made
a deeper impression on the soldiers than the attempts to explain
the principles of the American and Allied cause and the recital of
German "outrages" which GHQ ordered emphasized.

In the last week of September, after the American infantrymen
had run through some tactical problems in trench warfare, the
French officers offered their criticism. The neophytes failed to
give proper attention to details of supply and liaison; they called
for impossible artillery barrages and failed to position their machine guns properly. Then, in the imaginary attack, "Intervals
between men in waves were frequently insufficient and demoral-
izing casualties would have resulted."

Some of these lessons the doughboys would learn the hard
way. In particular, the high cost of the attack at Soissons in July
1918 would indicate that they had to learn the last point the hardest way of all.

This training period was a time of trial as well as of learning.
Brigadier General George B. Duncan commented, "This process
of training resulted in the relief of some older officers and placing
of responsibility upon more ambitious youngsters." An outstanding example of the latter, according to Duncan, was the son of a
famous father, Major Theodore Roosevelt, Jr., of whom he said,
"I have never known a harder working, more concientious leader."

Young Roosevelt even turned the daily hikes to and from the drill field into imaginative tactical problems for his battalion. Over in the 28th Infantry, the commander of Company G, Lieutenant Clarence R. Huebner, was another of those officers who was making the most of every opportunity to prepare his men. This Kansan, who had spent almost seven years in the ranks before he obtained his commission, was a firm believer in the rifle. He set up his own rifle range so that his men would get extra target practice. Every day each man fired five rounds at tin cans hanging on wires at ranges of 50 and·100 yards. (During World War II, Huebner commanded the First Division in the invasion of Europe and later a corps.) Duncan himself was one of the older generation who was succeeding while several of his contemporaries were failing. He arrived in France as the commander of the 26th Infantry Regiment. Within two and a half months he was a brigade commander in the First Division, and, in the next spring, he would wear two stars and take command of a National Army division.

The artillerymen of the First Division got a late start in their training. They did not arrive in France until mid-August, and then they went to Valdahon near the Swiss border rather than Gondrecourt. In the cool weeks of early fall, the cannoneers rapidly became acquainted with the French guns—75mm and 155 mm—with which they would fight their war. After the preliminary drills, the Americans went on the firing ranges every day except Sundays for some four and a half weeks, until they left for the front.

While the First Division was in the early stages of its training, Pershing put his staff to work constructing an elaborate school system to supplement unit training. Langres, a few miles south of Chaumont, was the Army Schools Center and the location of the General Staff College and several other schools. Others which offered instruction for specialists of all types from chaplains to cooks were scattered throughout France. Since these schools required faculty and students, the First Division had to furnish some of both. In late July, Pershing called on one of the brigade commanders, Brigadier General Robert L. Bullard, and Colonel James W. McAndrew, a regimental commander, to help set up the system.

This drain on divisional personnel provoked comment. One of the company commanders (Huebner) complained, "We had good noncom material but I found that as soon as I got a good man, he was sent off to school." At a higher level, Major George C. Marshall, chief of operations of the division, noted in the divisional war diary on November 26, 1917, "The departure for the Staff College or Corps Schools of nine out of twelve battalion commanders has seriously handicapped regimental commanders in starting the first week of the regimental training."

In the fall of 1917, the staff officers of GHQ drew upon their observations of the First Division to form several conclusions about training. Underlying a statement of general principles which the Adjutant General, Benjamin Alvord, issued on October 6 was a lack of satisfaction with the French dominance in this pioneering stage. Alvord made it clear that in the future training methods would be "distinctly our own." He added, "The standards for the American army will be those of West Point." Pershing wanted his men to break the deadlock on the Western Front, hence through his Adjutant General he emphasized the primacy of open warfare, a mobile offensive, over trench warfare. He also stressed strongly that officers should not be pessimistic. The G-5 (Training) section supplemented these principles with a specific program. During the first month in France, units should practice small unit tactics. Following this, the soldiers would occupy a quiet sector for four weeks and become accustomed to life at the front. Then, in the final month prior to their commitment to battle they would train at division level with artillery and aviation in offensive maneuvers. Although events in 1918 would force modifications, GHQ tried to put all of the divisions through at least an abbreviated version of this training program.

By the time this statement of policy came out of Chaumont, the First Division was in the final stages of preparation for the second phase of training and its initial move to the front. Since the departure of General de Pouydraguin and his Chasseurs in early September, General Paul E. J. Bordeaux and the 18th Division had assumed the training role, and they would supervise the American's introduction to the Western Front.

The plan was that a battalion from each of the four infantry regiments, together with a machine gun company and appropriate engineer and signal detachments, would occupy a sector for ten days. American officers would retain command of their companies, but the battalion and regimental commanders would be merely observers. At the same time the artillery regiments would each send forward a battalion, although the artillerymen would stay two weeks instead of ten days. Throughout the entire period, the French would retain control of the sector.

The scene of the American debut—the Sommerviller sector—was a quiet area some ten kilometers northeast of Nancy. There had been no heavy fighting in this sector since the first year of the war. Here the front line consisted of a series of company-size strongpoints. The French depended on the cordons of barbed wire and patrols to protect the gaps between these centers of resistance.

On the night of October 21, the first battalions moved into the line. As the first American combat units at the front, they collected a number of distinctions—first shot fired, first wounded, first prisoner (a mail orderly who wandered into the area of the 18th Infantry)—but there was no fighting during their tour. There would be more action for the second contingent.

After nightfall on November 2, the second battalions started to make their way forward through mud, mist, and pitch darkness. The men of Company F, 16th Infantry, one of the companies which had paraded in Paris on the Fourth of July, occupied the Artois strongpoint on a hill near Bathelémont. Earlier, as they waited in the ruins of Bathelémont, there had been some joking when they came under shell fire. Now there was tense excitement. By 9:30 p.m. the company commander, First Lieutenant Willis E. Comfort, could report the relief completed and his company in place.

The men had been at Artois less than six hours when the Germans began firing a heavy barrage which boxed in the strongpoint. The shelling cut the telephone wires and badly damaged the communications trenches before it shifted directly onto the strongpoint. Lieutenant Comfort wanted to call for a counter barrage, but the French lieutenant who was advising him talked him out of it. Simultaneously in the rear, the American battalion commander met initially with a similar response from a French major. Finally, however, the major did order a light and ineffective barrage.

By this time a raiding party of Bavarians had emerged from the heavy fog and smoke in the American trenches. After a hectic ten to fifteen minutes, they departed with eleven prisoners. They left behind a deserter, several Americans wounded, and the bodies of Corporal James Bethel Gresham, Private Thomas F. Enright, and Private Merle D. Hay.

The Germans considered "Jacobsbrunnen" (their code name for the raid) a success. For several days the soldiers in the Seventh Bavarian Landwehr Regiment had suspected that they were facing Americans. In order to obtain positive identification the commander authorized a raiding party of 213 officers and men. Although they lost two killed and seven wounded besides the one deserter, the Bavarians did establish the identification of the Americans. The leader of the raiders, Lieutenant Wolf, a schoolmaster in peacetime, also reported, "The enemy was very good in hand to hand fighting. . . ."

After daybreak on November 3, Captain George C. Marshall of the First Divison staff accompanied General Bordeaux on a visit to the scene. During their stay they questioned officers and men as well as the German prisoner and were able to determine the facts of the affair. Marshall reported to the division chief of staff that the men of Company F other than those in the platoon raided were "in very fair spirits," while Bordeaux acknowledged that they had "offered the utmost possible resistance."

The rest of their stay at Artois was less eventful for the men of Company F. Private Bernheisel remembered, "Duties of a soldier were carried on. Our rifles were kept clean and we tried to brush ourselves up a bit. Water was not plentiful but the chow was O.K." There were snow flurries and rain, but aside from some shelling and an occasional burst of small-arms fire the front was quiet. When their ten-day tour was done, they left under the same conditions as they arrived—at night in the cold rain.

By the end of November, the division was back in its training areas. After their tour in the trenches, the men were pleased to return to the billets. "Oh how welcome that barn" one soldier rejoiced. The scarcity of fuel combined with the severe cold lessened the comforts of life in these makeshift quarters; yet, stables and barns were far more comfortable than waterlogged trenches.

"The winter of 1917–1918 was godawful." Clarence Huebner bluntly summed up the opinion of those Americans who spent that season in Lorraine. The damp, pervading chill of one of the worst winters in years hampered but did not halt training. Soldiers grumbled as they carried full packs on long marches in the large scale maneuvers, which lasted up to two days in the icy weather. But they kept moving. There were shortages—winter clothing, gloves, leggings, shoes, and, for the animals, forage—but training continued. If, on occasion, weather made outdoor training impossible, the men assembled and disassembled their weapons and did the manual of arms in their billets. Frederick Palmer, the war-correspondent-turned-soldier, was not being too melodramatic when he referred to this period as the Valley Forge of the AEF.

While soldiers had to endure the rigors of maneuvers, a major purpose of these exercises was to train officers. Leaders had to master the problems of communications, logistics, and tactics. Staff officers from GHQ and often even Pershing himself watched them perform their jobs. Mistakes meant losing one's command. Success offered the opportunity of leading troops in battle.

One of the officers who excelled was the tall, sandy-haired new colonel of the 16th Infantry—John L. Hines. On horseback or in a motorcycle sidecar, he spent the daylight hours among his men. He organized the regimental staff in order to ensure the proper coordination of training. At night he studied tactics. Taciturn, thorough, firm, he suffered from nervous indigestion but no one who followed him throughout a day's activities would believe it. He earned the praise which one of his company commanders (Sidney C. Graves) gave him, "He made the 16th Infantry!"

Pershing had seen enough of the British and French leaders to be impressed with the necessity for energetic commanders. No doubt he was pleased with the performance of his former adjutant "Birdie" Hines. At the same time, he considered relieving the commanding general of the First Division.

Since the formation of the division, line officers had been chagrined with the assignment of an engineer to its command. Major General William L. Sibert had a distinguished record as an engineer, culminating in his work on the Panama Canal, but he had no experience as a combat leader. As early as August, Pershing had complained to the Secretary of War's representative, Felix Frankfurter, that Sibert could not "stand the 'gaff,'" and Frankfurter agreed. There were other complaints, justified or unjustified: Sibert depended too much on his staff; he was not enthusiastic enough about open warfare training; he was too inactive and had let the division decline in efficiency. Then Harbord, who was as close to Pershing as anyone, noted in his diary that Sibert was "a positive danger as the second senior officer in France."

Sibert never had much of a chance. Early in October, Pershing excoriated him in front of his officers when he fumbled through a critique of a tactical maneuver. On October 20, the C-in-C told Robert L. Bullard that he was considering promoting him to command of the division. Finally, on December 14, Pershing made the change, and Sibert returned to the United States where he became the Director of the Chemical Warfare Service.

Bullard understood clearly the Pershing method of command as he indicated in his diary on December 28, "He is looking for results. He intends to have them. He will sacrifice any man who does not bring them."

Other division commanders felt the Pershing touch even before their units reached France. During the winter when these generals came over on a month's tour in order to become familiar with wartime conditions, Pershing noted that over half were either physically incapable or too unalert to adjust to the demands of frontline duty. British division commanders who observed these officers for ten days sent him reports which corroborated his views. The visitors also impressed a First Division brigade commander, George B. Duncan, with their casual, sightseeing attitude. Pershing requested that those he considered inadequate be relieved, and the Secretary of War and the Chief of Staff carried out his wishes. The ranking major general, Leonard Wood, was among those embittered by Pershing's decision.

The month of November 1917 was momentous. In Russia, Lenin and his Bolshevik followers succeeded in overthrowing the provisional government of Alexander Kerensky and withdrawing Russia from the Allied camp. In northern Italy, the Central Powers pushed the Italians back some 70 miles and almost destroyed the Italian army. On the same day, November 10, that the Italians managed to establish a new line on the Piave River, the British called off their great Flanders offensive. Since July they had battered the Germans with little success at a cost of a quarter of a million casualties. About all they could claim for the offensive was that it had taken the pressure off the French army, which was recovering slowly from the debilitating losses and mutinies of the spring.

At the time, two other events of that month did not seem as impressive, but they were crucial in the evolution of the Allied war effort. Because of the Caporetto disaster, British Prime Minister Lloyd George was able to persuade the French, Italians, and, later, the Americans to join in a Supreme War Council. This political organization of the prime ministers with its military advisory body would provide for the first time, Lloyd George hoped, a coordinating agency for grand strategy. Before the month was out, the French Premier, Paul Painlevé, who helped form the Council would be out of power. But his successor, the indomitable old journalist Georges Clemenceau, brought the impetus of a strong will, a vigorous spirit, and a shrewd intellect to the helm of a country shaken and seriously weakened by three years of war.

The American role on the Supreme War Council was limited by the President's insistence on political independence from the Allies. On the other hand, Wilson strongly endorsed the Council as a means of unifying the Allied-American military effort. Thus he refused to name a permanent political delegate, while he appointed the Chief of Staff of the Army, General Tasker H. Bliss, as military representative. He was a wise choice. The position provided Bliss with an excellent opportunity to use his considerable diplomatic and analytic talents. Since he carefully subordinated his views to those of Pershing in matters concerning the AEF, there was virtually no friction between the two American four-star officers in France. Above all, Bliss knew where the line was between political and military affairs and never forgot that he was a military adviser.

Before Bliss arrived in January, the other military advisers on the Council reached an obvious decision: their strategy for 1918 would be defensive. The Allies would play a waiting game until the Americans arrived in enough strength to make a decisive move.

In early January, when the temperature hovered near the freezing point, the troops of the First Division wound up their training maneuvers. Bullard added a final touch with what he called "a hate-making campaign." Posters went up and speakers scattered throughout the division area to spread the word of German atrocities.

On January 15, the men of the First Brigade started for the front. The roads were icy, and the cold rain which turned to sleet increased the weight of the heavy packs and overcoats. "Little do I remember of the last part of this hike," Bernheisel commented. "As one in a trance, my legs moved. . . ." Exhausted, miserable, and cold, the infantrymen found the haylofts exceedingly comfortable that night. The next day they were back on the road. In their rear, the artillery and supply trains careened forward with horses slipping on the ice and sometimes overturning the equipment as they went down.

Their destination was the Ansauville sector, a seven-and-one-half-kilometer-wide section roughly from Seicheprey to Bouconville along one side of the St. Mihiel salient. The First Moroccan Division turned over to the American brigade a waterlogged trench line running through a low, marshy area—a defensive position dominated by the Germans. From Montsec, which rose to almost 400 feet behind their lines, the Germans could observe activities on the plain for miles. Since 1914, this had been a quiet sector where both sides could send weary divisions for recuperation. Sidney Graves, who was now back in command of Company F, 16th Infantry, remarked, "You could have stood on the parapet and hung up your laundry and so could the Germans when we came."

Three American battalions, each with three companies on line, occupied the front and settled into a routine. One hour before daylight and one hour before dusk, the men were supposed to "stand to" with fixed bayonets. The rest of the day, except for a few sentries, they tried to sleep as much as possible. Commanders emphasized sanitation. Colonel Hines bluntly instructed the 16th Infantry, "Any man committing a nuisance in the trench will be tried" and ordered each soldier to shave daily. Still, as the division commander indicated, there were "too few baths and too many cooties." Body lice would be an unforgettable experience for the frontline doughboy. At night, while patrols went out into No Man's Land to listen for any enemy activity, other parties went to the rear to bring up the marmite cans full of hot food. The men in the reserve battalions, waiting for their ten-day stint at the front, spent their time constructing trenches and fighting off rats.

During the first fifteen days, the French retained tactical control and restrained the exuberant Americans, thus the sector remained quiet. When Bullard obtained command on February 5, his first act was to encourage his men to stir up the Germans. There was no more laundry hanging after this. With the help of binoculars, an American sniper opened fire on one German soldier who was literally putting up his laundry a thousand yards away. As Captain Graves said, "We really made them mad."

The artillery contributed the most to this increased activity. In February, the Americans fired slightly more than a thousand shells a day. The next month, they threw 90,469 shells into the German sector. The Germans replied in kind but to a lesser extent. The 78th Reserve Division, which faced the doughboys, increased its daily artillery fire from less than 100 to more than 800 shells a day in February. During March, American observers counted 41,558 incoming shells. To a great extent, this was an extended artillery duel with each side trying to hit the other's gun positions. In the process, both used gas in perhaps as many as one out of every ten shells.

The French had warned the Americans that this was an active gas sector and had reinforced their warning by posting instructions in every dugout and shelter. As a result, there was an unexpected large number of false alarms, but the danger was very real. In the early morning hours of February 26 the men of the third battalion of the 18th Infantry on the right of the American line in the Bois de Remières were on the receiving end of about seven tons of phosgene. Eight died, and seventy-seven others who breathed some of the poison vapor had to be treated, in this first large German gas attack against Americans. A few days later Battery D of the 6th Field Artillery caught such a heavy dosage of mustard gas that all of the officers and men had to be evacuated.

Everyone feared the burning effect of the mustard gas. Many soldiers carried bars of soap to wash it off the exposed parts of the body as well as their genitals and under arms where blisters were apt to form.

The gas and high explosives, the rains and intermittent snows, and the days when food did not reach the front line made life miserable for the men in the trenches. Nor did they appreciate the many visitors: French and American staff officers, generals, and assorted civilians. On February 17, Pershing himself toured the front line trench with the brigade commander, George Duncan. Later Premier Clemenceau and Secretary of War Baker paid their calls. Everyone seemed eager to see the American sector. Since visitors attracted shellfire, the doughboys were not enthusiastic about such attention.

Between the American and German lines, No Man's Land varied from fifty to five hundred yards of barbed wire and bare shell-pocked ground. At night, both sides patrolled this area with small detachments in efforts to measure the wire, to detect enemy activity, and to deny the space to the enemy. On one patrol, Sergeant Anthony Scanlan of Company F, 16th Infantry, an illiterate Irishman but a tough, fearless veteran, attempted to pass on his experience to one of the youngsters. As Scanlan and the young soldier awaited the other section of their patrol, the sergeant saw some men approaching. He whispered, "Them is square-heads. I'll show you how we did it on Mindanao." He took a small piece of white paper, wrapped it around the muzzle of his Springfield so he could see the sight and fired. Unfortunately, the men were the rest of the patrol and he hit a corporal in the hip. The corporal survived.

Raids such as the one the men of Company F, 16th Infantry, suffered at Artois in November were also means of gathering information. During the First Division's stay in the Ansauville sector, the Germans showed particular interest in the Bois de Remières near Seicheprey. On two occasions they sent large raiding parties against the trenches in this area. Both times the American artillery caught the raiders and killed and wounded many of them. In the first raid the Germans killed twenty men of the 18th Infantry and wounded and captured others. Eighteen days later on March 19, the American artillery caught the second raiding party before it reached the trenches of the 28th Infantry. After elaborate preparation, two American raiding teams never got out of their trenches on the first of March because the engineers failed to arrive with the bangalore torpedoes necessary to blast through the wire. Ten days later, both raiding units succeeded in penetrating the enemy line but found no Germans; however, they suffered four casualties.

The Second Brigade relieved the First Brigade on March 9 and kept the sector active until it turned the trenches over to the 26th Division on April 3. The larger casualty list reflected the difference between this sector and that occupied by the division in the fall. In the Sommerville sector, the division had lost eighty-three officers and men killed, wounded, and captured, while its defense of the Ansauville area had cost 549 casualties.

Three other divisions shared the experiences of the First Division in the winter of 1917–18. Although the First seemed to be a favorite of GHQ, the others went through the joys and irritations of living among the French, the rigorous training, the supply shortages, and the bitter cold. In March, all three were at the front in quiet sectors—the Second and 42nd in Lorraine and the 26th in Chemin des Dames. Under French tutelage, they became accustomed to the sights, sounds, and smells of the trenches. The first shell fired, the first gas attack, the first raid, the first death— all were dutifully recorded.

The 26th was the first of these divisions to arrive in France. Because of the quick thinking of the division commander and his aide who grabbed some empty transports, the division beat the 42nd to France in the fall of 1917 but did not endear itself to GHQ in the process. The New England National Guardsmen who made up the Yankee Division were a proud lot who could trace their militia lineage back to the colonial period. From the beginning they had "a community spirit" which flourished amidst the anti-Guard attitude of many regulars in the AEF. Officers such as Charles H. Cole, former adjutant general of Massachusetts and a brigadier general, who enlisted as a private when the war began and, by August, was again wearing a star, and Albert Greenlaw, who resigned his position as brigadier general and adjutant general of Maine to become a captain in one of the infantry regiments, exemplified this Yankee spirit.

Yet, these Guardsmen permitted a regular and a West Pointer to call their division his own. Tall, with closely cropped white hair and moustache, Clarence R. Edwards, a major general in command of the Northeastern Department in Boston in 1917, organized the division and commanded it until the closing days of the war. No division commander in the AEF was as beloved or as controversial as Edwards. A Massachusetts captain, James T. Duane, wrote after the war, "Every lad in the 26th Division hails General Clarence R. Edwards as the Father of our Division. He was familiarly called (behind his back of course) 'Daddy.' . . ." Although Edwards had the respect and confidence of his men, his critics at higher headquarters considered him a politician who could not be trusted with the command of a division. As early as February, staff officers and superior commanders noted Edwards's faults: he did not carry out instructions; he tried to cover up errors; he talked too much. To the Yankees, this criticism was simply part of a plot of the regulars against their division.

When the New Englanders relieved the First Division, they also took over an adjacent sector from a French division and an additional regiment. The Ansauville sector—now doubled in length to fifteen kilometers—became known as La Reine sector. To compound the confusion, the sector was also called Toul throughout the American occupancy. A week after the Yankees settled into the muck of the marshy trenches, the Germans staged three raids against the 104th Infantry on the extreme left of the line in the Bois Brulé. Effective artillery fire combined with some hand-to-hand fighting ran the Germans off on April 10. Two days later, the 104th beat off simultaneous attacks at two points. In these melees, the American infantrymen took an estimated forty prisoners and gave up only one man as prisoner. The French were very much impressed and decorated 117 officers and men.

The next action—the largest single American battle up to that time—took place on April 20 at the extreme right of the sector. The night was quiet, and the moon was bright enough to permit visibility of a mile. Despite this, the first battalion of the 102nd Infantry was able to complete its relief of the third battalion without enemy interference. By 1:30 in the morning of the 20th, Company C was in position in the Bois de Remières and Company D was in front of Seicheprey. With three platoons on line and one in support, each company was responsible for a half-mile of the trenches.

Shortly after 3:00 a.m., the Germans opened up a heavy barrage which continued for two hours. At 5:00, under cover of the early morning fog, a force of an estimated 2800 Germans—spearheaded by a picked group of shock troops known as "Hindenburg's Traveling Circus"—overran both companies. The shelling had destroyed the two support platoons and broken communications lines. Even the battalion commander did not know what had happened until after dawn, and higher headquarters remained confused about the situation throughout the day. The shell-shocked captain of Company C stumbled into battalion headquarters and reported his company wiped out. Two patrols went out and found the survivors of Company D engaged in hand-to-hand combat. Lieutenant Daniel W. Strickland, who led one of the patrols, reported on the rest, "There they were, dead—in windrows almost, out in front of the fire trenches which by reason of the mud made poor places from which to fight."

The fighting continued throughout the day as reinforcements came up; however, a formal counter-attack planned initially for that night and then for early the next morning never came off. A major, who incidentally was not a Guardsman, disobeyed a direct order to carry out the assault. Later he was court-martialed and convicted for his poor judgment, but the attack was not necessary. By dawn of the 21st, the Germans had pulled back. The Connecticut Guardsmen were again in control of their old lines but less than 100 men remained from Companies C. and D.

The Germans reported 600 casualties, although the New Englanders estimated that they had inflicted more than twice that many. Pershing believed that the Americans lost 669 casualties, including 81 killed and 187 captured or missing. In callous military idiom, one could say that the 26th was bloodied.

The other National Guard unit in the first four divisions of the AEF was the 42nd. Unlike the Yankee Division, this division consisted of units from twenty-six states and the District of Columbia. In the summer of 1917, Douglas MacArthur conceived the idea of such an organization and gave its name when he told Secretary Baker—"It will stretch across the nation like a rainbow." With Baker's approval, the Chief of the Militia Bureau, William

A. Mann, began collecting the various Guard units, and MacArthur, who jumped from major to colonel when Baker named him chief of staff, started gathering a staff and planning to organize and equip the division. The infantry regiments which formed the core of the division were the 69th New York, Fourth Ohio, Fourth Alabama, and Third Iowa. Although these regiments lost their state designations and became, respectively, the 165th, 166th, 167th, and 168th, they retained their local spirit.

By November the Rainbow was training in France. Before it moved to the front, it gained a new commander and lived through a threat to its existence. General Mann, who was in his sixty-fourth year and looked it, returned home to retire. An artillery-man and West Point classmate of Pershing's, the genial Charles T. Menoher, took his place. For a time it appeared that his would be a hollow assignment. The rumor was that GHQ planned to use the division as a replacement base for a corps. Both Menoher and MacArthur appealed to Chaumont, and the 42nd retained its combat status.

In late February, the division began its month-long training stint in the quiet Luneville sector. According to the division historian, Henry J. Reilly, "The trenches were not quite like what the officers and men had expected to find. The front line was not always continuous." The line consisted of small defensive positions along the front separated by as much as 400 or 500 yards.

After the men had become more or less accustomed to the routine, their French tutors scheduled two raids on March 9. As the Iowans in Company F, 168th Infantry, waited under a German barrage to make one of the assaults, they noticed a visitor. "I saw a guy with a turtleneck sweater and a cap on, . . ." one soldier recalled, "and I couldn't figure what a fellow dressed like that could be doin' out there. When I found out who he was, you could have knocked me over with a feather." Colonel Douglas MarArthur was not one to wait at headquarters for news. On this particular raid, however, he and his companions reached the enemy trenches only to find them evacuated.

Already MacArthur was attracting the attention of higher headquarters. Lieutenant Colonel Hugh A. Drum, who stayed with the division as Pershing's personal representative throughout the Luneville tour, noted in his diary that MacArthur "is a bright young chap—full of life and go. He will settle down soon and make his name."

While in this sector, the Irish of the "Fighting 69th" celebrated Saint Patrick's Day. Since March 17 fell on Sunday, Father Francis P. Duffy had to say mass. Then the third battalion which was in the trenches was limited in its observance of the occasion, but the boys in the rear area had a fine time. Tommy McCardle sang funny songs and John Mullin serious ones; McManus and Quinn played their fifes for the Irish dances; and Lieutenant Prout recited the poem "Oh Ireland, I Bid You the Top of the Morning." Father Duffy concluded the celebration by reading a sad poem "Rouge Bouquet" by Joyce Kilmer and by directing the band "to follow me up with a medley of rollicking Irish airs. . . ." One wonders what the southerners and midwesterners, not to mention the French, thought about this curious affair.

During the Rainbow's stay in the Luneville sector, it had its share of visitors. Secretary Baker and General Tasker H. Bliss came as did Pershing, who toured a front-line trench within 300 yards of the enemy. The guest who stayed the longest was Lieutenant Colonel Drum. When he returned to Chaumont, he wrote that the division had made "an excellent showing." He was certainly impressed: "The men have undergone the hardships of long bombardments, gas attacks, and raids. They stand up against it well and never flinch. . . . All we lack is the majors and captains to make the team. They will come in time. The material is there."

The last of the pioneering divisions to reach the front was the Second, which entered the trenches in Lorraine near Sommedieue in mid-March. Half of the infantry in this outfit were Marines and the other half regulars, but a large percentage of both were recruits: 87.2 per cent of the soldiers and 74.3 per cent of the Marines had less than a year's service.

Although their recruiting campaign was based on the slogan "First to Fight," it looked in April and early May of 1917 as if the Marines would not even make it to France. Finally a presidential order swept aside army opposition, and the hastily organized Fifth Marine Regiment sailed with the First Division. There was no room in the First for another regiment—particularly a Marine regiment; so GHQ scattered the Marines throughout France and

England as military police. With the arrival of another regiment, the Sixth, Marine Brigadier General Charles A. Doyen collected the men of the Fifth and formed the Fourth Marine Brigade. The 280 officers and 9164 men made this the largest tactical unit in Marine Corps history up to that time. Doyen and other old timers remembered the 1890's when the entire Corps was less than a third the size of that brigade.

The other brigade was "Old Army"—at least in name and tradition—for the Ninth and 23rd Infantry Regiments had an impressive array of battle streamers on their regimental colors. And they were as eager to earn more battle honors as were the Marines.

From January until March the division trained. A sergeant in the Sixth Marines, who retired a full general after the Korean War, Gerald C. Thomas, said, "It was this period that made us tough. . . . We got tough, we stayed tough." They were also enthusiastic. The French tried to keep them quiet when they began their training at the front but to no avail. The French division commander, General Eugene Savatier, who supervised the 23rd Infantry during this phase of instruction, exclaimed, "But they were irrepressible!" On April 7, Pershing came to see them. When he talked with General Hirschauer, who commanded the French Second Army, about the division, he was pleased but not surprised with Hirschauer's reaction: "He said that without doubt it was then as efficient as any of his French divisions, confirming my own opinion. . . ."

These were big divisions. At a strength of 28,000 men, they were double the size of Allied and German divisions. Some of the French officers began to complain in the spring of 1918 that they were too big. No doubt the difference in size did lead to some confusion. Bullard observed that the French treated the American division "practically as a corps." Despite the criticism the Americans kept their divisions large. The reasoning was simple: because of its larger size, the American division should be able to sustain heavier losses and stay in battle longer. A secondary consideration was that, since there was a shortage of trained officers capable of commanding and carrying on the staff duties, fewer divisions would require fewer commanders and staffs. Heavy fighting would prove or disprove the soundness of the decision to keep the large division.

Before they became engaged in the great battles, all four of the pioneer divisions needed replacements to maintain their strength. The GHQ plan to replenish the ranks of the combat divisions caused disgruntlement. For each four combat divisions in a corps, GHQ wanted to keep two replacement divisions in support. The National Guardsmen from the West in the 41st Division and those from Michigan and Wisconsin in the 32nd Division arrived in France in December and February to find that they were to be used to sustain the four divisions already there.

They were bitter, as would be others who found themselves in the same predicament throughout 1918. About 12,000 men in the 41st went to the First Division and an equal number to the Second, while one regiment of the 32nd sent all of its captains and privates to the First. In April, the 32nd was able to regain combat status, but the 41st remained a depot division to the end of the war. In time Pershing authorized a change in policy so that one rather than two out of every six divisions would serve as a replacement unit.

The German offensives in the spring of 1918 brought into clear focus the Allied need for American reinforcement. After Russia left the war and the Italians suffered their defeat at Caporetto, it did not take military genius to recognize the situation and to prophesy that Germany would try to win a decisive victory on the Western Front. With the reinforcement of over 40 divisions which Erich von Ludendorff, the chief strategist of the German High Command, could draw from the East, the Germans would have numerical superiority and the initiative in the West.

In the face of this danger the Allies had moved toward greater unity in the creation of the Supreme War Council, but there was no unity of command, and the inter-allied reserve was little more than a gesture. In two of the first joint notes submitted by the military representatives of this Council, Allied generals recommended the logical strategy on the Western Front—defense until the Americans became a significant weight in the balance. The French commander—Pétain—endorsed this policy with his own estimate of the situation.

Both the French and British armies were short of manpower and were war weary. The costly slaughter of the 1917 offensives not only had reduced the British ranks but also had brought about a feud between the civilian and military leaders. Despite this manpower shortage, the British had to extend their front to help out the French, who were still recovering from the debacle of 1917.

While the Allies waited, the Germans prepared for their great blow. Behind their lines, divisions learned the so-called von Hutier tactics which had caused the earlier breakthroughs on the Eastern Front and in Italy. The artillerymen, Colonel Bruchmuller and Captain Pulkowsky, taught the techniques of surprise—targeting without actually firing and the massing of guns and their use in a rolling barrage. The infantrymen under the guidance of Captain Geyer learned to think in terms of the small group. The light machine gun, the light trench mortar, the flame-thrower, the close coordination of infantry with artillery and aircraft—all contributed to the mobility. When the day came, the small infantry attack teams would move close behind the artillery cover and continue to move, bypassing strong points, until the enemy's defense collapsed.

They prepared well—tactically. "Michael," the code name for the offensive, opened on a foggy Thursday morning, March 21. When the front stabilized two weeks later, the Germans could take pride in a signal tactical victory. They had made a penetration of almost forty miles and had crushed the British Fifth Army. Strategically, they had failed to win a decisive victory: their shock troops had not eliminated the British army and had failed to separate the two allied armies.

While "Michael" was in full course, the Allies at last achieved a unity of military control. On March 26, British and French leaders met at Doullens and, at Haig's insistence, conferred coordinating authority over both armies to Ferdinand Foch. The British commander needed help, and his French counterpart was reluctant to weaken his front to come to his aid. In his diary, Haig commented that Pétain had the appearance "of a Commander who was in a funk and has lost his nerve."

Within days Foch realized the impotence of his authority. At Beauvais, on April 3, the Allied leaders again met with both Clemenceau and Lloyd George present as well as Bliss and Pershing. They agreed, with the enthusiastic endorsement of the Americans, to grant Foch "the strategic direction of military operations." Although the commanders of the national armies retained tactical control as well as the right of appeal to their respective governments if they objected to a particular decision, Foch was the generalissimo. And Foch always looked forward to the attack.*

Before the Allies could take the offensive, however, they had to stem the German drive and hold on until their strength increased enough for an offensive of their own. Although a few Americans, engineer troops who were caught in the British Fifth Army area, were in the battle, thousands were needed. Immediately, Pershing fulfilled Haig's request for three regiments of engineers and promised that two heavy artillery regiments would follow. He was more generous with the French when he offered first Pétain and then Foch "all that we have. . . ." At the end of March, this meant a mere 318,621 officers and men. Including the 32nd, there were only five combat divisions. In negotiations which reached the White House level, the Allies dickered for the transport of more infantry rather than logistical troops and more control over the American reinforcements. But Pershing's generosity did not extend that far. He did order the Second Division to extend its sector and sent the 42nd and the 26th to the front to relieve French divisions and the First Division for more active sectors. The 32nd had to collect its people and undergo some more training before it could go to the front in late May.

The First Division underwent a brief period of rest and training before it moved to its new sector. Bullard, the thin, southern general who impressed a portrait painter with his aristocratic appearance, almost did not make the trip. Just before he left the Ansauville sector, a severe attack of neuritis put him in the hospital. Although the pain remained, he returned to his command and kept going for the rest of the war.

The Montdidier sector was at the point of the Germans' deepest penetration in the March offensive. By April 24, when the First

---

* John Terraine, the biographer of Haig, has given fair warning to those who attempt to view Foch's role from a World War II point of reference. In 1917–18, none of the Allies possessed sufficient preponderance of strength to permit a supreme commander to be really supreme. Then, Foch never had a Joint Allied staff comparable to the one Eisenhower used in the second war. *Douglas Haig: The Educated Soldier* (London, 1963), 375, 426.

Division took over the shell holes which passed for a front line, the Germans had hit the British with another drive to the north. Nevertheless, the Americans found activity enough along their front. Artillery fire seemed to be continuous, and there was a lot of gas.

As it became apparent that the Germans were not going to renew the attack in this area, the French began to plan a counter thrust. They soon dropped the plan to retake Montdidier; however, they did permit the Americans to stage a small attack in their sector facing Cantigny—a small village in ruins some three miles west of Montdidier. Originally the 18th Infantry was to have the task of seizing Cantigny on May 25th, but the Germans caught that unit in a heavy gas attack on the night of May 3rd and caused so many casualties (variously estimated from 700 to 900) that the plan was changed. Bullard asked for a delay of three days and designated the 28th Regiment for the assault.

Since this was the first American attack, First Division planners made elaborate preparations. They furnished not only detailed plans but also the division artillery and machine-gun battalions, the machine-gun companies of the 16th and 18th Infantry Regiments, a company of engineers and two additional rifle companies (from the 18th) to support the 28th. The French contributed more artillery, a group of twelve tanks, half of a flame-thrower platoon, and air cover. Prior to the attack, the infantrymen rehearsed with the tanks and aircraft against positions built to resemble the objective. General Pershing would be present, so perfection was in order.

The attack was virtually flawless. At 5:45 on the hazy morning of May 28th, 386 mortars and guns, including a few 280 millimeter monsters, began pounding the objective with high explosives and gas. One hour later, the infantry and tanks moved out close behind a rolling barrage and a smoke screen. By 7:30 they were digging in on the objective—an arc of some two kilometers encompassing Cantigny and representing an advance up to 1600 meters. In the ruined village, mopping-up squads were flushing stunned Germans out of the cellars and shell holes. Huebner, who took command of the second battalion when the major was killed, could never forget the horrible sight of seeing one German appearing "just as I had seen rabbits in Kansas come out of burning strawstacks [he] ran ten to fifteen yards then fell over singed to death." The Germans in the town were killed or captured.

As reports filtered up to their command hierarchy, the Germans were confused. At first they thought that the attackers were French. When they learned the truth, explanations were still in order as to why they lost the village: the men in the garrison had been there only since midnight; there was a lack of coordination since elements of two different regiments were in Cantigny; and the soldiers had never seen tanks before.

Infuriated by the loss, the Germans were determined to retake the salient. Two companies managed to force some of the Americans off the high ground beyond Cantigny before the morning was over, but the other German attempts failed. The Americans thought that they beat off as many as six counterattacks; however, the Germans were unable to provide artillery support for a single unified attack. The commanders of the 271st and 272nd Reserve Regiments failed to coordinate their efforts and did not establish close liaison with the artillery, so their understrength companies could not overcome the Americans.

Although the German artillery did not cooperate properly with the infantry, it did keep up a heavy bombardment which, together with machine-gun fire, made the Cantigny salient a very hot place indeed. With the withdrawal of the tanks and much of the supporting artillery an hour and a half after the attack, it was up to the 28th, with whatever support Bullard could muster from within the division, to hang on to the captured ground.

Colonel Hanson E. Ely, the gruff, forceful, former West Point football player who, as Huebner said, "really commanded the regiment," did not rattle easily. He had a reputation for pugnacity, and he was well aware of the prestige value of this attack. But on the night of May 29th, he warned that unless his regiment were relieved the next night he could not be responsible for what happened. As he bluntly put it over the telephone, "Front line pounded to hell and gone. . . ." Sleepless, short of food, water, and ammunition, suffering from casualties up to 40 per cent in some companies, the regiment was relieved by the 16th on the next night. The battle was not over, as the men of the 16th Infantry who endured the continued heavy shelling and machine-gun fire could testify, but the possession of the ruins of Cantigny and its shell-pocked surroundings was no longer in question.

The First Division at a cost of 1067 casualties took and held Cantigny, captured 225 prisoners, and killed and wounded perhaps as many as 1400 Germans. The commanders, staff officers, and men demonstrated clearly that they could plan and execute a successful operation. Admittedly, the enemy 82nd Reserve Division which lost Cantigny was not a crack unit (Intelligence officers rated it as third-class),* but this did not dim the luster of the victory. While the Americans probably exaggerated the impression their victory made on the Allies and the Germans, the success certainly bolstered American confidence, and those French officers who observed the battle were properly impressed.

The third German offensive, not Cantigny, was the focus of attention in the last days of May. An American Intelligence officer, Captain Samuel T. Hubbard, Jr., had predicted that the Germans would strike along the Chemin des Dames ridge, but the French had shrugged off his reasoning. On May 27, the Germans broke through the French lines in that sector. By nightfall they had advanced twelve miles. Three days later, German infantrymen were on the Marne—some fifty miles from Paris. By this time Pershing was giving less attention to the map of Cantigny and more to those of the Aisne-Marne.

---

* At GHQ, the Intelligence section maintained histories of all German divisions. Based on the interrogation of prisoners and captured documents, these officers assembled information about battle records, losses, morale, and discipline. In rating the enemy units, they took into particular consideration how and in what situation the enemy command used these units. If depended upon as an assault force under difficult conditions, the division would be rated first-class. If used primarily as a defensive unit, it would be considered fourth-class. Second-class and third-class designations represented variations of those classifications.

·VI·

A Divided Effort:
War Department and GHQ

The American war effort entered a new phase in the spring of
1918. By that time the foundation of the war-making structure
was in place, and new and greatly expanded old organizations
were beginning to function more smoothly under men who were
able to rise to the demands of the emergency. As Bernard M.
Baruch commented, "Our war effort was jelling at the time."

During the last eight months of the war, the nation approached
the crest of its war potential. The success of the German spring
offensives made this imperative and, with the Allied counterattacks, the developing expectations of victory served to accelerate
the war machine. Although the war ended before the full weight
of this effort reached the front, the results contributed decisively
to the victory.

As the tempo of the war increased and the American army
reached its peak in strength, there were clashes between the War
Department and the AEF over plans and personalities. The Secretary of War, through his diplomacy and basic common-sense,

alleviated the situation and prevented a let down in cooperation between the divided segments of the army.

In the winter of 1917–18, there occurred, in Newton D. Baker's term, "a period of questioning." An impatient people wanted results, and the evidences of preparation which they saw or, in most cases, heard about were discouraging. There were authenticated stories of men, still in civilian clothes, drilling with wooden sticks. The severe winter weather also brought complaints about living conditions in tents and hastily constructed barracks and about the lack of heavy clothing. The fuel shortage and breakdown of railroad service added to the national discontent. In those cold months at the end of the year, people were witnessing the result of a great war's impact on an unprepared nation. Yet, knowledgeable criticism could place some of the blame for the suffering of individual soldiers on the competition among the various inadequately coordinated supply bureaus.

Congress reacted to these problems by launching, in mid-December, an investigation of the War Department. Although the army by this time had remedied most of the specific complaints, the senators of the Military Affairs Committee who conducted the hearing believed that the situation demanded a reorganization of the government to provide for a strong centralized control of the war effort. As Senator James W. Wadsworth pointed out, "This has not been done thus far, it must be done in the immediate future."

After listening to explanations for several weeks, George E. Chamberlain, the chairman of the committee, made a dramatic accusation and proposed a solution. Before a group of notables, Elihu Root and Theodore Roosevelt among them, in New York City the Oregon senator announced, "the military establishment of America has fallen down, . . . because of inefficiency in every bureau and in every department of the Government of the United States." Chamberlain followed up with a bill to create a War Cabinet of "three distinguished citizens" who would assume the responsibility of planning and directing all war-related activities.

The reaction of the administration was quick and decisive. President Wilson, in a public statement, denied Chamberlain's charge as "an astonishing and absolutely unjustifiable distortion of the truth," and gave strong support to the target of the criticism, the Secretary of War. Although he had considered resigning, Baker appeared instead before the committee and delivered a comprehensive description of the accomplishments and of policy planning which even the hostile *New York Times* called "adroit and brilliant." More impressive than Baker's eloquent defense were his and the President's actions.

Within his department Baker created a War Council as a general supervisory agency, appointed a Surveyor General of Army Purchases, reorganized the General Staff, and brought in a new Chief of Staff. Across the street in the White House, Woodrow Wilson provided impetus to the economic sector, on March 4, with his appointment of a strong man with more authority to the post of chairman of the War Industries Board. In May, the passage of the Overman Act increased the President's power by a grant of the right to reorganize, abolish, or establish government agencies in whatever way he thought the war situation demanded. Without resorting to Chamberlain's proposed War Cabinet, Wilson centralized control.

In the War Department, Baker soon discarded the War Council and the office of Surveyor General as solutions to his logistical difficulties. The War Council, which he envisioned as a "thinking body" that would coordinate supply and relations with the AEF, was compromised from the beginning because two of the bureau heads who were members were under strong attack from the Senate committee. Then, this Council, which consisted of the Secretary, the Assistant Secretary, the Chief of Staff, and four bureau chiefs, started considering such details as fire-risk insurance and fraudulent enlistment of minors. After a month of existence the phrases "Item of unfinished business" and "Item of suspended business" appeared with increasing frequency in the minutes. A strong Chief of Staff made the body superfluous. As for the Surveyor General, the office lacked the requisite authority to take over Army purchases, and Edward R. Stettinius, a member of the J. P. Morgan banking firm, did not have the strength to overcome the lack. What Baker needed was a man to make decisions and the means to coordinate their execution. In his new Chief of Staff he found such a man.

Three officers had been in and out of this office in the first eleven months of the war with the predictable confusion. In Peyton C. March, Baker found the right man—a forceful, decisive soldier of balanced field and staff experience—for the difficult office of Chief of Staff. When March was a lieutenant colonel in the Adjutant General's Department in 1916, he had impressed the Secretary with his "grasp of the details of War Department business and," Baker added, "the boldness and simplicity with which he reformed the intricate record system. . . ."

Major General March inspired respect. Tall and wiry with the erect bearing characteristic of West Pointers, at fifty-three, he had an impressive reputation acquired during his thirty years in the army. The son of a distinguished scholar, he had graduated with Phi Beta Kappa honors from Lafayette College before he entered the Military Academy at nineteen in 1884. During the Spanish-American War and the Philippine Insurrection, he had won several citations for gallantry; first, as the commander of the unique, privately financed Astor Battery in the battle of Manila and then, during the pursuit of Aguinaldo, when he led a battalion of volunteer infantry. After his return from the Philippines, he continued to add to his reputation as a member of the first General Staff, as an observer with the Japanese army during the Russo-Japanese War, and as the commander of an artillery battalion and later a regiment. His tours of duty in the Adjutant General's Department supplemented his service in the line. The excellence of his record caused Pershing to select him as the chief of the AEF artillery. In the seven months he spent in France, March commanded the first brigade of artillery and established the foundation for the artillery program in the AEF.

When he arrived in Washington, March began building what he customarily referred to as a "machine." He eliminated those men whom he considered unsatisfactory and brought in more efficient officers whom he supported "100%" as one of his selections, the Acting Quartermaster General, Robert E. Wood, recalled. Wood added, "He was a severe chief but a very fair one."

Above all, he assumed power over the heretofore independent bureau chiefs—a step his wartime predecessors had been unable to take. Indeed, during the period of John Biddle's tenure, at the turn of the year, the most powerful of these men, Enoch H. Crowder, who was the Provost Marshal General as well as the Judge

Advocate General, apparently became the dominant soldier in the War Department. March restricted them by controlling their access to the Secretary and by replacing them in the two most important supply bureaus by men of his own choosing such as Wood and the equally successful Chief of Ordnance, Clarence C. Williams. In another limiting move, he abolished their separate personnel offices and consolidated the handling of commissioned personnel matters in a branch of the General Staff. The Senate investigation had publicized evidence of the basic inefficiency of the overlapping supply bureaus in purchasing war matériel. As the war came to an end, March was in the process of consolidating procurement under a division of the General Staff.

As Chief of Staff, March brought to the pinnacle of military power in this country a ruthlessness which had been lacking in his predecessors. "My position was," he wrote in *The Nation at War,* "that under the war power of the President I could do anything necessary to carry out the military program, and I invariably acted on that assumption." Under him the General Staff swelled in power and in numbers, so that by Armistice more than a thousand officers were on this duty in Washington in contrast to fewer than twenty in April 1917.

According to one of the generals in the War Department at the time, March "lived, breathed, and slept efficiency." A brilliant and hard man of quick decision, March tolerated no wasteful amenities. Within weeks he achieved results but frequently at the cost of making enemies both in and out of the army, including numerous politicians whose efforts to secure favors he scorned. He shrugged off criticism, "One is proud to be hated, if it is a consequence of doing one's work well." Although the more diplomatic Secretary of War deplored the abrasive manner of his Chief of Staff, he appreciated his accomplishments. In 1936, Baker looked back on the hectic war period and paid March this compliment, "The war was won by days. Your energy and drive supplied the days necessary for our side to win."

On the same day—March 4—that General March became Chief of Staff, Bernard M. Baruch became chairman of the War Industries Board and, in President Wilson's terms, "the general eye of all supply departments in the field of industry." By bestow-

ing power on Baruch, Wilson made possible the solution of the
supply problem which had goaded the Senators to their mid-
winter attacks on the administration.

The need to coordinate the civilian and military demands on
industry had been evident since before the war. A week before the
United States entered the war, the Council of National Defense
had created a General Munitions Board for this purpose and,
when this proved unsatisfactory, in July 1917, the War Industries
Board. Yet these agencies suffered from a fatal weakness in the
months of chaotic competition for available goods. They could
only advise, and Secretary Baker was determined to keep them in
that advisory capacity.

The first chairman, Frank A. Scott, a Cleveland manufacturer,
collapsed physically under the strain of attempting the impossible. After a prominent shipbuilder refused the important post,
Daniel Willard, the president of the Baltimore and Ohio Railroad,
tried, but resigned in two months. At this point, in mid-January,
Senator Chamberlain was preparing to launch his appeal for a
War Cabinet, but Wilson would not be hurried. Although it would
be almost seven weeks before he named Willard's successor, the
President overruled the Secretary of War and granted Baruch the
requisite authority. "I won't overrule you," he assured Baruch in
this regard. The difference between Baruch and the previous
chairmen was crucial. "He could do things," General March recalled, "instead of recommending them."

Since the first stirrings of economic preparedness, Baruch had
been prominent in the planning agencies. A member of the original Advisory Commission of the Council of National Defense, he
had served also as Commissioner of Raw Materials on the War
Industries Board. This handsome man of dignified appearance
was a Wall Street speculator who gave evidence of his success by
calmly writing out a five-million-dollar check for a bond purchase
during the first Liberty Loan drive.

Although his career on Wall Street disturbed some—among
them Newton D. Baker—and probably delayed his appointment
to a position of such great responsibility, once in office, Baruch's
skills were invaluable. He had made his great fortune in speculation because he had the ability to assimilate and correctly inter-

pret a myriad of facts about the varied industries as well as the general economic situation. President Wilson testified to this trait by nicknaming Baruch "Dr. Facts." There was another virtue to consider. As a speculator, Baruch owed his allegiance to no one, no particular firm, nor field of business. He was an independent man and, above all, he had the unrestricted support of the President. The combination gave him great personal power in 1918.

Baruch set about his task with characteristic energy and optimism. He picked capable subordinates—generally the managers of large industrial firms—and gave them the authority, and he avoided butting in. Although he softened the edge of his authority with a pleasant personality, he was decisive and firm when necessary.

As a middle man between the military consumers and the civilian producers, Baruch was the coordinating authority who filled the gap so evident in the first year of the war. And he used his power in both directions. When it appeared necessary to curtail severely the production of civilian automobiles, he called in the various Detroit manufacturers and explained the situation. He brought them to terms by placing phone calls in their presence and ordering the commandeering of their raw materials and transportation facilities. On the other hand, he demonstrated his authority to General March soon after both entered office. March was irritated because the War Industries Board had allocated a number of ammunition wagons to the French. But there was not much argument with Baruch who recalled, "I told him that the dispute would be taken to the President . . . [and] that he knew what the President's decision would be." The army did not get the wagons at that time, and March then understood the chairman's position. After that they dealt with each other in mutual respect.

"The means of controlling the war effort," Baruch stated later, "is priority," which he defined as "the power to determine who gets what and when." In his memoirs, he elaborated on what he termed this "absolutely essential" wartime economic tool. "Through the use of priority rulings, WIB was able to direct, restrain, or stimulate war production as the ever-changing situation required. Priority enabled us to allocate scarce materials where they were needed most, to curtail less essential production, to break bottlenecks, to end reckless and chaotic competition and hoarding, to conserve fuel, to save shipping space, to pool and ration."

The Armistice came at a time when American industry, under the supervision of the so-called "Czar of Industry," was nearing its peak in war production. Baruch's performance had stilled effectively the congressional criticism of a lack of centralized control. In the 1950's a member of the Senate Military Affairs Committee of the First World War period, James W. Wadsworth, said that Baruch's appointment was a key result of the wartime investigation. Although the senators did not get their version of a War Cabinet, they did get the desired result.

The administration of the army's supply program remained a problem until the end of the war. In contrast, the navy handled its logistics relatively well and gave Baruch a modicum of worry. The supply bureaus in the War Department were sensitive of their independence, although this meant overlapping functions and, as demonstrated in the early months of the war, chaos. Gradually informal arrangements lessened the confusion, but there remained the basically inefficient procurement. In his reorganization of the General Staff in February 1918, Secretary Baker created two new divisions, Purchase & Supply and Storage & Traffic, to supervise supply activities, but these organizations, within the limits of General Staff theory, could not take over supply administration.

After March came to power, there was an evolution toward centralization with the ultimate goal of the General Staff going beyond its supervisory role to the actual control of the handling of supplies. In this period, the builder of the Panama Canal, Major General George W. Goethals, became, in Baruch's phrase, "army supply."

Upon his return March found his old friend Goethals wearing two hats as Acting Quartermaster General and Director of Storage & Traffic Division of the General Staff. After a few weeks the Chief of Staff combined the two General Staff divisions into the Purchase, Storage & Traffic Division and named Goethals as its head. His instructions to Goethals were characteristic of his method: "You are given complete charge of all matters of supply. You can make any changes in personnel, methods, and general set-up necessary to get results and don't bother me with details, I hold you responsible for results, and I will take all the responsibility for anything you have to do to get them. When you need more authority or specific authority in any particular case, come to me, and you will get it."

The sweeping provisions of the Overman Act, which authorized organizational flexibility, gave March the means of increasing General Staff power in the logistical area. In August, Goethals persuaded March to use this authority to permit the General Staff to move into the bureau domain and to take over most of the supply function. Thus, the army's primary supply agency, the Quartermaster Corps, became a subsidiary of the P.S. & T. Division. At this point Goethals, who had the title of Assistant to the Chief of Staff, became an executive rather than a supervisor with merely advisory authority. When the war ended, General Staff officers were still trying to untangle the myriad strands of supply, but at last they did have a centralized supply agency.

In the 1950's when General of the Army George C. Marshall was reminiscing about the First World War, he praised Secretary Baker highly and commented, "He rode a very difficult horse . . . between General Pershing and General March, and he did it extraordinarily well." Here Marshall was referring not only directly to a clash of strong personalities but also implicitly to a cardinal factor in the American conduct of the war. With his initial delegation of authority to Pershing, Baker, in effect, divided the army into two segments with himself as the controlling link. In a 1919 letter to James G. Harbord, the Secretary explained his attitude toward Pershing, "my duty to the country and its cause was to support General Pershing at every point, to give him complete freedom and discretion, and if the time ever came when I could not do that, to replace him." But, in his anxiety to avoid the dangers of running a war from a headquarters distant from the field, Baker, to a certain extent, ignored the peril of permitting a field commander to make military policy.

This relationship was not particularly difficult, despite a certain amount of inevitable confusion and friction, until the spring of 1918. From that point to the end of the war, the great increase in the flow of men and material to the AEF and the pressure of large numbers of Americans taking part in the battle multiplied the stress on the divided organization. Prior to this period, Bliss and Biddle alleviated the situation by accepting the status of Pershing's agents in this country. Although the Chief of Staff was by law the military adviser to the Secretary of War, Bliss considered his function as wartime Chief of Staff, as he wrote Pershing in 1921, to be that of the "Assistant Chief of Staff to the Chief of Staff of the AEF." Within this self-imposed limitation, Bliss would advise the Secretary, but he believed himself to be distinctly subordinate to the "Commanding General"—Pershing. Apparently Biddle followed his example. When March came, he did his utmost to carry out Pershing's requests, but he refused to take a subordinate role.

The situation was also complicated by President Wilson's desire to avoid too intimate political association with the Allies. In the amalgamation controversy, for example, it was difficult to separate political from military policy.

After the initial discussion in the spring of 1917 of using American soldiers in British and French ranks, the Allies did not press the issue until early December. Then, as they pondered the course of the war, the Allied leaders were appalled by the possibility of heavy German reinforcements coming from the Eastern Front to northern France. Where could they obtain the men to stop the expected German offensive? The British and the French were scraping the bottom of their manpower resources and on their own could not maintain a balance of strength on the Western Front. The obvious solution was to appeal to the Americans for more men.

Up to this time, as Prime Minister David Lloyd George said, the Americans were arriving "with what seemed to be disconcerting and perplexing slowness." And John J. Pershing was in complete agreement on that point. On November 30, there were elements of four divisions and support troops totaling 126,000 men in the AEF, but the First Division was the only one nearly ready to occupy even a quiet sector. The Allies, who desperately needed riflemen, looked askance at the large numbers of noncombatant troops taking up valuable space on the transatlantic transports.

While Colonel E. M. House, the President's personal representative, was in Paris, the British Prime Minister proposed the amalgamation of American infantry companies or battalions in their units. Although House was at the head of a mission with the task of coordinating the American and Allied efforts, he considered such a decision beyond his authority and passed the plan on to the President and to Pershing.

Throughout December and January in frequent conferences, British civilian as well as military leaders tried to obtain Pershing's assent to amalgamation. The French also tried to obtain American units to reinforce their weakened divisions, but they soon shifted their arguments to support of the British. Later, Pershing described the negotiating conditions, "In all these discussions, the British were bargaining for men to fill their ranks and we were trying to get shipping to carry over our armies."

Although Pershing was determined to resist persuasion, his position was somewhat ambiguous. The British, as well as the French, considered the issue important enough to require the personal approval of the President. Hence, Lloyd George had opened the question with House and pursued it in Washington through his ambassador, as did the French. Wilson and Baker, however, interpreted it as a military decision. Wilson's instructions, which Baker cabled to Pershing in late December, indicate their attitude.

After he informed the General that the British and French were pressing him on the issue, Wilson advised in the Baker message, "We do not desire loss of identity of our forces but regard that as secondary to the meeting of any critical situation by the most helpful use possible of the troops at your command. . . . The President, however, desires you to have full authority to use the forces at your command as you deem wise in consultation with the French and British Commanders-in-Chief."

The message itself seemed clear enough. The President and the Secretary would condone amalgamation but, since they considered it a military matter, they delegated the decision to Pershing. However, Lloyd George and Clemenceau were unwilling to relinquish such a crucial question to their generals. Rather than conferring merely with his military counterparts, Pershing found himself dealing directly with the prime ministers, while the dynamic Welshman and the famous old Tiger kept the question alive in Washington through their ambassadors.

Unfortunately for Pershing, Secretary of State Robert Lansing hurt his bargaining position by giving the gist of this message to the French ambassador. The British also promptly learned of its contents. As a result the Allies knew that Pershing's civilian superiors were sympathetic to their proposal. Since they also knew that the power of decision belonged to Pershing, they stepped up their efforts against him.

The minutes of a conference on January 30 at Versailles indicate the pressure as well as the difficulty in separating the political from the military aspects of the question.

> Mr. Lloyd George said he gathered that the question was now left to General Pershing to decide.
>
> General Pershing said he thought Washington wanted a straight recommendation from him.
>
> Mr. Lloyd George remarked that what the government wanted was a statement from General Pershing as to whether a military necessity exists; that, speaking from a politician's standpoint of view, the government wanted a recommendation from General Pershing; that he, himself, knows what Mr. Baker wants; that he wants a statement from General Pershing that a military emergency exists. . . .

If Wilson and Baker were not aware of the political ramifications of the issue, Pershing certainly was. In the agreement which he signed with the British, he put into writing six objections to amalgamation; the first three were political in nature.

> 1st.—The national sentiment in the United States against service under a foreign flag; 2d.—The probability that such action by the United States would excite serious political opposition to the Administration in the conduct of the war; 3d.—The certainty of its being used by German propagandists to stir up public opinion (in the U.S.) against the war; 4th.—It would dissipate the direction and effort of the American Army; 5th.— Differences in national characteristics and military training of troops and consequent failure of complete cooperation would undoubtedly lead to friction and eventual misunderstanding between the two countries; 6th.—Additional manpower on the

Western Front could be provided as quickly by some plan not involving amalgamation.

The agreement which Pershing and Lloyd George signed on this occasion was that the British would provide shipping above their present contribution to bring over American troops who would train with them. Thus, they obtained the men and the implicit promise of using them at the front if necessary during the training period. Although the actual terms of the agreement did not specify numbers, Pershing and the Chief of the Imperial General Staff, Sir William Robertson, worked out details. The British did not get the 150 infantry battalions they wanted. Instead Pershing forced them to accept his terms: they would bring over 150,000 men—the personnel of six full divisions, which meant only 72 infantry battalions. Eventually ten divisions did spend some time training with the British and two—the 27th and the 30th, which comprised the American II Corps—stayed at the British front. During the spring, the French also received American aid in the form of four Negro infantry regiments which became organic parts of French divisions.

Woodrow Wilson may have erred in this instance in delegating too much authority to a soldier. Certainly, he complicated the issue by letting the Allies know that he was sympathetic to their proposal. Nevertheless, he and Baker did leave the decision to Pershing and they gave him their support when he made it. Within two months, they would have another opportunity to endorse the field commander's broad authority.

In late March the impact of the German offensives caused the Military Representatives of the Supreme War Council, including Bliss, to recommend that that the Americans ship only infantry and machine-gun troops—combat men who could be sent rapidly to the front in Allied units. At that time, Baker, who was in France on his first inspection tour of the AEF, conferred with Bliss and Pershing. The Secretary approved the appeal with the qualifications that Pershing be given the discretion as to the training and use of the men and that the goal of an independent American army not be forgotten.

The British followed up this appeal with an offer to the War Department to supply the supplementary shipping necessary to take 120,000 troops per month for four months. Baker, who was now back in Washington, and March approved this program. In the meantime, Pershing had gone to London to talk with the British War Minister, Lord Milner, about bringing over the infantry and machine-gun men. While there, the British told him of the agreement reached in Washington, but Pershing refused to accept it and agreed only to a shipment of the combat troops plus the engineers and signal corps troops of six divisions in the month of May.

When he returned to Chaumont, the AEF commander was shocked to find a message with the terms of the Washington agreement. In his opinion, "This concession went further than it was necessary to go and much further than I had expected." Also, the British were testing his authority again by going over his head to Washington. At this time, there was no need of worry on the latter point. As soon as Baker learned that Pershing had made a different arrangement, he promptly recognized its precedence. He informed the President of his conversation with the British ambassador, Lord Reading, "I told him . . . that I felt he and I were too far from the situation to see this as clearly as those in Europe and that so far as I was concerned I felt it my duty to cooperate to carry out the arrangement which plainly seemed wise to Lord Milner and General Pershing."

A few days later, the Secretary wrote Bliss that he had also made it clear to Reading "that as General Pershing is the American Commander-in-Chief we must continue to be guided by his judgment of the military exigencies in France in the matter of the transportation of troops there."

The situation was tense as the Allies again turned to Pershing. Both the British and the French thought in terms of the battle and their desperate need for reinforcements, while Pershing considered their appeals as efforts to thwart the formation of an independent American army. The British believed that the agreement Pershing had made with them in London was inadequate. The French were angry because the British had made an unilateral pact with the Americans. Besides, it seemed to Clemenceau that his ally conceded too much to Pershing.

When the Supreme War Council held its fifth session on the first of May at Abbeville, the aged but vigorous French Premier confided his views to a member of the British delegation, Sir William Wiseman. As they walked from their quarters to the conference, Clemenceau told Wiseman of his doubts as to Lloyd George's abilities and then, in front of a butcher shop, he pointed his cane at a sheep and exploded, "Pershing is getting all of the meat. I want some of the meat."

Although Clemenceau opened the meeting with an attack on the London agreement, he soon laid this aside and joined Lloyd George, Foch, and the other Allied leaders, including Premier Orlando of Italy, in a frontal assault on Pershing. For two days they tried to persuade him to extend the time limit of shipments of the combat troops beyond the month he agreed to in London.

On the first day, Pershing, with the silent Bliss sitting beside him, was adamant even in the face of their predictions that the Germans would win if he remained obstinate. Wiseman remembered "that Pershing was black as thunder the first day. . . . He was very sulky." Near the end of the afternoon, as the three Allied premiers stepped up their arguments, Pershing ended the discussion with an emphatic, "Gentlemen, I have thought this program over very deliberately and will not be coerced."

Even Pershing could not completely withstand what he called "all the Allied 'heavy artillery,' " but he succeeded in obtaining favorable terms. On the afternoon of the next day, he conceded a one-month extension of the program of transporting 120,000 infantrymen and machine gunners and agreed to discuss the possibility of another extension in June. In return, he forced acceptance of two provisions: the Supreme War Council must formally endorse the principle of an independent American Army and the British must provide shipping for an additional 40,000 men over the two-month period. The Allied dignitaries, who did not want to risk a deadlock with the American commander at this crucial stage of the war, reluctantly accepted the compromise.

A few days after the meeting adjourned, General Bliss, who disagreed privately with Pershing, wrote the Secretary of War, "The whole thing is in a muddle so far as the understanding of the English and French is concerned." In the emergency, when it seemed as if the Germans might score a decisive victory, the Allies wanted as many combat troops as possible as soon as possible. If the Germans did succeed, Pershing's plans for a large independent army would be tragically pointless. Pershing made his estimate of the situation and gambled with extraordinarily high stakes. Since the Germans did not succeed, events proved Pershing correct. Yet, it takes little imagination to appreciate the desperation of the Allied leaders and why they were so perplexed with the American commander that May.

The Allies were disgruntled with Pershing's intransigence, and their dissatisfaction was increased by a belief that Wilson, Baker, and Bliss were more sympathetic to their arguments. Neither Lloyd George nor Clemenceau would have tolerated such independence in a soldier on what they considered a political question. On May 4, Lloyd George wrote his ambassador in Washington, "I do not believe that we shall ever get allied arrangements working satisfactorily until there is a civilian of first rank with real powers on this side. . . . It is maddening to think that though the men are there the issue may be endangered because of the shortsightedness of one General and the failure of his Government to order him to carry out their undertakings."

Both Lloyd George and Clemenceau, through their representatives in Washington, tried to bypass Pershing and plead their cause to President Wilson. Because of the close relationship of Sir William Wiseman with the President's confidant, Colonel Edward M. House, the British had a better opportunity to reach the President. Indeed, the British Prime Minister had thought of House as a good possibility for the role of an American proconsul in Europe.

Wiseman and Reading explained the situation to House, who immediately relayed the information to the President. Both of these Englishmen were more candid with House than Lloyd George would probably have desired. Reading was particularly frank when he confessed to House, as the Colonel wrote Wilson, "that he thought it would be a mistake for me to go, or for you to send anyone, because it is evident that what Lloyd George wants is someone to overrule Pershing." Since Wilson was not willing to weaken Pershing's position to that extent, he refused to send a civilian superior to France.

One aspect of the situation drew a strong sympathetic response, however, from House as well as Baker and March. In the course of a lengthy cable to House, on May 11, Wiseman explained the Allied case against Pershing and added, "Size of the American Expeditionary Force is, however, growing far too large for the present Staff and organization. This is beginning to constitute a serious problem which needs early attention." In the copy of the cable which he sent to the President, House added the marginal comment, "This I think is true."

After Wiseman had returned to the United States and had discussed with House the progress of American affairs in Europe, the Colonel made a recommendation to the President. "What I have in mind to suggest to you is that Pershing be relieved from all responsibility except the training and fighting of our troops. All his requirements for equipping and maintaining these troops should be on other shoulders." In this letter of June 3, House suggested Stettinius as the man to take charge of American logistics in France.

Wilson forwarded House's letter to Baker, who replied that both he and March had made the same suggestion to Pershing earlier but that he did not think Stettinius was the proper choice. The Secretary then suggested General Goethals as a much better qualified man for the position. As an officer, Goethals could command the Services of Supply and be coordinate with Pershing rather than serve under him.

The congested ports in France, the failure to reduce the time ships spent in those ports, and various other problems reflected, in part, the need for a stronger officer than the general, Francis J. Kernan, Pershing put in command, plus the need for a different relationship between GHQ at Chaumont and the Services of Supply. Nevertheless, it was not until Pershing learned in late July of the proposal to send Goethals to France that he acted to correct the situation.

Since Baker still supported Pershing's virtual independence, he asked for Pershing's approval before he put the plan into effect. Always jealous of his power, Pershing considered this a threat and reacted swiftly. He persuaded his good friend Harbord, an energetic, tough officer who had just won high praise as a combat commander, to relinquish his command of the Second Division in order to take over the SOS. Then, he transferred the responsibility for routine supply matters from GHQ to the SOS with the privilege of establishing direct cable communication on those affairs with the War Department. For a week, he and Harbord toured the SOS installations throughout France. Upon his return, Pershing attempted to ease the Secretary's mind with a glowing report of the logistical establishment.

Baker viewed Pershing's flurry of activity with a touch of amusement but endorsed his decision. It was apparent to him that Pershing unjustifiably doubted the completeness of his support. Indeed, at the time, a rumor circulated in the AEF that the proposal to send Goethals to France was part of a plot which had the ultimate goal of replacing Pershing with March. There was no truth in this rumor, but it engendered suspicion which carried over into the postwar memoirs.

Baker, March, and Pershing agreed on fundamental principles. All accepted the premise that the United States, represented by an independent force, would make its major effort on the Western Front. And there was no question either of Pershing's command of the combat troops or of his authority to decide strategy and tactics without interference from Washington.

By appointing Harbord as Commanding General of the SOS with increased power, Pershing settled the command question as far as AEF logistics were concerned. But, while the proposal to send Goethals to France was under consideration, Pershing made a recommendation which muddled logistical matters for the rest of the war.

As he agreed at Abbeville, Pershing attended the next session of the Supreme War Council at Versailles on the first two days in June. Again the question of American reinforcement was a lively topic, particularly since the German attacks were exacting a heavy toll of the Allied armies.

In the late afternoon of June 1, Pershing, who was not feeling very well, conferred with Foch and Lord Milner. He summarized the conversation in his diary: "He [Foch] wanted all the transports used for bringing over infantry and machine gun units. I pointed out that our program has been seriously interrupted by the concessions already made to this idea; that the French railroads are on the point of breaking down for lack of skilled workmen to repair their rolling stock, that the ports are going to become congested because of breakdown of the railroad service and that there are not sufficient men now in France to unload the boats; that we are pushing the shipbuilding, but that it is useless to do this unless we take steps to be ready to unload the ships. Along this line of argument, I pointed out that this could be a short-sighted policy which would lead us to a very complicated situation."

Pershing came to terms on the following day, despite his argument, and signed with Foch and Milner a recommendation to the War Department. In this he agreed, that if the army could send 250,000 men in June and also in July, 170,000 of these soldiers in June and 140,000 the second month would be in infantry and machine-gun units. The rest, except for 25,400 railroad troops, would be in categories of Pershing's choosing unless the 250,000 were exceeded. In that case, all over 250,000 would be combat troops.

At the same time Lloyd George, Clemenceau, and Orlando sent their own recommendation to President Wilson. Rather than contradict the request Pershing had endorsed, the political leaders extended it in a general way. The crux of their message was that Foch had said that he needed 100 American divisions to win, and they were asking for those divisions "at as early a date as this can possibly be done."

One hundred divisions was an astonishing figure. The fact that the Allied leaders would name such a figure reflected their desperate assessment of the recent German successes. According to Pershing, that many divisions would mean "at least 5,000,000" Americans in France and a combat force greater by one-fourth than the entire Allied armies then on the Western Front.

During June the situation at the front combined with this urgency of the Allies' request must have made a deep impression on Pershing. A little over two weeks after the meeting at Versailles, he cabled an urgent request for 66 divisions (3,000,000) men by May 1919 and reinforced this with personal letters to both Baker and March. In the latter, he confided to the Chief of Staff, "our allies are becoming so war-weary that I do not believe they will hold out beyond another year."

When Clemenceau and Foch visited Chaumont on June 23, they found Pershing in an entirely different mood from the man with whom they had argued at Abbeville and Versailles. In disregard of the arguments he gave Foch on the first of the month, the

American general readily agreed to throw his influence behind their desire for 100 divisions by July of the next year. Apparently, the only person present who expressed doubt about the possibility of the attainment of such a huge program was the French High Commissioner to the United States, André Tardieu. Although, after the war, Pershing stated that he did not think the program was possible and that he wondered if Clemenceau and Foch did either, he gave no indication of these doubts at the time. In his memoir, he explained, "I was willing to ask for the greater numbers, feeling, however, that the War Department would do wonders if it could carry out even the 66 division program."

Throughout the summer Pershing exerted as much pressure as he could to secure acceptance of the 100-division program. In July he wrote March, "There is nothing necessary to win this war too stupendous for us to undertake, and I am firmly of the view that unless we carry out the program that has been outlined for next year the war will drag on indeterminably. . . ." A month later he cabled both Baker and March, "Wish again to urge 80 divisions by April and that the 100-division program be adopted as minimum by July. On account of shortage in manpower of allies, it is my fixed opinion after careful study that this is the very least American force that will insure our victory in 1919."

When Pershing made recommendations of the ultimate strength of the AEF, he based his proposals on what he believed the situation demanded. In its preparation of such plans, his staff had comparatively little information about conditions in the United States. Once the AEF proposal reached Washington, a thorough study was necessary of the nation's capacity to fulfill such demands. For the War Department General Staff, this meant the awesome task of correlating the availability of men and raw materials, the rate of training and industrial production, the procurement and distribution of supplies, and the transportation of men and material within this country and across the Atlantic. While the General Staff was working out the details of the problem, the presidential decision to send troops to Russia in response to Allied requests gave the planners another factor to consider. However, as it developed, the demands of the Russian expeditions on manpower and resources were too small to affect

the AEF program. Before March and then Baker could approve
sending 100 divisions to France, they had to know whether or not
the army could actually carry out such a program

The first problem was to determine in round numbers how
many men were involved. Unless the planners on both sides of the
Atlantic used the same figure, they could not possibly hope to get
together on the many details of supply schedules. Although Pershing did not give a specific figure in his request, he evidently
thought in terms of "at least 5,000,000 men." On the other hand,
Clemenceau believed that he was asking for an AEF of 4,160,000
soldiers. When he heard about the recommendation, Bliss
thought that it must mean 3,375,000 men for the 1920 campaign.
In Washington, Goethals made his estimates on the basis of
4,260,000—a figure the Chief of Staff accepted—but Brigadier
General Henry Jervey of the Operations Division came to the conclusion that the program included 4,160,000 men. Obviously
such differences heightened the confusion in discussions of the
program in France and in the United States.

The initial response of the War Department to Pershing's great
proposal was cautious. Although they promised to do their utmost, both Baker and March warned the AEF commander that
the goal might be impossible. The Secretary of War, on July 8, in
a lengthy letter to Bliss, explained:

> March and I are studying together the 100-Division program, but
> are finding it full of burrs. The latest one presented to me is, that
> all the ports in France, and all the berthing space there, if de-
> voted to the exclusive use of America, would not, on present cal-
> culations, be adequate for the 100-Division program. . . . As
> you know, our intention has for some time been to develop 100
> Divisions by 1920, but to push that consummation ahead a whole
> year is not easy, to say the least of it, even if it should turn out
> to be possible with the maximum aid from the British and
> French. . . , I am not willing to believe that anything is im-
> possible, no matter what it is, but at present it looks as though I
> would need Aladdin's lamp for the 100-Division program. . . .

At the regular Wednesday morning meetings with civilian experts, Baker and March discussed the requirements of the large
program with Baruch and the shipping people—Edward N. Hur-

ley (Shipping Board), P. A. S. Franklin (Shipping Control Committee), and others. Earlier, in June, they had recognized that the large shipments of combat troops, agreed upon at Abbeville and Versailles, was a gamble. Then Hurley had stated that he could not provide enough American shipping to supply the increased numbers of troops, but March and Baker were still optimistic. The Chief of Staff cut off complaints of inadequate shipping with a curt, "We'll pack them in like sardines," as far as the soldiers were concerned, and, in regard to cargo, with a decision to eliminate less essential supplies. Merely clothing an army of such large size would require virtually all of the available wool in the United States. And, as it was discovered in September, the steel requirements of a much smaller program (80 divisions) combined with Allied commitments were in excess of American capacity.

On July 18, March made his recommendation to the Secretary of War. Based on the General Staff estimates of the demands not only for 100 divisions but also the lesser demands for 60 and 80 divisions, he told Baker that it was flatly impossible to carry out the largest program within the time limit Pershing had set. Indeed, his memorandum continued that the smallest figure was "the only one that we are absolutely certain of our ability to accomplish." However, he was willing to recommend the median program of 80 divisions (3,360,000 men).

Baker carried the recommendation to the White House. Although Wilson approved the 80-division program, he did so, perhaps, with reluctance in view of its large logistical demands. A few days later, he warned Baker and others that "the supplying of war needs, either directly or indirectly, are in some instances far in excess of the productive capacity of the country and in other instances almost as great as the full capacity of our present organized industries. . . ."

After the President gave his approval, several obstacles remained. Congress had to agree to appropriate the necessary sums and to approve an expansion of the draft limits to cover 18 to 45 years. The War Department would also have to ask guarantees from the Allies to supply ships and artillery. But it was assumed that these qualifications would soon be overcome. Despite Pershing's urgent reassurances, however, there was also the question of the ability of the AEF as well as the capacity of the French ports and railroads to handle the logistical burden. It was at this time that the problem of the command of the SOS arose.

Although there was ample reason to doubt that they could carry out the 80-division program by June 30, 1919, the military and civilian leaders in Washington planned on that basis. The AEF did not. To the end of the war the staff officers in the expeditionary force made their supply schedules and requests on a radically different estimate. What they chose to call an 80-division program included 80 combat and 16 depot divisions, which with support troops amounted to a total of 4,585,000 men—a figure 1,225,000 larger than the War Department envisioned. Statistical confusion compounded when Pershing indicated on October 2 that he thought the AEF version amounted to 4,770,000 men, and, a week earlier the Secretary of War added 400,000 replacements, thus making a total of 3,760,000 in what he considered an 80-division AEF.

These discrepancies meant that the logistical planning and processes had an Alice-in-Wonderland aura. For this, March, Pershing, and the Secretary of War were equally to blame. Neither March nor Baker directly informed Pershing of the decision to adopt the 80-division program until September when Baker visited France and March explained the program in a cable. Nevertheless, Pershing apparently knew of it as early as mid-August when he referred to it in a cable. Since March had informed Bliss in late July, the former Chief of Staff presumably told the field commander. Then the fact that an AEF board had met in August to work out an 80-division program (80–16 formula) indicated knowledge of the War Department decision.

When March finally on September 25 stated explicitly what the official program was and told the AEF commander that it was "impracticable" to carry out his larger program, Pershing remained adamant. He cabled in reply: "The needs of the American Expeditionary Forces and the orders in which they should be met are best known here . . . If our calls can not be met because of insurmountable difficulties I ask that I be so informed in order that necessary revision in the schedules to meet such conditions be made here and not in the United States." March so informed him, but, with the Armistice only a month away, the dispute was rapidly becoming a source of reminiscent bitterness.

Regardless of the argument over the maximum attainable program, the Americans took a great gamble by risking the imbalance in shipments of men (approximately 2,080,000 reached France) and supplies. Goethals wrote his son two weeks before the end of the war: "We're in bad shape in shipping not having the requisite bottoms to carry what Pershing says are his minimum requirements. We are hustling men over while the cargo end gets worse & worse." A few days later, Harbord warned Pershing that the pounds of cargo per man received from the United States had dropped from 49 in June to 22 in September.

With the help of the British, whose ships carried to France 49 per cent of the AEF, the War Department sent across the Atlantic more men in the last eight and a half months of the war than there were in the entire army at home and abroad on April 1, 1918. In the six months May through October the smallest number of men to make the passage in a month was 245,945 and the largest, in July, was 306,350. During these months, with the exception of June, cargo shipments increased steadily but they could not keep pace with the flow of men. The General Purchasing Board of the AEF under Charles G. Dawes, a civilian turned brigadier general and an old friend of Pershing, did help by procuring supplies in Europe. But it was necessary to step up cross-Atlantic supply at a rapidly increasing rate anyway.

In order to transport and sustain the AEF, the government's fleet of transports and cargo ships grew from 13, with a total tonnage of 94,000 on July 1, 1917, to an armada under its control of 616 vessels representing over 3,500,000 tons. The government seized German vessels, appropriated neutral shipping, and built, bought, and rented other ships to make this possible. Much of the credit for this effort belonged to the civilian Shipping Board and its related agencies, Emergency Fleet Corporation and the Shipping Control Committee. Within the army a section of the War Department General Staff, the Embarkation Service under Brigadier General Frank T. Hines, had the task of coordinating the men and supplies with the ships.

The war ended in November, and so the fears of those who watched the shipping statistics did not materialize. By early October it was apparent to the Allied generalissimo that the 100 divisions he had pled for in the summer were no longer necessary. At that time Baker, who was still worried about the discrepancy between the War Department and GHQ versions of the 80-division program, asked Foch how many divisions he needed to win. Foch startled him with his reply, "Forty!"

The end was in sight, since the United States already had that many divisions in France or en route. But, in the first week of October, when the difficult situation in the Argonne was a burden, Pershing wanted as many men as possible to ensure victory.

During the summer and fall of 1918, there were rumors about differences between the two army leaders on opposite sides of the Atlantic. Some assumed that the command of the SOS was one aspect of the "Pershing-March Feud." Others undoubtedly pondered the ramifications of War Department General Order # 80 (August 26, 1918). A passage in this order granted the Chief of Staff "rank and precedence" over all other officers and delegated to him the responsibility for carrying out the army program. Accustomed to his supremacy and his privileged relationship with the Secretary of War, Pershing was hypersensitive of any real or apparent effort to dilute his authority.

Within a few days after his arrival in the spring in Washington, March aroused his former superior's suspicion by an apparently innocent policy. The then Acting Chief of Staff wanted to exchange a certain number of General Staff officers between the War Department and the AEF. In this way, he hoped to bring about in Washington a better understanding of conditions in the AEF while giving capable officers an opportunity to serve in France.

Pershing's chief of staff, Harbord, seized on this and wrote a venomous note to his commander. In a complete rejection of any good intention on March's part, Harbord wrote: "This order . . . is a distinctly unfriendly act. It shows no consideration for your needs, and undermines your well-laid foundation, with what wild ambition in mind we can only guess."

After a cable exchange, Pershing sent the officers, but a War Department board found that only three of the thirty dispatched were capable of General Staff work. With this less than half-hearted cooperation the policy collapsed.

March and Pershing also failed to get together on the crucial question of promotions to general rank. From April until the Armistice, although they corresponded frequently about the matter, they never reached an understanding. Pershing felt so deeply about this difference that he devoted two entire letters and significant portions of others to the Secretary of War on the subject.

Pershing wanted complete control over these promotions in the AEF, and he thought that his officers should be given preference over those in the United States. March had to consider the entire army in this regard. Because of his artillery background, he also wanted to make sure that artillerymen commanded artillery brigades. With the great expansion of the army and the resulting formation of new brigades and divisions, he needed new generals to command those units. Based on past experience, he knew that it was difficult to pry newly commissioned generals away from France.

Pershing's greatest irritation, carefully nourished by Harbord, was that the Chief of Staff had gotten stars for several younger colonels in the AEF—among them Douglas MacArthur—without Pershing's recommendation. (Before the war ended, however, Pershing did recommend MacArthur for promotion to major general.) At the same time other officers whom Pershing had recommended did not receive their stars. Regardless of the merit of the officers involved, there was no justification for March to continue to take such actions which obviously antagonized the AEF commander.

The dispute over promotions, the proposal to send Goethals to France—Pershing told Baker that he understood "General March wanted to order it out of hand"—and, most of all, the difference between March's attitude and that of his predecessors provoked Pershing to complain to the Secretary of War. On the same day (July 28) that he wrote Baker his reasons for not wanting Goethals, he sent a second letter which he devoted entirely to promotions and March. In this he accused March of assuming "a very curt tone in his cables to me" and "the attitude of Commanding General of all the armies rather than that of Chief of Staff speaking for his Chief." He then indicated the source of the complaint, "There may be nothing in this but all my staff notice it."

In August and September, Pershing and Harbord, reiterated this protest. On August 17, Pershing wrote the Secretary about the lack of "satisfactory teamwork" between the AEF and the War Department General Staff. In this letter, he suggested March's relief without mentioning his name. When Baker came to France in September, Harbord went over the entire relationship with him. The Secretary assured Harbord of his support of Pershing. He said that he had no intention of forcing Goethals or anyone else on Pershing and that he would make certain that Pershing's recommendations of promotions would be followed. Baker expressed surprise when Harbord told him that he thought March was ambitious to succeed Pershing and responded by saying that if the death or disability of Pershing forced him to name a new commander, he would choose the successor from among the generals in the AEF. He added that he would tell March of this policy. Harbord promptly passed on this information to Pershing. Although Pershing saw Baker on several occasions during the visit, neither left any evidence that they had discussed March. However, Baker did act to reconcile the different versions of the 80-division programs.

During the war the Secretary handled the difficult situation diplomatically. He did not let March know about Pershing's and Harbord's suspicions and constantly reassured Pershing of his support. When the AEF commander published his memoirs, March read the letter of August 17 and sharpened his wit for acid criticism of the "C-in-C" in his own book. Much of the legend of the "Pershing-March Feud" stems from these exchanges in the 1930's. Although Baker deplored March's part in the postwar controversy, he did say as he read portions of Pershing's book, "He saw his own problem but seems wholly to have failed to grasp ours."

These were two strong, hard men who had served together briefly prior to the war in the same cadet company at West Point and in the same office as members of the first General Staff. As

Chief of Staff and a four-star general, March raised his position to a status coordinate with Pershing, but Baker did not permit him to act as a superior to the AEF commander.

There is no evidence that March had any hopes of supplanting Pershing or made any effort to do so. In fact, March, with the exception of the promotion dispute, apparently supported Pershing wholeheartedly. Below the top-level relationship, the War Department complaints of the failure to adjust shipping schedules and of the various changes in requests balance the agitation of AEF staff officers over the failure to send supplies as requested and the lack of training for replacements.

Douglas MacArthur, who knew both Pershing and March and who was involved in the promotion dispute, later said that he thought Pershing's staff "poisoned his mind toward March." "I am convinced," he concluded, "that there would have been no trouble between Pershing and March if they could have conferred."

After the war, in 1923, Pershing asked his aide George C. Marshall to examine the War Department records to see if Baker had erred in not drafting larger numbers of men in the spring of 1918. In order to pass judgment on this point, Marshall explored the whole question of War Department support of the AEF programs during that period. On the basis of this analysis, he stated that both Baker and March had strongly sustained Pershing. He also told his chief that, while he was unable to answer his query directly, he did believe, "When one considers the inevitable confusion incident to coordinating industries in the United States, training, shelter, and shipping, it is surprising that the demands from the AEF were met to the extent they were. . . ."

In 1956, Marshall commented to his biographer, Forrest C. Pogue, about the Pershing-March relationship. "I think they were both at fault. . . . What saved the situation was Newton Baker."

·VII·

The Romance and Reality
of the Air War

"The only interest and romance in this war was in the air." Although Brigadier General William Mitchell, who made that statement, was certainly prejudiced, it is true that no other aspect of World War I so captured the public imagination. Even after a half-century, this popularity is reflected by the enthusiasts in the Society of World War I Aero Historians and the whimsical homage the cartoon character "Snoopy" regularly gives to the fliers of 1917–18. The romance and the horror was in the skies of France where it was man against man, a personal war. But before American men and planes could make their mark in combat, great problems in production, training, and administration had to be overcome.

When the United States went to war, each of the armed services had pitifully small and ill-equipped air components. In the army, navy, and Marine Corps, there were approximately 1500 officers and men to handle the less than 300 obsolescent airplanes

—none of which were fit for combat. In contrast, the French, by
May of 1917, had 1700 airplanes at the front.

The American air pioneers in uniform were junior officers in
their thirties or younger; hence they did not have much force in
the councils of their separate services. The army, which had 65
officers and 1120 men and a large proportion of the aircraft in
April 1917, had bought its first plane less than eight years before
from the Wright brothers with the stipulation that it could be
packed into a wagon for transportation purposes. Two years later,
the navy ordered three airplanes.

In the few years prior to the war, Americans had made some
advances in military aviation but on a very small scale in comparison with the European powers. A civilian pilot had flown a plane
from a ship. Army aviators had experimented with ground-to-air
radio communication and had fired a machine gun from the air.
A former Coast Artillery officer had even devised a bombsight and
had used it. But these were all tentative, experimental measures.
The trouble with Mexico provided, on the other hand, active service for the flyers under rather unusual conditions. Captain Benjamin D. Foulois and the pilots of the first air squadron with the
Punitive Expedition flew reconnaissance missions in a moun-
tainous area higher than the maximum altitude ceiling of the
planes and suffered the consequences in crashes. Earlier at
Tampico and Vera Cruz in a better operating terrain the navy
had used some of its planes for the same purpose without the
accidents. From these flights the senior officers drew the obvious
conclusion that aircraft had a reconnaissance value.

Most officers already had accepted the airplane on this premise. In 1914, before the Pershing expedition, the Chief Signal
Officer wrote in his annual report, "But the useful, approved, and
most important work of air craft is probably to be found chiefly in
reconnaissance and the collection and transmission of information in the theater of military operations; for this reason aviation
must be reckoned as a vastly important branch of the Signal
Corps of the Army. . . . [however] in view of present conditions it appears that the use of air craft for attack alone does not
warrant the expense of production of air craft for this purpose. . . ." The events of the developing air war in Europe failed
to change this basic concept of the military leaders. When the

United States became a belligerent, the army still maintained its air unit as a subordinate section of the Signal Corps.

At first the armies in Europe had not used their airplanes for fighting either; however, by 1915, both sides had developed airplanes which could give battle, and an air war was in progress. For the remainder of the war each nation competed to stay ahead of its opponent in creating superior aircraft. In this contest which would have crucial repercussions in the American air program, the British developed sixty-seven different types of observation, pursuit, day-and-night bombing aircraft, and the French sixty-four.

The men who flew these planes were heroes to a public appalled by the monotony of the horrible trench stalemate. In the gruesome mass slaughter in the trenches, there was little opportunity for the romantic, while high above the ground the aces, soaring at 100 miles an hour, fencing with each other until the quick kill, called up images of knighthood. By 1916, Americans could read with vicarious thrill of the exploits of a few of their countrymen scattered throughout the Allied squadrons—in particular the handful in the celebrated Escadrille Lafayette. Formed in April 1916, this squadron of American volunteers commanded by French officers won its share of victories and excited the admiration of many Americans.

During this period in the United States, the preparedness movement had its effect on military aviation. Through the large appropriation bills of 1916, the services received authorizations for expansion and, during that fall, a joint army-navy board began a study of the problems of coordinating their air arms. The military men already had available a means of coordination with industry in the civilian preparedness agency—the National Advisory Committee of Aeronautics (NACA).

As the nation moved closer to war in early 1917, army planners prepared two air programs in compliance with General Staff requests. The first, submitted on February 16, called for expenditures of more than $43,000,000. At the end of March the now Major Foulois and two other officers turned in another estimate, which provided for 1850 flyers and 300 balloonists with appropriate equipment in a reconnaissance and observation force at a cost of $57,450,000. These were ambitious plans for a service which had received a total of less than $15,000,000 throughout previous years. A concurrent survey of industry by the NACA placed these estimates in perspective. The chairman of that agency reported that only twelve companies were capable of manufacturing aircraft for the government and warned, "Though millions may be available for a specific purpose in time of great need, no amount of money will buy time."

For a few days following the declaration of war, the NACA apparently dominated the air planning. On April 10, it recommended the creation of an Aircraft Production Board to consider "the quantity production of aircraft," and, two days later, it proposed an appropriation of $300,000,000 for a combined army and navy program to train 7500 pilots in the next two years and to produce just under 20,000 airplanes by the end of 1920. During the first week of the war, the members of the committee believed that 3700 planes would be the maximum capacity of American industry in 1918. Within five weeks, the Council of National Defense established the proposed board, and the service secretaries formed a joint Army and Navy Technical Board to attempt to standardize the designs of the airplanes.

On May 23 a dramatic appeal from the aged French Premier, Alexandre Ribot, changed the scope of American planning and became the basis for the military aviation program. The key paragraphs of the cable were:

> It is desired that in order to cooperate with the French Aeronautics, the American Government should adopt the following program: The formation of a flying corps of 4500 airplanes—personnel and matériel included—to be sent to the French front during the campaign of 1918. The total number of pilots, including reserve, should be 5000 and 50,000 mechanics.
>
> 2,000 airplanes should be constructed each month as well as 4000 engines, by the American factories. That is to say, that during the first six months of 1918, 16,500 planes (of the latest type) and 30,000 engines will have to be built.

Although Ribot did not actually set the time limit "during the campaign of 1918"—after the war it was discovered that apparently a member of the French mission had inserted the phrase—this request was still a tremendous one. When Major Foulois completed his detailed estimates based on the cable, he had a total of 22,625 airplanes and 45,250 engines at a cost of $640,-000,000. Since the French had built up to a force of some 4700 training and combat planes in three years, they obviously viewed the American productive capacity with unalloyed optimism.

In early June the chairman of the Aircraft Production Board, Howard E. Coffin, decided to publicize widely the program in order to gain public support for rapid congressional approval of appropriation. Coffin, who had skillfully used publicity previously in advancing industrial preparedness, appealed to newspaper editors. The glamor of the air war, the challenge and compliment to America's pride in quantity production, and the underlying appeal of a quick and easy victory if the nation fulfilled Ribot's request made the program attractive to newspaper editors. There was no shortage of metaphors. The Chief Signal Officer of the army spoke of "winged cavalry." Orville Wright pointed out the advantage of putting out the eyes of the enemy. And Coffin was at his best when he said, "The road to Berlin lies through the air. The eagle must end this war."

Congress responded to the official endorsement and public opinion by passing the huge money bill virtually without opposition in mid-July. There were a few dissenters to the great enthusiasm for the program. One warning came from Fiorello H. La Guardia, who would be an air officer within a few weeks. This New York Congressman declared, "This war will be won in a much more cruel and less spectacular manner." Although many army officers probably shared La Guardia's apprehension, the Secretary of War gave the measure his full support and stated that aviation "furnishes our supreme opportunity for immediate service. . . ." On July 24, President Wilson signed the bill, and military aviation had a program and money. At that time, it lacked a large aircraft industry, technical knowledge, and a well-organized administration. But dreams of masses of airplanes over the Western Front were more attractive than the fact, which few knew, that American industry had delivered only 78 airplanes during the month of July.

Two years later, in 1919, Secretary Baker gave in his introduction to Arthur Sweetser's *The American Air Service* an analysis of the enthusiastic acceptance of this air program, so out of proportion in a balanced war effort and seemingly with such little basis for actual realization. According to Baker, this program impressed the war leaders as the major means of the nation's participation in the war, since transportation difficulties evidently would bar the dispatch of a large expeditionary force. "We were dealing with a miracle," the Secretary wrote:

> The airplane itself was too wonderful and new, too positive a denial of previous experience, to brook the application of any prudential restraints which wise people would have known how to apply to ordinary industrial and military developments. As a consequence, the magicians of American industry were expected to do the impossible for this new and magical agency, and this expectation was increased by the feverish earnestness with which all Americans desired that our country should appear speedily, worthily, and decisively in the war.

Before the air program came before Congress, two business executives, temporarily in uniform, attempted to solve one of the most difficult problems in the air war—rapid improvement in design versus mass production. As Professor I.B. Holley, Jr., in *Ideas and Weapons* stated, "The objectives of more weapons and better weapons tend to pull in opposite directions." Colonels E.A. Deeds and S.D. Waldon hoped to obtain an engine which could be a standard model, hence mass-produced while efficient enough to retain its superiority in competition with the changing European designs. In the last days of May they put two engineers, J.G. Vincent and E.J. Hall, to work on the idea. The result was the Liberty engine. The designers succeeded in overcoming the production objective, since some 15,000 of these engines were produced during the war; however, they were not entirely successful in solving the design problem because the engine required modifications as the war progressed and was too heavy for high speed fighters. Yet a British expert later called this engine "about the most reliable power plant that the world had seen up to that date."

Other problems thwarted the ambitions of military aviation planners. At home, the lumber industry was unable to supply enough spruce for aircraft bodies. In order to meet quotas the government virtually took over the spruce industry and brought out the lumber. Abroad, Americans found French airplane manufacturers asking high prices and anxious to work out payment procedure before they would release design information. But the materialism of the French was only one aspect of the major problem of obtaining and handling information.

Before the American military leaders could make proper decisions and the manufacturers could begin to produce to their capacity, they needed complete, accurate, and timely information about aircraft designs. In obtaining and processing this information, they were primarily hampered by the lack of an efficient organization. A grant of clear-cut authority to a specific agency should have eliminated much of the confusion which stemmed from the conflicting reports of various boards, missions, and assorted individuals. As it was, there were coordination difficulties within the AEF, and between the AEF and the War Department, and, in the United States, between the Aircraft Production Board and the Air Service. Later, future General of the Air Force H.H. Arnold, an assistant to the Director of Military Aeronautics in 1918, who became commanding general of the Air Force in World War II commented, "The separation of functions caused by the everchanging channels in the Signal Corps was the worst problem of all." In the spring of 1918, after a large amount of adverse publicity about the failure of the air program to fulfill the early grandiose estimates, reorganizations took place on both sides of the Atlantic. While the AEF apparently settled its problem, in Washington the crucial division of responsibility remained, with a military agency charged with training and determination of airplane requirements and a civilian bureau made responsible for supervision of production.

Initially, in the AEF, Major Townsend F. Dodd, a flyer who had been with Pershing in Mexico, was the Chief Aviation Officer; however, Dodd's tenure was brief. For when Pershing and his staff arrived in Paris, Lieutenant Colonel William Mitchell met them at the rail station. Since Mitchell outranked Dodd and also had the advantage of having been on the scene a few weeks, he became the leading American air officer in Europe.

Mitchell, the son of a former Senator, had learned to fly at his own expense on weekends in 1916. When war seemed imminent, he wangled a post in Spain as a military observer. Upon the entrance of the United States into the war he went to France. In the intervening two months before Pershing's arrival, Mitchell toured the Allied front, talked with various military leaders, and sent back not only reports but also a plan for an American air program, which the War Department evidently ignored. Aggressive, self-confident, and, above all, flamboyant, Billy Mitchell, at thirty-seven, was a man with a future.

It is indicative of the organization problem of the time that the War Department sent abroad a mission in June to do what Mitchell had done in part in April. This mission of more than a hundred technical experts under the direction of a newly commissioned major, Raynal C. Bolling, was supposed to select specific aircraft models for American production and, in general, to work out methods of cooperation with the Allies in aviation affairs. By sending such a mission rather than supplying the necessary technicians to the Chief of AEF Air Service with the request that the tasks be done under that official, the War Department undercut the authority of the agency which would be responsible for combat results.

For five weeks the mission gathered information and settled some of the problems of collaboration in each of the three Allied countries. At the end of July, Bolling recommended four planes which he thought the United States should produce. The fighters he chose were the British Bristol and French Spad. As the observation and day bombing plane, he advocated the British DeHaviland (DH-4) and as the night bomber the Italian Caproni. Because of a variety of reasons, including failure to obtain detailed plans in time, technical difficulties, and, in the case of the Spad, later cancellation by the AEF, the DH-4 was the only one of the four to be mass-produced successfully in the United States.

When Bolling advised Pershing that the United States would be unable to provide the necessary aircraft to the AEF until the summer of 1918, the General conferred with the French about supplying his command with planes until American production could take over the burden. The French agreed on August 30 to provide 5000 airplanes and 8500 engines by the next June with the help of American tools and raw materials; however, they were unable to fulfill this agreement.

The Air Service in the AEF continued to expand despite its difficulty in securing planes. In the summer of 1917, Pershing had wisely separated it from the Signal Corps and granted it status equal to the other branches of the army. As it grew, however, it went through a series of reorganizations and changes in command which kept it in an unstable condition until May 1918.

During its first year the AEF Air Service had six different commanders. Mitchell had taken over from Dodd at the beginning. Then when the Bolling mission broke up, Bolling stayed to share authority with Mitchell. In this arrangement Bolling was in charge of the Zone of Interior (the logistical aspects of the AEF Air Service) and represented the United States on the Interallied Aircraft Board, while Mitchell was responsible for the Zone of Advance. (Since there were no actual combat units at the time, he was concerned with plans and preparation.) Within a few weeks, Pershing designated an artillery officer, Brigadier General William L. Kenly, as Chief of Air Service while retaining Bolling and Mitchell in their assignments. In November, Foulois, now a brigadier general at thirty-seven, came over with a large group of officers and supplanted Kenly. During this reorganization, Foulois relieved Bolling but kept Mitchell, who was seething with resentment at the change in command. Finally, in May 1918, Pershing named one of his West Point classmates, an engineer officer and an excellent administrator, Mason M. Patrick, to the post of Chief of Air Service, which he held for the remainder of the war.

The administration of the Air Service galled Pershing. He later said: "Differences in the views of the senior officers of the corps were not easily reconciled. Jealousies existed among them, no one had the confidence of all the others, and it was not easy to select from among the officers of the corps any outstanding executive." By selecting an older man and an experienced administrator who had not been involved in the internal feuds of the Air Service, Pershing achieved stability in the junior service. Patrick, in the judgment of one of the air staff officers, H.A. Toulmin, Jr., "applied a strong hand calmly, but it was always firmly held upon the throttle of affairs."

Changes in planning also compounded the confusion. As Toulmin, who was Chief of the Coordination Section of the AEF Air Service, recalled, "New programs blossomed and withered day by day. Great prospects involving thousands of planes came and went." Several of these programs, ranging from the initial goal of

59 combat squadrons to the grandiose program of 260 squadrons, received official sanction. Although the large figure meant a much greater ratio of airplanes to ground troops than either the French or the British maintained, the AEF planners based that plan on the ambitious estimates of the Ribot message. By the summer of 1918, personnel shortages and the failure of industry to fill the quotas caused the reduction of the program to 202 squadrons. When the war ended, only 45 squadrons were actually at the front.

In the United States military aviation also ran the gamut of changes in plans and organization and had the added problem of supervision of production. General Arnold recalled, "Until the spring of 1918 our situation, despite constant minor changes, was more a state of affairs than a chain of events." The air officers in Washington were caught between the cancellations, constant changes, and new requests in AEF cables and the incessant problems of a rapidly developing industry which they hoped would fulfill its expanding and inconstant goals.

Until the spring of 1918 the Signal Corps retained control of military aviation operations with an agency of the Council of National Defense, the Aircraft Production Board, responsible for production. It was a move toward better coordination when, in May 1918, President Wilson created two organizations within the War Department to perform those functions: the Bureau of Military Aeronautics (under Kenly who had returned to the United States) to take the place of the old Aviation Section of the Signal Corps and the Bureau of Aircraft Production (with John D. Ryan, former president of Anaconda Copper Company at its head) to supplant the Aircraft Production Board. Now aviation was independent of the Signal Corps, but cooperation was faulty between the operations bureau and the civilian production agency. In the last week of August the Secretary of War attempted to alleviate this difficulty with the appointment of Ryan to the offices of Director of Air Service and Second Assistant Secretary of War. But Ryan was not able to effect any basic improvements during the two and a half months left in the war. In November he wrote, "I have not taken over the actual direction of Military Aeronautics and my connection with it has not made any real change in its operations." Thus the control of aviation was not unified at any time during the war in the United States, and the air program suffered accordingly.

While the army was in the throes of its aviation problems, the navy was expanding its own air force, to the chagrin of some of the soldiers. Billy Mitchell, for one, complained, "The navy was going to conduct an air war of their own somewhere, nobody knew where exactly. This performance just meant a tremendous waste of money, men, and energy." In turn, the navy men criticized the obstructionist attitude of the army officers. When they asked for material to develop a separate bombing group, they found Foulois in opposition. Foulois knew that the army needed all of the equipment it could obtain, and he did not relish the idea of sharing the supply of Liberty engines and aircraft with the navy, but he was overruled by the Secretary of War. In Italy, where both services had small detachments, the navy found the army most uncooperative. Naval Lieutenant John L. Callan commented on the attitude of the army's Captain Fiorello H. La-Guardia, the Congressman, "It is very important for us to know whether he is actually working for us or against us." Within five weeks he had apparently found the answer to his question and suggested to his superior that LaGuardia be sent from Italy.

Despite its difficulties with the army, the navy air arm flourished. The Northern Bombing Group did carry out operations against the German submarine bases and other units stationed in England, France, and Italy played a role in the naval war. By the Armistice, the navy had serving overseas 17,524 officers and men of its total of 37,409 in its aviation branch. Among its fliers were two future Secretaries of Defense, James Forrestal and Robert A. Lovett, and the one naval ace, David S. Ingalls, who later became an Assistant Secretary of the Navy. During the war the navy established a firm foundation for future development of its air program. Mitchell who dreamed of a single air force might well complain of the division of effort, yet the Northern Bombing Group did put into effect his theory of strategic bombardment.

After the war the chief of staff of the AEF Air Service, Colonel Edgar S. Gorrell, stated, "The basic task we faced was that of training men." Since there were fewer than 1200 officers and men on aviation duty in the army when the war began and more than

190,000 at the time of the Armistice, training was obviously a major task.

Soon after the declaration of war the army contracted with several universities to give aviation candidates basic ground training. After completion of this course, the cadets then entered flying schools in either the United States or Europe. If in this country, the flyer would then have to complete his advanced training in Europe because of the absence of combat planes here.

In order to provide a few more instructors as well as trained leaders, the United States granted citizenship and commissions to some officers in the Royal Flying Corps. One of these men, Major Harold E. Hartney, a Canadian lawyer who had shot down five planes and had become a captain in the RFC, commanded the American First Pursuit Group in the St. Mihiel and Meuse-Argonne campaigns.

During this training process the clash between the "Old Army" men and the new air men was particularly evident. Since there was a marked shortage of regular army aviators, the army had to draw upon other branches as well as civilians to run these schools. Hiram Bingham, a Yale history professor and famous discoverer of Inca ruins, who became successively Director of Military Schools of Aeronautics, Chief of Air Personnel, and commander of the training base at Issoudun, was shocked by the ineptness of many of the regulars in dealing with the aviators. Bingham had learned to fly at forty-one, and he could not understand the adamant refusal of nonflying regulars serving in the Air Service to learn even the basic aviation terms. At one flying school he knew, the cavalry officer in command had a hitching post constructed in front of his headquarters. When he started on horseback to inspect the flying field, he ran into trouble, according to Bingham: "His horse took exception to the noise caused by several machines whose engines were being warmed up 'on the line' in front of the hangars. As his horse pranced around in front of the planes, he waved his hands, and as soon as he could make himself heard, shouted out the order, 'Stop those fans! Don't you see they scare my horse?'" Somehow, young men still learned how to fly.

The first and largest American flying school in France was at Issoudun on a clay plain 65 miles south of Orleans. About the time training began in October, heavy rains turned the area almost into a morass. The mud was more than an inconvenience, since the airplane wheels would throw it up against the propellers and break them. The engineering officer, Lieutenant Edward V. Rickenbacker, solved the problem by designing a wheel fender to prevent this.

One of the students who was there at this time, Charles R. Codman, left a description: "A sea of frozen mud. Waiting in shivering line before dawn for the spoonsful of gluey porridge slapped into outstretched mess kits, cold as ice. Wretched flying equipment. Broken necks. The flu. A hell of a place, Issoudun."

In those early days, Issoudun did have an impressive staff to deal with the headaches of running a base under difficult conditions. Besides Rickenbacker, who became the leading American ace, Lieutenant Douglas Campbell, who would be the first official ace, was the adjutant for a brief period and Lieutenant Quentin Roosevelt, the former President's son, served as post quartermaster. The commanding officer and training officer for several months was Major Carl Spaatz, who commanded the Strategic Air Force in World War II.

At Issoudun, fliers who had learned on the Curtiss "Jennies" in the United States virtually started all over again with the French pursuit ship—the Nieuport. In time, they progressed from dual flying to soloing, then acrobatics, and formation flying. Toward the end of the war, the development of camera guns permitted the teaching of combat flying, but, in the early period, acrobatics was the closest approach to simulated combat and the most dangerous phase of the training. The French instructor would demonstrate the handling of the stick on the ground, watch the student go through the motions, and then send him up to try it out alone. Sometimes the novice failed to come out of the *vrille* (tail spin) or one of the other maneuvers. This was a calculated risk, for without the knowledge of these maneuvers the pilot would be helpless in combat.

Until the Americans opened their own aerial gunnery school in August 1918 their pilots had to learn that skill at the French school at Cazaux, where they flew and fired live ammunition at the balloons and towed sleeves. Here the student also found out how to deal with gun jams, so that he could tell at a glance if he could fix the malfunction or if he should leave it alone. After this training, the pursuit pilot, hopefully, was ready for action.

Other schools in France prepared officers for observation and bombardment work and a few for duty in the unwieldy observation balloons. The English helped out by training some pilots and thousands of mechanics, while the Italians instructed a handful of pilots.

Then, the front. The first pursuit pilots to enter this last stage were members of the 94th Squadron. The insignia of this squadron appropriately was a symbol of the United States throwing its hat in the ring—Uncle Sam's top hat with a ring around it.

The ground force of the squadron organized at Kelly Field, Texas, in August 1917 and completed its training at Issoudun. In early March the squadron picked up eleven of its pilots and entrained for the First Pursuit Organization Training Center at Villeneuve-les-Vertus in the Champagne sector. Seven more novice pilots joined it here as well as four veterans of the French Lafayette Flying Corps. Major Jean Huffer took command and Captains Kenneth Marr, James Norman Hall, and David McK. Peterson became flight commanders. The training officer at the center was the famous Major Raoul Lufbery, who was the leading American ace with 17 victories in the Escadrille Lafayette. These experienced men helped the squadron through the early days until it could develop its own leaders.

For about two weeks the fliers merely observed the French air unit stationed there in action. Then, in mid-March, the Nieuports 28's arrived. The next day, March 19, Lufbery led the first patrol over the lines north of Rheims. For this mission he picked Rickenbacker and Campbell. Since they did not yet have guns, Lufbery saw that they did not get into any trouble. But the initiation did include some anti-aircraft ("archy") fire which put some holes in Rickenbacker's plane.

After their return, "Luf" asked them if they had seen anything and chuckled when both replied negatively. He had seen about fifteen planes, friendly and enemy, during the flight. This lesson was not lost on his students. Campbell later remarked that a lot of the fliers who were killed "were shot down in the early part of their career before they had really learned how to see." The combat pilot had to learn not to focus his eyes on a point but to keep them unfocussed and to stare vacantly as he continually twisted his head so that he would notice anything that moved. Lufbery gave them other helpful ideas such as carrying a small hammer strapped to the wrist to use in clearing up gun jams. Very intense and businesslike, Lufbery left his mark on the squadron in the two months before he fell or leaped to his death from his burning plane.

From early April until the last of June, the 94th squadron gained combat experience in the quiet Toul sector near St. Mihiel. After they received their machine guns, they were ready for action. On their first day in actual operation, it came to them.

Sunday, April 14, was a foggy day and not conducive to flying, but the Americans learned shortly before 8:45 a.m. that two German planes were enroute to the base. The two pilots on alert—Lieutenant Alan F. Winslow, a veteran of the French flying corps, and Douglas Campbell—set out to stop them. Winslow had reached a height of only 250 meters when he saw an enemy plane coming out of the mist about 100 yards to his front and above him. He opened fire, maneuvered to counter the German's acrobatics, got behind him, and forced him to a crash landing 100 yards from the airfield. Campbell, meantime, had heard Winslow's initial burst and, as he recalled, "I noticed his tracers were going toward an airplane which had black crosses on it. I had never seen a German airplane before but that obviously was one." As he started to turn to go to Winslow's help, Campbell saw another stream of tracers from above and behind him streak past his plane. In the excitement he forgot about the low altitude and, in the process of maneuvering to get the advantage, he stalled and fell into an involuntary dive. When he pulled out of this, he had enough speed to zoom up behind the Pfalz and shoot it down in flames over the airfield.

The two victories within a few minutes on the first day at the front and in full view of the rest of the squadron on the ground was a boost to the morale of the young fliers. Later, Billy Mitchell concluded that this double victory "had a more important effect on American fighting aviation than any other single occurrence. It gave our men a confidence that could have been obtained in no other way."

One of the pilots who reached the field in time to see Camp-

bell's victim crash was Eddie Rickenbacker. At twenty-seven
Rickenbacker was not only older than most of the others but, because of his experience in racing automobiles, was already tough-
ened in a field of dangerous competition. In the spring of 1917 he
was a well-known professional racing driver at a time when
Campbell, in contrast, was completing his undergraduate work in
chemistry at Harvard. Rickenbacker's experience on the racing
tracks was, as Major Harold E. Hartney pointed out, "priceless in
his work as an aviator. It gave him two great assets—patience
and a marvelous judgment of speeds and distances."

For many of the young pilots air fighting was a sport or an
adventure as they dueled with an enemy who might be as close as
fifty feet. "The fact that maybe you wouldn't get back," Campbell
recalled, "was not something one thought about much." He added,
however, "Nobody had any plans for tomorrow." They did not
even have parachutes.

With Rickenbacker the air war was a sport and an adventure,
but he did have plans for tomorrow. He had come to France with
the Pershing party as a chauffeur, transferred to the aviation section, learned how to fly, and, after his stint as engineering officer
at Issoudun, joined the 94th. At the front, he carefully noted and
analyzed his experiences. In the process, he amassed the knowledge that together with his competitive instinct made him one of
the most skillful pursuit pilots.

On April 29, "Rick," with the help of Captain Hall, brought
down his first German. During the last two weeks in May he tal-
lied four more victories, but then he went without a confirmed kill
until the middle of September. In the interim, he had developed
such a severe pain in his ear that he had to go to the hospital
twice—the second time for a mastoid operation. He used his time
in the hospital to sort through his experiences again and to plan
for elimination of any unneccesary obstacles to his success in the
sky. Jamming of machine guns, for one, was a critical factor
which, to a great extent, he could remedy. More than anything
else, this analysis of the air war made him more self-confident. In
the last two months of the war, he scored twenty-one more victories
in addition to serving as squadron leader for most of the period.
Mature, cautious, quick-thinking, and virtually nerveless, Rickenbacker understood and mastered this dangerous game.

On his first day as squadron commander, September 25, "Rick" demonstrated his skill. In the morning he took off in his Spad for a long flight over the lines. Pilots could do this if they wished in addition to their regular missions. Many of the air victories resulted from these hunting expeditions rather than the regular missions, particularly during the period in the Toul sector.

After flying past Verdun and into the German territory, "Rick" saw below him a couple of enemy photographic (two-seater) airplanes with an escort of five Fokkers above them. Since they had not seen him yet, he climbed rapidly for altitude so that he could approach with the sun at his back. He dived for one of the Fokkers and opened fire. The German attempted to swerve, but too late. Originally, "Rick" had planned to shoot this man and then get away, but in a few seconds, he saw that the four other German pursuit pilots were confused so he continued his dive toward the photographic planes. In the face of the firing of the observers he maneuvered for a favorable position, but these Germans evidently were more experienced than their friends in the escort planes, who were still milling about. At one point one of the Halberstadts got on Rickenbacker's tail, but he climbed and doubled back out of the situation. Finally, after about ten minutes of maneuvering for the best position, "Rick" sideslipped, got off a good burst of fire into the side of one of the planes, and watched him go down in flames. By this time the Fokkers had recovered from the initial surprise and were moving in to get the American. The pleased ace headed for home as fast as he could and outran the Fokkers. For this doubleheader victory, the army in 1931 eventually awarded Rickenbacker the Medal of Honor.

The greatest fighter pilot, Rickenbacker believed, was Frank Luke. An impetuous undisciplined boy, Luke showed no fear in carrying out the most difficult of missions—shooting down observation balloons. Because of the anti-aircraft batteries and the pursuit planes which protected these balloons, the attacker played with the odds against his getting out alive. Luke took the chance frequently and amazed everyone by succeeding—temporarily. In four days he shot down eight. Within a few minutes on September 18, he destroyed two more balloons and three planes. During September he scored a total of 18 victories (the second highest American total) and won the Medal of Honor, but the odds won out. On

September 29, he shot down three balloons and strafed some enemy troops while under constant attack by the enemy planes. Forced to crash behind the German lines, he refused to surrender and shot it out, unsuccessfully, with the Germans.

The air war was changing its scope during the summer and fall of 1918. On the individual level, the sporting and adventurous approach of the spring gave way, for some fighter pilots, to a greater awareness of their mission. Douglas Campbell experienced this when he shot down his fifth plane.

While on a lone hunting expedition on the last day of May, Campbell engaged a German two-seater photographic plane. With guns in the back as well as in front, these aircraft were not easy opponents. As he maneuvered, Campbell noticed that the rear gunner was using up his ammunition by firing at him while he was out of range. In time the firing stopped. When the American came in for a closer look, he saw the empty ammunition belts trailing over the side. Although he might hesitate to shoot him in that condition, Campbell reasoned that the German probably had photographs of the Allied lines. Almost half a century later, he recalled the combat and commented, "So I just had to get up behind him and shoot him down—cold—it made me sort of sick." But he realized that he could not let the plane escape with valuable photographs even though he was sorry for the fliers, "War isn't like that."

On a broader basis, in the summer and fall of 1918, Colonel William Mitchell was able to put into effect some of his beliefs about the proper use of airpower. In May 1917, Mitchell had visited the headquarters of the British air commander, Major General Sir Hugh Trenchard. For Mitchell this was a highly instructive experience. Trenchard believed that the best way to gain and to maintain air superiority at the front was to keep up an offensive against the enemy's rear areas, thus drawing off aircraft from the front to protect supply dumps and communication centers. In Mitchell he found an enthusiastic disciple.

In July 1918, Mitchell had his first opportunity to try out this policy. When he collected his small force in the Chateau-Thierry sector, he found that his men were outnumbered while fighting some of the best German squadrons. The large enemy formations proceeded to take a heavy toll from the smaller American patrols.

(Among those killed in this period was Quentin Roosevelt, TR's son.) The Americans reacted immediately by starting to fly in larger formations, but Mitchell also thought of Trenchard's idea. He obtained a British force—to carry out the mission of drawing the enemy planes from the front. After the bombing raid on their major supply point in the area, the Germans pleased Mitchell by reacting as Trenchard had predicted.

July was a good month for Billy Mitchell. When the Americans made their attack on Soissons, he was able to gain control of the air. Even Pershing overlooked his many hot arguments with Mitchell and praised this achievement. In his memoirs Pershing wrote, "The usefulness of our Air Service during this period could hardly be overestimated, as previously the enemy had seemed to have the superiority whenever he cared to use it." As a culmination of his good fortune, at the end of the month, Mitchell became Chief of the Air Service of the First Army and took command of all American air combat units.

Foulois, who held that position, had asked for his own relief and recommended Mitchell as his replacement. A tough little ex-infantryman, Foulois had flown one of the initial test flights with Orville Wright in 1909. He was not as flamboyant as the enthusiastic but rather recent convert to flight, and there was no affection between him and Mitchell. The latter indicated in his post-war memoir that he was harshly critical of his superior officer from the time Foulois arrived in France, certainly Mitchell was not an ideal subordinate. In the spring Foulois found him so irritating that he recommended his return to the United States. After Pershing talked with Mitchell and obtained his assurance of loyal cooperation, he passed the word on to Foulois that he expected him to cooperate with Mitchell. Soon, Mitchell's tactlessness and zeal annoyed others, and in early July brought on an investigation of his activities by the Inspector General. It was easy to criticize Mitchell, but one could not overlook the results he secured. Foulois discussed these matters with André W. Brewster, the IG, and presumably with Patrick and then made his decision to relinquish his command. For the remainder of the war, Foulois was in charge of air logistics in the AEF.

The pursuit pilots had done well in the summer, and Mitchell was proud of them; however, the fledgling American bomber units were not as impressive. When Mitchell took the fighter units into the Chateau-Thierry sector, he left the 96th Daylight Bombardment Squadron in the Toul area. On July 10th, the regular army major commanding this squadron led a flight of six planes on a mission. In the air they became lost in the fog and mistook Coblenz for Metz. When all of them landed, almost out of fuel but still armed with their bombs, they discovered their mistake and became prisoners. The humorous aspect of this escapade was not lost on the Germans nor on quite a few Americans, but it was a hard blow to the morale of the 96th. And Mitchell was furious, "I know of no other performance in any air force in the war that was as reprehensible as this."

Morale did not improve with the arrival of the first American-built planes at the front in August. The DeHaviland-4s had certain drawbacks. By the time the first squadron of them flew over enemy lines they were obsolete as combat aircraft. Then, because of the location of the gas tank between the seats, the plane was subject to a sudden fire between the pilot and observer when hit by an incendiary bullet. After the war, the Air Service historian, Colonel Edgar S. Gorrell, argued with statistics that the DH-4 was no more dangerous in this respect than other aircraft. Nevertheless, the label of "Flying Coffin" or "Flaming Coffin" stuck. Yet, before the war ended, the AEF used 417 of these planes at the front in bombardment and observation squadrons. Despite the great expectations about American production in the summer of 1917, these DH-4s were the only American planes to serve in combat.

As commander of the American air combat force, Mitchell was in his element. The young flyers admired him, and he seemed to have rapport with them. One of the aces remembered him as a "bundle of energy." He moved fast, worked hard, and would wear a star before his thirty-ninth birthday. In his memoirs, he showed his pride in having the fastest automobile, a Mercedes racer, and the "fastest airplane on the western front." And he used them in constant inspection trips. Frequently, he flew over the front as a part of what he termed "my work of watching everything." Afterwards, he claimed that he slept only three hours a night during the last six months of the war. He must have relied on excitement and ambition to keep going at such a pace.

Shortly after the war, his superior, Major General Mason M. Patrick, described his noted subordinate in a letter to Pershing:

> He thinks rapidly and acts quickly, sometimes a little too hastily. He is opinionated but I have usually found him properly subordinate and ready to obey orders. While he has worked well with the men and material which it was possible to furnish, his own ideas of what were necessary to accomplish his tasks I have found sometimes exaggerated. In other words, he has asked for more in the way of personnel and transporation than I believe to have been absolutely necessary for the performance of his duties. He has some tendency to act on his own initiative; it is not meant that this is a fault, as it is frequently a virtue, but there have been a few times when it has been uncertain just where he was or what he was doing. He is at all times enthusiastic and full of energy.

In the St. Mihiel campaign Mitchell commanded his largest force of men and planes. For six weeks he prepared for this formal debut of the First Army. Because he believed that the Germans would concentrate 2000 planes within three days, he requested and got a huge force to counter the enemy. According to General Patrick's final report, the 1481 planes under Mitchell's command were "the largest aggregation of air forces that had ever been engaged in one operation on the western front at any one time during the entire progress of the war." The Allies were generous in making this possible with the French lending him 742 planes and the British another 130 aircraft.

Two days before the attack, Mitchell flew over the sector for a final reconnaissance. On the following day, he personally read the attack order to his assembled officers. He planned to use his armada in large formations to strike alternately from both sides of the salient, as he said, "just as a boxer gives a right hook and a left hook successively to his opponent."

Unfortunately for Mitchell, the weather during the battle limited his forces. The log of one of the American squadrons explained succinctly, "September 12th, which opened the St. Mihiel offensive, was on all counts the worst flying day in many months."

Despite the miserable conditions the men did fly and harassed the enemy with their strafing and bombing, but the rain and high winds limited their efficiency for two days. However, the 14th was a clear day, and the photographic planes were able to fly their missions for the first time.

The good weather also brought out the enemy planes. This was the third day, and the German air strength did increase but not to the extent predicted by Mitchell. By September 16th, the Germans had only 243 planes in the sector, and Mitchell's strategy and overwhelming force kept most of them behind their own lines in defense of their rear area installations. Pershing was pleased that Mitchell had maintained supremacy of the air and commended him and his men.

The final campaign of the war was more of a challenge to the American Air Service than the brief affair at St. Mihiel. The weather remained generally unfavorable for air war throughout the Meuse-Argonne offensive. Then, although Mitchell still had more aircraft than the Germans could put up in opposition, the ratio had narrowed considerably. A postwar survey of the opposing forces by the Air Service historian Colonel Gorrell reflected the marked change in the situation since St. Mihiel during the six and a half weeks of the campaign. On one day (September 26) Mitchell mustered a total of 842 French and American planes to face 302 enemy aircraft. By mid-October (October 15), his force had dwindled to 756, while the Germans had increased their number of planes to 504. In the last phase of the operation (on November 1), Mitchell had 697 planes to oppose the 486 of the enemy. Although on each occasion more than 100 British planes were available, they were not under Mitchell's personal command. This difference in ratio did not change Mitchell's tactical ideas. If anything it made him more certain of the advantages of rear area raids to attract the enemy away from the front.

While Mitchell could argue with justification for his approach, he was willing to compromise with the ground commanders. Infantry officers wanted help in taking machine gun nests and in finding out what was on the other side of the hill. At St. Mihiel they had a relatively easy time of it, and their need for close air support had not been as pressing, but they wanted all of the help they could get in the difficult days of the Meuse-Argonne. The air officers, however, complained that the ground troops did not signal them properly and did not know how to use their support

Warming up for the Kaiser. Recruits learn to doubletime on their first day in the army during the fall of 1917.

"Juggy" Nelson at Corfu in the fall of 1918.

William S. Sims introduces King George V to an American baseball player at an interservice game on July 4, 1918.

The Secretary of the Navy is ready for action. Josephus Daniels checks out a gunsight on the USS *Wyoming* in February, 1917.

U.S. Signal Corps

Issoudun

Ralph Curtin

Enroute to France and the war. John J. Pershing (in the center) chats with James G. Harbord (in civilian clothes) and Benjamin Alvord on board the *Baltic*.

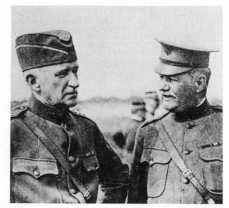

U.S. Signal Corps

Hunter Liggett (on the right) explains the situation to Clarence Edwards in May, 1918.

State Historical Society of Wisconsin   U.S. Signal Corps

Engineers cleaning up Cierges after the 32nd Division captured it during the Aisne-Marne offensive.

U.S. Signal Corps

A quiet moment and a bite to eat in the frontline trenches of the Rainbow Division in March, 1918.

Soldiers of the 92nd Division inspecting their gas masks behind the front in August, 1918.

State Historical Society of Wisconsin   *U.S. Signal Corps*

U.S. Signal Corps

Robert L. Bullard Confers with Philippe Pétain on the day before the initial attack in the Meuse-Argonne.

A dangerous moment for these First Division infantrymen in Exermont, October, 1918.

U.S. Signal Corps

U.S. Signal Corps

One of the reasons why the going was slow during the early days of the Meuse-Argonne offensive. This often reprinted photo of the traffic jam at Esnes clearly indicates the problem.

A gathering of the generals. Left to right: John J. Pershing, James W. McAndrew, Billy Mitchell, John L. Hines, William M. Wright, and Charles P. Summerall. The officer with the handlebar moustache on the extreme right is the Inspector General of the AEF, André Brewster.   *Hines Family and Charles L. Bolté*

Charles P. Summerall (on the left) poses with Frank Parker on October 31, 1918, a few days before their attempt to take Sedan.

Three of the stalwarts of the First Division in the summer of 1918. John L. Hines is seated in the front. The chief of staff of the division and later chief of staff of the III Corps, Campbell King, is on the left with George C. Marshall on the right. The armbands worn by King and Marshall indicate that they are staff officers.

Hugh Drum in his office at Souilly at the end of the war. As he wrote his wife: "I look somewhat worn but still in the ring." The cord on the map behind him marks the First Army front line on November 10, 1918.

Secretary of War Newton D. Baker with his towering Chief of Staff, Peyton C. March (on his right), welcome Omar Bundy who had just returned from France in November, 1918.

The aces are glad to be going home. Left to right: Douglas Campbell, Eddie Rickenbacker, James Meissner, and Paul F. Baer on board the *Adriatic* in February, 1919.

Men who fought at Belleau Wood in the 96th Company, Sixth Marines. Joseph G. Stites is on the left in the top row.

Joseph G. Stites

Miss Elizabeth Satterthwait

Illinois in the World War

Frederick Trevenen Edwards

Clayton K. Slack

SOME OF THOSE WHO FOUGHT

Sidney C. Graves

Harris and Ewing

Mrs. Ben H. Bernheisel

Frederick A. Pottle

Ben H. Bernheisel

Frederick A. Pottle

effectively. Thus, under the pressure of heavy fighting, the ground and air units had to work out liaison procedures in order to make air support effective. Infantrymen visited airfields and went up in the planes, while pilots and observers visited the trenches. Observation planes flew what their crews called "cavalry reconnaissance" missions to obtain information for the infantry, and fighter pilots strafed front line strong points. One of the pursuit pilots, Carl Spaatz, recalled that the slow rate of fire of the machine guns of that period limited the effectiveness of the strafing. Nevertheless, the observation reports and the damage inflicted by the strafing raids were helpful and, above all, it helped the morale of the ground troops to see friendly planes in action.

Mitchell correctly refused to spread his force in a thin cover over the lines. He would supply help in the infantry when needed, but he also maintained strong formations and kept up bombing raids. At times, of course, he could combine the bombing missions with infantry support. The largest bombing raid under his command took exactly that form.

On October 9 he learned that the Germans were building up a force less than five miles to the rear of their lines near Damvillers —on the right of the American position. He asked for and got more than 500 bombers and escort planes from the French to stop this potential counterattack. Late that afternoon, this huge flight passed over the lines and hit the concentration with 32 tons of bombs (about one-fourth of the total bombs dropped under American control during the war).

This mission also had a side effect which demonstrated the validity of Mitchell's theory. Just as convoys drew submarines to them, these bombing formations attracted enemy fighters. Not only did they pull the enemy aircraft away from the front but they also provided the opportunity to destroy the fighters in large numbers. In the Damvillers raid, German pursuit ships attacked and brought down one of the planes but at a loss of twelve of their own. General Patrick stated that over two-thirds of the enemy aircraft destroyed in the Argonne offensive were shot down "by just such concentrations and under similar conditions."

Whether used on front line positions or on rear area raids, an air attack did have an important psychological effect. Both American army commanders, Hunter Liggett and Robert L. Bullard, remarked on this in their brief comments on the air war in their postwar memoirs. In reference to a period of enemy air superiority earlier in the war, Bullard recalled "a bitter feeling of helplessness and terror, as if you were right under his hand or heel, completely at his mercy." The Second Army commander added, however, "The reality never justified this feeling." Liggett agreed, "Our experience demonstrated that aerial bombardment of towns, railroads, bridges, etc., produced little material effect; it has a moral effect, however, if constantly repeated." Bullard supplied an example, which H.H. Arnold corroborated, "Day after day for almost a year the Allied communiqués told of the 'successful bombing' of the Metz-Sablons railway station, which to the day of the armistice calmly went on functioning." Technique and equipment had not yet met the demands of the problem. The famous World War II commander Carl Spaatz, who flew escort on a World War I bombing mission, later commented that bombing of that day was not very effective simply because it was not accurate.

If the war had lasted into 1919 the Americans would have had better bombers and would have raided deeper. The British already had a strategic bombing force in action and had worked out an agreement with the United States to produce jointly Handley-Page bombers and to train crews. The war ended before any of these planes reached American units at the front. In fact only one night-bombardment squadron, equipped with obsolete planes, reached the front by the Armistice, and it arrived on November 9.

The original goals and the propaganda of the summer of 1917 overshadow the results of the American air program. Yet, by November 1918, industry had produced 11,754 planes and the armed services had some 227,000 officers and men in their air arms. But the Americans ranked far behind the British and French in numbers of aircraft at the front. At their peak, shortly before the Armistice, the AEF had 45 squadrons (740 planes), of which only twelve at the front consisted of American-built planes. Although they were in action less than seven months, the American fighter units made an impressive record. The number of enemy planes they shot down was more than double the number the Germans downed of theirs.

At the time of the Armistice, the Air Service was perfecting equipment and theories that one usually associates with World War II. Electrically heated flying suits and oxygen masks would make high altitude flying possible, and air-to-air radios certainly would facilitate communication. One of the top secrets in the United States was the "Bug," an unmanned air bomb which General "Hap" Arnold compared to the German V-rockets of the later war. In October 1918, Billy Mitchell suggested to Pershing that they equip an infantry division with parachutes and drop it behind enemy lines. And strategic bombardment was already a cardinal factor in Mitchell's thinking, even though he did not have the planes to demonstrate it during the war.

After World War II, General Arnold, in a review of the First World War period, said of Mitchell, "For Billy, the Armistice was an untimely interruption—as if the whistle had ended the game just as he was about to go over the goal line." In a sense this conclusion would serve for the entire American Air Service.

·VIII·

"They Are Putting New Life into the Game."

During the summer of 1918, for the first time, large numbers of Americans fought the Germans. Initially, they helped blunt German offensives, but, after July 18, they were on the attack. Nine divisions saw action in the provinces of Aisne and Marne during this period, and, in August, two corps, under American commanders, occupied adjoining sectors. In these battles, however, it was the French who set the time, named the place, and gave overall direction to the Americans.

On the Western Front, the numerical balance shifted in favor of the Allies as hundreds of thousands of Americans crossed the Atlantic. The AEF passed the million mark and was over a third into the second million by the end of August. That number included Negroes who labored and fought in segregated units.

During the last four days of May there seemed to be no stopping the Germans as they swept toward Paris. The Allies were

Chapter title quoted from H. A. Drum (June 15, 1918).

taken by surprise. Even the German leader Ludendorff, who had planned the offensive as a diversion to draw French reserves from the British, was amazed at its success. For the French, despair soon set in as they saw German infantrymen approach the scene of the great battle of the Marne of 1914. In Paris it was almost unbearable. The government planned to move to Bordeaux, and there was panic in the Chamber of Deputies.

On May 29, when a staff officer visited the command post of General Joseph Degoutte whose 21st Corps was falling back before the German attacks, he saw Degoutte "silently weeping over a tattered remnant of a map. . . ." After his return to Paris, General Mordacq wrote in his diary, "I left him with no hope of ever seeing him again."

There were 650,000 American soldiers in France, but, to some Frenchmen, it appeared that they had arrived just in time to witness the collapse of a nation. At the American Embassy and the offices of the American military personnel on the Supreme War Council, trucks waited to evacuate men and papers on notice. Even Pershing would soon issue secret orders to plan for the evacuation of his headquarters at Chaumont.

In this charged atmosphere Allied political and military leaders met at Versailles in the sixth session of the Supreme War Council, June 1 and 2. Again they strongly pressed Pershing for American reinforcements. An excited Foch kept repeating, "The battle, the battle, nothing else counts." Although Pershing still stood by his eventual goal of an independent American army, he did agree to disrupt his shipping program for June and July in order that thousands of additional combat troops could make the crossing ahead of schedule. Earlier, on May 30, he had promptly responded to Pétain's urgent request for aid by sending two divisions to him.

The first Americans to reach the battlefield were two companies of the Seventh Machine Gun Battalion, Third Division. Coincidentally, the companies of the Sixth Engineer Regiment which had been with the British in the "Michael" offensive were also from this division. Regulars in name, if not in experience, the men of the Third had been in France only a matter of weeks. Except for the engineers, none of them had been at the front—

even for a training period in a quiet sector. As a result, the French took the regiments and, in some cases, battalions into their own divisions along their defensive line.

The machine gunners arrived on the afternoon of May 31 after a 110-mile journey which took 22 hours in their overloaded trucks. Immediately, they took up positions to protect the bridges across the Marne at Château-Thierry. For the next four days, these men played a key role in helping the French stop the German advance.

During June, American attention focused on the Second Division and, in particular, the Marine Brigade. In part this was the result of GHQ censorship policy which would not permit newsmen to designate units, branches of the army, or even regulars, but the reporters could mention Marines. The news coverage that the Marines got that month would rankle soldiers for 30 years. More to the point, however, the Marines did bear the brunt of the heaviest fighting in June and, in the end, a Marine major was able to report, "Woods now U.S. Marine Corps entirely." Maurice Shearer, commander of the third battalion of the Fifth Marine Regiment, referred, of course, to Belleau Wood.

This hunting preserve, in the shape of a kidney, measured roughly 1000 yards across its widest northern section and some 3000 yards in length from the southern to the northern tips. When the Marines first saw it the trees and thick undergrowth were in full foliage, which hid the many huge boulders and ravines.

Later, some military analysts would say that the Marines should have ignored the wood; that artillery could have neutralized it with a heavy gas barrage; that infantry should have bypassed it and forced the withdrawal of defenders by isolation; that as a military objective it was of little value—certainly not worth the cost that Marines and some soldiers (from the Second Engineer and Seventh Infantry Regiments) paid for it. While one can argue that initially the artillery did not have enough gas to neutralize the area; that men in the wood could have controlled the immediate surrounding area and stopped units from bypassing; still the most telling criticism is the last. A historian can say that the Fourth Marine Brigade could have waited through the days until the artillery was prepared and that the woods were not worth the lives it took except as a symbolic gesture. Even then, the questions remain: Was this the place? Was this the time? Was it worth the cost? It is not a complete and certainly not a coolly reasoned answer, but the fact remains that the officers and men of the Fourth Marine Brigade thought so in that summer month of fifty years ago.

They fought in the way men fought at the West Wood near Antietam Creek and in the little clump of trees on Cemetery Ridge at Gettysburg. The military value of any of these small areas can be questioned. But at one time at one particular place, one group of men desperately wanted to take that ground away from another group equally desperate in their desire to hold. In the process, their actions dictated decisions and events.

The Civil War analogy is apt. Marine First Lieutenant John W. Thomason, Jr., who lived through the battle and later earned a considerable reputation as a writer and an illustrator, thought of the Civil War; but he saw little resemblance between the color and glamour that he believed the Civil War battles to have and what he saw of exhausted men in drab uniforms fighting for their lives. Yet today there seem to be marked similarities between the experiences of those men in 1918 and their grandfathers in the 1860's. Mounted dragoons with lances at rest; horse-drawn cannon wheeling into firing position; lines of infantry, dressing right as if on parade, marching across open field toward the enemy— all seem to belong to an earlier time, but they were part of the experience of the men who fought at Belleau Wood. More than the sights, there was the same basic dependence of commanders on the courage and spirit of their men rather than technique to win the battle. But in the 1860's the cruel test was over in hours. At Belleau Wood the hours ran into days and on into weeks, with gas barrages intensifying the horror.

Originally GHQ had planned to use the Second Division to relieve the First but, when Pétain asked for help, Pershing sent him the Second. They got their orders on the afternoon of the 30th and left early the next morning. They rode most of the way in trucks driven by Annamites and Tonkinese (we now call them Vietnamese). Throughout that day into the night and on into the next day, they rode and then marched into the confusion of a retreating

army. Mile after mile on the dusty roads, they passed refugees
with their pots and featherbeds, clocks and bird-cages, or whatever frightened people could think to carry or load on their carts.
There were French soldiers mixed in the stream—dragoons, artillerymen with their horse-drawn guns and caissons, and beaten
infantrymen—moving as fast as they could away from the Germans.

French officers gave orders, countermanded them, and presented new orders to American commanders who had lost touch,
in some instances, with their units. Marines and soldiers had to
change the direction of their march to keep up with those changes
in orders. On the morning of June 1, about 8 o'clock, the Ninth
Infantry reached its destination. By dark the Twenty-third Infantry and the two Marine regiments reported that they were also in
position west of Château-Thierry. During the next four days, the
artillery and other support units arrived. Here were some 26,600
fresh but tired, and in many cases hungry, troops ready to bolster
a faltering French army.

Apparently, the first senior American officer to report to the
French corps commander, General Degoutte, was Brigadier General James G. Harbord. In the first week of May, Harbord had left
Pershing's staff to take command of the Marine Brigade in place
of General Doyen, who was in poor health. Harbord and the division chief of staff, Colonel Preston Brown, would be more prominent in the division throughout June than the commander, Major
General Omar Bundy. A short, dapper man who reminded Frederick Palmer of a typical "meticulous post commander," Bundy did
not impress Pershing either. On June 9, Pershing wrote in his
diary, "General Bundy disappoints me. He lacks the grasp. I shall
relieve him at the first opportunity." Harbord never lost the confidence of his commander. Brown, an alert, very intelligent, witty
but blunt soldier, irritated the French at times, but he stopped
Degoutte from breaking up the Second and using its units as
piecemeal reinforcements. A Yale graduate and a lawyer, Brown
had enlisted as a private in 1894 and had served almost three
years in the ranks before he won a commission. Brown spoke
French and did most of the talking when he and Bundy met with
the French commanders. A pair of strong personalities, Harbord

and Brown; one wonders if Bundy ever got to say much at all in their presence.

For three days the Marines and soldiers withstood shelling and an occasional enemy foray, but most of the time the four regiments on line waited. In the distance across the rolling countryside, at times, some of the Americans could see the German infantry and artillery moving closer. During this period the Germans occupied Belleau Wood, the tiny village of Bouresches, and various other points as they pushed the French back through the lines of the Second Division. When one French officer ordered a Marine captain to fall back also, the Marine snapped: "Retreat, hell. We just got here."

Degoutte turned the sector over to the Americans on the fourth with the understanding that they would hold their nine kilometers of the front at all costs. Obviously his spirits had risen since Mordacq had left him on May 29, for on June 5 he ordered an advance. General von Conta, who commanded the German corps which now faced the Second Division, also ordered his men forward. The offensive was over for Conta, but he wanted his units to secure a better defensive position. The Americans, however, made the first move.

On June 6, the Marine Brigade made two attacks—one at 5 A.M. against German positions to the west of Belleau Wood and another, twelve hours later, against the wood itself and the nearby village of Bouresches. In well-aligned waves, Marine companies crossed the wheatfields dotted with poppies. Here a corporal stopped to pick a poppy to stick in his helmet buckle; there Captain Donald Duncan continued smoking his pipe as he waved his men forward with his swagger stick; and the veteran Gunnery Sergeant Dan Daly, already the winner of the Medal of Honor twice, led in a different manner as he bellowed to his platoon, "Come on, you sons of bitches. Do you want to live forever?" And nearly everywhere, men crumpled and sprawled when the enemy machine guns criss-crossed the formation. They took Hill 142 to the west of the wood and Bouresches, as well as a small section of the wood, but they suffered 1087 casualties. (This remained the most costly single day in Marine Corps history until twenty-five years later at Tarawa.)

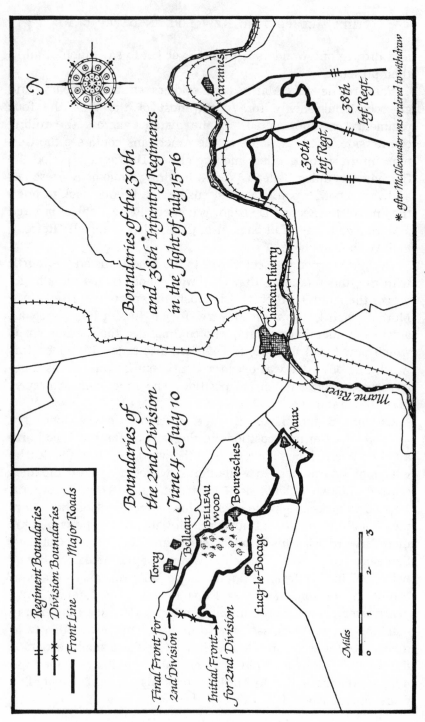

Legend:
- ⫛⫛ Regiment Boundaries
- ✕✕ Division Boundaries
- ■ Front Line
- ─── Major Roads

Boundaries of the 2nd Division June 4–July 10

Boundaries of the 30th and 38th* Infantry Regiments in the fight of July 15–16

← Final Front for 2nd Division
← Initial Front for 2nd Division

Torcy
Belleau
BELLEAU WOOD
Bouresches
Lucy-le-Bocage
Vaux

Château-Thierry
Marne River
Varennes

30th Inf. Regt.
38th Inf. Regt.

* after McAlexander was ordered to withdraw

Miles
0 1 2 3

N

THE BATTLES OF BELLEAU WOOD AND CHÂTEAU-THIERRY

For 20 days the battle in and near Belleau Wood raged. They were, as Private Hiram B. Pottinger of the Sixth Marines said, "days of hell." On June 11, Harbord requested the relief of his brigade. He told his superiors that "officers and men are now at a state scarcely less than complete physical exhaustion." But they stayed on in the shallow foxholes which they also called, half-jokingly, "graves." There were shortages of water, and many never saw hot food but lived on the obnoxious "monkey-meat" (canned Madagascar corned beef) or raw bacon and hardtack, which the men in Bouresches supplemented with potatoes and carrots they found in gardens. They wore the same clothes for weeks. The shelling never seemed to stop, and there was gas on all but four days of the five weeks they spent in this sector. Many suffered from diarrhea, and some had temperatures of 105°, but they got up from their foxholes and formed for the attacks. The division inspector reported on June 19 that the second battalion of the Sixth Marines had lost more than 64 per cent of its men; yet, he added, the morale was excellent. They lived on pure nerve. Their only respite was for six days, June 16–21, when the Seventh Infantry Regiment took over their wooded front.

Time and again companies went into what the colonel of the Sixth Marines called "the dark, sullen mystery of Belleau Wood" and struggled in hand-to-hand combat with the Germans. Attack after attack achieved only a few more square yards of the devastated forest or resulted in no gain. Then, the Germans, also racked with diarrhea and, in addition, influenza, counterattacked.

At Bouresches, the Marines fought members of the crack Tenth Division—a first-class combat unit. Throughout most of the month, the defenders of Belleau Wood were the 461st Regiment of the 237th Division. Although rated as a fourth-class division, the 237th had excellent regimental commanders including the canny veteran of African fighting, Major Bischoff, who made good use of the defensive possibilities in the wood. As the Marines continued hammering, the German 28th, a second-class but considered with the Tenth to be one of the better German divisions, came to the aid of the 237th. Finally, the 87th, another fourth-class division, had to relieve the survivors of the 237th and 28th, and it was this unit which lost the wood.

Before Shearer sent his victorious message on the morning of

June 26, the Germans underwent a solid 14-hour bombardment followed by another assault by Shearer's battalion. Even then Shearer had to beat off counterattacks during the night before he could make his report. But it was definitely over by that morning.

Why did it take so long? Harbord answered, in part, when he wrote in his diary on June 23: "You wish more than anything else in the world to know the exact position of your troops, and exactly where the enemy is with reference to them. . . ." Not only the brigade commander but also, on many occasions, regimental and battalion commanders did not know where their men were in the wood. Nevertheless, they issued orders based on the neat lines drawn on their maps; orders which were frequently irrelevant to the real situation. On June 11, one battalion commander, Lieutenant Colonel Frederic M. Wise, reported that his men were in possession of the wood after an attack. Wise did not know where his men were, nor for that matter did they know exactly where they were. Admittedly, the maps were poor and in short supply, but one cannot help wondering about the ability of officers to read the available maps and to recognize the appropriate terrain features. Communications also were a crucial problem: telephone wires were often cut; it took time for runners to make their dangerous journeys; and in the excitement of the fighting, officers sent messages and forgot to put the hour on them. Then the situation frequently changed before even the properly dated message got back to brigade headquarters. Often, during attacks, the initial reports were too optimistic; thus, unaware of the actual heavy casualties, Harbord issued orders to battalions too weak to carry them out.

It was difficult to coordinate properly artillery and infantry in such conditions. Besides, on occasion Harbord showed a lack of appreciation for the need of artillery support. In the portion of his papers preserved in the National Archives there are several memos prepared by the French on open warfare which he read in May 1918. In these memos the underlined sections refer to the importance of emphasizing the rifle and machine gun rather than artillery. More than that, Harbord depended on the willingness of his Marines and the soldiers from the Second Engineers, who came to supplement their ranks, to fight beyond a reasonable threshold of endurance.

There were some 5200 casualties (including approximately 750 killed)—more than 50 per cent of the brigade's strength. During June, Frederick Pottle, who was in Evacuation Hospital # 8 at Juilly, recalled "a long, brown, almost unbroken line of ambulances filling the road from Château-Thierry to Juilly." And he remembered the most horrifying casualties, the mustard gas cases with their blistered bodies. After a heavy mustard gas barrage which caught virtually all of the men in the second battalion of the Sixth Marines, Pottle described the scene at the hospital, with hundreds of men "nearly all blinded, many delirious, all crying, moaning, tossing about." About all one could do was spread zinc ointment on the blisters and put castor oil in the blinded eyes of the sufferers until the blisters healed and the men recovered their vision.

The French changed the name of Bois de Belleau to Bois de la Brigade de Marine, and the Americans awarded medals to some of the Marines—including one Medal of Honor to Gunnery Sergeant Charles Hoffman.* But valor was so common that it was difficult to distinguish individual acts. Sergeant Joseph G. Stites, who was one of the mustard gas victims in the Sixth Marines, later recalled, "There was no special bravery that I know of by any special men except that they did their duty . . . to the limit of their endurance."

The Germans were impressed. An intelligence officer rated the Second Division "a very good division" and added: "The spirit of the troops is fresh and one of careless confidence." A Private Hebel who fought in Belleau Wood wrote home, "We have Americans opposite us who are terribly reckless fellows." And it was a German general, Böhm, the commander of the 28th Division, who best explained, in an order to his troops on June 8, the significance of Belleau Wood: "it is not a question of the possession

---

* Four future commandants of the Marine Corps fought at Belleau Wood: Wendell C. Neville (1929–30), Thomas Holcomb (1936–43), Clifton B. Cates (1948–51), and Lemuel C. Shepherd, Jr. (1952–55). Several other Marine officers would play leading roles in the amphibious operations in the Central Pacific during World War II. Among them was Holland M. Smith, who served on Harbord's staff and who later commanded assaults on Tarawa, Saipan, and Iwo Jima. In his memoir, *Coral and Brass* (New York, 1949), p. 45, "Howlin' Mad" Smith said, "I always took Harbord as a model. . . ."

or nonpossession of this or that village or woods, insignificant in itself; it is a question whether the Anglo-American claim that the American Army is equal or even the superior of the German Army is to be made good."

The rest of the Second Division also fought, and many soldiers, such as the cocky, little colonel of the 23rd, Paul B. Malone, would bitterly resent the attention the Marines received. After all, the Third Brigade suffered more than 3200 casualties in this sector. On July 1, this brigade carried out a "mechanically perfect" assault on the town of Vaux. Men in the ten German divisions who faced the Second at one time or the other during this period were aware of the Third Brigade even if the American public was not.

Interservice bickering aside, the crucial fact, well recognized at the time, is that the Americans were beginning to assume a share of the burden of fighting. As one of the French staff officers exclaimed in mid-June to an American liaison officer at Pétain's headquarters, Major Paul H. Clark, "You Americans are our hope, our strength, our life."

On June 16, the *New York Times* featured in a banner headline the statement—"1,000,000 Americans to be in France by July." The Germans knew that a large number of Americans were in France and that a great many more were arriving. Ludendorff was surprised and Hindenburg was dismayed by the rate of the American reinforcement. Time was running out. Their mighty blows had failed to gain a decision. The most recent one, a relatively small offensive conducted by the 18th Army in the Montdidier-Noyon area, had been called off on June 11 after only two days. But the German high command continued to think in terms of attack.

The peace offensives—*Friedenstürme*—were to end the war. First, three armies would improve the Marne salient by clearing the French from the area about Rheims. After the successful completion of this attack, Ludendorff hoped to follow up promptly with a decisive attack against the British in Flanders.

Again, German troops made elaborate preparations for the assault. The men did not need training, since they were veterans of the Chemin des Dames offensive, but they had to move into position, and there was the large number of artillery pieces to put in place. Secrecy was crucial; surprise was the essence of success.

But there was no surprise. Everyone assumed that the Germans would attack, and prisoners divulged exact information including the hour. The French prepared a defense in depth to stop the German attack. Thus the heavy artillery preparatory fire would fall on a virtually empty front, while the main line of resistance would await the German attackers in the rear. Since the French knew the hour that the German artillery was to begin its fire of preparation, they gave their artillery orders to lay down barrages a few minutes prior to the German bombardment. Shortly before midnight on July 14, the French surprised the Germans with their shelling of artillery positions, ammunition dumps, and assembly positions.

To the east of Rheims, General Henri Gouraud, the one-armed veteran of Gallipoli, made certain that the proper preparations were completed in his Fourth Army sector. Then, on the afternoon of the fourteenth, he entertained the American generals and colonels of the 42nd Division at dinner. Gouraud appreciated the three battalions of the Rainbow which were with his front line troops and the support which the remainder of this division provided. While he did not invite anyone from the 369th Infantry Regiment, which was also in his sector, at least one French officer did the honors. A young artillery lieutenant shared his supply of champagne with Lieutenant Chester V. Easum of Company D. This was an enjoyable respite, as Easum later reminisced, "while we waited for the war to begin."

Early in the morning, the Germans came, but they could not penetrate the main defense line. Fighting developed into hand to hand combat for some of the infantrymen of the Rainbow Division who beat off repeated assaults near Souain. Gouraud had planned well, and his men, French and American, were equal to the task.

The other French Army commanders whose troops had to face the German onslaught on the morning of July 15 were not as thorough as Gouraud. In particular, they did not evacuate their front to the same extent, with the result that the Germans broke the French lines west of Rheims. Indeed, von Boehn's Seventh Army seemed to be moving on schedule except for a disturbing hold-up on the extreme right, where the first-class Tenth Division and the second-class 36th Division struck the defensive line of the American Third Division.

From the eastern edge of Château-Thierry for some twelve kilometers east, nearly to Varennes, these Americans held the Marne river line. Each infantry regiment had a battalion up in the rifle pits and along the railroad embankment near the river's edge and two other battalions in supporting positions in the hills and woods further to the rear. Unlike Gouraud, Degoutte, now the commander of the Sixth Army, wanted front line defenses maintained and even reinforced; he virtually ignored the instructions to defend in depth. The commander of the Third, who considered himself a tactical expert, demurred and did not put more men on the front. Major General Joseph T. Dickman, a burly, strongminded former cavalryman, did not like the French much anyway.

Fortunately, Degoutte did go along with the decision to fire the surprise counter barrages prior to the German preparatory fire. Even then, the Germans were able to deliver a shattering bombardment. The gas forced the Americans to wear the uncomfortable masks for hours, while the high explosives killed and wounded many of the defenders, since they were in shallow trenches and rifle pits with virtually no overhead protection. Most withstood the avalanche of shells, but others simply could not. A medical officer in the 30th Infantry, Major William E. Boyce, described the shell shock cases: "Some of them cursed and raved and had to be tied to their litters; some shook violently . . . some trembled and slunk away in apparent abject fear of every incoming shell, while others simply stood speechless, oblivious to all surroundings." Among those who had to be relieved was a regimental commander.

While the entire division had to withstand the shelling, the two regiments in the eastern half of the sector and a few men in the Seventh Infantry Regiment had to fight off the German infantry. About four o'clock, the Germans crowded into their boats and started across the deep but rather narrow (50 yards) Marne through the smoke screen and early morning fog.

Although the American artillery took a terrific toll, enough Germans reached the southern bank to gain a strong beachhead in the area held by the 30th Infantry. First Lieutenant James R.

Kingery of Company B threw grenades at the boats until he was shot down, and other survivors of the two companies near the river did all they could to keep the Germans from landing—but land they did. At the front there was confusion and chaos; in the rear, at regimental headquarters, there was confusion and ignorance.

Throughout the night and into the early morning hours, Colonel Edmund L. Butts and his staff studied a map in their dugout. Since communications were out, he had no idea of what the situation was. Finally, the first battalion commander reported that his two companies along the river were destroyed. Major Fred L. Walker knew that he had heard nothing from them, despite his efforts to regain contact, so he assumed that they no longer existed. On the basis of this erroneous information, Butts requested that artillery fire on their positions. This caught some of the Americans still fighting. When his own artillery fire started coming in, Lieutenant James H. Gay of Company C decided to withdraw his platoon. By this time, Butts had pulled back his entire advance line, so Gay had some difficulty locating other Americans. But he eventually found someone to whom he could turn over the 150 German prisoners he and his men had taken.

In the 1930's, when officers at the Infantry School, Fort Benning, Georgia, studied this action, they concluded that Butts had made the correct decision based upon the information he had available. While they did not comment in *Infantry in Battle* on Butts's decision to withdraw to his support position, the division commander apparently approved, since he commended him. At any rate, the Germans failed to penetrate this second line.

Colonel Ulysses Grant McAlexander, if asked, would probably not have approved the withdrawal of the 30th Infantry. At that time he and his men of the 38th were fighting for their lives, and the departure of the 30th left his flank open. The French, on his right, had departed much earlier, in fact, about four o'clock; but McAlexander had prepared for that contingency by having rifle pits dug on his right flank. Despite the French assurance that they would not retreat, McAlexander took no chances.

This was the second regiment McAlexander had commanded in France. GHQ had relieved him from the 18th Infantry because a staff officer found him asleep in his dugout at nine o'clock one morning in the Sommerviller sector, and a later report had indicated that he did not do well in one of the winter maneuvers. It was not until his brigade commander, George B. Duncan, explained to Pershing that McAlexander customarily spent the nights with his men in the front-line trenches and gave him a strong endorsement that Pershing gave him another chance. A short, hard, perverse West Pointer, McAlexander showed the "C-in-C" that he had made a wise decision. In his *Final Report,* Pershing took particular note of the stand McAlexander's 38th Infantry made on July 15th when he said that this regiment "wrote one of the most brilliant pages in our military annals."

McAlexander had three companies along the river line. Actually the bulk of each company was at the railroad embankment about 350 yards from the Marne, while two platoons waited on the river's edge in each company area (except G, which had only one platoon forward). With the help of accurate artillery fire, Companies E and H repulsed German attempts to cross in their front; however, after the Germans annihilated the advance platoon of Company G, they were able to establish themselves on the southern bank. Then many other Germans were running across the footbridge in front of what had been the positions of the 30th Infantry. Captain Jesse W. Wooldridge used every available man in Company G and picked up several men from the 30th to fight off the Germans on his front and his left. By 10:40 A.M., the Germans were supposed to be eight kilometers south of the Marne, but they were still stalled at the railroad line, and Wooldridge, who had fourteen bullet holes in his blouse, was even counterattacking. McAlexander, according to Wooldridge's testimony, was "everywhere" during the battle. With Germans on three sides of his embattled second battalion, McAlexander did not have to go far to find himself in the midst of the fight.

For fourteen hours, until they received orders from what McAlexander called "higher authority," these infantrymen fought viciously even with their fists. In his operations report, McAlexander summarized the result in one sentence: "This regiment fought the German 10th and 36th Divisions to a standstill and captured prisoners from each of their six attack regiments." He claimed that his men had destroyed the Sixth Grenadier Regiment and "all but destroyed" the Fifth Grenadiers as well. After the war

the chief of staff of the German Seventh Army, Walther Reinhardt, corroborated his estimate at least as it concerned the Sixth,
for there were only 150 or so survivors of the 1500 to 2000 men
who went into the assault. The adjutant of the Fifth, Kurt Hesse,
admitted that it was the "heaviest defeat" of the war and commented on the "savage roughness" which the Americans displayed. On July 16, the German leaders ordered a cessation of the
offensive.

The American role in the second battle of the Marne carried a
tragic footnote. Four rifle companies of the 28th Division, the
Pennsylvania National Guard division, were integrated into
French units to the right of McAlexander's position. Since the
French did not tell these Pennsylvanians that they were retreating, the four companies found themselves surrounded and had to
fight their way out. A few survivors made it to the old support line
some five kilometers to the rear, where they found other units of
the 28th fighting off the Germans.

While some Americans were helping turn the tide on the Western Front, thousands more were arriving daily as the transatlantic movement reached its peak. In July 1918 a German prisoner
of war, working at a French port, watched one of the large convoys come in. He turned to an American and asked how many
troops were arriving. When the American answered forty or fifty
thousand, the German, with tears in his eyes, exclaimed, "Mein
Gott in Himmel."

The figures were staggering. Beginning with the handful in
Base Hospital # 4 who sailed on the Cunard liner *Orduna* on May
8, 1917, more than two million Americans crossed the Atlantic to
go to war. The initial group of the first and most strongly guarded
convoy, carrying the First Division, set out on June 14, 1917. For
the next months, crossings were rather infrequent until the German spring offensives forced the British to release a large amount
of their tonnage to the Atlantic Ferry. From April 1 to October 31,
more than 1,600,000 made the trip. The largest monthly total
was in July when 306,350 landed in French and English ports.
The British carried slightly more than 48 per cent and the Americans, relying heavily on commandeered German passenger ships,

took a little over 46 per cent across the Atlantic. French, Italian, and Dutch vessels provided passage for the remainder.

For the soldiers, overseas orders meant a flurry of activity as they packed equipment, greeted replacements who came in to bring the unit up to strength before it sailed, and cleaned up the barracks or tent areas. Finally, the men marched to the trains for the first lap of their journey. In the case of the 32nd Division, it took 61 special trains to move the 23,685 men from Camp Mac-Arthur, Texas, to Camp Merritt, New Jersey, and two trains to take the horses and mules to Newport News, Virginia, in early 1918.

The train trip to the embarkation camp was a pleasant change from the routine. Frederick A. Pottle remembered the one he made in the spring of 1918 as being "one mad panorama of noise and excitement." At the stations, men, women, and children shouted and waved small flags; whistles blew and bells rang; girls ran up to the soldiers leaning out of the coach windows to touch hands (an occasional daring young lady might even give a hasty kiss or her name and address); women passed out coffee, apples, ciga-rettes.

Four out of every five men in the AEF left from New York har-bor. (Most of the others departed from Newport News, Virginia.) In the New York area Camp Merritt was the last stop for more than half a million eastbound soldiers. Here they underwent final inspections, waited until all the paperwork was in order, drew new clothing, if needed, steel helmets, and gas masks. During the summer of 1918, when transports were waiting in harbor, many soldiers did not stay at the camp long enough to see the interior of the barracks.

In order to be at the Hoboken piers at 8 a.m., the men had to get up about midnight, eat breakfast, and march to the trains or fer-ries that would take them to their ships. On the pier a long line of soldiers with full packs moved steadily, more or less, to the check-out desk at the foot of the gangplank. There was time for coffee and rolls or ice cream and milk which the Red Cross women pro-vided and a few moments to fill out a safe arrival card which the army would mail when the ship reached its destination. Then they boarded the ship and went below decks, where they stayed until the transport cleared the harbor. In the summer of 1918 the army abandoned this needless security measure and permitted the men to come on deck for a last look at the USA.

There were some men who were not enthusiastic about going to France. Yet of the more than 1,600,000 who passed through the New York Port of Embarkation only 5000 deserted. Many others went absent without leave to see New York, to spend a little time with their families, or to delay their voyage, but they returned within the ten-day limit and were not declared deserters. Some soldiers committed suicide, and others wounded themselves, but apparently not many took such drastic actions.

Nearly all those who made the voyage did so under the protection of the American navy. The Cruiser and Transport Force, headed by Vice Admiral Albert Gleaves, carried out this mission. Gleaves, a Tennessean who remembered hearing the cannon at the Battle of Nashville during the Civil War, was in charge of the First Division convoy and remained at the task throughout the war. Understandably, the admiral took pride in the fact that not a single American soldier under his care was lost en route to Europe because of enemy action. The U-boats did sink four transports on the return voyage as well as the *Tuscania*, the *Moldavia*, and the animal transport *Ticonderoga* while eastward bound. Thirteen members of the 32nd Division lost their lives on the *Tuscania*, 56 men from the Fourth Division died on the *Moldavia*, and 215 soldiers and sailors went down with the *Ticonderoga*. Since Gleaves's cruisers were not protecting these vessels at the time of the sinking, however, his boast is correct.

Although it seems incredible that the dreaded submarines were so unsuccessful against the transports, there were several good reasons for this failure. The transport convoys and cargo convoys steamed along in widely separated lanes. Since 85 per cent of the traffic was in the supply lane and these vessels were slower and less protected than the "troopers," they were much easier targets. A U-boat commander might patrol for days in one of the 60-mile-wide transport lanes without even seeing a ship. If he did see one, he would need a lucky shot to hit one of the fast moving ships and even more luck to get away from the horde of destroyers. As a result, the Germans concentrated on the cargo ships. Despite the odds, there were occasional attempts against eastbound transports, but as a rule destroyers succeeded in beating them off. As one might expect, actual attacks were fewer than the number of alarms. Nearly every soldier who made the trip had his story of a sub scare.

The navy also attempted to foil U-boat commanders by creating optical illusions and by carrying out routine evasive maneuvers. A convoy was a startling sight because of the brightly colored dazzle-painted ships. These gaudy designs were intended to confuse a viewer as to the shape of the vessel and its direction. The zigzag maneuvers followed at various times during a voyage were actual changes in direction—a complicated business for convoys. William D. Leahy, who commanded the transport *Princess Matoika* on a crossing in May 1918, explained the problem in his diary.

> This convoy consists of 12 vessels, all of different characteristics, all as hurriedly slapped together as was my command, most of them provided with inexperienced officers, and some being commanded by their merchant masters who never before saw a ship in formation.
>
> Steering zig zag courses in formation under these conditions with the great unwielding vessels one thousand yards apart left very few dull moments for the skipper.

While many vessels of various sizes and backgrounds took part in the Atlantic Ferry, the largest and fastest, ironically, was the largest German passenger liner, *Vaterland*. Launched in 1914, this great ship was interned in New York when the war began that summer. The Americans seized the ship in 1917 and rechristened her *Leviathan*. In ten trips, the *Leviathan* carried 96,804 soldiers to Europe in an average time of just under eight days. Since she was so fast, the ship, as was the case with a few other fast transports, frequently crossed without cruiser escort.

The carefully recorded statistics of the *Leviathan,* or of any one of the other tranports, convey little of the experiences of the two million men who crossed the Atlantic to go to war. The tons of food consumed; the average length of serving time (on the *Leviathan,* 9000 men ate their meals in 90 minutes), afford no information as to how palatable the food was or how many men were too seasick to eat. Whether or not a soldier had a good voyage depended on the type of ship, the weather, and his rank. Officers had better quarters and, even if they ate the same food, they enjoyed their meals in more leisure and in more pleasant dining facilities.

Wartime passengers usually spent twelve days at sea. During the day in good weather, soldiers swarmed over the decks. "You can't stay there, buddy. Move along," was an all too familiar refrain. Aside from abandon-ship drills and cleaning the quarters, there was little to do: read, play cards, chat, watch the other ships in the convoy, and wait for the next meal, unless seasickness made all activity virtually impossible. At night, the strict light discipline limited the soldiers. They had to give up their matches when they boarded ship. Portholes were closed and the only light came from tiny blue bulbs.

In the troop holds there were columns of canvas or wooden bunks—three or four to a tier. Frederick Pottle christened the enlisted quarters on the *Caserta*—"Our dungeon"—and most doughboys would think the term appropriate. Sardines in a can was another inevitable analogy which occurred to the soldiers. During the spring and summer of 1918, the navy compounded the crowded conditions by overloading the faster transports up to 50 per cent in excess of their rated capacities. On these ships, men slept in shifts as soldiers had to share their bunks. Private Clayton K. Slack spoke for two million others when he said, "We'd had all the boat ride we wanted."

A familiar sight for the doughboy arriving in a French port was the Negro stevedore. These soldiers in their blue denim uniforms unloaded much of the AEF supplies. About one out of every ten soldiers in the AEF was a Negro. Early in the war, Pershing had made it clear that he wanted men—black or white. The War Department responded by including in its great troop shipments approximately 200,000 Negroes. While the majority—some 150,-000—of these men were labor troops, four separate infantry regiments and the 92nd Division did see action on the Western Front.

In France, the Negroes found a white people who would accept them as social equals. As much as possible, however, the AEF tried to impose American racial mores on the French. Indicative of this attempt was a secret memo which Colonel Linard, the French liaison officer at the American GHQ, sent in August 1918 to both military and civilian officials. In order to placate the American whites, Linard warned that the French attitudes of "indulgence" and "familiarity" were "matters of grievous concern to the Americans." After describing American racial prejudice, he concluded by urging French officers not to accept Negro officers as equals and to avoid overpraise of Negro troops. As for civilian officials, Linard asked that they "make a point of keeping the native cantonment population from 'spoiling the Negroes.' "

The cardinal fear of white Americans was of Negro soldiers associating with French women. Lurid rumors in which rape was a term freely misused circulated in the AEF. On one occasion the commander of the 92nd allegedly referred to his command as the "rapist division." Yet, apparently, only one Negro out of the more than 25,000 in this unit was convicted for actual rape. Indeed, there seems to have been little trouble between the Negroes and the French. After the war, the mayors of several communities where the army had quartered Negroes praised the conduct of the Negroes.

French authorities also made good use of American Negro combat troops. In fact, the four Negro regiments did all of their fighting within units of the French army. They carried French rifles, ate the French ration (although one captain noted that additional sugar was substituted for the wine), and, at first, wore French helmets.

The first Negro infantry regiment to reach France established the precedent. During their first two and a half months in the AEF, the men of the 15th New York worked as laborers. The only thing that differentiated this regiment from the other labor units, other than its title, was its famed band conducted by Lieutenant Jim Europe, a well-known dance-band leader. In March, however, Pershing sent the newly designated 369th Infantry Regiment to serve with the French. Within a month, the French reorganized and equipped the New Yorkers as a French infantry regiment, gave them a brief training, and placed them in a quiet sector at the front.

On its second tour in the trenches, the 369th suffered its first casualties and provided the first Negro heroes of the war. While on outpost duty in the dark, early morning hours of May 14, two privates engaged a German raiding party. Although wounded at the beginning of the action, Needham Roberts continued to throw grenades. This left Henry Johnson, a former New York Central red cap from Albany, New York, to carry on most of the fight. Johnson was up to the task, using his rifle as a club after he emptied it pointblank and then going after and killing one German with a bolo knife as the enemy attempted to capture Roberts. Finally, the Germans withdrew leaving Johnson and Roberts still holding their post despite their multiple wounds.

There would be numerous other Negro heroes who earned the right to wear the coveted Distinguished Service Cross, the Medaille Militaire, or the Croix de Guerre—more than a hundred in this regiment alone—but Johnson and Roberts were probably the most famous. Both received the Croix de Guerre and recovered from their wounds.

By the time of the Armistice, the 369th had spent 191 days at the front; a longer period than any other regiment, its colonel, William Hayward, a well-known New York lawyer, believed. Although the regiment took part in some of the heaviest fighting, its veterans claimed that they never lost a prisoner or a trench. According to reports, it lived up to its motto of "Let's Go."

The other three Negro regiments arrived in France in April and soon joined French divisions, where they remained throughout the war. Although the 8th Illinois, which had become the 370th, lost its Negro colonel, it kept a predominant majority of Negro officers. In the fall of 1918 it won praise from the French for its part in the final offensive.

The 371st and 372nd served together in the French 157th Division. In their weeks at the front, both units favorably impressed the French. After a severe battle in Champagne during the Meuse-Argonne offensive, the division commander, General M. F. J. Goybet wrote both regimental commanders, "The bravery and the dash of your regiments are the admiration of the Moroccan division and they are good judges." After the war the French showed their regard for these regiments by awarding a Croix de Guerre unit citation to the 371st and 372nd as well as to the 369th. Their request in June 1918 for all the Negro infantry regiments which the Americans could send was an even more concrete illustration of French regard of these troops.

In their offensive of late May, the Germans had gained a salient roughly 37 miles in length at its base (from six miles west of Soissons to just west of Rheims), which bulged out in a crude crescent some 20 miles to Château-Thierry. On July 15, they had pushed out along the eastern face of this salient. As long as they kept their enemies on the defensive, this salient was a threat—a possible base of attack; yet, once the coin turned and the Allies moved to the offensive, the bulge became a vulnerable liability. Generalissimo Foch thought in terms of moral ascendancy—of the will of a commander dominating that of his opponent. The psychological meaning which possession of this salient connoted is a case in point.

The most obvious area for a counterattack was along the western face near Soissons. If an Allied force could penetrate to the heights south of Soissons where artillery could interdict traffic on the highways and the key railroads in the salient, the Germans would have to evacuate the salient. If the attacking force was strong and swift enough and could retain its momentum, there was the alluring possibility of trapping the bulk of the Germans. In mid-June, Foch ordered Pétain to prepare plans for such a move.

While there would be subsidiary attacks, the main role was to be played by General Charles Mangin's Tenth Army. Within this army, the XX Corps under General Pierre E. Berdoulat had the crucial mission of seizing the heights below Soissons. Perhaps it was a coincidence or maybe it was a sentimental gesture that this corps was Foch's command when the war began. For the initial assault, Berdoulat would have three divisions: the First Moroccan which included the legendary Foreign Legion as well as Senegalese and Moroccans, and the First and Second American. All were large—the First Moroccan also had twelve rifle battalions—and all had reputations as spirited assault troops. Along the western face of the salient, twenty-three other divisions and a cavalry corps were also available to Mangin and Degoutte, whose Sixth Army would supplement the attack.

While the French were planning their counterthrust, the Germans were working up their offensive on the eastern face of the salient. Although they realized the value of the Soissons area, the

Germans misestimated French intentions. The chief of staff of the German Seventh Army, Walther Reinhardt, noted that the French had pulled back their artillery as far as possible in an obvious defensive position; thus the Germans considered the sector safe enough to move their artillery closer to the front. There seemed to be little risk involved for the Germans in maintaining a shallow defensive line with exhausted, under-strength, and flu-ridden divisions while the bulk of the Seventh Army moved eastward for the offensive. Then, even if their attack was not successful on July 15, the Germans assumed that the Allies would shift their reserves toward Rheims. Common sense would dictate such action. In fact, Pétain did order the suspension of counterattack plans and called for the reserves on the morning of July 15. Within two and a half hours, however, Foch telephoned to countermand Pétain's instructions. The will must dominate even over common sense. In this case, the Generalissimo was right.

While the generals and their staffs on the highest command level looked at maps and pondered their opponents' intentions, the men in the First and Second Divisions pondered their future. Both divisions had left the line on July 8. Naturally, rumors went the rounds. In the Second Division, there was hopeful speculation about a month in a rest area and leaves, but the men of the First had more colorful imaginations. A staff officer, R. H. Lewis, wrote to a friend on July 8: "I have heard rumors varying all the way from a return to America to root for the Liberty Loan to a trip to Ireland to supress [sic] the Irish rebellion with side rumors of trips to Italy and Russia thrown in."

Before they joined the XX Corps, both divisions acquired new commanders. Always close to Pershing's heart as well as to his mind, Harbord got a second star and the Second Division. The First went to Charles P. Summerall, who also sported a new second star. An artilleryman, Summerall had not made friends at GHQ when he had argued for more artillery as a member of the Baker Board in the summer of 1917, but since then he had proved himself as commander of the First Division artillery brigade. There were many hard drivers among the AEF generals from Pershing on down, but there were none as colorful or as histrionic as Summerall. Contemporary writers thought of Cromwell, Stonewall Jackson, and crusaders when they described him. He knew how to use artillery; he knew how to command; and he got results.

Secrecy enveloped the move of the American divisions to the XX Corps area. In order to guarantee surprise, the French did not explain movement orders and issued them in somewhat unorthodox fashion. When Harbord arrived, after a brief respite in Paris, to take over the division on the morning of July 15, he found that the artillery and trains were gone. No one knew exactly their ultimate destination or mission. And Preston Brown was extremely irritated to receive movement orders without an explanation from a French transport officer—a mere captain. On the afternoon of the 16th, the infantry and machine gun units of the Second boarded uncomfortable trucks again driven by Annamites and began their journey. The troops might not know their destination, but it was obvious that they had left rest and leaves behind. By the time the footsoldiers started their trek, those in the First Division were hiding in the Forest of Compiègne. Their truck journey over, they would march the rest of the way to the jump-off position.

Since the French wanted to keep the Germans off guard, they planned to have the two American divisions rush forward to the front just before the scheduled hour of the attack—4:35 a.m., July 18. This meant an unforgettable night for the troops. Heavy rain, thunder, and lightning helped shield the activity but made marching more difficult. Conditions were particularly bad in the Forest of Retz, where the Second Division slogged forward. In the dark woods, men, plodding through the mud, had to hold onto the packs of those in front to keep from getting lost. Trucks, animal-drawn guns and caissons, cavalry, and tanks, which many Americans saw here for the first time, forced the foot columns to the sides of the narrow roads. Lieutenant John W. Thomason, Jr. of the Fifth Marines recalled, "No battle ever tried them as hard as the night road to Soissons. . . ."

The infantry made it barely in time. Some of the men in the First Brigade of the First Division reached the jump-off line only five minutes before H hour, while the Ninth Infantry and Fifth Marines reached the line at doublequick just in time to continue running forward after the rolling barrage. Only one of the machine gun battalions in the Second Division arrived on time, and it was short of both guns and ammunition. Since the First Moroccans were holding this section of the front, they merely had to pull in their flanks to make room for the Americans.

The terrain where many of these men would die was generally a rolling plateau covered with fields of waist-high wheat. Within the XX Corps, the going would be easiest initially for the First Division, for their 2800-meter front was already on the plateau. In the center of the corps front, the Moroccans would have to gain the high ground of the plateau and then clear a small woods before they would have an open front. On the right flank of the corps, the Fifth Marines must fight their way through an outlying section of the Forest of Retz to reach the open ground. If the attack progressed over three kilometers, however, the left brigade of the First Division would run into Missy ravine, and the Second Division would have to cross Vierzy ravine, almost five kilometers from the jump-off position. Farther on in their sector, the First Division assault troops could expect to find two other ravines— Ploisy and Chazelle—transversing their axis of attack. These ravines were formidable obstacles. Missy, for example, was more than a kilometer in width and contained cultivated fields, a village, a stream, some marsh land, woods, and was bordered by steep, rocky slopes 50 to 60 meters in height.

This counterstroke was different from earlier large-scale offensives. For the first time the Americans would take part with their spirits undiminished by three years of a trench stalemate. Where veterans were cautious, the Americans rushed to danger even after Cantigny, Belleau Wood, and Vaux. Mangin's chief of staff, Joseph Hellé, commented: "We were quite unprepared for such fury in an attack." Reinhardt, his counterpart in the German Seventh Army, also remarked on the bravery and stamina of the Americans and compared their enthusiasm with that of the German volunteers of 1914.

The attack was also distinguished by the complete lack of artillery preparation and by the extensive use of French tanks. The fact that the Americans had had little if any experience in tank-infantry tactics mitigated the value of the tanks; nevertheless, the tanks were effective. In the War Diary at the headquarters of the German Crown Prince, who was in command of the army group

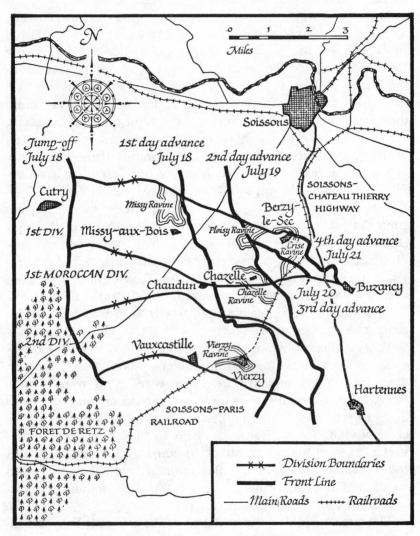

THE BATTLE OF SOISSONS

holding the Marne salient, special emphasis was given to the use of armor. Heretofore the Germans had underestimated the tank's effectiveness, but as the staff officer who kept the War Diary stated: "The experiences of July 18, 1918, for the first time, taught us differently." According to Harbord, there were 48 tanks with the First Division and 28 with the Second, while more than 300 others were employed along the Tenth and Sixth armies' fronts. Finally, the opposing forces had not established a complex network of trenches on the western face of the salient such as one found in areas where the lines had remained in the same general position for months or even years.

It was still dark on the morning of July 18 when the rolling barrage began with 108 guns firing on the behalf of each American division. The men had to move steadily forward to keep up with the pace of the barrage, which moved up 100 meters every two minutes. Summerall had placed all four of his regiments on line in battalion columns (assault battalion followed by support battalion with reserve battalion bringing up the rear). Harbord thought that he would need only three regiments on line (also in battalion columns) to carry his 2.5 kilometer front.

The attack opened on schedule. A few minutes prior to 4:35, the Germans had fired a brief and rather feeble barrage which had failed to disrupt either the Allied infantry or artillery. When their own barrage started, the Americans moved out with surprising energy, considering their lack of sleep and their hard trip to the jump-off positions. Initially, they met virtually no resistance, since the Germans were obviously very surprised. Within an hour, all of the American units reported that they had reached the first objective.

The assault battalions continued moving forward. By 7:00 a.m. the Second Division had advanced a total of four kilometers, and its light artillery was displacing forward. The First Division was also keeping up the pace, yet a couple of problems were developing. The Moroccans were having difficulties and were not keeping up with the Americans, which meant exposed flanks for both American divisions. And to the left of the First Division zone, the Second Brigade was nearing Missy ravine—the first significant obstacle.

Despite the attention which the Allied 155 mm guns had paid

to this ravine, a lot of Germans, ready to fight, were still there. In the woods and heavy brush, machine gun nests and infantrymen had excellent positions to protect the artillery emplacements. Major Clarence R. Huebner found that the going was indeed hard for his second battalion of the 28th Infantry. Not only did the Germans destroy his supporting tanks but also hit his battalion on its left flank, since the 153rd French Division had failed to carry their sector of the ravine. Soon, the lead battalion of the 26th Infantry was also drawn into the fray. As the Germans held up these two units, the infantrymen in the 16th had to begin fending off Germans at the head of the ravine. In order to protect his flank, Huebner ordered his men to seize enemy positions in the French zone of attack. Throughout the hot, sunny day, the Second Brigade fought its way through the ravine until the surviving Americans carried the far heights overlooking the valley that afternoon. By this time Huebner was the only officer left in his battalion and he consolidated the remnants of his companies into five small platoons commanded by sergeants.

John L. Hines, now a brigadier general and commander of the First Brigade, was having less trouble to his immediate front than was the Second Brigade commander, but his flanks were worrying him. While part of his left regiment, the 16th, had to help out the Second Brigade, his right regiment moved into the zone of the lagging Moroccans to fight hand to hand in order to take the German strong points at the village of Chaudun. In this action, the second battalion of the 16th, which came up to help the 18th Infantry, lost all of its officers and more than half of its men, whereupon the old soldier of F Company, Sergeant Anthony Scanlan, although severely wounded, took command and reorganized the battalion.

By afternoon the Second Division was beginning to slow down. On the right, the 23rd Infantry was held up temporarily by the Germans in the village of Vauxcastille, while the Ninth Infantry had to begin the hard task of capturing Vierzy ravine. The Fifth Marines had to worry about their left flank, exposed by their outdistancing of the Moroccans, but when necessary they moved into the Moroccan zone to squelch enemy resistance. During the attack, two immigrant sergeants in the 66th Company, Louis

Cukela and Matej Kocak, each won a Medal of Honor by capturing machine gun nests at the point of the bayonet.

Harbord could be proud of his men's performance, but it was questionable how much longer they could keep going. The toll of the hard trip, the arduous night march, and the rigors of the day's battle was beginning to tell on them. In the Fifth Marines, Lieutenant Thomason saw men fall asleep on their rifles at noon. The division was nearing a state of physical exhaustion.

Control was also a problem. The rapidity of the advance, together with the loss of many leaders, contributed to the confusion, which was further compounded by the change in direction of the advance from east to southeast after the first objective. Marines and infantrymen intermingled as individuals, and units drifted from their proper zones, while at the same time some Senegalese were showing up in the Second Division's assault units. The Marine Sergeant Kocak led twenty-five of these French colonials in a successful attack on another machine gun nest.

Early in the afternoon—about 1:30—Harbord ordered the commander of the Third Brigade (Ely of Cantigny fame—now a brigadier general) to advance at 4:30 p.m. Because of the lack of communications, Ely personally had to find his two regimental commanders to give them the attack order. Since he did not locate them until after 4:30, he set a new time for the attack—6:00 p.m. But the French commander of the support tanks wanted even more time. Finally, the 23rd Infantry jumped off at 7 p.m. followed by the Ninth 15 minutes later. With the help of the Marines, the infantrymen conquered Vierzy ravine and the village of Vierzy and began to dig in on the plateau about 1200 meters east of the village. They were exhausted, short of food and water, and both flanks were in the air, but the men of the Second Division had made the deepest penetration, some 8.2 kilometers, of any Allied division on that day.

Orders too frequently do not mesh with the real situation. That thought may have occurred to Harbord when in the middle of the night—about 2 a.m.—a French officer came into his headquarters with orders for the Second Division to resume the attack at 4 a.m., July 19. The Frenchman indicated that corps headquarters did not know exactly where the division was. Since wire communications were out, there was no quick way that Harbord could inform the corps commander of the impossibility of getting off an attack at the correct hour because of the condition of his command. The Sixth Marines could make an attack, but they would have to march three or four kilometers before they reached the front. The order went out at 3 a.m.; yet the Sixth did not leave its bivouac area until three and a half hours later and did not cross the front to go into the attack until 8:30 a.m. This was not an area where one could make a peaceful approach march in broad daylight.

The Marines' objective was an arbitrary line beyond the main Soissons–Château-Thierry highway. With two battalions on line and a third battalion as well as a battalion of the Second Engineers backing them up, the Marines started across the open fields. Some French tanks were available, but artillery support was insufficient for the needs of the assault troops on that day. After a couple of hours in the attack, during which more than half of the Marines in the two assault battalions became casualties, the survivors dug in along a line of incomplete German trenches. Here they withstood heavy shellfire and the deadly enfilade fire of machine guns for the remainder of the day and suffered from the lack of water and food. They had advanced just under two kilometers with both flanks in the air, but the Soissons–Château-Thierry road lay 800 meters beyond their endurance.

During the day, Harbord wrote a formal letter to Berdoulat, explained the situation and the condition of his men, and made this request: "I desire most strongly that they [the men of the Second Division] should not be called upon for further offensive effort." After midnight, the remnant of the division, except for the artillery, left the front. There were only three officers and some 200 men on the Sixth Marines' front left to withdraw. In two days, this division had advanced 11 kilometers and captured some 2900 prisoners and 75 guns at a cost of approximately 4000 casualties. It would have been not only inhumane but also irrational to expect these hungry, thirsty, and utterly exhausted men to do more. The French, incidentally, did not pass the objective line set for the Sixth Marines on July 19 until August 2.

The First Division began its second day of battle in better condition than its sister division. Summerall had his command more in hand than did Harbord. Then, the First had not advanced as far on July 18 as had the Second, and the men of the First were not exhausted. When Berdoulat ordered the First to jump off at 4 a.m., Summerall received the orders early enough and had good enough communications within his division to get his regiments into the attack at the proper time.

The corps commander expected much from his Americans. He required the Second Brigade to advance four kilometers and the First Brigade a little more than five kilometers to a map line from Berzy-le-Sec to Buzancy exclusive. In order to reach the objective, the regulars would have to cross two ravines, Ploisy and Chazelle, which cut into the plateau and narrowed it a half kilometer in width, as well as a third ravine, Crise, closer to the objective. And these ravines presented the same problem which the already notorious Missy had provided on the 18th.

Although the regulars made two concerted attacks, one at 5:30 p.m. in addition to that during the early morning, they were able to move forward only half the distance to their goal. This was enough, however, to gain a foothold in Ploisy ravine and to reach the head of Chazelle ravine. As one might expect, Summerall made certain that his men got proper artillery support, and the tanks were helpful until all were destroyed, but the French 153rd Division still failed to keep up on the left. Again, the Second Brigade had to stop in order to defend its open flank, and the First Brigade had to hold up and divert its attention to its left flank. On this day, however, the Moroccans did maintain their advance on the right of the First Division. The Germans were stiffening their resistance: the 3000 casualties in the First Division (among the wounded were Huebner and Major Theodore Roosevelt, Jr.), doubled the toll of the previous day, a testimony to the effectiveness of the German defenses. Although stymied, the infantry regiments of the First and the Sixth Marines in the Second Division hit hard enough on July 19 to worry the chief of staff of the German Seventh Army, who commented that the situation "assumed a decidedly critical aspect."

For the third consecutive hot summer day, the First Division attacked. The battle weary infantrymen still had the objective of the previous day with one significant difference: Berdoulat gave them the mission of taking Berzy-le-Sec, which had previously been assigned to the 153rd Division. At 2 p.m., after a two-hour artillery preparation, the infantry, supplemented by companies from the First Engineer Regiment, followed a rolling barrage across the two ravines. The First Brigade and the Moroccans fought their way over the Soissons-Paris railroad and stopped still short of the objective, but they covered two kilometers in their advance. The story was all too familiar on the division's left flank: the French lagged and exposed the Second Brigade's flank. The 28th and 26th Infantry Regiments—what was left of them—started out in good order at the sound of leaders' whistles, and they forced their way to within half a kilometer of Berzy-le-Sec; however, they simply could not keep moving in the face of the German fire. On this day, American intelligence officers identified elements of four German divisions (two first-class, a second-class, and a third-class division) in front of the First.

That night, the French sent reinforcements to the 153rd Division and relieved the Moroccans but left the First in action with the same mission. The First Brigade must cross the Soissons–Château-Thierry highway and a final ravine, Crise, and secure the heights overlooking Buzancy, while the Second had to take Berzy-le-Sec. As he went among his men, Summerall promised them relief on the following night. In the Second Brigade, Brigadier General Beaumont B. Buck, a southerner who had come to France with the First as the commander of the 28th Infantry, visited his men in their front-line shell holes and explained the morrow's attack order to them. Everybody, cooks, clerks, kitchen police, military police, as well as the faithful engineers, would have to join in this final effort.

Although the Second Brigade did not have far to go to achieve its objective, the village of Berzy-le-Sec, it needed all it could muster to take this formidable strongpoint. Located on the edge of the plateau, Berzy had the Ploisy ravine on one side and the steep Crise ravine on two other sides. This left one approach across level ground for the Americans. If they could overcome the Germans here, they would be on the high ground overlooking the Crise ravine, through which the Soissons-Paris railroad and the Soissons–Château-Thierry highway ran. Some five kilometers up the ravine was Soissons. After three hours of artillery preparation, General Buck rallied the survivors of his brigade, who then moved forward with Lieutenants John R. D. Cleland and James

H. Donaldson in the lead and seized Berzy in a furious 45 minutes. By 9:15 a.m. they were on their objective.

The First Brigade also carried its objective. Hines had a longer way to go so he started his men out at 4:45 a.m. with only a rolling barrage to aid them. It was a hard fight, since they had to guard their left flank as well as keep up the attack to their front; nevertheless, they made it across the ravine and highway on to the Buzancy heights.

Despite the promised relief, the First Division had to spend another 24 hours at the front. The relieving unit had not reached the battlefield in time to move into position at night. There was not much the Americans could do on July 21 except wait. That night, the 15th Scottish Division took over the sector. The artillery brigade would stay another day, but the Soissons campaign was over for the infantry.

It was an 11-kilometer walk back to where they had started on July 18. This was valuable terrain won by this division at the cost of 7317 casualties. During their four days in the attack, the division had captured nearly 3400 Germans and 75 guns.

In the Forest of Retz where the survivors gathered about the rolling kitchens on the morning of July 23, regimental bands played the regimental airs and men shouted and joked as they rebounded from the pressures of the battle. When they formed in their respective units, the losses were particularly apparent. General Buck recalled: "Battalions looked like companies, companies like squads." All of the battalion commanders in the four infantry regiments were casualties, and the 26th Infantry, which lost its colonel as well as all of its field officers was commanded by a young captain, Barnwell R. Legge. Many of the companies were commanded by non-coms and at least one by a private. Altogether, 60 per cent of the officers and half of the men in the infantry units were lost in the five days of fighting.

A week after July 18, Corporal Pierre Teilhard de Chardin, a Jesuit priest and a brave stretcher bearer in the First Moroccan Division, attempted to describe the sights and sounds of the great battle to a friend: "There was something implacable about all this, above all; it seemed *inanimate*. You could see nothing of the agony and passion that gave each little moving human dot its own individual character and made them all into so many worlds. All you saw was the material development of a clash between two huge material forces."

All that remains of the exhilaration, the exhaustion, the fear— the complex emotions which Soissons provoked—are the memories of men now grown old. For those who were not there, there are only the words. A rabbit jumping from a hedge in front of an assault line; the flies on the corpses; twigs and leaves falling gently, cut by a hail of a machine gun bullets; French mounted curaissiers drawing sabers and charging machine guns with the inevitable result; the incessant din; lines of sullen prisoners moving to the rear; the wounded, thirsty and in pain, lying in the sun ———Soissons.

There were cowards who skulked and excited men who failed to set their rifle sights or who did not remember to use them or who perhaps shut their eyes when they jerked the triggers. Some soldiers wandered about the battlefield in search of their units. (Ben Bernheisel now a corporal in the 28th Infantry was one. He was wounded after he found his company.) But, together with any other Americans or French they found, they kept fighting Germans. French generals pontificated: the Americans stayed too close together, that was the reason for their high casualties. The French were also critical of leadership and training. One might add that the difficult missions, the Germans, and lagging French units on American flanks also contributed to the number of American dead and wounded.

Despite their criticism, the French, from general to private, praised the spirit of the Americans. Teilhard de Chardin, who survived the war to become a distinguished scientist and philosopher, told his friend: "We had the Americans as neighbors and I had a close-up view of them. Everyone says the same: they're first-rate troops, fighting with intense *individual* passion (concentrated on the enemy) and wonderful courage. The only complaint one would make about them is that they don't take sufficient care; they're too apt to get themselves killed. When they're wounded, they make their way back holding themselves upright, almost stiff, impassive, and uncomplaining. I don't think I've ever seen such pride and dignity in suffering. There's complete comradeship between them and us, born fully-fledged under fire."

Lieutenant Colonel Hugh Drum was not in the battle; he was

still working on plans for the future. In a letter to his wife on July 21, however, he attempted to explain the meaning of the victory on the Soissons plateau:

> Our troops are doing fine work. They gave the Hun the hard knock of the last few days. The success in this particular has had a very good effect materially and psychologically. The spirit of every one is away up. This is what we wanted. The French and all the Allies now take off their hats to the American fighting man. We can well be proud of him. The Hun will come back with a counter blow, but our success has blocked a serious offensive by him. This may be the "turning of the tide."

From a higher vantage point, Foch, soon to be named a Marshal of France, stressed the significance of Soissons in a memo on July 24: "These [Allied] armies, therefore, have arrived at the turning point of the road. They have recovered in full tide of battle the initiative of operations; their numbers permit and the principles of war command them to keep this initiative."

At Pétain's headquarters, on July 18, there was horseplay in the operations bureau as officers mimicked the reactions of German leaders to the events of the day. Major Paul Clark, Pershing's liaison officer, described the scene to his chief: "And between laughs they would read the latest message, mark it on the map, shake my hand and utter eulogies about the Americans. . . . Several have said 'Without the Americans this would never have been possible.'" Less than four months later, on the night of November 10, in a conversation with Clark, a French major general named Duval thought of Soissons when he talked about the American role in the war: "Take the all important attack of July 18. Without the presence in the attack of your troops the attack would have been an utter impossibility—it would never have taken place. Your presence was absolutely essential."

Prior to Soissons, there were other offensives in which, after an initial success, the general situation had again fallen into a stalemate. But in July 1918 the flood of American reinforcements made the crucial difference: Allied forces were steadily growing, while the Germans had to merely fight on with what they had. When Field Marshal von Hindenburg described the battle, he referred to the heroism of the German defenders but he added, "even heroism such as this could no longer save the situation; it could only prevent an utter catastrophe."

Immediately, the Germans had to plan the evacuation of the Marne salient, since the Allies could now interdict the key transportation lines into the salient. Also, they had to cancel preparations for their offensive against the British in order to send reserves to help stave off the attack. Hindenburg poignantly wrote, "How many hopes, cherished during the last few months, had probably collapsed at one blow!" The counteroffensive coming hard upon the collapse of the offensive of July 15 forced a hallucination of failure even on the Kaiser. While lunching with Wilhelm II on a train from Hindenburg's headquarters on July 23, Admiral George A. von Müller noted that "the Kaiser admitted he had not closed an eye all night. He had seen visions of all the English and Russian relatives and all the ministers and generals of his own reign marching past and mocking him."

It would take the signal victory of the British near Amiens on August 8 to give Ludendorff his "black day." However, the defeat at Amiens put the seal on what had happen in July. Soissons could have been considered a fluke, a temporary setback, but Amiens made it crystal clear that it was not. There would be no German counterblow.

The First and Second Divisions won the laurels in the Soissons attack; yet, they were not the only American combat troops who went into action against the western face of the Marne salient on July 18. In Degoutte's Sixth Army, elements of the Fourth Division served with the French II and VII Corps, and the American I Corps operated as the hinge of the great forward movement of its right flank at the apex of the salient.

Although I Corps headquarters had been in existence since January, it had not taken over a sector until July 4. Early in the year, prior to the German offensives, Pershing had planned to have this corps assume the responsibility of the quiet Toul sector, but he had shelved this idea when the German attacks forced the use of American troops to bolster Allied units. Meantime, the corps had administrative responsibility for various American divisions which fought under the tactical control of French corps. The corps commander, Major General Hunter Liggett, was no prima donna, however; he could wait for his opportunity with equanimity.

At sixty-one in the spring of 1918, Liggett could take quiet pride in the fact that he was universally admired in the regular army officer corps—if he ever gave the fact a thought. Frank D. Baldwin, a retired major general who earned the Medal of Honor twice in the Civil War and in an Indian War, said of him in 1919: [he] "has no equal in professional ability or noble character among our American generals." And Billy Mitchell, who was so critical of many of his army contemporaries, called Liggett "one of the ablest soldiers I was ever brought in contact with."

In March 1917 Liggett became a major general in the regular army. Since his graduation from West Point in 1879 he had commanded various infantry units, including a brigade, and had headed the Philippine Department. During his career he had also been at the Army War College as a student, later as teacher, and finally as president. Even his hobbies were professionally oriented. He was fond of military history and maps.

While his colleagues respected Liggett because of his professional ability, he was held in high esteem for another reason as well. Field Marshal Lord Wavell of World War II fame, in his biography of Field Marshal Viscount Allenby, wrote: "In all professions, and especially in the military, character is of greater importance than brains or experience." Liggett possessed all three attributes. Trustworthy, loyal both to superiors and to subordinates, he also had the necessary trait of moral courage. In times of crisis he was imperturbable. Officers were also well acquainted with his good humor, his tact, and, above all, his lack of self-centeredness, which enabled him not only to recognize but also to appreciate another man's situation and point of view. Finally, as General Bullard said of him: "Liggett had the valuable faculty of seeing what was important and what not; and he did not waste his time or attention on what was not going to count." In sum, he was well prepared for high command.

The obvious obstacle to Liggett's attaining combat command was his physique. The general was a very fat man. Since Pershing demanded relatively young and active commanders, it appeared likely that his age and overweight would condemn him to a train-

ing camp or to staff work. Early in the war he commanded the
41st Division which consisted of National Guard troops from several western states. In the fall of 1917, when he went to France
along with other division commanders, he perhaps realized that
his party was being looked over while they observed the Allies and
the embryonic AEF. Indeed, British division commanders reported
in writing their views of the visiting Americans to Pershing. In his
report, the commander of the Guards Division flatly stated that
Liggett "was very much too old to command a Division in the
field."

Pershing recommended reassignment for several of these generals, but he did not want to lose Liggett's services. He suggested
his name for the post of military representative on the newly created Supreme War Council, but Secretary Baker wanted Tasker
Bliss for that position. In December the 41st Division arrived in
France to become a replacement division. The next month Pershing decided to make Liggett his first corps commander. He
never regretted the decision.

Liggett probably never discussed the matter with Pershing.
However, ten years later, he did say that he understood that the
question of his physical fitness had arisen at Chaumont. His comment was characteristic: "I never have inquired and the report
continues to be only hearsay to me, but unquestionably there is
such a thing not only as being too old to fight but too fat. That
disqualification is the more serious if the fat is above the collar."

In mid-July, Liggett's corps consisted of two divisions—the
167th French and the 26th American. Originally, GHQ organization planners had intended a corps to consist of six divisions (four
combat, a base, and a replacement division); however, before the
I Corps actually took over a sector, this policy was abandoned.
The more flexible French system of having a corps comprise a
headquarters, a few technical units, and some artillery and whatever infantry divisions were available and necessary for a particular mission was more suitable.

Liggett had nothing but praise for his French division, which
was commanded by an able general with the unlikely name of
Schmidt. But he had his reservations about Clarence Edwards
and the 26th. Throughout the spring he had administrative control over this division and had seen a good deal of Edwards. Dur-

ing this period he knew that his own chief of staff, Brigadier General Malin Craig (later Chief of Staff of the Army, 1935–39) had become prejudiced against Edwards and the division. For the most part, Liggett considered Craig's views just. Personally, he was not pleased with the officers of the 26th and their talkative commander. The events of the first week of the counteroffensive reinforced this attitude.

On the morning of July 18, the 52nd Brigade of the 26th Division attacked and seized its objective. Although the front was lightly held by understrength German units, the skillful placing of machine guns made any advance difficult. Despite Liggett's explicit instructions to avoid crowding assault troops into dense formations, the infantrymen, not only in the 26th but also in the other divisions which took part later in the campaign, persisted in making this mistake. Liggett praised the enthusiasm but deplored the costly results of this lack of caution which the relatively inexperienced troops displayed. The New Englanders were not lacking in heroism: one of them, Private First Class George Dilboy, when fired on while reconnoitering, drove several Germans away from a machine gun by himself. He won the Medal of Honor but died from wounds.

What troubled Liggett was that he could not depend on the division to do what he wanted it to do when he wanted it done, and Liggett blamed the senior officers of the division for this lack of coordination. An incident on July 18 illustrated the problem. One of the assault units, the third battalion of the 104th Infantry, was supposed to jump off from the edge of Belleau Wood at 4:35 a.m. along with the multitude of other battalions on the western face of the salient. An enemy barrage of gas and high explosives hit the battalion and disorganized it while it was moving through the woods that night. Because only a few of his men were in position at H hour, the battalion commander decided to call off the attack. Since he thought it was only a local operation to straighten out his immediate frontline, he did not think it particularly important anyway. Finally, at 6:05 a.m., he sent a message which explained his decision via carrier pigeon to the brigade commander. An hour later, the regimental commander, who was furious, ordered another battalion commander to take over the third battalion and to attack in 25 minutes at 7:30. It was 8:20 before the third battalion actually started moving forward. Despite the delay and the confusion, the battalion did reach its objective.

A more crucial failure to carry out orders took place on July 22. Since the corps front was becoming more narrow as the advance continued, Liggett ordered the 26th to take over the sector which the French 167th was holding. The maneuver was simply beyond the capacity of the division, and Liggett had to suspend the order after Edwards failed to put it into effect. There were extenuating circumstances. The 26th had been fighting for four days; hence the men were tired and their ranks depleted by heavy losses. During the advance, they had to change direction from east to northeast, which caused confusion and intermingling of various units. The orders did not reach the division until late on the night of the 21st, and thus there was not enough time to pass them on to the subordinate commanders so that the 167th could be relieved during the early morning hours of darkness. It does not take an apologist (although the division had more than its share) to grasp the difficulty of the situation, and one can assess Liggett and his staff for some of the blame.

But Liggett analyzed such incidents within a context of other problems with Edwards. In fact, later he asserted that neither he nor Edwards could locate one brigade (the 52nd) for three days. He was very much impressed by the fact that when he asked Edwards and other senior officers where their infantry was, they frequently did not know. Then, Edwards constantly complained and, on occasion, tried to beg off from attacks which, when he did carry them out, were, at times, hours late. Finally, on July 24, Liggett had it out with his recalcitrant subordinate. He bluntly told Edwards that his trouble was that neither he nor his officers obeyed orders. As corps commander, he expected exact obedience rather than varying interpretations and qualifications of his instructions. He also suggested that Edwards relieve some colonels. Three weeks later, Liggett made these same points a matter of record in a letter to the Adjutant General of the AEF. He concluded his letter of August 13 with this recommendation: "It is my belief that the usefulness of the 26th Division as a dependable fighting unit can be restored only after a period of thorough basic training and reconstruction. . . ."

At the time, the details of their beloved commander's relations with his superiors were not known to the men in the 26th. They were too much concerned with the battle they were fighting from July 18 to 25 to give high command much thought. The Germans were retreating, but the infantry pressed them in a series of attacks about 18 kilometers into the Forest of Fère. On July 22, two days before he was killed, Major George J. Rau, commander of the first battalion of the 102nd Infantry, sent a message which described the all too frequent situation of the troops in the attack: "For Christ's sake, knock out the machine guns on our right. Heavy casualties. What troops should be on my right and left, and where are they?"

The French on both flanks of the 26th were more cautious in their attacks. They preferred, understandably, to call for artillery rather than to attack machine-gun positions in frontal assaults. This is a key reason why each of the flank divisions suffered about one-third of the losses sustained by the New England division, which had over 4000 casualties during its week in the offensive.

On the nights of July 25 and 26, the infantry brigades of the Rainbow Division took over the corps front from the 26th, an attached brigade of the 28th and the 167th French division. At this time the enemy appeared to be in retreat, but they were merely falling back to an excellent natural defensive position along the Ourcq River. The New York Irishmen in the 165th, according to legend, insisted on calling the small, shallow stream the O'Rourke, and their chaplain, Father Duffy, teased a French officer about the size of the river: "I told him that one of our soldiers lay badly wounded near the river, and I offered him a pull at my canteen. Raising himself on one elbow and throwing out his arm . . . he exclaimed, 'Give it to the Ourcq, it needs it more than I do.'"

But the Ourcq was no joke in the five days and nights (July 28 to August 1) during which the 42nd attempted to break the German hold on the hills, woods, and small villages which provided deadly fields of fire for the defenders. The Fourth Guard Division, one of Germany's finest, contested every move and was quick to counterattack. On July 28 the village of Sergy changed hands seven times. Liggett sent up two battalions of the 47th Infantry from the Fourth Division (one of them under Major Troy Middleton, who would command a corps in World War II) to help the

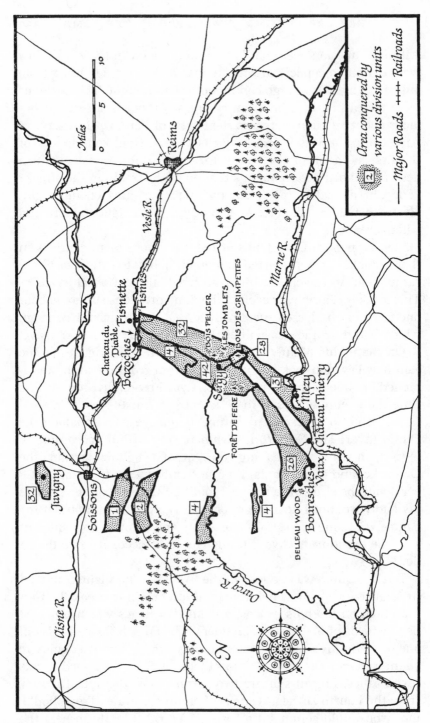

THE AISNE-MARNE OFFENSIVE

Rainbow keep up the attack. This was the first time under fire for the Fourth Division infantrymen, and their initiation resulted in heavy casualties. Finally, when the French corps caught up on each flank, the bloody stalemate was broken. Actually it was another American division, the 32nd in the French XXXVIII Corps, which came to the aid of the Rainbow Division by driving the Germans out of their strongpoints of Les Jomblets, Bois Pelger, and Bois de la Planchette.

When the 42nd left the front line beyond the Ourcq on the night of August 2, the Germans were again in retreat. In its eight days of action, the division had suffered some 5500 casualties, including Sergeant Joyce Kilmer, the poet, who was killed on July 30. Liggett, impressed by the division's performance, wrote: "It proved itself a first class Division in every sense; swift in attack, and tenacious in both attack and defense." During the battle he relieved a brigade commander, Robert A. Brown, who virtually collapsed under the strain of the fighting, and gave the brigade to Douglas MacArthur, a new brigadier general. But he had no qualms about leadership in this division. One could not hope to improve on such National Guard officers as Major William J. "Wild Bill" Donovan (chief of OSS during World War II), commander of the first battalion in the 165th New York; Colonel Benson W. Hough of the 166th Ohio; or Colonel Henry J. Reilly of the 149th Illinois Field Artillery.

Liggett sent the Fourth Division forward to relieve the Rainbow Division. Although the infantrymen in the Fourth had fought in earlier stages of the battle, the division as such was entering action for the first time. As was the case so often in the war, the distinction of being regulars did not disguise the fact that the young officers and nearly all of the men were inexperienced. They made the same mistakes of bunching together and of rushing machine guns that the Guardsmen had made. In the advance to the Vesle River, early on the morning of August 4, the 39th Infantry committed a cardinal tactical sin when it presented the Germans with an artilleryman's dream of marching in columns of squads across open terrain. The Germans were quick to take advantage of the spectacle and hammered the column with artillery and, since it was within range, with machine guns.

There were also at first some problems of control within the

division, but Liggett was lenient and had faith in the senior officers. What he may not have known was that the division, because
of the severe winter, had actually had little training in the United
States. In the six weeks it spent in Europe prior to the opening of
the Aisne-Marne campaign, it had trained briefly with the British
and at greater length with the French but not enough to satisfy
some of its officers. Only two days before one of his regiments
attacked with the French on July 18, Brigadier General Benjamin A. Poore, commander of the Seventh Brigade, wrote in his
diary: "They all seem to be feverishly anxious to get us into
line, even before we are ready, and everybody wants a hand in the
game of playing with the Am. division, their new toy." Despite his
misgivings, there was not much that Poore or the division commander, a cavalryman with snow-white hair and a neat moustache, Major General George H. Cameron, could do about it.

The Fourth entered the battle in a pursuit phase. On their right,
in a French corps, the Wisconsin and Michigan Guardsmen in the
32nd were also following the retreating Germans. Both had problems with their transportation. There was a paucity of good roads,
and the hard rains added to the misery of the troops. Lieutenant
Edmund P. Arpin, Jr., in the 128th Infantry Regiment, 32nd Division, recalled: "An advance of this sort entailed merely a matter
of putting them down and picking them up out of about three
inches of mud at each step." During this wet period, Father William P. O'Connor, the chaplain with the 120th Field Artillery,
thought that a dry shirt was "one of the foretastes of Heaven." In
the advance, there were times when men did not have food or
water and, at no time, could one escape the flies and the stench of
death. Dysentery went its rounds and included Liggett among its
victims. Men and units got lost as one might expect. When the
58th Infantry was marching forward in pouring rain one night
the regimental operations officer, Lieutenant Charles L. Bolté
(who retired a full general and Vice Chief of Staff of the Army),
was shocked to find one entire battalion missing. On this occasion
the battalion commander located his men by ordering some cooks
to start preparing coffee. As soon as the odor of the hot coffee got
around, he found not only his missing men but a goodly number
from the rest of the regiment collected about the rolling kitchens.

While the battle never reached the breakthrough stage, French cavalrymen hovered about as they did at Soissons. The operations officer of I Corps was disgusted and commented in his report that they "complicated the supply problem and use of roads." Yet, Lieutenant Arpin, who saw them on the battlefield, did have praise for the cavalry. He was impressed by the technique used by small groups of horsemen to clean out machine-gun nests. When they spotted one they would dismount, order their horses to lie down, assemble a 37 mm gun, shell the position, follow up with hand grenades at close range, and then mount and search for more Germans.

The pursuit came to an end for the Fourth and the 32nd Divisions when they found the Germans waiting for them in another good defensive position on the heights commanding the Vesle River Valley. The river, some thirty feet wide and up to six to eight feet deep, was not much of an obstacle, even though the Germans had thoughtfully laid barbed wire in the creek bed. But it was necessary to cross the open terrain in full view before the enemy positions could be reached. Patrols and probing attacks soon made it clear that this was not a rearguard but a main line of resistance. Cameron brought up his entire division while on his right the 32nd followed suit. On August 4, Bullard and his III Corps headquarters came up and took charge of the adjoining sector, which at this time was held only by the Wisconsin and Michigan Guardsmen. For nine days, the two American corps were side by side on the Vesle, but the offensive was over.

In support of the 32nd on the Vesle was the 28th Division, at last together as a unit, and the Sixth Brigade of the Third. All three of these divisions had participated in the fighting since mid-July under French corps commanders, although Degoutte had assigned the 56th Brigade of the Pennsylvania Guard Division to Liggett for a few days.

The Third Division had preceded the 32nd in combat with the French XXXVIII Corps. It crossed the Marne in pursuit of the Germans on July 20 and began to have the same difficulties with the rearguard as the other French and American units. By the time the 32nd relieved it in the vicinity of the Bois de Grimpettes, it was, according to its chief of staff, Colonel Robert H. C. Kelton, a "shattered division." Within a week, nevertheless, one of the brigades was back at the front on the Vesle.

For a month, from the first week in August to early September, the Germans stalled the French and Americans on the Vesle lines. The Americans held roughly six kilometers from St. Thibaut to Fismes and bitterly fought the Germans in see-saw actions for the possession of bridgeheads at Bazoches, Château du Diable, and Fismette. It did not make sense to the American generals to maintain a frontline along the river in full view of the enemy and to hazard men's lives in attempts to establish the vulnerable bridgeheads. Afterwards Bullard commented: "I have rarely, if ever, seen troops under more trying conditions . . . they were on the spot and they stayed there. . . ." Any movement by day brought down fire, as the Germans used cannon to snipe at careless soldiers. They were also lavish with mustard gas. Both Liggett and Bullard complained, but Degoutte was adamant. The idea was that Foch hoped to make the Germans think that the troops on the Vesle were preparing for what he called "a vigorous attack."

Throughout most of the month in "Death Valley," a name the Pennsylvanians gave the Vesle front, the 28th under portly Charles H. Muir shared the sector with the 77th Division. These draftees from New York City and its suburbs had served a stint in a quiet Lorraine sector before coming to the Vesle in August. On one moonlit June night in Lorraine they had passed the Rainbow Division behind the lines. As the columns marched past in opposite directions, the solders in the 77th and the New York Irish regiment yelled out their sections of the city and listened for responses. Inevitably someone started singing "Sidewalks of New York," and one man in the 77th sighted his brother in the Rainbow.

During its first five months in France, the 77th had two major changes in command. Pershing promoted George B. Duncan from his brigade in the First Division to command of the 77th Division in May, but Duncan had to give it up because of doctor's orders in August. His successor was Robert Alexander who, like Harbord and Preston Brown, had entered the army as a private. Alexander, a proud man who, according to one of his staff officers, "boned gruffness," took particular pride in his heterogeneous division. Among his junior officers were businessmen, lawyers, at least one actor and a college professor of English literature (Captain Wardlaw Miles, who won a Medal of Honor in September for continuing to command his company although wounded five times). As for the enlisted men, Alexander reported: "It was currently said that there were 43 languages and dialects in use among the men, and there were quite as many shades of religious belief and disbelief." The general did not make that statement in a snide manner. If he had any doubts about the capability of his troops, he soon dismissed them.

What finally broke the deadlock on the Vesle was an attack by the French Tenth Army north of Soissons in late August. Although understrength and not yet recovered from the rigors of their fighting on the Ourcq and Vesle lines, the 32nd Division took part in this operation. In fact their capture of Juvigny on August 30 was a crucial blow against the German defenders.

The French used the nickname "Les Terribles" to praise this division's prowess in battle. These men had come from an Alsace sector so quiet that they could enjoy the German band music from the other side of No Man's Land. They had helped out the Rainbow in July. By the time they joined Mangin's army they were veterans. The battles of late July and early August had been hard, but the Juvigny fight was much tougher. The German defenders fought hard and made effective use of the caves in the area to protect their machine guns but "Les Terribles" were stubborn in their determination to force the Germans back. They succeeded in capturing the ruins of the village of Juvigny and in advancing some two and a half miles in five days of constant battle. The division historian referred to this period as "five days of hell on earth."

There were many men of German descent in the 32nd. If his parents had waited to emigrate, the division commander would have been born in Germany. As it was they left Germany with three children and added to the family in Indiana. A regular army officer, William G. "Bunker" Haan was a solid sort who, unlike Clarence Edwards, retained the affection and respect of both his Guardsmen and GHQ. He and his division were dependable.

The Germans gave up the Vesle line only to fall back a few kilometers nearer the Aisne River where they again stabilized the front. They could be proud of their defensive actions since the collapse of their last offensive. The attack at Soissons had surprised them, but, after a couple of anxious days the German commanders had regained control of the situation. True, they had to give up the Marne salient, but they succeeded in withdrawing their forces to pre-planned phase lines on the Ourcq and the Vesle on schedule. Their losses were heavy; indeed, so severe that Ludendorff had to break up ten divisions to provide replacements. Significantly, the German definition of success changed in July in terms from how many kilometers they advanced to how well they conducted a retreat.

In their analysis of the American role in the campaign, the German generals criticized the leadership and used the heavy losses sustained by the American divisions to support their criticism. At the same time they praised the spirit of the soldiers who committed themselves so recklessly to the attack. When they discussed the American *élan,* the German officers used an analogy of their own men in 1914. The comments of the French professional soldiers about the Americans were similar to those of their adversaries.

The Americans also had their views. They respected the Germans as formidable opponents. While, at the time, they did not know of the German withdrawal schedule, their repeated attacks made certain that the Germans did not stay a day longer than planned in positions within the salient. One might expect some criticism of the French. American inexperience undoubtedly brought on confusion and mistakes and the resulting casualties, but the constant pressure of Degoutte and Mangin to push hard against the enemy contributed its share. A particular sore point was Degoutte's insistence on keeping them in the death trap of the Vesle valley rather than permitting them to hold on the safer high ground. Also, French staff work had hardly been model throughout the summer campaigns. It seemed to American officers that the French were always sending them into battle confused by repeated changes in orders, with little advance warning, and without reasoned consideration of logistical problems. In early June, Preston Brown's criticism of the French was so vocal and continuous that it came to Pershing's attention. Although the "C-in-C" was not noted for his affection for the French, he was concerned enough with good relations to clamp down sharply on Brown. Finally, in the attack, French units frequently lagged on the flanks and left them open to German fire and counterattacks.

It was a hard summer, one that many Americans did not survive. Lieutenant Frederick T. Edwards, now gas and flame officer of the 18th Field Artillery in the Third Division, did survive. During that season, the former theological student saw much of war. From a château in a rest area on August 3, he wrote his father: "I am hanging my soul out to air, which it needs badly,—there have been too many horrible smells lately and this clean sweet air is like a cool drink of water."

But this was merely a respite.

·IX·

The AEF Comes of Age

With the formation of the First Army and its success at St. Mihiel, Pershing's dream of an independent American army came true. Until then, the battle story of the AEF was one of individual units from company level to corps fighting with the Allies. The organization of this army and its conduct in battle required talents other than raw courage as young, trained professional officers demonstrated their capacities for staff work. Even after an American army entered the field, Pershing contributed divisions to reinforce Allied ranks. Two of these remained with the British throughout the war while others came and went as needed.

"I never saw General Pershing looking or feeling better. He is sleeping well. He is tremendously active." Charles G. Dawes jotted these remarks in his diary on August 25. The reason for Pershing's well-being at this point was obvious and Dawes stated it in his next sentence: "He will soon strike with his field army." Since his arrival in France, Pershing's battles had been those of an administrative or diplomatic nature. Now, the fruition of his efforts was at hand.

At Abbeville, during the first week in May, he had forced the English and the French to a formal agreement with his aim of a separate American army. His constant argument was that American manpower would have the most telling effect on the Germans if used in an independent force rather than dispersed as replacements among the Allied units. In the intervening weeks, while American soldiers were playing an increasing role in the fighting, Pershing had continued his campaign for the formation of this army. To his delight, Foch told him on July 10: "To-day, when there are a million Americans in France, I am going to be still more American than any of you. . . . The American army must become an accomplished fact." Together, they concluded that the First American Army should assemble in the vicinity of Château-Thierry within the next three weeks.

The events of the remainder of the month made this decision even more plausible. Liggett's corps was in action there, as were several American divisions. All that was required to bring the plan to culmination was another corps headquarters (Bullard's was immediately available) and the actual establishment of an army staff and headquarters. Pershing announced the latter in a general order on July 24, with the qualification that the order would go into effect on August 10. Actually the headquarters was in operation during the last week in July, and Bullard took over a corps sector on August 4. Premier Clemenceau wired his congratulations on the formation of the field army: "History awaits you. You will not fail it."

In early August the situation changed in that Foch no longer wished to press the offensive across the Vesle. While the sector was hardly quiet, it no longer presented the opportunity for a positive stroke which Pershing wanted his army to make as its debut. The alternative was a project, which he had never discarded—the reduction of the St. Mihiel salient. In June 1917 he and Pétain had tentatively agreed on this as an American objective. When the GHQ staff officers—Fox Conner, LeRoy Eltinge, and Hugh Drum—completed their strategic study in September 1917 they endorsed the operation as the major American effort in 1918. Since then many of the divisions had served their training tours on that front. Most recently, in a program on future offensive actions which he presented to Pétain, Haig, and Pershing on July 24, Foch gave this mission to the Americans. Even when it seemed logical to organize the First Army for action in the Marne salient, Pershing still intended to create a second army to fight on the St. Mihiel front. With the folding of the offensive, Pershing naturally turned to the St. Mihiel idea. Although, as commanding general of the First Army, he took over the Vesle sector from Degoutte for one day (August 10), he issued orders that same day to move the army headquarters to Neufchâteau and to plan for the St. Mihiel operation.

The organization and administration of an army headquarters and all of the complex problems involved in planning and conducting a campaign forced the Americans to disprove the Allied charge that the American army did not have officers prepared to carry the responsibilities of high command and staff positions. After the war Pershing's most distinguished commander, Hunter Liggett, commented: "The more mechanical and complex war grows the greater importance the staff must take on. It is the nervous system and the brain center of the army." Pershing, Liggett—all of the American officers who held high command in this war—had to depend on a relatively small coterie of graduates of Fort Leavenworth Staff College to carry on the key staff work. Resented, if not hated, by many line officers, the Leavenworth men symbolized a break with the past.

More than West Point—indeed, many were not West Pointers —the common tie of Leavenworth training bound together a professional elite. At Fort Leavenworth, these young officers (most of them were in their late thirties and early forties in 1918) studied their German textbooks and learned how to recognize and analyze all of the important factors in a tactical situation and how to prepare a proper comprehensive order. Above all the Staff College broadened the horizons of young officers. George C. Marshall (Class of 1908), who became the Chief of Operations of the First Army, put it this way, "I learned how to learn." This training provided graduates with a common outlook on tactics and the same military vocabulary. Charles D. Herron (also Class of 1908), chief of staff of the 78th Division, explained the importance of this background: When you talked with another Leavenworth man, "he understood what you said and you understood what he said."

The older officers who commanded the divisions and corps frequently lacked this exact understanding, since most of them did not have the advantage of the Leavenworth training. These generals who learned their trade in what Herron called "the drill regulation army" had to depend a great deal on younger, professionally educated officers. Of course there were qualifications. Some of the older men who were not Staff College graduates had attended a short course at Leavenworth, others had pored over the Griepenkerl and Buddecke texts on their own, and quite a few had attended the Army War College. In turn, not all of the division chiefs of staff were Staff College graduates.

Hopefully, the commanders and their staffs would work together in this manner: the commander would state the problem in a broad sense, whereupon the staff under the supervision of the chief of staff would develop a solution in all of its tactical and logistical aspects or possible solutions. After the commander decided to accept a particular plan, the staff then made the appropriate arrangements to put it into effect and to supervise its execution. Thus freed from administrative detail, the commander could make decisions, visit subordinates, inspect and attempt to inspire his men, and, more or less, act as a troubleshooter. As Herron recalled, his division commander would get up each morning and go to that section of the line where the firing was heaviest, while Colonel Herron, the chief of staff, stayed at headquarters to pull "all loose ends together" and to keep "track of everything that goes on."

This relationship demanded on the part of the commander explicit confidence in his chief of staff and, on the part of the chief of staff, a sense of proportion and understanding of his proper role. Mutual loyalty was also a requisite for success. The chief of staff had to know that the commander would support him when he issued orders in the general's name. In turn, the general had to trust the judgment of the younger officer. The obvious danger was a domineering chief of staff presuming too much and taking over the commander's role. It was a fine line which some overstepped.

In a period when there was the difference in training between the older and younger men, the personal element was even more important than it would be later in the twentieth century when one could assume a general similarity in the professional education of commanders and staff officers. During the pre-World War I era, the officer corps was small enough so that an officer of long and varied service would know personally a fairly large percentage of all of the regular officers. Thus, John J. Pershing remembered Malin Craig as a schoolboy on an army post; recognized Herron, whom he had not seen since he was his tactical officer at West Point in the 1890's, at Chaumont; and knew Hugh Drum from his work in the Southern Department of 1916 and early 1917. From his own class at West Point, there came eleven division commanders. As a tactical officer, he had occasion to know cadets who would be at the staff age in World War I. (Herron's class of 1899 alone included twelve key staff officers.) And there were many other opportunities for Pershing, who had a strong memory, to evaluate other officers' personalities and performances. In France this acquaintance paid off when the older officers often had to depend on their knowledge and judgment of men at first rather than their own technical training to put their trust in their juniors. Later, of course, they could judge on the basis of results.

Three of the staff officers who got results in important positions were Fox Conner (Staff College, Class of 1906), Hugh A. Drum (Class of 1912), and George C. Marshall. Conner and Drum accompanied Pershing to France and participated in virtually all of the basic planning for the AEF. Marshall, who came over as operations officer of the First Division, helped develop the training program and plan for the early actions of the pioneer division. When the war ended, Brigadier General Conner was chief of operations at GHQ, Brigadier General Drum was chief of staff of the First Army and had as his chief of operations, Colonel Marshall. All Leavenworth graduates, they began the war as a major, a senior captain, and a junior captain, respectively.

Tall, robust Fox Conner was, according to Herron, "a fine professional soldier with an open mind and of great intelligence . . . one of the really ablest men in the Army." Others, including Dwight D. Eisenhower, who became Conner's protégé in the 1920's, would agree with that opinion. A Mississippian with a deep interest in military history, Conner could be sardonic, and he was always frank. Of particular advantage at this time was his fluency in French, cultivated during a year he spent with a French artillery regiment in 1911. Pershing depended on him as his principal battle planner. In 1939 he wrote Conner's wife: "You know what great confidence I had in him and the high regard in which I have always held him, dating from the time he was a cadet at the Academy." A year earlier, he paid Conner the highest tribute: "I could have spared any other man in the A.E.F. better than you."

Marshall, at thirty-seven, was already known as a soldier of brilliant promise. Long before his years as Chief of Staff, Secretary of State, and Secretary of Defense, long before he was venerated and maligned, Marshall was respected by his contemporaries as a man who knew what he was doing and could always be depended upon to do it well. Even then, one did not presume on the dignity of the soft-spoken but high-strung Virginia Military Institute graduate. Intensely dedicated to his profession, Marshall disciplined himself rigidly. Although he was ambitous, if he thought it necessary he would risk crossing even Pershing to state his opinion.

When the United States went to war, Hugh Drum, despite his youth, was one of the army's most experienced staff officers. He had served on the staff of the commander of the Vera Cruz expedition, and in 1916 during the mobilization of the National Guard he had been the staff officer in the Southern Department charged with planning the organization, employment, and training of the Guard on the Mexican border. A short man whose large nose marred his handsomeness, "Drummie" had been in the army twenty years by the time he reached his thirty-ninth birthday in September 1918. When his father, a regular captain, was killed in action in Cuba, Hugh received a direct commission from President William McKinley. A man of boundless ambition, Drum was denied the culminating prize of his career when Franklin D. Roosevelt chose Marshall rather than him to be Chief of Staff of the Army in 1939.

On July 14, 1918, Pershing told Lieutenant Colonel Drum that he would be chief of staff of the First Army. Earlier in the year, Drum had been scheduled for a similar position in a corps, but Pershing had refused to release him from the Operations Division at GHQ. Now Drum had his chance. At the end of the month he wrote his wife: "While the work is extremely hard you can realize how happy I am in this work. It is the position I have always desired." On September 1, he was also explicit: "This is my opportunity and I am at it from 8:00 a.m. to 12 midnight each day. The results are worth it." It was Drum's job to select the staff officers, organize the headquarters, and plan for the organization of the field army. After he had brought together thirty-five officers (eventually there would be 600), he coordinated their planning for supply, transportation, and tactical utilization of the army.

Since Pershing was the commanding general of both the AEF and the field army, he had to divide his time between the two headquarters. This left Drum with more freedom and more power than if he had been under the constant supervision of a commander. Douglas MacArthur later said that Drum actually ran the army. The point is that he provided continuity of supervision in the First Army. It was a difficult feat Pershing was attempting, and he had to depend heavily on his chiefs of staff to help him carry the double load. Fortunately, Drum and James W. McAndrew, the chief of staff at GHQ, were old friends, and apparently there was generally a good relationship betwen the two headquarters.

Throughout August and into September, both staffs wrestled with their complex assignment. The build-up for the St. Mihiel attack involved over half a million Americans and 110,000 Frenchmen, as well as 2971 guns, 200,000 tons of supplies, and 50,000 tons of ammunition. Some of the men, guns, and matériel were in position, but the majority had to be transported into the area. In order to make the most efficient use of the available roads, the staff officers had to prepare detailed march tables to provide units with specific information as to how fast they should travel, how much road space they should take up, and where they should be at what time. All this was in addition to the planning of the transportation of supplies and material. While part of the staff worked out these problems, others planned the battle: how many units should be employed in what positions to ensure attainment of what specific objectives. In the Operations Section at GHQ, two lieutenant colonels, Walter S. Grant (Staff College, Class of 1915) and George Marshall, worked on the operations plan while at First Army headquarters Drum directed similar planning. Before the end of August, Pershing assigned Grant and Marshall to the First Army staff to help complete the final plan and to draft specific instructions for the units.

While his staff labored, Pershing negotiated with Haig, Pétain, and Foch. From Haig, he wanted all five and eventually got three American divisions previously assigned to the British for training and which Haig had hoped to use as reinforcements. His business with Pétain and Foch took up more time. Since he was short of service troops and artillery because of the shipping program, he had to ask Pétain to furnish both men and equipment to supplement his infantry and relatively meager artillery units. He pressed Foch on the necessity of his requests. The French would also have to supply virtually all of the transportation as well as one corps in the attack.

In fact, the American dependence on the French was so great at this time that Pershing, as commander of the First Army, agreed to serve under Pétain. This curious command arrangement, Pershing hoped, would assure cooperation of all of the French units under his immediate command. Although Pétain remained in nominal supreme command over the First Army until October 16 and reviewed First Army plans, he handled the situation with delicacy and permitted the Americans virtual independence. In the parlance of the day, the French "played the game" and were most generous in their aid to Pershing.

It was Pétain who suggested to Pershing on August 19 that the Americans should attempt to fool the Germans as to their intentions. Since so many people knew about the upcoming offensive, one could assume that the Germans would find out about it also. Why not try to mislead them by making some preparations for an attack elsewhere? Pershing thought it an excellent idea. After he let Conner and a few other GHQ officers in on the secret, he dispatched Omar Bundy with a corps staff to Belfort with instructions to begin planning for an attack toward Mulhouse. French guns in that vicinity began ranging, aircraft flew reconnaissance missions, radio traffic increased, and Bundy, his staff and the twenty-one reconnaissance officers from seven divisions supposedly destined for the offensive played their roles realistically. Their realism was unfeigned, for they honestly thought that they were going to conduct an attack. At Belfort, only Colonel A. L. Conger from the Intelligence Section at GHQ knew that it was a ruse. The scheme worked: not only Bundy and his officers were duped, but, more to the point, the Germans were convinced enough to send three divisions to back up their defenses in that area.

Pershing also found Foch very helpful at first. August was a happy month for Foch. He wore his cap at a jaunty angle. As the generalissimo, he was pleased with the British successes. As a man, he had reached the summit of his profession when President Poincaré presented him with a marshal's baton. He could afford to humor Pershing now. After all the American offensive could not help but add to the general discomfort of the Germans. In mid-August, when he looked over the plan of the St. Mihiel attack, he even extended its objective. Then, on August 27, he received a letter from Haig which markedly changed his views on the American offensive.

Sir Douglas envisaged an immense German salient from the Meuse River almost to the North Sea. He argued for combined offensives, with his armies moving against Cambrai, and French and American forces together making a concentric move toward Mézières. Given this conception, it would be a strategic error to continue the St. Mihiel offense toward Metz, since the Americans would be going away from Haig's vast salient.

Foch accepted Haig's proposal with alacrity. As he explained earlier on July 24 in his program of offensive action, he wanted to encourage several offensives with the primary goal of keeping the initiative and the secondary purpose of clearing railway lines to use in later operations. In this memorandum, he asserted: "It is impossible to foretell at present where the different operations . . . will lead us. . . ." Now, Haig had provided the prophecy in the form of an over-all strategic plan.

Foch told Pétain of the new plan and then went to Ligny-en-Barrois, advance headquarters of the First Army, to explain it to Pershing. He wanted the Americans to furnish four to six divisions to fight in the French Second Army between the Meuse River and the Argonne Forest and to provide eight to ten divisions in a separate American army which he hoped would take part in the grand offensive on the left of the French Second. The target date he set was September 15. Foch also outlined modifications he considered necessary in the St. Mihiel plan in order to make the new project feasible. He thought that Pershing should eliminate the secondary attack on the western face of the salient, reduce the number of divisions scheduled for the operation, and limit his objective to a mere reduction of the salient. Since Pershing would be involved with this offensive, the generalissimo also suggested that Degoutte and an artillery general might supervise the American staff work for the new American army he wanted to fight in the great battle.

This came as a shock to Pershing. On the same day (August 30) he assumed command of the 42 miles of front lining the St. Mihiel salient, Foch seemed to be moving to wreck the operation and destroy the independent American army. Pershing could accept the grand strategic concept, although he wondered if the Allies had enough strength to carry it out at this time. And he acknowledged the necessity for limiting the St. Mihiel offensive, but he believed it necessary to include a secondary attack. (Foch thought the Germans would pull out as fast as they could once the attack began on the southern face of the salient. Pershing wanted to be absolutely sure of victory.) For him, these were minor points, however, compared with the basic matter of the future of an independent American army. When Foch, irritated by Pershing's harping on this fact, blurted: "Do you wish to take part in the battle?" Pershing bluntly replied: "Most assuredly, but as an American army and in no other way."

On the following day, Pershing went to see Pétain. These two generals had more in common than did Pershing and Foch, aside from the fact that both held analogous positions as national commanders under the supranational command of the generalissimo. In their conversation on board Pétain's headquarters train, Pershing found Pétain agreeable. Both thought that Foch overstepped his authority in attempting to dictate the abandonment of the secondary attack on the western side of the St. Mihiel salient. As a tactical matter, this came under the prerogative of the army commander. When Pershing broached the question of strategy, he learned that Pétain did not favor a continuation of the St. Mihiel offensive toward Metz. While this might be worthwhile in the future, Pétain thought that Foch's project (apparently neither

Pétain nor Pershing knew at this time that Haig originated the plan) should have precedence. Besides, before the Americans should launch an attack against Metz, they or the French would have to push the Germans back on the Meuse in order to secure their flank. Pétain then suggested that Pershing assume responsibility for the line westward from his present sector at St. Mihiel to the Argonne Forest—some 48 miles of additional frontage. Thus, if an attack were to be made in the Meuse-Argonne sector, an American army would make it rather than the French Second. Pershing had mentioned this possibility to Foch on the previous day, so he was pleased to accept Pétain's suggestion.

Pétain was more amenable than Foch, in part, because of his basic concern for his army. Undoubtedly, Pétain was more acutely aware of the effect of four years of war on the French army than was Foch, and he wanted to conserve his tired men as much as possible. The fresh American troops, he believed, would have to strike the final blow in the war. If Pershing was willing to accept the challenge at this time, Pétain was delighted to let him.

Two days later, Pershing, Pétain, and Foch met to settle the questions Foch had provoked at Ligny. They soon reached mutual agreement. Foch accepted the Pershing-Pétain solution of extending the American front to the Argonne. Although Pershing reluctantly offered to cancel the St. Mihiel operation in order to stage the Meuse-Argonne attack, Foch did not think it necessary. By delaying the latter until September 25, he hoped that Pershing would be able to wind up a limited St. Mihiel campaign and have enough time to get his army into position for the Meuse-Argonne offensive.

This new plan presented a formidable task to First Army staff officers. They would have to change their plans for the St. Mihiel operation, carry out that battle, and plan an entirely different battle. Normally, staffs would spend two months or longer working out a battle plan: they would have three weeks. Pershing broke the news to Drum on September 3.

Actually the modifications in the St. Mihiel plan were not drastic. The Americans had to do without a supporting attack of five or six French divisions immediately to the west of the salient, but they just reduced the total assault force against the salient by only one-half of a division in the secondary attack. Instead of thirteen assault divisions with seven in reserve, there would now be twelve and one-half with five and one-half in reserve (including fourteen American). Because of the limited objective, the staff had to change slightly the directions of both the primary and secondary attacks. The new orders were ready for distribution on September 7. Foch wanted the attack to take place on September 10, but the Americans had to wait until French heavy artillery units arrived from Mangin's army. As it was, the exact hour and date of the attack were not set until the tenth.

The object of all of this consideration was a bulge of some 200 square miles with the village of St. Mihiel near the apex of the rough triangle. The wooded heights of the Meuse River were the dominant terrain feature along the western side of the salient, while forests, Montsec and lesser hills covered the southern face. Within the salient was part of the Woëvre plain which, American intelligence officers knew, would become swampy when the rains came in mid-September. On most of the salient front the Germans had the advantage of the high ground. In the four years they had held the area, they had made skillful use of the terrain in constructing strong defensive positions supplemented by a great amount of barbed wire. Since early 1915, when the French attacked but failed to budge the defenders, the sector had been quiet. On both sides of No Man's Land, divisions came to recuperate, and here, in 1917, the Americans came to train their divisions in trench warfare.

Throughout his negotiations with Foch and the other Allied leaders, Pershing naturally had made it clear that he wanted his first battle test as an army commander to be an obvious success. The reason for the elaborate precautions and the overwhelming superiority of force is understandable. Because of the task he had set for himself to lead a separate American army, Pershing, as an untried army commander, would be gambling on a new army staff, two new corps commanders and their staffs, and four untried divisions.

Against the eight war-weary enemy divisions and one brigade holding the line of the salient, Pershing would send four corps including four French and eight and one-half American front-line divisions. The French II Colonial Corps with three French divi-

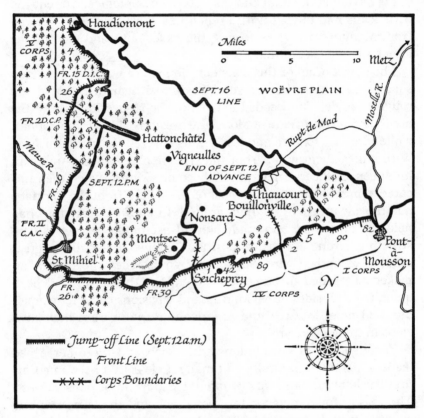

THE ST. MIHIEL OFFENSIVE

sions had a follow-up mission around the apex of the triangle. On the southern face the I and IV American Corps would conduct the primary attack with seven divisions, while in the west the V American Corps, containing a French division as well as the 26th and a brigade of the Fourth, was charged with the secondary attack.

In mid-August, Pershing had promoted Joseph Dickman and George Cameron to command the IV and V Corps respectively. These two former cavalrymen, so unlike in appearance and manner, had made a good impression as division commanders on the "C-in-C" during the fighting in July. Now they had less than a month to complete the organization of their staffs and to ready their headquarters for battle. The dependable Liggett, of course, already had an experienced, efficient staff in I Corps headquarters.

Although this would be their first offensive, all four of the untested divisions had spent a few weeks in the trenches. Two of them, the 89th and the 90th, had begun their first tour at the front on the southern face of the salient in August. These soldiers were draftees, many of whom had been in the army less than six months. Most of the men in the 90th came from Oklahoma and Texas, while those in the 89th were from the tier of states spanning from Missouri to Arizona. The All-American Division (the 82nd), with its southern mountaineers and farmers and a large contingent of foreign-born, drafted from northern cities, had completed its training stint at the front also on the south side of the salient in August. Like the other regular divisions, the Fifth consisted of a majority of wartime volunteers. They had gained their trench experience in the Vosges mountains.

The major generals who commanded these divisions were an interesting group. Henry T. Allen of the 90th was an impeccable dandy who had balanced attaché duty in Berlin and Moscow with combat assignments in Cuba and the Philippines. In early September, Allen frequently visited corps headquarters to discuss relatively minor matters. On September 11, Liggett told him, "Allen, you have on a new pair of boots every time you come to see me." Perhaps, this was Liggett's manner of hinting that Allen came too often. He might be a little nervous over his debut as a combat division commander, but no one questioned Allen's courage. The 82nd Division had as its commander William P. Burnham, who enlisted after he failed to graduate from West Point and then worked his way up through the ranks. John E. McMahon of the Fifth was an Academy classmate of Pershing's. Although he was slightly younger than the "C-in-C," he looked much older, and some wondered if he could stand the physical strain. The controversial Leonard Wood had organized the 89th Division, but the Secretary of War, upon Pershing's strong recommendation, had removed him from command just before the division came to France. During the first week in September, Pershing named his former West Point roommate, William M. Wright, to command this division. He knew that he could depend on his close friend Billy.

Pershing also knew that he could depend on the three divisions —the First, Second, and 42nd—he expected to give the momentum to the primary attack. On the other side of the salient, the one brigade of the Fourth on line merely had a holding mission, but Pershing entrusted the major role in the secondary attack to the New Englanders of the 26th Division. Since the summer campaigns, the veterans in these divisions had been in rear areas and quiet sectors. Bathing, delousing, enjoying a clean uniform and a clean billet were blessings: the maneuvers and return to the trenches were not. But officers and men had to try to learn how to avoid mistakes which had been so costly in the summer. There were replacements; so many came to the Second that it had 1400 men over the authorized strength. Visitors also came. The young, personable Assistant Secretary of Navy, Franklin D. Roosevelt, visited the Marine brigade. More appreciated however, was the AEF's most popular entertainer—Elsie Janis. Chaperoned by her mother, Elsie sang, danced, told stories, and turned handsprings on makeshift stages in front of grateful audiences.

The Second and the Fourth had new commanders as other replacement officers joined all five veteran divisions. John A. Lejeune, whom Harbord called "a splendid man," had not joined the Second until late July. A Marine major general and a graduate of the Army War College, he had failed earlier in the summer to persuade Pershing to permit him to form a Marine division. After three weeks in command of a brigade in the 32nd Division and less than three days as commander of the Marine brigade, he was Pershing's choice to replace Harbord. An experienced campaigner, Lejeune also had the great advantage of knowing many of the senior AEF officers because of his tour of duty at the War College. John L. Hines came to the command of the Fourth with the reputation of a successful combat leader. Upon his arrival he made a favorable impression when he called together all of the officers above the rank of captain and explained his policies. The men came to know him as a thorough inspector—a major general who would get down on his knees in the muck to check the under- side of a truck. Without flamboyance, he was forceful, and, while he did not overlook minor matters, he had the gift of recognizing the major.

The New Englanders still had Clarence Edwards, but they also had two new infantry regimental commanders. One of them, Ma- rine Colonel Hiram I. Bearss, would soon show the 102nd why Marines called him "Hiking Hiram." Another Marine colonel, Frederic M. Wise, who commanded a battalion at Belleau Wood, took over a regiment in the Fourth. Two other combat veterans joined new divisions as brigade commanders. At last McAlexan- der got his star, and the men in the Texas Brigade (the 180th) of the 90th Division began to understand why the "Rock of the Marne" veterans respected him. In the Fifth Division, Paul B. Ma- lone, bitter because he still wore eagles, came from the Second Division to take over the Tenth Brigade.

As the time of attack drew near, the plans worked out by the staff officers materialized in the form of long columns of rain- swept infantry slogging in roads which became wide streaks of mud, of horses struggling to pull guns, caissons, and wagons through the mire, of trucks inching forward through the mass of men, horses, and equipment. The divisions, not already in the sector, had to travel an average of 100 kilometers, and trucks and trains could go only so far before the walking began. Because of secrecy, the army, concentrating around the salient, moved only during the night and then without lights. By day, the soldiers had to hide themselves, their animals, and their paraphernalia in woods or billets and try to sleep. The horses suffered more than the men, since forage and water, despite the rain, were difficult to obtain. Some fell dead in harness.

Even the units in position had to do some moving in order to make way for the incoming troops. In this manner, for example, the sector of the 89th Division narrowed from sixteen kilometers to four. The attack orders each division prepared explained such arrangements in detail. In fact, as Lejeune said, these orders and their multiple annexes, which might be anywhere from 19½ to 50 or more typed pages in length, were "compendiums of information and instruction."

While preparations were in full progress, a debate took place at First Army headquarters as to the amount of artillery preparation that would be necessary for the attack. Liggett and others argued for little or no preparatory fire in order to ensure surprise. Those who advocated the pre-attack bombardment pointed to the need of damaging positions and wire as much as possible, as well as the psychological effect on both the defenders and the attackers. Pershing heard the arguments and decided not to use preparatory fire. On the night of the tenth, however, he reconsidered his decision and ordered a four-hour preparation on the southern face and a seven-hour fire on the western side of the salient.

The plan was now fixed. On the south side, six divisions would attack at 5 a.m., September 12, while the 82nd, which was on the shoulder of the salient, would stay in position. An hour later the French troops near the apex of the triangle would join in the advance. On the other side of the salient, the 26th and the French Fifteenth Colonial Division would jump off at 8 a.m., to be followed by the other French troops on their right an hour later. In the position analogous to that of the 82nd, the brigade of the Fourth would stay put during the assault.

The night of September 11 was pitch black, and the steady rain chilled the thousand of men waiting for battle. Many of them did not file into the forward trenches until a few hours prior to H hour. About 8 p.m., Sergeant William L. Langer of the First Gas Regiment carried ammunition through the labyrinth of water-logged trenches and found them empty. On his return, rows of soaked, miserably cold Second Division infantrymen crouching in the muck filled these same trenches. One of the officers in the Ninth Infantry Regiment, Second Lieutenant Herbert Snyder, later told what he carried that night—pistol, papers, gas mask, maps, a slicker, a pound of chocolate and a can of milk to supplement his half pound of "corn willie" and two packages of hard bread, 180 cigarettes, and a cane. A few kilometers down the line, in the Rainbow Division sector, Lieutenant Colonel William J. "Wild Bill" Donovan was apprehensive. He had survived the terrible days on the Ourcq, but his battalion of the New York Irish Regiment had 75 per cent new officers and 65 per cent new men. Donovan knew that the Germans were in good defensive positions, and he thought that his men would suffer awesome casualties in the attack.

Precisely at 1 a.m. the artillery opened fire. Almost three thousand guns brightened the sky with continuous flashes and deafened men with the roar of the detonations. The Germans were surprised. Although they had anticipated an attack for days and had planned to evacuate the salient when it came, they had just started moving some of the war matériel out. As a precautionary measure General Fuchs, the commander of the defenders, Army Detachment C, had ordered two divisions, which, as it developed, would face the primary attack, to fall back to a secondary line. Many of these Germans were in the process of moving to the rear when the barrage began, but the commander of one of the divisions (77th Reserve) misinterpreted the order and left two-thirds of his infantry in their old positions virtually without artillery support.

Donovan was relieved when he noted that the German artillery did not seem to reply to the preparatory fire. Apparently they were pulling out, and all he and his men would have to do was to push them and they would surrender. At H hour, he led his men out of the trenches and across the narrow stream, the Rupt de Mad. While there were some pockets of resistance, the advancing line all along the front soon overwhelmed them. If anything, the barrage at a rate of four minutes for every 100 meters was too slow in some areas. The wire which everyone worried about was there in great quantity, but it was old and rusty. The teams with wire cutters and bangalore torpedoes opened gaps. Tanks were some help, but, because of the soggy ground, they could not keep up with the infantry. Donovan pressed his men: "Get forward, there, what the hell do you think this is, a wake?" And he tried to keep them moving in the proper zone.

Over in the Rainbow's 166th Infantry, a medic, Private George A. Dennis, drove the battalion medical cart forward. He noticed some infantrymen shouting at him, but he could not hear them because of the shelling. When he reached St. Benoit, he unloaded the cart and set up a dressing station. The foot soldiers had been trying to tell him that he was passing the advance line. By the time the first assault troops reached the village, Dennis had been there a half hour.

Major Terry de la Mesa Allen, a regular cavalry officer who was commanding an infantry battalion in the 90th Division, ran into considerable more difficulty. Just before his men went into the assault, Allen was wounded and stunned. When he came to in an aid station, he tore off his first-aid tag and ran to catch up with his troops. Finding a few stragglers, he collected them and continued forward. While they worked their way through the wire and the trenches, they came across some enemy machine gunners. In hand-to-hand combat, Allen and his men bested these Germans. The major, missing some teeth and with his face covered with blood, paused to pick up one of the German identification tags and then resumed his search for his battalion. Before he could find it, some soldiers from another regiment stopped him. Like other officers he had removed his insignia prior to the attack, so when these Americans searched him and found the German ID tag, they thought he might be an enemy in disguise. Eventually, Allen convinced them of his proper identity, but, by this time, he was so weak that they sent him back to an aid station. Less than twenty-five years later, Major General Allen led the First Division against the Germans in North Africa and Sicily.

Unlike the machine gunners Allen fought, many Germans were eager to surrender, as Sergeant Harry J. Adams of the 89th Division discovered. When Adams saw an enemy soldier run into a dugout at Bouillonville, he ran after him. He had two rounds left in his pistol, so he fired both of them through the door and called on the German to surrender. As the sergeant stood dumfounded, over 300 German officers and men filed out of the dugout. Adams was equal to the occasion; he brandished his empty pistol and marched the prisoners toward his platoon. His startled platoon leader thought the gray column was a counterattack force.

Letters written by Germans in the area indicate the desperate state of their morale. A noncom wrote: "The men are so embittered that they have no interest in anything and they only want the war to end, no matter how." Another soldier said: "I am so nervous that at the sound of every shell I fall to my knees and trembling overcomes me." These men were in the Tenth Division, the only first class unit in the salient. It had already suffered severely at the hands of McAlexander and his regiment on the Marne, however.

When Captain Walter Lippmann of the Army Intelligence interrogated prisoners, he found them convinced that Germany would lose and delighted that they were out of the war. Already a well-known commentator on public affairs, Lippmann reported to President Wilson's adviser, Edward M. House, his analysis of the German soldier and his political views: "He is a highly trained and technically competent peasant, but fundamentally a peasant in his political relations. . . . Even the most sensitive among them refuse flatly to believe that America has any ideal purpose. They simply do not believe such things exist among nations."

By the afternoon of the twelfth, the attacking troops had passed beyond the scheduled first day's objective. Tired though they were, it was exciting to enjoy the greetings of the French civilians, crawling out of their cellars, and to pick up souvenirs or to eat one's fill of food left steaming in German field kitchens. The doughboys were amazed by the panelled dugout with electricity and running water and by others with elaborately furnished dining and recreation rooms. Liggett's corps intelligence officer was also amazed when he heard that the Second Division had picked up prisoners from 57 different units. Upon investigation, however, he learned that these Germans had come from other sectors of the Western Front to attend a machine gun school at Thiaucourt. When the Americans caught them, they were trying to catch a train out of the salient.

In the confused, fluid situation of a retreat, a cavalryman such as Pershing, Dickman, or Cameron might well yearn for some mounted troopers. Dickman did have a few in a provisional squadron of four troops from the Second Cavalry under Lieutenant Colonel O. P. M. "Happy" Hazzard. Most of the troopers had been in uniform only a year, while the officers, with the exception of Hazzard, were young and inexperienced. All were anxious to do their share, even if their horses, convalescents from veterinary hospitals, were untrained as cavalry mounts when they got them in August. Dickman used B Troop for courier duty but attached

Troops D, F, and H to the First Division. With Troop F in the lead under a young West Pointer, Captain Ernest N. Harmon, they attacked a German column with their automatic rifles. Some machine gunners forced them back, but not before the cavalrymen had knocked two of the machine guns out of action. The next day, at dawn, the troopers were out again. While D and G Troops secured the interior of the salient, Harmon and his men carried out the traditional mission of reconnoitering ahead of the infantry. He located the enemy positions, captured 73 Germans and a battery of heavy artillery. In the next war, Harmon gave up his horse and led the First and Second Armored Divisions and, later, the XXII Corps in battle.

The secondary attack which began at 8 a.m. did not move as rapidly as the primary attack. The New Englanders admitted that resistance was light, but they had to hold up because the French on their left flank were not advancing fast enough over the rough, hilly ground. Nevertheless when Edwards got the order that night to push as hard as he could to reach the First Division and seal off the lower part of the salient, he showed how fast his people could move. On that clear night, the 102nd Connecticut with "Hiking Hiram" Bearss in the lead marched nine kilometers and occupied Hattonchâtel and Vigneulles. Edwards promised that they would do this by four the next morning; they did it by 3:15. Within four hours, a scout platoon from the 28th Infantry entered Vigneulles and closed the salient.

Pershing celebrated his army's triumph and his fifty-eighth birthday on September 13 by escorting Pétain into St. Mihiel. As they left the village they met Secretary of War Baker; soon there would be other distinguished visitors—President Poincaré, Foch, and Clemenceau. During this day the First Army, with Pétain's permission, pushed beyond the limited objective set by Foch until the soldiers began to run into the Michel line which the Germans had hastily prepared at the base of the salient. For the next few days, Americans and Germans clashed along this line in what military commentators call "local operations," but the battle was over.

In two days the First Army had achieved several important results. Foch had wanted the offensive in order to open up the Paris-Avricourt rail line for Allied use. By driving the Germans out of the salient, the Americans not only did this but also deprived the enemy of a base from which he could have harassed the rear of the American force in the upcoming Meuse-Argonne offensive. Now, the Americans were in position to threaten Metz, the Briey-Longwy industrial complex, and the crucial railroad passing through that area. Closest to the hearts of the American commanders and staff officers, however, was the proof that they could successfully plan and conduct an independent operation of this magnitude. And, within the context of other Western Front offensives, the 7000 casualties were light.

The most the Germans could claim was that the battle had not been a catastrophe. Although they lost about 17,000 men (of whom some 2300 were killed and wounded and the rest prisoners), approximately 450 guns, war stores, and the salient, they did get the bulk of the defenders out and re-establish a defensive line. They had planned to evacuate, but they did not want to take this step until it was absolutely necessary. General Fuchs hesitated until almost noon on September 12 before he ordered the withdrawal. After all, his superior officer, the Army Group commander, General Max von Gallwitz had instructed him on September 3, "not to concede an easy success, particularly since we are dealing with Americans." As it was, two weeks later, Field Marshal von Hindenburg telegraphed Gallwitz: "The severe defeat of Composite Army C on September 12 has rendered the situation of the Groups of Armies critical." Hindenburg assumed that "faulty leadership" was the reason, since in the past (apparently he was thinking of the Aisne-Marne campaign) he claimed that weak divisions had beaten off American attacks.

The Field Marshal did not have to impress on Gallwitz that his situation was critical. The fortress of Metz was vulnerable; the army had taken much of the artillery for use at the front, and Gallwitz feared that the Americans might know this and continue their advance through the partially completed Michel line. They had the momentum of victory, and the Germans wondered why they did not sustain it. Some of the Americans, of whom Douglas MacArthur was the most vocal, shared this view. Liggett did not agree: "The possibility of taking Metz and the rest of it, had the battle been fought on the original plan, existed in my opinion, only on the supposition that our army was a well-oiled, fully coordinated machine, which it was not as yet. . . . As I see it, the American army engaged to its uppermost, would have had an excellent chance of spending the greater part of the winter mired in the mud of the Woëvre, flanked both to the east and the west." Actually the issue did not come up except in conjecture. Pershing had committed his army to the Meuse-Argonne, and that is where it would strike its next blow.

On September 3, the day after Pershing met with Pétain and Foch to determine the role of his army in the St. Mihiel and Meuse-Argonne offensives, he received an important visitor with an astonishing request. General Armando Diaz, the commander of the Italian Army, asked him for 25 divisions, which together with appropriate auxiliary units meant a million American soldiers. Pershing showed no surprise as he listened to Diaz explain his needs. There had been so many requests and so much pressure from the Allies for American soldiers that he no longer reacted emotionally to such appeals. Already, he had dispatched one regiment, the 332nd Infantry, to Italy, and he politely told Diaz that there would be no more.

Despite Pershing's efforts, he was never able to collect all American troops together in his field armies. During the fall of 1918, Americans who went to war to fight the Germans turned up in Italy in the 332nd Infantry pursuing Austrians and in "fantastic sideshows" in North Russia and Siberia. A reinforced infantry regiment, the 339th, actually fought Bolsheviks near the Arctic Circle, while some 9000 other Americans found themselves sharing uneasy occupation duty with the Japanese and other Allied forces in Siberia. Then, even in the midst of the Meuse-Argonne campaign, Pershing sent divisions to aid the French and the Belgians. The veteran Second and the Oklahoma and Texas National Guard Division (36th) gave invaluable support to Gouraud's Fourth Army in Champagne. Reputedly, Pétain said that the Second's capture of the Blanc-Mont ridge was "the greatest single achievement of the 1918 campaign." And the 37th and the 91st Divisions took part under French corps commanders in the closing days of the fighting in Belgium. King Albert of the Belgians, in a postwar tribute to the 37th summed up his debt when he wrote, "You came when your help was needed."

The British also wanted American troops, as Lloyd George had made clear in the various Supreme War Council meetings, but Pershing's early decision to locate his army on a sector of the French front virtually excluded Americans from the British area. To be sure, there were a few American medical units with the British and occasional visits from American commanders and staff officers, but these were gestures rather than contributions. Even in the terrible days of the German spring offensives, there were only a few American engineer troops available to the British commanders. It was extremely frustrating for those political and military leaders who pondered the increasing casualty lists and the decreasing source of replacements to be denied access to the reservoir of American manpower.

Finally, after conferences on both sides of the Atlantic, the British gained the concession of training American combat troops and of using them, within Pershing's qualifications, at the front. Beginning with the arrival of the 77th Division in April, the infantry and machine gun troops, together with assorted other divisional units but no artillerymen, of ten divisions came under the supervision of Field Marshal Haig. The British equipped these soldiers, fed them, and trained them, but as it developed only four of these divisions actually reached the British front.

American troops did not relish this arrangement. It was difficult to forget what every schoolboy learned about the king, the embattled farmers, redcoats, and all the rest. Of course many overcame the stereotype and the suspicion to respect and to like the British; but apparently most soldiers disliked the "Limeys" and never let anything change the situation. Australians and Canadians seemed to share this feeling and, on occasion, in bar-room brawls in the French villages behind the lines, they would join with the Yanks against the English.

Language problems and rations were constant sources of friction and confusion. Mark H. Ingraham, who commanded the Supply Company of the 309th Infantry Regiment, 78th Division, commented: "A foreign language doesn't cause as much irritation as your own language spoken differently." Differences in accents might be amusing, but calling a railroad car a truck could lead to difficulties when supply officers of the two armies discussed logistics. And what American soldier would guess that when a British

officer reported from the front—"Things here are a bit fruity"—
that he meant that his unit had suffered heavy casualties. The
tendency to avoid technical terms and constantly to use initials
utterly unintelligible to the Americans also complicated matters.

In the ranks, the food ration was a daily reminder of the British. The men did not think that they got as much as when they
were on American rations, and they certainly did not get the same
kind of food. Tea and jam were no substitutes for coffee and
sugar, and one soon got enough of bread and cheese, not to mention frozen Australian jack-rabbits. A Wisconsin private in the
33rd Division, Clayton K. Slack, however, liked the cheese and
never forgot the generosity of a British company which halved its
ration to feed Slack's company for a few days in the summer of
1918.

Five divisions of Americans—4th, 28th, 35th, 77th, and 82nd
—did not stay with the British long enough to become well acquainted or to complete their training. Foch asked for these men
in early June to bolster the French front, and the British submitted gracefully to the generalissimo's decision. When the 307th Infantry Regiment of the 77th Division left its British mentors, the
British division commander came out and saluted the departing
infantrymen, while his band played them out of the area. This display of what Captain W. Kerr Rainsford of the 307th called "true
sporting spirit" was particularly remarkable, since the British division was about to return to the front and Major General Sully-
Flood had expected the Americans to reinforce his command.
Sully-Flood had previously made a good impression when, after
watching a baseball game, he had taken a turn at bat and hit a
home run. Some Americans understandably hated to leave this
division.

Just as he had done with his units which trained with the
French, Pershing established a corps headquarters to control the
five divisions remaining with the British. In June he named Major
General George W. Read as commander of the II Corps with this
specific mission. Read, a handsome, tall cavalryman who looked
to one acquaintance as if he might have been a model for one of
Frederic Remington's drawings of a frontier cavalry officer, gave
up command of the 30th Division to assume his new responsibilities.

At this time there were three National Guard and two National Army divisions under Read's jurisdiction. New York Guardsmen filled the ranks of the 27th Division, while those from Illinois were the cadre of the 33rd, and the War Department had brought together Guard units from the Carolinas and Tennessee to create the 30th—"Old Hickory"—Division. The 78th consisted primarily of drafted men from New York and New Jersey, while the last division, the 80th, drew its personnel from Pennsylvania, Virginia, and West Virginia drafts.

Although several British units helped train the American divisions, the Australians led the Americans into their first attack on the British front. The Yanks liked the Diggers: they could appreciate the exuberant, businesslike approach of these allies more than they could the reserved, unhurried, and, in some cases, pessimistic, manner of the English. The Australian corps commander, Lieutenant General Sir John Monash, was hardly a typical British general. In his photographs he looked the part, with his jaunty stance and his riding crop tucked under one arm, but in fact he was not even a professional soldier. An Australian Jew, he had made his reputation as an engineer before the war. In France he applied his organizational and analytical talents to the business of war and in so doing demonstrated, according to B. H. Liddell Hart, "the greatest capacity for command in modern war among all who held command in the last war."

The battle of Hamel showed Monash at his best. Near the Somme River the Germans held a ridge containing the Bois de Vaire and the town and wood called Hamel. The high command could justify an attack on this ridge in terms of testing the enemy defenses and of seizing a better position, but Monash was particularly interested in trying out some new techniques. To drive the Germans back some 2500 yards on a 6000 yard wide front, Monash planned to use eight battalions of Australians and eight rifle companies from the American 33rd Division, together with 60 attack tanks. Prior to the battle he rehearsed the assault troops over and over again until the infantrymen perfected their coordination with the tanks. The "curious monsters" (in his words) fascinated Monash, who thought that they would be of greater value if they went into battle under the exclusive command of the infantry commander and if they stayed up with the infantry close to the rolling barrage. Supplying ammunition to an assault force after it had seized its objective had been a troublesome problem. Monash attempted to solve this by training pilots to parachute boxes of ammunition on pinpoint targets. He also used gas effectively by having his artillery fire some gas shells with smoke shells prior to the attack. Then, at zero hour, when only smoke shells hit in the enemy lines, he expected the Germans to don masks, while his troops would not be hampered by masks.

The Australian general believed, "A perfected modern battle plan is like nothing so much as a score for an orchestral composition. . . . ." And he demanded that "every individual unit must make its entry precisely at the proper moment, and play its phrase in the general harmony." To ensure success, Monash personally explained the plan in detail to his senior officers and then, once he was convinced that everyone understood perfectly, he would not permit any alterations in plans that could lead to confusion.

On June 30, Monash held his last conference. All was set, he thought, for the attack on July 4th—a date he chose with due regard for the Americans. Despite his careful preparations, Monash overlooked the diplomatic implications of using Americans in the attack. Perhaps his superior, Sir Henry Rawlinson, commander of the Fourth Army was thinking of this when he ordered Monash to reduce by half the number of Americans involved on the next day. Grudgingly, the Australian did as he was told. There was still time for such a change, but he was not prepared for the next development.

John J. Pershing was in the British zone to check on his divisions when, on July 2, he learned about the planned attack. Immediately, he told Read to withdraw the American infantrymen from the scheme. He followed this up by personally telling Haig the next day and by telephoning Read to impress him with the urgency of the matter. Word reached Monash less than twelve hours before H hour. In a tense meeting with Rawlinson, Monash flatly stated: no Americans, no battle. Rawlinson passed this on to Haig, who deferred to the corps commander's ultimatum; hence the battle went off as scheduled with approximately 1000 Americans in their appointed places. Pershing was furious. To him this was simply an indication of the British desire to wrest control of the American troops away from him. He gave explicit orders that Americans were not to be used in this manner again.

The battle itself was a success. As Monash recalled, "No battle within my previous experience . . . passed off so smoothly, so exactly to time-table, or was so free from any kind of hitch." Within 93 minutes after the infantrymen and tanks jumped off from the white tape line at 3:10 a.m., they were in possession of the objective as well as 1472 prisoners and two guns. The men in Companies C and E of the 131st and A and G of the 132nd Infantry Regiments who fought in separate platoons attached to the Australian battalions won the praise of their allies for their role. They lost in killed, wounded, and missing, 176 officers and men, some of whom were victims of one hitch which Monash overlooked—short rounds from the supporting batteries. In the fighting, when a machine gun stopped a platoon of Company E, 131st, Corporal Thomas A. Pope won the Medal of Honor by rushing the nest alone and killing several of the Germans with his bayonet.

During the remainder of the month, many other Americans began their tours in British trenches in less hectic circumstances. As a regular part of their training, the 27th, 30th, 33rd, and 80th Divisions sent units to the front. They shared experiences already familiar to thousands of their compatriots: the long march at night, the first shelling, the sounds, sights, and smells of the trenches. And, as Private Clayton Slack said, "Those that weren't scared, weren't there."

When the British made the attack that so profoundly rattled Ludendorff on August 8, the 131st Infantry was a part of the reserve of the British III corps. After clearing with higher headquarters, the corps commander ordered the regiment into the battle on the second day, August 9. The tired infantrymen had been up all of the previous night on a twenty-mile hike to reach the area. At 3:30 p.m., they received orders to jump off at 5.30 p.m. from a point almost four miles away. In the hot sun, Colonel Joseph B. Sanborn led his men with full packs to the attack position. Despite the fact that they were exhausted and had had no rations and very little water since the previous day, these men double-timed the last mile and arrived to follow the rolling barrage. Although he was sixty-two years old and a thirty-eight-year veteran of the National Guard—he had commanded the "Dandy First"

Illinois, the parent regiment of the 131st, since 1898—Sanborn personally led the march and deployed the battalions along the line. Under the leadership of their doughty old colonel with the huge moustache, these men fought throughout the night and drove the Germans out of Gressaire Wood and off the bare Chipilly Ridge which overlooked the historic Somme River.

While the 131st was still at the front on August 12, Pershing met with Haig on the British commander's headquarters train and asked for his men. Understandably, Haig was bitter. Although he had continually criticized the American commanders and staff officers for their inexperience, he desperately wanted to keep the American troops. He had equipped and trained them, and now, when they were beginning to take some of the burden off of his own men, Pershing wanted them. More than that, after four years of frustration, it seemed to him that victory was possible if he could mobilize a strong enough offensive on his front. He wrote in his diary: "What will History say regarding this action of the Americans leaving the British zone of operations when *the decisive battle* of the war is at its height, and the decision still in doubt!" He needed the Americans, but he could only persuade Pershing to leave two divisions temporarily with him.

The 33rd Division was the most experienced of the three divisions which left the British in late August. While the men of the 78th had not seen any front-line service, various units in the 80th had, including some who had participated in the closing days of the offensive begun on August 8. Yet, none of these units could match the record of the 131st Infantry. The commander of the Prairie Division, George Bell, Jr., a portly gentleman with a white goatee, could be proud of his men. Up to this point Bell had not actually commanded the 33rd in battle, but he had kept a tight rein on all aspects of division affairs other than tactical operations. In the process, Bell took a controversial step when he relieved the commander of the 65th Brigade and placed him under arrest during a routine training exercise in mid-July.

Many officers were relieved at various levels of command during World War I. National Guard generals were particularly vulnerable under the severe scrutiny of regular army superiors, but what makes the case of Henry R. Hill unique is that Hill took the option of commanding a combat infantry battalion as a major rather than more sedate office work as a colonel. A bachelor who owned a furniture store in Quincy, Illinois, Hill had been active in Guard affairs since he enlisted as a private in 1894. By the time of the Mexican border call-up, he was a brigadier general, and he held that rank throughout the early days of the war when many other Guardsmen were losing theirs. The official account of his relief remains in records still closed to public scrutiny in the National Archives. According to one version, the immediate cause for his relief was that Bell found some of the men in Hill's brigade not wearing steel helmets, contrary to the division commander's explicit orders. It will never be known how effective Hill would have been as a brigade commander in combat, but it is known that he was killed on October 16 while leading his battalion in the 128th Infantry Regiment, 32nd Division, and that he won a Distinguished Service Cross.

The two divisions, 27th and 30th, which stayed with the British throughout the rest of the war were commanded respectively by John F. O'Ryan and Edward M. Lewis. Another West Point classmate of Pershing's, Lewis had demonstrated his abilities as commander of the army infantry brigade in the Second Division during the fighting in the early summer. O'Ryan, who turned forty-four in August, was not only the youngest man to command an American division for an extended period of time during the war but also the only National Guard officer to remain in such a position throughout the war. A trim, athletic lawyer whose abiding interest was the military, O'Ryan, unlike Lewis and many other senior regular officers, was a graduate of the Army War College, where, incidentally, he had known George Read. He had also been a division commander on the Mexican Border. By mid-September, these generals and their troops had already experienced some fighting on the British front, and presumably they were ready to carry their load in the fall offensives.

On four successive days, September 26 through 29, the Allies launched offensives against the Germans. First, the American First Army and the French Fourth struck between the Meuse River and Rheims. On September 27, the British moved out in the Cambrai sector. The following day, the British Second Army, the Belgians, and some French divisions jumped off in Flanders. As the last of these drives, the British Fourth and the French

First Armies attacked the Hindenburg Line in the vicinity of St. Quentin. The 27th and 30th Divisions, as part of the British Fourth Army, shared the mission of breaching this formidable defense line. For this battle, General Rawlinson, the Fourth Army commander, combined the II Corps with the Australian Corps. This meant that Sir John Monash commanded the Americans as far as operations were concerned, with Read present as an observer.

The key terrain feature in the sector was the St. Quentin canal, a legacy of the Napoleonic era. When possible the Germans placed their main line of resistance behind this obstacle, but in the particular zone assigned to Monash the canal went underground into a tunnel some 6000 yards long. In his plan Monash recommended that no attempt be made to cross the canal itself but that the major attack be made on the trenches in the tunnel area. Since his own units were understrength and worn, he advocated that the two large American divisions take over the entire corps front of about 7000 yards and make the assault. Rawlinson approved his plan with two qualifications. Where Monash had suggested that his forces should go through not only the three lines of the Hindenburg or Siegfried system but also the Beaurevoir Line, Rawlinson was not as optimistic and limited the objective to a penetration of the third line of the Hindenburg system. The army commander did not want to dismiss the canal from consideration either. Although he did not give the chore to Monash, he ordered the adjacent corps on the right to prepare to cross the canal.

Monash started implementing the plan in his usual meticulous way. In order to ensure that the Americans understood his methods as well as the British technical terms, he assigned 217 Australian officers and NCO's, so that someone who did would be with all American units from corps headquarters to a company post of command. Then he held two conferences, in which he explained with the help of maps and diagrams the plan to the American generals. The attack seemed to him to be a simple matter. After a 60-hour bombardment, during which the British would use mustard gas for the first time, the men and tanks would move straight ahead through the lines. In the tunnel area, the terrain was rolling and posed no significant difficulties. Once the Americans had conquered the third line, the Hindenburg support line, then two Australian divisions would take over the advance and exploit the breakthrough.

There was one significant flaw in Monash's plan: he assumed that the attack would begin from a jump-off position which was then in German hands. Indeed, the projected start line was roughly along the outpost line of the Hindenburg position. Prior to September 29, in the right half of the sector, his Australians pushed the Germans back close enough to the line so that the 30th Division was able to secure the attack position without too much trouble. The 27th Division, which relieved two British divisions in the left half of the sector, was not so fortunate. Since the British had made no effort to take the attack position, this left the 27th with the task of advancing over 1000 yards and of seizing the German trenches before it would be in the proper position.

At 5:30 a.m. September 27, the infantrymen of the 106th Regiment, with the ineffective aid of a few tanks, attempted to gain the proposed jump-off position. Throughout the day, fighting raged about the three German strongpoints: the Knoll, Guillemont Farm, and Quennemont Farm. A reinforced battalion took the Knoll three times and lost it each time. By the end of the day German counterattacks had driven the survivors of the 106th back to their own trenches, except for an unknown number of Americans, some of them wounded, who remained isolated in No Man's Land and within the German line. Monash was dismayed: "The non-success of this operation . . . considerably embarrassed the preparations for the main attack on the 29th."

The dilemma was acute. Already the artillery had its barrage tables computed on the assumption that the Americans had possession of the German outpost line. There was not enough time to prepare new ones which would coincide with the actual situation. Besides, this would mean firing on the lost American parties as well as the Germans. O'Ryan asked for a delay of one day to gain time, and Monash passed the request along with his approval to Rawlinson, but the army commander disapproved. Three armies were involved in this attack, and he refused to change the plan to benefit one division. All he could offer was a few more tanks, the

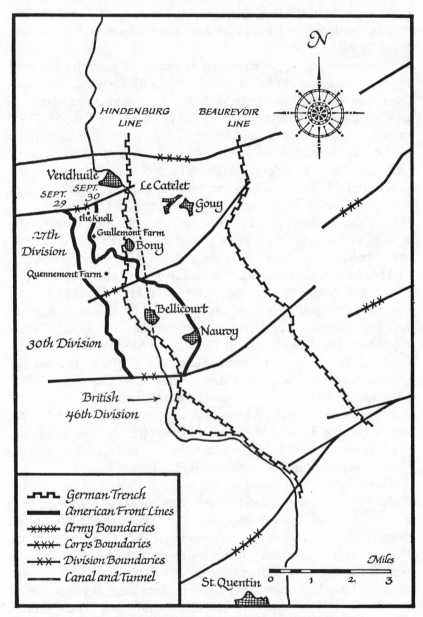

N

HINDENBURG
LINE

BEAUREVOIR
LINE

Vendhuile

Le Catelet

SEPT.   SEPT.
29   30   Gouy

the Knoll

27th   Guillemont Farm
Division   Bony

Quennemont Farm

Bellicourt

30th Division   Nauroy

British
46th Division

German Trench
American Front Lines
Army Boundaries
Corps Boundaries
Division Boundaries
Canal and Tunnel

Miles
St. Quentin   0   1   2   3

THE BATTLE FOR THE ST. QUENTIN TUNNEL

advice to have the 27th attack an hour earlier than everyone else, and the consolation that he was willing to accept partial failure in order to preserve the original plan.

Zero hour was 5:50 a.m., September 29—a foggy Sunday morning. The four assault battalions in the 30th Division left the tape on time and advanced, more or less, on schedule. Because of the fog and smoke, as well as the shock of battle, commanders found it difficult to control their troops, but the men collected in small groups and acted on their own initiative in clearing out machine gun nests and in maintaining the momentum of their attack. With the help of some British tanks, they broke through the main trench line within two hours, and most of them reached the objective during the afternoon. Rawlinson had been callous toward the problem of their sister division, but he had made one decision that worked to the advantage of the Old Hickories when he ordered the 46th British Division to cross the canal. Equipped with life belts, small floating piers, light collapsible boats, mud mats, life lines, scaling ladders, and courage, these Englishmen crossed the narrow canal and threw the Germans off balance on the right of the 30th Division. The left battalions in the 30th did not advance as rapidly because of the difficulties of the 27th Division.

A thousand yards and many well-entrenched Germans separated the New Yorkers from the protective barrage. But this was only the beginning of the problems of that awful day. The British unit on the left lagged and exposed the flank battalion. Tanks, which Monash had used so effectively at Hamel, were not of much help. The American tank battalion (the 301st) was able to get 34 of its 40 Mark V tanks to the battlefield, but those assigned to support the left regiment never gained contact with the infantry. Accurate German artillery fire and a forgotten British mine-field knocked out 16, while the others continued to search for the infantry in the dense fog and smoke. Visibility was so poor that the tankers had to use compasses, some of which were defective, to keep on course. Only one tank actually reached the tunnel line.

The four assault battalions in the 27th Division jumped off at zero hour, and the shouts "All right, boys, *let's go!*" echoed down the line. A soldier in Company A, 107th Infantry, the regiment on the left, recalled the end of the suspenseful waiting: "Cheers, laughter, and the battle cry of the 27th, 'Mineola!' Cigarettes were lit along the line." Amazingly, many of them kept going through the outpost line and on through the main line of resistance. When the men in Company H, 107th, reached these trenches, they threw grenades and then fired at the Germans, who stood up to toss their "potato masher" grenades. With their bayonets, the Americans charged the defenders, who began to run except for one who turned and fought with his bayonet. A soldier parried the thrust and drove his bayonet into the German. Private First Class Raymond R. Williams, who watched the terrible scene, remembered: "The German gave a yell as he dropped that could be heard above the noise of battle. Everyone on the scene of the fight stood still and looked on with bated breath." The other Germans stopped, dropped their weapons, and shouted "Kamerad."

At corps headquarters, Monash sifted the reports. Throughout most of the morning, the messages indicated satisfactory progress, but he was too experienced to assume that the battle was over even when a flyer came back with the information that he had seen Americans on the objective. Only two days before, quite a few men in the 106th Infantry had also reached the objective, but that battle was lost. In the early afternoon, he began to get disturbing reports from the two Australian divisions who were running into stiff opposition as they followed the Americans. Despite his admonitions, the Americans had obviously failed to mop up after their advance units passed through the enemy trenches. The situation was extremely confusing. Some men were on the objective but, in the words of a staff officer in the II Corps: "everybody was fighting everywhere throughout the width of the contested area without there being any well defined front."

What had happened was that, after the American advance had gone past, Germans in the tunnel had come up through hidden passages and emerged on the battlefield behind the leading elements of both American divisions. As one American officer said: "The Boche just seemed to ooze out of the ground." The under-strength, under-officered, and relatively inexperienced American units simply could not handle this situation and needed all the help the Australians could provide. The Diggers managed to secure most of the area in the 30th Division zone, but those on the extreme left of the 27th Division area were unable to reach the German main line.

When Monash learned about this situation, he scrapped his original plan and concentrated on cleaning the Germans out of the town of Bony and the northern end of the tunnel and capturing the remainder of the Hindenburg main line in this sector. He withdrew the American divisions and gave orders to his Australians to attack on the morrow. It would take them two days to achieve the goal he initially had hoped the Americans would reach on the morning of September 29.

That night, in a steady rain, the survivors trudged to the rear. In the machine gun company of the 107th, Lieutenant Kenneth Gow, who would lose his life two weeks later, wrote: "The muster after the company came out was the saddest, most heart-tearing experience I ever want to go through." At the time, no one could know the exact number of casualties; some men were still isolated within the enemy lines, while others were intermingled with the Australians. The 107th, however, did lose over 50 per cent of its assault troops—approximately 1000 men. Apparently, this was the most casualties suffered on a single day by an American regiment during the war.

After a week of recuperation, the American divisions relieved the Australians on October 6. By this time, the Australians had taken the Beaurevoir line. Read was in full command now, and he used the 30th Division to press the Germans. For five days these southerners kept up the advance. As other Americans had learned earlier in the Aisne-Marne campaign, a retreating German army was a formidable adversary. During this fighting, which resolved into the taking of one machine gun position after another, enough men in this division won the Medal of Honor to give the 30th a total of 12 such awards, more than any other division. When the Selle River caused a pause in the advance, the 27th took over the corps front and consolidated the position for several days until the 30th was again ready for action. On the seventeenth, in concert with a general advance along the Fourth Army front, both divisions fought their way across the river. After three days, Rawlinson gave them a respite. Since September 27, the two divisions had lost 13,182 men, roughly divided equally between them, and they had not received any replacements. The 27th and the 30th had done their share and, for them, the war was over.

Both the British and the Australians praised the effort these Americans had spent. Monash later summed up the praise and the criticism in two sentences: "They showed a fine spirit, a keen desire to learn, magnificent individual bravery, and splendid comradeship. But they were lacking in war experience, in training, and in knowledge of technique." In general, Read could agree with that.

The Germans were in a hopeless situation, and they knew it. They simply could not continue to hold out against the Allied offensives. "Unlike the enemy, we had no fresh reserves to throw in," Hindenburg wrote. "Instead of an inexhaustible America, we had only weary allies who were themselves on the point of collapse." On September 28, he and Ludendorff agreed that they must ask the government to seek an end to the war. Almost seven weeks of fighting remained. During this period, in which the II Corps fought its battles, the bulk of Americans were caught up in their greatest battle of the war between the Meuse River and the Argonne Forest.

·X·

The Final Blow

The Meuse-Argonne campaign was the culmination of the American effort. It began with a gamble, continued through days of bloody, hammering attacks, and ended with a spectacular breakthrough. More than a million Americans participated in this battle, and for most of them it was their introduction to warfare. Their inexperience and that of their officers compounded the losses caused by a stubborn and skillful German defense. It was 1926 before the War Department published a final tabulation—26,277 dead and 95,786 wounded.

When Pershing agreed to commit his army to the offensive between the Meuse and the Argonne Forest, he took on a formidable task. Aside from worrying about the difficulties of working out the complex logistical and tactical problems with a staff yet to conduct its first battle, Pershing must have had misgivings when he looked closely at a terrain map of the area. To be sure, the jump-off line was closer to the vital German railroad—Carignan-Sedan-Mézières, a key supply artery—than was any other Allied front. But the configuration of the terrain was in itself an explanation why the French had not advanced in this direction previously, although there had been bitter fighting there during the battle of attrition for nearby Verdun.

The Meuse River, the right boundary, was unfordable and was bounded by a number of hills—the heights which furnished observation and positions for guns to fire into the sector. The left boundary, not quite twenty miles away, was in the midst of the Argonne Forest. The heavy growth and the steep ravines made walking, much less attacking, difficult in the Argonne, while the bluffs, which overlooked the Aire River on the eastern edge of the forest, provided observation and gun positions with advantages similar to those on the other side of the Meuse. While these two terrain features dominated the defile up which the Americans would have to advance, there were ridges and hills such as Montfaucon and various woods in the defile itself. As one would expect, the Germans had made skillful use of the advantageous terrain features when they established four defense lines in the sector. If any attacker succeeded in advancing some ten miles through the crossfire from the heights of the Meuse and the bluffs of the Argonne and in penetrating the first two German lines, he would then be confronted with the main line—the Kriemhilde Stellung or Hindenburg Line—which crossed the right boundary at the Meuse north of Brieulles and passed through the Cunel heights and across the left boundary north of the Argonne near Grandpré. Then, there still remained Freya Stellung along the Barricourt ridge. Afterwards, Drum flatly stated: "This was the most ideal defensive terrain I have ever seen or read about. Nature had provided for flank and crossfire to the utmost in addition to concealment. . . ."

In early September, while most of the First Army staff concentrated on the St. Mihiel operation, Drum assigned others to the task of planning the Meuse-Argonne attack. By September 7, they had a plan which 13 days later, in the form of Field Order #20, became the attack order.

The plan was to overwhelm the Germans and make two deep penetrations through the German lines on each side of the commanding high ground of Montfaucon. Upon the completion of these turning movements, there would be a single powerful thrust through the Kriemhilde Stellung in the vicinity of Romagne and Cunel. The terrain limited the tactical options as did the boundaries. Drum later stated: "There was no elbow room, we had to drive straight through." And they had to do it quickly. The order specified that the assault troops should reach their objective in the afternoon of the first day, and Drum hoped that they would penetrate the Kriemhilde Stellung by the morning of the next day at the latest. This meant an advance of ten miles in one day, double the distance required of the foremost attack divisions on the first day of the St. Mihiel operation.

This was an audacious gamble but one the planners thought that they should make in view of the situation. The terrain was difficult and the fortification system, formidable, but the Americans knew that the sector was lightly held. Intelligence reports indicated that they would face five understrength divisions. Once the attack began, however, Intelligence officers believed that the Germans could bring fifteen divisions into the area within three days. Such reinforcement would make the position virtually impregnable. Pétain had predicted that they might spend the winter stalled in front of the second line at Montfaucon. Unless they hit very hard and very fast, that was a reasonable possibility.

Surprise was essential. Logically, the Germans would expect a continuation of the St. Mihiel offensive in the direction of Metz or Briey; thus there seemed to be a good chance of catching them off guard. In order to fool them, the French and elements of the 33rd Division occupied the outposts in a screen across the front until the night of September 25, and reconnaisssance officers donned French overcoats and helmets when they visited the line. Artillery registration and radio messages were held to a minimum in an attempt to maintain the illusion of a normal quiet sector.

The First Army tacticians also depended heavily on the advantage of strength. Not only did they hope to overwhelm the Germans with nine large assault divisions in three corps but also they expected these divisions to keep pouring more men into the attack. Drum summed up this view in the Field Order: "Deployment will be made with sufficient depth to insure several fresh impulses during the advance and the holdings of the various objectives."

The plan was vulnerable in two principal areas: control and

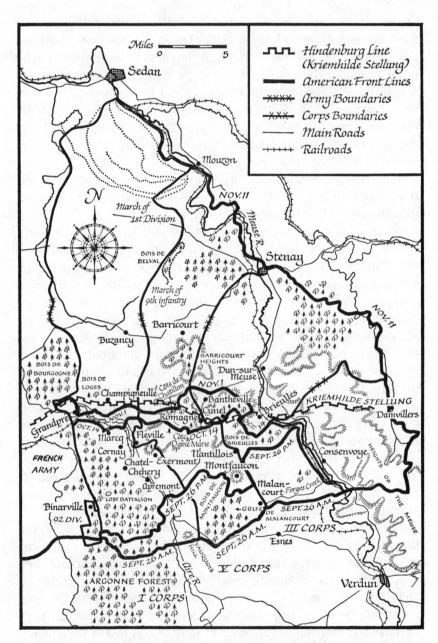

Miles
0 — 5

Hindenburg Line
(Kriemhilde Stellung)
American Front Lines
Army Boundaries
Corps Boundaries
Main Roads
Railroads

Sedan

Mouzon

NOV. 11

March of
1st Division

Meuse R.

Stenay

BOIS DE
BELVAL

NOV. 11

March of
9th infantry

Barricourt

Buzancy

BOIS DE
BOURGOGNE

BARRICOURT
HEIGHTS

Dun-sur-
Meuse

Brieulles

KRIEMHILDE STELLUNG

BOIS DE
LOGES

Côte de
Chatillon

NOV. 1

Damvillers

Champigneulle

Bantheville

Romagne

Cunel

OCT. 14

Grandpré

OCT. 14

NOV. 1

Côte de
Dame Marie

BOIS DE
BRIEULLES

OCT. 14

HEIGHTS OF THE MEUSE

Marcq

Fleville

Consenvoye

FRENCH
ARMY

Cornay

Nantillois

SEPT. 26 P.M.

Chatel-
Chehery

Exermont

Montfaucon

Apremont

Malan-
court

Forges Creek

BOIS DE
MONTFAUCON

SEPT. 26 A.M.

Binarville

LOST BATTALION

SEPT. 26 P.M.

GOLFE DE
MALANCOURT

SEPT. 26 A.M.

III CORPS

92 DIV.

SEPT. 26 A.M.

Esnes

VAUQUOIS
HILL

V CORPS

Verdun

SEPT. 26 A.M.

Aire R.

ARGONNE FOREST

I CORPS

THE MEUSE-ARGONNE OFFENSIVE

transportation. Liaison and communications were always problems in an attack, but with such a large number of divisions, several of them inexperienced, involved in a headlong advance, one could assume a great deal of intermingling and confusion. In an effort to avoid some of this confusion and to assert control, there were intermediate checkpoints established in the form of corps objectives where all divisions were to halt and wait for the lead of the center corps to advance to the army objective—Kriemhilde Stellung. To support the advance, it would be necessary to move artillery and supplies forward. The planners knew that there were only three main roads, each in dubious condition, one in each corps sector, but apparently they hoped the initial attack would drive the Germans back far enough and neutralize the enemy gun positions in the Argonne and beyond the Meuse to the extent that engineers could repair the roads and get the necessary support forward. A failure in either control or transportation would jeopardize the success of the plan.

After the optimistic First Army staff drew up the tactical plan, they had to consider the logistics of moving 222,000 men out of the area and 600,000 into the sector to set the scene for the offensive. On the average, this entailed a move of about 48 miles for combat troops. Drum gave Colonel Marshall the task of planning and coordinating the troop movement from the St. Mihiel concentration to the Meuse-Argonne—a chore involving at least 400,000 men. To simplify the problem, Marshall decided to put the motor vehicles on one road and marching men and horses on two others. This meant splitting up some units, but it would make the most efficient use of the roads. Throughout, he had to work closely with a French captain, Gorfu, to avoid entangling his columns with the French troops coming in the same general direction to build up the French IV Army for its offensive west of the Argonne. Since Marshall usually did not know more than twenty-four hours in advance exactly which units could move, and since he could not foresee such instances as an artillery outfit's losing many of its horses in a shelling just before it was scheduled to take its place on the road, he had to be flexible and to stay close by the telephone. Despite the complications and the necessity of moving only at night, all of the units reached their destinations at the proper time. The Germans, incidentally, did notice that there were some movements in progress, but they were unable to find out enough to interpret the purpose correctly.

An infantryman in the 80th Division, Private Rush S. Young, summed up the march: "Every one and everything was trying to get along at the same time." After nightfall, they boarded trucks or started out on foot. In either case, they were prepared to change places within minutes. Crammed into trucks, unequipped with springs, one soon passed beyond endurance but never became numbed to the jolting and wanted only to get off. Nevertheless, a soldier, slogging for hours through the mud, churned by a cold, steady rain and thousands of feet, could only wish for a seat on anything that moved. Staff officers in autos which splashed mud on the columns gave many men a desire to live if only to meet one of those officers after the war. Some men in the 307th Infantry Regiment never forgot the staff officer who drove up in the rain while they were on a ten-minute break near the end of a twenty-mile hike and sharply ordered them to put out their cigarettes. During daylight the soldiers slept in the dripping woods or in crowded billets and waited for the night and another march.

In the sector, the change-over from French to American control began on September 10, when Bullard moved his III Corps headquarters into the area and the 33rd Division took over a section of the front. As soon as they could get away from the St. Mihiel front, Liggett and Cameron brought their I and V Corps headquarters to the sector. When they received their orders, they learned that each would have three attack divisions in the offensive, with Bullard on the right, Cameron in the center, and Liggett on the left. Meantime, fourteen other divisions marched to their positions on the line or in reserve, and Pershing housed his advance headquarters of First Army in the town hall of Souilly—the building Pétain had used as his office during the Verdun campaign.

On the night of September 25, which unlike the eves of the Soissons and St. Mihiel attacks, was not stormy, the last of the assault troops moved up to the line. Right to left were ranged the following divisions: the 33rd, 80th, Fourth, 79th, 37th, 91st, 35th, 28th, and 77th. The 33rd and 80th had the mission of moving forward to take up blocking positions along the Meuse River at the same time that the Fourth, 79th, 91st, and 35th were making the deep penetrations on both sides of Montfaucon. The 28th was supposed to drive a wedge along the eastern edge of the Argonne, which together with a similar move by the French on the opposite side of the forest would isolate it. This left the 77th and the 37th Divisions with the task of conducting holding attacks strong enough to contain the Germans to their front until the other moves succeeded.

The Fourth, 28th, 33rd, and 77th Divisions were veterans of the summer fighting, but the other divisions were relatively inexperienced. Yet, even in one of these so-called veteran divisions, the 77th, 4000 of the infantrymen arrived within two days of the jump-off time. These were westerners, drafted in July. Since most of their six weeks in the army had been spent in traveling, their training was severely limited. In the 305th Infantry, an enterprising New Yorker earned an easy five francs by demonstrating how to insert a clip into the rifle for the newcomers. One company commander was philosophical about his seventy-two replacements: "They had at least no prejudices to be overcome. . . ." The Pennsylvania, Virginia, and West Virginia draftees who made up the 80th had been in quiet sectors; so had the Guardsmen from Kansas and Missouri in the 35th and those from Ohio and West Virginia in the 37th. However, the drafted men from the Pacific Coast and Rocky Mountain states in the 91st and those from Pennsylvania and Maryland in the 79th actually saw the front for the first time when they took over their sectors on the Meuse-Argonne line. Indeed, over half of the enlisted men in the 79th had been in uniform only four months.

Why were the two least experienced divisions selected to participate in the crucial penetrations in the corps upon which planners had keyed the entire advance? If the plan were to succeed, the 91st and the 79th would have to perform extraordinarily well in their first battle. According to Drum, the officers in the G-5 (Training) Section of GHQ rated both divisions very high. Apparently, on the basis of this glowing report, First Army planners decided to gamble on the two untried units.

Division commanders who were going into their first battle in that capacity were West Pointers Adelbert Cronkhite (80th), Charles S. Farnsworth (37th), and Peter E. Traub (35th), the last another Pershing classmate. All were officers of good reputation, as was William H. Johnston (91st), who had entered the army as a paymaster's clerk. Joseph E. Kuhn of the 79th was a West Pointer with a particularly interesting background. Not only had he been President of the Army War College and considered a possibility for the office of the Chief of Staff of the Army in 1917 but also as an observer at the German maneuvers in 1906 and as a military attaché at the German General Headquarters in 1915–16, he had an unmatched acquaintance with enemy leaders.

At 11:30 p.m. September 25, the long-range guns began firing on the German rear areas. Three hours later, in a terrible burst, all of the artillery—over 2700 guns—opened up. Until 5:30 a.m. (H hour), this shrieking pounding noise and the spectacle of a reddened night sky fascinated the men waiting in the trenches. Dawn came, but fog, thickened by a smoke screen, obscured the battlefield. The preparatory fires lifted as the guns shifted to a rolling barrage. At H hour, officers looked at their mimeographed maps, their watches, and their men, and signaled forward. Along the twenty-mile front, infantrymen started walking. There were no visible landmarks and, at a distance of fifty feet or so, men disappeared into the mist. In the Fourth Division each company commander in the assault battalions had an engineer with a compass to help him stay on course. Occasionally, one heard the sputter of a machine gun, which, together with the light defensive artillery fire, did cause a few men to fall, but the shell-torn ground, overgrown with brush and covered with the tangles of barbed wire, offered the principal impediment initially. It was enough to make some of the attackers lose contact with their protective barrages.

Generals anxiously awaited news. On this line and in this fog, there were no observation posts where they could watch the advance. They could go along with the attacking force and risk the possibility of getting lost or of spending the day as company commanders. The more reasonable choice was to stay at their headquarters with occasional visits to their subordinates' command posts in an effort to maintain control, a course which meant that they had to depend on messages for information. Unfortunately the messages were sometimes inaccurate and frequently out of proper sequence, if they got back at all.

What news there was initially was good. The 33rd Division was able to cross the Forges brook and get to its objective in three and a half hours with the help of good artillery support and an overhead machine gun barrage. The division G-3, Major William H. Simpson, who wrote the attack order, later remarked that while it was a "very ticklish operation . . . it went very smoothly." (In World War II Simpson commanded the Ninth Army.) On almost the entire front, resistance was slight, and the attackers moved steadily forward with few casualties.

In front of Montfaucon, which dominated the sector some four miles behind the German line, however, trouble developed in the zone of the 79th Division. Here the 313th and 314th Infantry Regiments, each with two battalions in the attacking line, early lost the rolling barrage. Thus, when the two companies in the advance of the 313th reached a clearing, called the Golfe de Malancourt, at nine o'clock they were pinned down by Germans in a trench line on high ground in front of the Bois de Cuisy. Machine gunners and snipers thwarted every effort to get across the mile of open area or to flank the trenches. At this time, the men in the sister regiment were unable to help out because they were trying to clear the enemy out of the ruins of Malancourt and other strong points. In the rear, reserve troops ran into enemy machine gunners, which the inexperienced infantrymen had failed to mop up. For several hours, Colonel Claude B. Sweezey tried to get his regiment going again. By midafternoon, after the divisions on either side of the 79th had made the Golfe de Malancourt a salient, Sweezey launched another frontal assault. This time, with the help of French tanks and a flank attack by the 314th, he was able to push through the clearing and into the Bois de Cuisy. The Germans were falling back to Montfaucon, but the 313th was immediately in no condition to take advantage of the situation. Sweezey tried to collect his men, who were scattered in the woods. At dusk, he ordered one battalion, supported by seven or eight tanks, to attack Montfaucon. After 45 minutes in the deadly valley in front of the heights, the French commander of the tanks refused to go on. At 6:45 p.m. it was pitch dark. Although Company K had reached the outskirts of the town of Montfaucon, Sweezey called it back and stopped the attack. The key position on the Meuse-Argonne front remained in German possession.

Two other divisions were involved in the fighting about Mont-faucon that day. In midafternoon, since the fog had lifted, the infantrymen in the 145th Regiment of the 37th Division could see clearly the ruins of the town about a mile away. Although it was in the sector of the 79th Division, these men tried to seize it but were driven back. Later, when Sweezey came up and made his attempt, they tried again but also failed. On the opposite side, the Fourth Division had the most favorable opportunity to capture or to cut off the garrison of Montfaucon.

Why the Fourth did not take advantage of this opportunity was a topic of discussion within army circles after the war. Of course, Montfaucon was neither the division objective nor that of the III Corps. In order to carry out such an operation properly, coordina-tion of the move of the Fourth with the advance of the 79th would have been necessary at army level since the divisions were in different corps. It would have been a dangerous step to turn part of the Fourth into the zone of the adjacent division without mak-ing certain that the infantry and artillerymen in the 79th under-stood what was going on to their front. Given the lack of experi-ence of the 79th and the communications problem of the day of battle, this would have been a difficult task. Anyway, there is no indication that anyone at Fourth Division or III Corps head-quarters considered the possibility until late in the day. Then the move considered was an attack on Nantillois (a town less than two miles behind Montfaucon) by the reserve brigade of the Fourth. In later years, Brigadier General Ewing E. Booth, the bri-gade commander, maintained that his troops could have captured this village and cut off the garrison at Montfaucon on the morn-ing of the 27th. Why they did not illustrates the effect of restric-tive orders carried out inflexibly. For fear of the loss of control, the opportunity was forsaken.

Prior to the battle, when the III Corps attack order reached divi-sion headquarters, Colonel Christian A. Bach, the chief of staff, was concerned about the instructions as to how the Fourth was to assist the 79th. In fact, he later commented that this section of the corps order was "as clear as mud." In his draft of the division order, he attempted to clarify the role by specifying that the Fourth would envelop Montfaucon from the north and the east, but the corps chief of staff, Brigadier General Alfred W. Bjorn-

stad, revised the division order to read that the Fourth would aid
the 79th "not by an advance into the area of the division on its
left but by steady progression to the front. . . ." This was clear
enough, but events during the battle changed the situation.

First, there was an accidental intrusion into the zone of the
79th during the morning by the support battalion of the 39th Infantry Regiment. The advance had begun promptly with a battalion each from the 47th on the right and the 39th on the left in the
lead. Roy W. Winton, who commanded the support battalion,
soon found that the company he had assigned to keep liaison
with the 79th was melting away. The 79th fell so far behind that
he eventually gave up trying to keep in touch with it. By this time
he had another problem: his two advance companies had lost
their direction, despite the engineers and their compasses, and
were drifting straight toward Montfaucon. When he reached
them, they were already in the trench system in front of Montfaucon. One of his company commanders told him that patrols reported the place unoccupied and urged that they take it. Winton
refused because, if this information was wrong, the six or seven
platoons actually available would not stand much chance in an
assault against such a position. Besides, it was in the zone of the
79th; if he was able to take it, his men might be attacked in the
confusion by the 79th. Anyway, he was overdue back in his own
sector where his battalion was supposed to leapfrog the lead battalion. He got back as soon as he could, reported to his regimental
commander, was "chewed out," and, later in the day, was
wounded.

While Winton's men were on the outskirts of Montfaucon, the
rest of the division was making steady progress. Major James A.
Stevens, in command of the assault battalion of the 47th Infantry, reported that he lost only one man to enemy fire in the advance to the corps objective. By 12:30 the lead elements of the
division were on this objective. While he waited with his men, at
this point, Stevens sent patrols to his front into the Bois de
Brieulles. They returned with the welcome news that there was no
enemy in the woods. But orders held the assault brigade to this
line until the center corps reached the same line and was ready to
advance. Unfortunately, at this particular time, the 79th Division,
whose lead the Fourth was to follow toward the Kriemhilde Stel-

lung, was over three miles behind the Fourth in the vicinity of the Golfe de Malancourt. For five hours the men of the Fourth waited. During the afternoon, Stevens watched enemy infantry and batteries of artillery move into Nantillois, a little over a mile to his left in the zone of the 79th. He opened fire on them with his machine guns and one-pounders, but his weapons were no match for those of the Germans, who returned the fire with more effect. Meantime, Germans also came back into the Bois de Brieulles. At 5:30, the brigade moved forward on corps orders, but it was too late. Without artillery, the infantrymen could not budge the Germans to their front.

Even though this attack was not successful, there was another possibility: the lead brigade could serve as a base for an attack against Nantillois by the reserve brigade. General Hines realized this and telephoned corps headquarters for permission. The corps chief of staff gave his approval but later retracted it. (After the war, Bjornstad told Pershing that he regretted having done this.) It was after midnight before the change in orders reached the reserve brigade then marching to the attack position. Booth was embittered at what seemed to him to be the loss of a great opportunity to knock the Germans off balance early on the morning of the 27th. Although the 79th captured Montfaucon by noon on that day, it took that division another twenty-four hours to take Nantillois. Whether or not Booth's attack would have had a major influence on the course of events is a matter of speculation. Certainly, if successful, it would have given the Americans Nantillois a full day before they captured it. But it is unlikely that such a move would have prevented the stalemate that developed. A local victory at Nantillois could not have untangled the traffic on the vital supply roads across the old No Man's Land.

Hope of success in the terms of the original plan went aglimmering on September 27. "Where it had been possible, twenty-four hours before, to walk upright," Colonel Bach noted, "the men now had to crouch or crawl. . . ." When Pershing sifted the news of the first day and the ominous reports of the stiffened German resistance, he ordered a continuation of the attack. The III and I Corps had performed relatively well and, in both cases, apparently they could have made further progress, had the attack order not held them at the corps objective. Even in the center corps, the 91st had advanced eight kilometers and the 37th had done as well as one could expect. But the 79th had not lived up to expectations, and their failure to achieve a spectacular gain in their debut at the front held the other divisions back. Too much had been asked of these "green kids," as an experienced artillery officer called them. Indeed, too much had been required of the First Army. For the remainder of the month, the divisions beat against the Germans and slowly pushed them back. Casualties were heavy and, in a few cases, organizations began to disintegrate as the constant fighting took its toll.

The division which lost the most men in this period and its cohesiveness as a unit was the 35th. Whether there were 8000 or 7000 casualties (as the division historian asserts on different pages) or less than 6000 (the War Department figure), everyone agrees that the division had a difficult time in this battle. The first day went well. The Guardsmen took the strong point of Vauquois Hill and seemed to be well on their way up the Aire River valley, but they faced the crack First Guard Division, and these troops, the best German soldiers on the Meuse-Argonne front, began to react strongly. The 35th continued to advance, but under this severe pressure an internal problem developed to such proportions that it brought about disintegration of the unit.

Friction between regular officers in key positions and Guardsmen racked this division. (Among the Missouri Guardsmen was the commander of Battery D, 129th Field Artillery Regiment— Captain Harry S Truman.) While this friction existed in nearly all Guard units, the other divisions were able to work out a relationship with which people on both sides could live. The 35th, however, never had the opportunity because of a profound shake-up during mid-September. In the few days before the battle the commanders of both of the infantry brigades, three of the infantry regiments and one of the artillery regiments, and the chief of staff were replaced. Obviously, the new officers did not have the time either to learn their jobs or to gain the trust and cooperation of their subordinates. Thus, the division went into battle not only with new leaders but also with bitterness, since Guardsmen blamed regulars for these changes.

The 35th was supposed to advance rapidly during the offensive. The success of their mission depended upon excellent internal communications as well as liaison with adjacent divisions. Since so many officers were new and since the division had not gone through the open warfare training with maneuvers which should have prepared it for this task, the result of heavy fighting —five attacks in four days—should have been predictable. Individuals fought well, but organizations virtually ceased to exist as heavy losses of company and field grade officers severely damaged the chain of command. On one occasion, the night of the 27th, the commander of the 139th Infantry Regiment went forward, got lost, and wandered about the battlefield for over twenty-four hours until he found the command post of the 28th Division. While he was lost, his replacement could find neither the regimental command post nor the regiment when he hunted for both on September 28, nor was the location of either known to brigade or division headquarters. Even the brigades became so intermingled that there were no infantry units available for support or maneuver. Near Exermont, on the 29th, when the Germans stopped the division's last attack and drove the survivors back, the 35th reached its limit of endurance. Early on the morning of October 1, the First Division relieved the exhausted men. Except for a stint on a quiet sector, the war was over for the 35th Division; however, the controversy was just beginning. An army investigator, who did not spare regulars in his criticism, blamed "poor discipline, lack of leadership, and probably poor preparation," but to people in Kansas and Missouri it was simply a case of misuse of the division by regulars. Objectively, when one considers the division's lack of open warfare training and experience and the recent turnover in command and staff positions on top of the regular–National Guard friction, it is amazing that the Kansans and Missourians did as well as they did.

The Provisional Squadron, Second Cavalry and the American light tank brigade, commanded by Lieutenant Colonel George S. Patton, Jr., supported the 35th. The horse cavalrymen won commendation for their patrol and liaison efforts, but the pioneer armor unit was obviously better suited for this type of warfare. There were 189 French Renault six-ton tanks (141 manned by Americans) available to help the 28th and the 35th divisions. This was not an introduction to battle for the American tankers since they had been in the St. Mihiel campaign but, in the Aire River valley, these men saw their heaviest fighting.

The exuberant Patton had come to France as an aide to Pershing; but in October 1917 when he learned that the AEF was going to have a tank corps he applied for the new service. In his letter he stated his qualifications: "I believe that I have quick judgement and that I am willing to take chances. Also I have always believed in getting close to the enemy. . . ." Before he saw action, he had to train men to fight in this new arm—a chore in which Lieutenant Colonel Dwight D. Eisenhower was also engaged at Camp Colt, near Gettysburg, Pennsylvania. Although Brigadier General Samuel D. Rockenbach was the chief of the Tank Corps in the AEF, Patton was the combat leader of the American tankers.

Tank-infantry teamwork had to be makeshift on September 26, for apparently there was no combined training prior to the battle. As a result, the tanks and infantry fought their own battles at times. For this reason, the tanks captured Varennes at 9:30 on the morning of the 26th but had to wait four hours for the infantry to arrive. During that morning, Patton rallied some infantrymen and led them behind his tanks until he was wounded. After the loss of its commander, the brigade continued in action until its tank repair rate reached 123 per cent—long enough to impress Hunter Liggett, who wrote: "The tank has a great future in war." Much of that future belonged to George S. Patton.

On September 30, Pershing wrote in his diary: "The three things which give me most concern are the roads and circulation, the building of light railways and the communication between corps and division headquarters." After four days of incessant pounding, his army had not yet reached the objective set for the afternoon of the first day. At this point, failures in both control and transportation had reduced the offensive to a struggle for local gains, with the hope that, sooner or later, German morale would crack.

There were two aspects of the control problem. During the first day, the attempt to impose too much control held most of his divisions to the corps objective when they could have picked up another kilometer or so almost without opposition. Then the concern for fixed boundaries had kept the Fourth Division from taking advantage of its opportunity to capture the Germans on Montfaucon. And it was also difficult to get units to do what you wanted them to do at a specific time and to find out promptly whether or not they had carried out their mission. When communications were down between divisions and corps, as Pershing complained, or within the divisions, as in the case of the 35th, it was impossible to coordinate units and to direct the conduct of the battle.

Despite the difficulties of control, Pershing was more worried about his transportation problem. On the three shell-pocked traces called roads, men, horses, guns, trucks, and tractors were snarled in perpetual traffic jams. Wounded, waiting for evacuation, lay in the same place for twenty-four hours, while the trucks and wagons, filled with ammunition and food, inched forward. Engineers and infantrymen worked day and night in an effort to fill in the holes and to strengthen the roadways while others were trying to use them. Trucks bogged down, and men pushed them off the roads. Colonel Carl Penner, the commander of the 120th Field Artillery Regiment in support of the 79th Division, could not forget the frustration of trying to get his 75 mm guns forward. To anyone who was there the reason for the jams was obvious. "The damage was done," as Penner said, "by trying to put too many units through a space that would not accommodate them."

During the initial phase of the offensive, American Negroes were involved in a series of actions which had little influence on the course of the battle but which had broader social significance than the military effort of all of the other American units. The conduct of the 368th Infantry Regiment of the 92nd Division during its five days in the Argonne Forest was long remembered and emphasized, while the excellent records of other Negro regiments were forgotten. Two battalions of this regiment disintegrated and, with some exceptions, the officers and men, despite their relatively light casualties (official army figures were 332), ran from the enemy. Although the first battalion went beyond its orders in making a considerable advance, the actions of the second and third battalions served to stigmatize the Negro soldier and to bolster the belief that Negro officers were useless as combat leaders.

What happened to this regiment of Pennsylvania, Tennessee, and District of Columbia draftees is perhaps less important than why it happened, yet both are necessary to an understanding of the incident.

In June and July 1918, two months after the arrival of the last of the four separate regiments, the 92nd Division debarked in France and began an abbreviated training program. By the end of August it was occupying a quiet sector of the front in the Vosges Mountains. After this tour in the trenches, the division joined I Corps as part of its reserve in the Meuse-Argonne offensive. Shortly before the battle, in a move to strengthen liaison with the French Fourth Army, also scheduled to attack on September 26, Drum asked Liggett to send a regiment to the French on his left. The French would then brigade it with one of theirs so that the bridge between the two armies would be under French control. Liggett selected the 368th and sent it on an overnight march to the French area. In the great battle which began on September 26, this regiment and two machine gun companies in support would be the only units of the 92nd to see combat.

When the regiment went into position, Colonel Fred R. Brown, a West Pointer with nineteen years of service, put his second battalion on the front, held his third battalion in reserve, and turned the first over to the French for use in division reserve. As the officers of the second battalion scattered their men along the lengthy sector of a little over two kilometers, they studied the terrain—heavily wooded and interlaced with undamaged barbed wire. Despite a shortage of maps and wire cutters, they were supposed to make their way through this formidable obstacle. Nevertheless, if the First Army planners were correct, the enemy would fall back and offer little resistance.

For the first four hours of the attack on the morning of September 26, the plan proceeded as scheduled. There was no opposition; yet, because of the terrain and the width of the sector, the battalion commander lost contact with some of his units, which were picking their way through the woods. As the Germans began to resist, the Americans continued to advance but in a disjointed fashion. When darkness fell, the battalion commander ordered a withdrawal to the starting point, apparently in the hope of regaining control over his units. On his left the French had not advanced but the American 77th Division had moved forward on the right.

Colonel Brown attempted to improve the situation the next day by dividing his sector in half and bringing up the third battalion. Despite the appeal of the second battalion commander that the fresh battalion take over the entire sector so that he would have more time to get control of his companies, Brown ordered him to continue in command of half of the sector during the attack.

On the 27th, the Germans provided stiffer resistance, but the third battalion and F and G companies of the second advanced. Again, the second battalion commander lost contact with his units, and this time, with the third battalion as well. After a few hours, G company drifted back to the original position.

For the third time, on September 28th, Brown ordered an advance. On this occasion, for the first and only time during its stay in the Argonne, the 368th received some artillery support—an ineffective half-hour barrage in the afternoon. Twice the second battalion, except for two platoons of F company which did advance, failed to overcome German resistance. After the second attempt the bulk of the battalion fell back in disorder. The regimental commander then relieved the battalion commander. The third battalion fared even worse. It tried two attacks, but both times its officers and men ran back to their own lines.

On the fourth day, the French sent the 9th Cuirassiers in to take over half of the sector. The following day, Brown withdrew the two battalions and replaced them with the first battalion. Although he was not under orders to attack, the first battalion commander, Major John N. Merrill, a soldier of fortune who had briefly attended West Point and had served as an enlisted man in the American army, as an officer in the Philippine constabulary, as chief of the Persian gendarmerie, as a colonel in the Persian army, and as a captain in the British Indian army, kept up with the advancing Cuirassiers. For more than three kilometers to a point beyond Binarville, this white officer forced his men forward, according to him, at times at pistol point. In contrast to the other battalion commanders, this experienced soldier maintained not only control over his men, albeit in a ruthless manner, but also liaison with the units on each flank.

The immediate consequence of the actions of the 368th was

the relief of the 92nd from the Argonne front. While the regiment had been fighting, First Army had turned over the entire 92nd Division to the French, who planned to use it to replace one of their divisions. After the debacle, however, the French corps commander changed his mind and returned the division, including the 368th, to First Army, which sent it back to the rear areas.

As the white regimental commander and battalion commanders tried to explain the problems of the 368th, they promptly laid the blame on Negro officers. All three battalion commanders considered the Negro company officers, with some exceptions, incompetent cowards who could not control their men. Colonel Brown endorsed this complaint, and General Ballou relieved thirty officers as unfit to command troops. The third battalion commander, who wanted more drastic action, preferred formal charges of cowardly misconduct in the face of the enemy against five officers. Court-martial boards convicted all five, sentenced four to death by firing squad and one to life imprisonment at hard labor. Later all five were freed.

In turn, Negroes pointed out the good work done by some of the Negro officers—a few in the regiment even won the Distinguished Service Cross—and accused the second and third battalion commanders of cowardice and incompetence. But whites were running the army, and the debacle to them simply confirmed the general belief that Negro officers could not command combat troops.

In 1919 the army held an investigation of the affair. After listening to the various white and Negro witnesses, the investigating officers concluded that the reasons for the trouble in the Argonne were the inexperience of the unit, the difficult terrain and wide sector, the lack of sufficient maps and wire cutters, the change in mission from liaison to attack, and the lack of artillery support. They also indicated in their report that "the operations would have been more successful had the majority of company officers shown more individuality and personal resourcefulness." Apparently the board did not censure the commanders of the second and third battalions, although their competence seems a more than debatable point.

The board and, in 1923, the Historical Section of the Army War College tried to make an objective analysis of the conduct of the 368th, but both groups of officers failed to grasp the underlying fact which caused the unit to have difficulties. Their minds apparently were closed to the effect of racial prejudice on the operation of the regiment and the division.

Bullard, by then a lieutenant general and commander of the Second Army, recommended clemency for the convicted officers in the belief that "these Negroes could not be held as responsible as white men," and thus supplied unwittingly the key to the problem in his candid memoirs. Bullard obviously believed that Negroes were inferior and when he visited the division following its service in the Argonne, he found that the ranking officers agreed with him. Except for Ballou, he wrote: "Not one of them believed that the 92nd Division would ever be worth anything as soldiers. Every one of them would have given anything to be transferred to any other duty. It was the most pitiful case of discouragement that I have ever seen among soldiers."

Certainly, the white officers of the 368th shared this attitude. They put their contempt and distrust of Negro officers on record, while the first and second battalion commanders added that they also questioned the value of Negro combat troops generally. Long before the battle test, Negro officers and men were aware of this attitude and the general animosity. First Lieutenant Howard H. Long, a Negro with a master's degree in experimental psychology from Clark University, was at the headquarters of the second battalion during the battle. Twenty-five years later, he wrote, "Many of the field officers seemed far more concerned with reminding their Negro subordinates that they were Negroes than they were with having an effective unit that would perform well in combat." In such an atmosphere morale was low, and the whites and Negroes were not able to develop a relationship to withstand the difficulties of the situation in the Argonne. As Long concluded, "Only a miracle could have achieved that."

The dissimilarity of the Negro officers in this regiment also contributed to the lack of cohesiveness of the unit. Although all were company grade officers, some were middle-aged, while others were in their early twenties. Then, there was a bloc of over thirty former regular army enlisted men. While some of these men had attended college, many others, who were semi-literate, did not have much in common with the younger college contingent. One second lieutenant with twenty-five years in the ranks had been in the army before some of the younger men were born. In the college group there were more than twenty men who had attended or graduated from various colleges and universities. Besides Long, another first lieutenant had a bachelor's degree from Amherst and a third had attended Harvard for three years. Spanish War veterans and long-time regular non-coms, lawyers and teachers, and even two former officers of the Liberian Frontier Force—they were hardly a homogeneous group.

The major casualty of the incident was the concept of Negro combat officers. After all, the army considered the use of Negro officers as an experiment, and, on the basis of the experience of the 368th, it could consider the experiment a failure.

Although by law Negro officers were equal to white officers, in practice, they were second-class citizens. When the 368th boarded the *George Washington* to sail for France, the Negro officers were assigned to second-class quarters, while the white officers had first-class staterooms. Throughout their service, Negro officers frequently did not have the privileges to which their rank entitled them. At times whites barred them from officers' clubs and refused to allow them to stay in officers' quarters, while many white enlisted men refused to salute them. It seemed that white superior officers, from the commanders of the three separate regiments which had some Negro officers through the various units in the 92nd Division, had one standard policy—to get rid of Negro officers as soon as possible. The argument against Negro officers centered upon their inferiority and their inability to gain the confidence and support of their men. Thus the 92nd, which started out with 82 per cent of its officers Negroes, had 58 per cent Negro officers at the end of the war. Pershing later expressed the standard opinion of the whites: "It would have been much wiser to have followed the long experience of our Regular Army and provided these colored units with selected white officers."

Colonel Charles Young, the West Point graduate who was the senior Negro in the service, summed up the attitude of the Negro officers: "The black officer feels that there was a prejudgment against him at the outset, and that nearly every move that has been made was for the purpose of bolstering up this prejudgment and discrediting him in the eyes of the world and the men whom he was to lead and will lead in the future." In a letter he wrote in

1920, General Ballou corroborated this view: "It was my misfortune to be handicapped by many white officers who were rabidly hostile to the idea of a colored officer, and who continually conveyed misinformation to the staff of the superior units, and generally created much trouble and discontent. Such men will never give the Negro the square deal that is his just due."

The war did not end for the 92nd when it left the Argonne, yet the few weeks it spent in the quiet Marbache sector and even the advance one brigade made on the last day of the war were anticlimactic. Minds were made up. In the future the whites would emphasize the failure of the 368th in the Argonne and forget the achievements of the four separate Negro infantry regiments. On the very days in late September that the 368th had its difficulties, the Negroes in the 369th, 370th, 371st, and 372nd were carrying out successfully their missions in general attacks with the French in Champagne and the Oise-Aisne sectors. And the 370th was officered largely by Negroes. The French praised these regiments but white Americans chose to remember the 368th.

The Negroes who had hoped that the war would give them an opportunity to demonstrate their loyalty and to bolster their appeal to the whites for reforms were disappointed. The wall of prejudice was too high. Even well-meaning northerners could not rise above stereotypes. On July 26, 1918, an editorial writer on the Milwaukee *Sentinel,* when he praised two of the separate Negro infantry regiments, wrote: "Those two American colored regiments fought well, and it calls for special recognition. Is there no way of getting a cargo of watermelons over there?"

Too few whites grasped the vision which Dr. W. E. B. Du Bois described the month the war ended: "We did love our country because we deemed it capable of realizing our dreams and inspiring the greater world . . . all loved and loved passionately not America, but what America might be—the Real America, as we sometimes said." A half-century later, Negroes would still be awaiting the fulfillment of this dream.

When he reminisced about the war, Pershing wrote: "The period of the battle from October 1st to the 11th involved the heaviest strain on the army and on me." Although the German government approached Woodrow Wilson with a request for an armistice during this period, this did not lessen Pershing's immediate problems. His army still fought to reach the objective set for Sepember 26. While the Germans were unable to reinforce their Meuse-Argonne sector as much as the American intelligence service had anticipated, they had strengthened their force to nine divisions and elements of three others. Transportation across the old No Man's Land remained a serious problem, and influenza began to run its course. During the damp, cold weather of the week which ended on October 5, some 16,000 soldiers came down with the disease.

Under pressure from Foch, Pershing set 5:25 a.m., October 4, as H hour for a general attack. Its basic purpose was to penetrate the Kriemhilde Stellung and to seize the high ground behind the line. He gave Bullard the task of capturing the Cunel heights with his three divisions—the 33rd, Fourth, and 80th. In the V Corps, Cameron had two experienced and fresh divisions, the Third and 32nd, to take the heights northwest of Romagne. On the left, Liggett had the mission of capturing the formidable Argonne bluffs and the ridges north of Exermont with the 77th, 28th, and First Divisions. This time the order specified that the corps were to advance independently; there would be no holding back as there had been on the first day of the offensive.

It was another foggy morning when the Americans again started forward. By the end of the day, Pershing knew that the attack had not achieved its aim. The German guns east of the Meuse helped keep Bullard's corps from reaching its objective, and machine gunners and accurate artillery fire held down the advance of the other two corps.

The First Division gained the most ground on this day, as the Sixteenth Infantry fought its way four kilometers up the Aire River valley to Fléville. But the Germans in the First and Fifth Guard Divisions, among the best in the German army, made this advance costly. By one p.m. the third battalion of the 16th had only two officers and 240 men left of the 20 officers and 800 men who started that morning. Despite the heavy punishment from gas, shelling, and machine gun fire, the units of the First held together.

Lieutenant Maury Maverick of the 28th Infantry Regiment described the shelling: "We were simply in a big black spot with streaks of screaming red and yellow, with roaring giants in the sky tearing and whirling and roaring." The sensation of an over-head shell burst was unforgettable: "There is a great swishing scream, a smash-bang, and it seems to tear everything loose from you. The intensity of it simply enters your heart and brain, and tears every nerve to pieces." Before the day was out, Maverick was wounded, but he survived to become a prominent Texas Con-gressman in the 1930's.

On October 5, the American divisions renewed the attack, but the heights of Cunel and Romagne were again beyond their reach. North of Montfaucon, the Third Division was unable to make much progress toward Romagne. Some of its artillery, however, did move closer to the front.

In the Eighteenth Artillery Regiment, the adjutant, First Lieu-tenant Frederick T. Edwards, spent the morning at headquarters. While he waited in the concrete dugout, he wrote his father and described the day: "The first real fall morning I've seen since I've been over here. It's not yet nine o'clock; there's been a heavy mist all night which the sun is trying to burn away. The woods are very blue and hazy and one rubs his finger tips every few minutes to try and keep them warm." Early that afternoon, Edwards started forward with six men and a wagon toward the advance headquar-ters. When the group reached Montfaucon, Edwards and the ser-geant major left the others behind. About 75 yards from the ruined church at Montfaucon, a 77 mm "whiz-bang," a high explosive shell, hit within eight feet of Edwards. He half-turned and fell; the uninjured sergeant-major yelled and the rest of the party ran up to the lieutenant. Edwards regained consciousness briefly, pointed to his groin, and said: "I'm hit here, Silva," to one of the sergeants. They carried him in a blanket to a nearby aid station as the shells fell about them. It was about 4:15 p.m.

After a dreadful ambulance ride, during which Edwards was conscious, he reached an American Red Cross hospital at Fleury-sur-Aire at 11:00 that night. He had lost a lot of blood from his eight wounds, three of which were in his lungs, and was cold. Nurse Marjorie L. Work dressed his wounds and gave him a stim-ulant. As she washed his face and hands, he spoke of his parents and his half-sister. Just before the litter-bearers took him into the operating room, the nurse asked if he wanted her to write his family. He was obviously pleased: "Will you!" and gave her their address. Within fifteen minutes he was dead: one among the 1366 of the Third Division who lost their lives in this battle.

Although the attacks on October 4 and 5 were not successful, the wedge which the First Division drove into the German lines provided the base for a solution to two problems which plagued the I Corps. Since the second day of the month, seven companies and two machine gun sections of the 77th Division had been trapped near Charlevaux Mill in the Argonne about a half-mile within German territory. Despite Alexander's efforts, he had been unable to reach these men in the so-called "Lost Battalion." Something had to be done about those men. Then, the Germans still controlled the heights in the Argonne and were able to hurt the First Division with their artillery fire on its left flank. If a large American force could attack westward into the Argonne from the base line Fléville-La Forge, it could take the pressure off both the First Division and the "Lost Battalion." This would be a daring maneuver, since the right flank of the attack force would be in air—that is, open toward the enemy—while the infantry moved laterally across the front. It would be an imaginative stroke in a period characterized by direct frontal assault.

On Sunday morning, October 6, the idea occurred simultaneously to Liggett and to Colonel Ralph T. Ward of the Operations Section at First Army headquarters. That noon, Drum and Major General McAndrew conferred with Liggett and his chief of staff, Brigadier General Malin Craig, about the move. It was a gamble and, except for Craig, Liggett's staff disapproved, but Liggett, Drum, McAndrew, and finally, Pershing, believed it worth the chance. The decision made, Craig called in the commander of the division in corps reserve and outlined the plan to him. Now it was a matter of execution.

George B. Duncan, who had been in command of the 82nd Division only two days, was somewhat mystified. Craig had not briefed him on either the friendly or the enemy situation; he had merely told him of the plan. In less than sixteen hours, he would have to move a brigade of infantry and his artillery brigade eight miles over a road which the First and 28th Divisions used to capacity and place them in an area neither he nor most of his offi-

cers had ever seen and then attack. This was a task which would
have strained a veteran division. Although the 82nd had served
on quiet sectors and played a small role in the St. Mihiel campaign, it was not a veteran division.

The men started their march to the front that afternoon, while
the 164th Brigade commander, Brigadier General Julian R. Lindsey, and a few officers attempted a reconnaissance. When the
written order came from corps headquarters, Lieutenant Colonel
Jonathan M. Wainwright (later of Bataan and Corregidor fame)
drafted the division attack order. The infantry would take over a
sector between the 28th and First Divisions during the night and
attack without artillery preparation at five o'clock the next morning. This order reached the regimental commanders about midnight while their men were still trying to get through the cold rain
and the heavy traffic on the road.

The assault battalion of the 327th Infantry Regiment and some
of the artillery did reach their assigned positions on time but the
others were late. Altogether only six companies of the entire infantry brigade got into action that day, but they managed to capture two hills on the west side of the Aire River. The next day the
164th Brigade attacked again. During this attack, a corporal in
Company G, 328th Infantry Regiment, Alvin C. York, who was
drafted despite his religious objections to war, singlehandedly
broke up a German battalion. He brought in 35 machine guns and
132 prisoners and left behind possibly as many as 28 dead Germans whom he killed. No one knew exactly how many Germans
he did kill near Châtel-Chéhéry. When General Duncan later
asked him how many he thought he had hit, York replied; "General, I would hate to think I missed any of them shots; they were
all at pretty close range—50 or 60 yards."

It would be some time before the American public would find
out about Alvin York, but the story of the "Lost Battalion" was
already well known. Because of the pressure which the 82nd Division exerted to their rear, the Germans who surrounded the New
Yorkers withdrew. The siege ended on the night of the seventh,
but Major Charles W. Whittlesey, the tall, gaunt Plattsburg graduate, who commanded the "Lost Battalion," waited until the next
afternoon to take his men off the hillside. There were 194 sur-

vivors able to walk away of the 554 who had started out on the morning of the second.

On October 10, the Argonne Forest was in possession of the Americans. The flank attack of the 82nd, together with advances by the 77th and 28th Divisions, cleared this area which had dominated the left of the Meuse-Argonne sector since the beginning of the offensive. Yet, Liggett was not satisfied. His plan had worked, but the thought of what might have been the result if Lindsey had been able to get his full brigade of the 82nd into action on the seventh galled him. Possibly, they could have captured the bulk of the German force in the forest, and they might have prevented the enemy from establishing a strong position at Grandpré and the Bois des Loges, north of the Argonne. Liggett regretted the lost opportunities particularly since, if the attack had reached its full potential, he thought that it could have saved several days of costly, frontal assaults. As his disappointment mellowed after the war, he realized the unusual demands he had made on the 82nd. "However the difficulties were great," Liggett wrote Drum in 1927, "& the Div comparatively green & I think they did well under all the circumstances." In his conception of this daring maneuver, Liggett demonstrated his flair for tactics. He showed his understanding of men and war in his acceptance of the results.

An attempt to seize the heights east of the Meuse was not as successful as Liggett's maneuver to drive the Germans from the Argonne. Since the beginning of the battle, Foch, Pershing, and almost any soldier in the III Corps recognized the necessity of silencing the German guns beyond the Meuse. Finally, Pershing reinforced the French XVII Corps, which had remained in place east of the Meuse up to this time, and ordered it to attack on October 8. Two French divisions, six Senegalese battalions and the 58th Brigade of the 29th Division—Guardsmen from Delaware, Maryland, New Jersey, Virginia, and the District of Columbia—were to attack early that morning. As they pushed the Germans back along the river, three battalions and supporting machine gun troops from the 33rd Division would cross the Meuse on two hastily constructed foot bridges. At first the attack progressed satisfactorily; the men in the Illinois division were able to cross the river without too much difficulty.

That afternoon, as Company D, 124th Machine Gun Battalion, followed the first line of infantry near Consenvoye, Private Clayton K. Slack noticed a couple of Germans carrying ammunition boxes off to his left. When he told his sergeant, the sergeant replied that he would tell the infantrymen. Slack remonstrated that the Germans might shoot them in the back. The noncom retorted: "If you are so damn brave, go after them yourself!" Since he only had a pistol, Slack looked about for a rifle, picked one up from a wounded man, and then started after the Germans. As he came up behind them, he saw that there were three with two machine guns. "Hands up!" he shouted. The startled Germans stood up. Then, as Slack recalled: "Everything happened so fast, before I realized what had happened, there were ten of them. . . ." The private marched his prisoners back to an infantry unit he saw coming forward, turned them over to an officer, and ran to catch up with his company. Undoubtedly, his action saved the lives of many of those infantrymen. After the Armistice, Pershing awarded him a Medal of Honor.

The next day, the attack continued. The Germans, however, not only hardened their resistance but also counterattacked. Both sides received reinforcements, as six more battalions of the 33rd crossed the river and the Germans brought up another division. In the first two days the 33rd gained five kilometers, but for the next week the battle see-sawed at that point as the Germans stopped the advance of the entire XVII Corps.

In this pocket, east of the Meuse, American and French infantrymen fought a desperate battle. German guns to their front and on their right flank pounded them with high explosives and poison gas. Under orders to use gas lavishly, the German artillery put the Americans and the French through an ordeal. The 33rd had the awful distinction of having more men gassed than any other American division (more than 2000). By mid-October, the men in this division were exhausted; many of them had worn their clothes to shreds; the skin on some men's feet peeled off with their filthy socks. They had been on the Meuse-Argonne front for over a month and, since September 26, they had been under constant gas and high-explosive harassing fire. During most of this period they were unable to change clothes or to get water with which to wash. On October 21, Pershing withdrew the 33rd from the line. The Germans still held the crucial gun positions, and they continued to hold them until the last week of the war.

Between the Meuse and the left boundary of the First Army, just north of the Argonne, on October 10, the Americans confronted the Kriemhilde Stellung. After Drum and the First Army operations officers pondered over their maps at Souilly, they decided that a pincer movement similar to the plan for the attack of September 26 might break the German line. Although all seven of the American divisions would attack, the planners designated the Fifth and 42nd Divisions to make the deep drives. Pershing accepted the plan and, in order to conform with a general attack by the French Fourth Army, west of the Argonne, set the date—October 14.

Both Pershing and Drum believed that the key position in the Kriemhilde Stellung was the Côte Dame Marie, west of Romagne. This crescent-shaped ridge, which measured five-eighths of a mile in length, had two prominent hills near each tip of the crescent. If the Fifth and 42nd succeeded in their attacks, the ridge would be pinched off. Nevertheless, Pershing ordered the 32nd Division to attack this ridge three hours before the other divisions would jump off in the hope that this would hold the Germans there and possibly mislead them as to his intentions. He could not expect more of the men in the 32nd. They had been in the fight since the first of the month, in contrast to the Fifth and the 42nd Divisions, which had been at this front only two days.

The 32nd had earned its reputation as a good division in the Aisne-Marne campaign and at Juvigny and suffered over 6800 casualties in the process. In September about 5000 replacements joined the division, but many of these men, drafted in July, were virtually untrained. A company commander in the 128th Infantry complained of his replacements, "with their unfamiliarity with weapons, a gun was about as much use as a broom in their hands." Although the 32nd, even with so many new men, had pushed the enemy back during its first ten days on the front, the Germans on the Côte Dame Marie stopped their advance and held them in place for three days.

The men who had to get out of their foxholes and attack Côte
Dame Marie early on the morning of October 14 probably did not
know that they were supposed to be the bait holding the Germans
in place while the Fifth and 42nd Divisions sprang the trap. The
division had orders to take the ridge, and they intended to do it—
if possible. At first it looked as if the objective would be too much
for them. On the left, the 127th Infantry was stymied as it attempted to get through the wire to the main part of the ridge. In
the center, the third battalion of the 126th Infantry found a gap
in the wire near the southeast tip of the ridge, but they also
learned that the Germans had concentrated their artillery and
machine guns on this gap. A battalion of the 128th, however, was
able to get past the right of the ridge and flank the Germans in
nearby Romagne. This seemed to have little effect, though, on
the Germans, who still had firm control of the formidable ridge.
The men in the 32nd were certainly holding the enemy on the
ridge, but the Germans seemed to be getting the better of this particular action.

What changed the course of the battle was an act of desperation which succeeded beyond all expectations. The third battalion commander of the 126th, after several attempts to get
through the gap in the wire, sent Captain Edward B. Strom and
seven men forward to take the machine guns which covered the
gap. Under heavy fire, Strom and his men worked their way up
the steep slope until they advanced within 150 yards of the guns.
They fired rifle grenades into the German position and then
rushed the survivors. When Strom reported to his commander, he
turned over ten machine guns, fifteen prisoners, and the key to
Côte Dame Marie. The most amazing aspect of this exploit is that
none of the patrol were killed. The rest of the battalion and the
second battalion of the 126th were now able to get on the ridge.
During the afternoon, the 127th also began to move around the
side of the ridge. That night, they found Côte Dame Marie deserted.

Neither the Fifth nor the Rainbow Divisions were as fortunate
as the 32nd that day. Although the Americans did make slight
advances at various points on the line, the projected pincer movement was blocked. Indeed, even though they tried on the next two

days, they could not make the breakthrough envisioned by the
First Army planners. Nevertheless, Douglas MacArthur's brigade
did capture the Côte de Chatillon, northwest of the Côte Dame
Marie on the 16th. With the capture of these two ridges, the dominant terrain features on the Romagne heights, the Americans
had decisively cracked the Kriemhilde Stellung, and Pershing
could say, at last, "The main objective of our initial attack on September 26th had now been reached."

The general attack in mid-October was Pershing's finale as a
field army commander. Earlier he had decided to give up this position and to divide the huge army which held some 83 miles of
the front from Port-sur-Seille, east of the Moselle, to the Argonne.
Since the strength of the First Army had reached 1,031,000 (including 135,000 French soldiers), it was becoming unwieldy. Even
before the St. Mihiel campaign, he had ordered Colonel Stuart
Heintzelman to form a staff for a Second Army. On October 12,
he named Bullard the commander and assigned responsibility to
him for 34 miles of the front, from Port-sur-Seille to Fresnes.
Until the last week of the war, this remained a quiet sector.

Liggett was the obvious choice as the new commander of the
First Army. No one could match him in experience or in reputation as a corps commander. Pershing told him on October 3 that
he would turn the army over to him. Nine days later, the call
came to report to First Army headquarters and to take command
immediately. That night, Liggett dined with Pershing and Drum
on Pershing's private train near Souilly. After a lengthy conference, Pershing deferred to Liggett's request not to assume command until the end of the upcoming battle. This would give him a
few days (until October 16 as it developed) to visit the various
units and to learn the condition of the army. Liggett once wrote:
"War provokes more muddled thinking than any human activity I
know of." He wanted information and time to avoid that problem.

The three corps commanders whose men went into the assault
on October 14 did not have any respite. Dickman hurried from his
corps on the quiet sector in front of the old St. Mihiel battlefield to
take command of Liggett's former corps, while Summerall and
Hines left their divisions to become, respectively, commanders of

the V and III Corps. Muir took Dickman's place in the IV Corps, and others rose to division command to replace the new corps commanders.

Pershing could break men as readily as he could make them. One wrong decision or the appearance of an error could cost an officer his career, and many knew the humiliation of reporting to the Classification Depot at Blois after failing in combat. During the first week of the campaign, Pershing relieved four infantry brigade commanders. Before the end of October, three division commanders and the V Corps commander fell.

The corps commander, George Cameron, never understood why Pershing removed him and blamed his ill fortune on Drum's dislike. The circumstances indicate, however, that Pershing wanted a more dynamic leader, and Summerall was just the man for that role. After all, the V Corps had not lived up to expectation in the initial attack and, apparently, Pershing did not believe that Cameron had done very well since then. The "C-in-C" relieved Beaumont Buck of the Third Division and John McMahon of the Fifth because he thought that they mishandled their divisions in the attacks of mid-October. Buck brought his reserve up too soon, and McMahon withdrew one of his brigades from a salient which he should have held. Then, there were reports of an inordinate number of stragglers from these divisions. Preston Brown and Hanson Ely were Pershing's choices to replace Buck and Mc-Mahon.

The most controversial relief Pershing made during the entire war was that of Clarence Edwards on October 22. Edwards had never been popular with Pershing—who considered him contentious—and the GHQ officers. As early as spring, there had been talk about relieving Edwards, and few regulars indicated any regard for him or his division. Pershing made his move in the form of a letter from McAndrew, in which the chief of staff simply told Edwards that he was needed for a comparable command in the States. Since the 26th was then fighting east of the Meuse, the timing was unfortunate. Although there was no explanation at the time, Edwards had made a report on October 19 that conceivably may have triggered his relief. He had the poor judgment to send to Liggett personally an account of fraternization between two of his soldiers and the Germans. Edwards was impressed by the information the two men picked up during their visit with the Saxons, who told the Americans that the war would soon end and that they did not intend to shoot anyone. Liggett was furious: "To my mind, this constitutes a flagrant case of the most insidious and dangerous propaganda we have yet run up against, its intent being to weaken the fighting determination of our men." Then Liggett ordered Edwards, in this letter on the 20th, to suppress absolutely any such fraternization. Perhaps, on that day, during Pershing's visit to Souilly, Liggett told him of the incident. Whatever the cause, Edwards got the letter from McAndrew two days later. The division resented his removal and aroused many civilians in New England over the treatment of their general. Again, the regular army-National Guard prejudices, at the root of so much friction in the AEF, caused bitterness. Whether or not Pershing was justified in removing Edwards, it is clear that he should not have taken the step in late October and that his personal dislike for the man hampered any objective consideration of his case.

Although Pershing spared Liggett the uncomfortable chore of relieving those division commanders, he left him the task of getting the army in shape to resume the offensive. For three weeks the army had fought hard, and it had paid dearly in lives for the advance of ten miles. Infantry units were understrength, some were disorganized, and many were exhausted. Liggett had to gain time for recuperation.

He was in a much better position to obtain the rest than Pershing. Although he understood as well as Liggett the condition of the army, Pershing by the nature of his position as "C-in-C" was exposed to pressure from Foch and Pétain to keep up the hammering attacks. As long as he was both commander in chief and First Army commander, he did continue the attacks. Even after he appointed Liggett, he pressed him to attack; however, Liggett calmly stated the situation and won the respite. While Liggett never said so, one gets the impression that he thought Pershing was rattled. After several conferences, according to Liggett's aide, Major P. L. Stackpole, Liggett told Pershing to go away and to forget the problems of the First Army. He intended to stage limited attacks to obtain a better base line for a general attack, but he would not continue the constant and costly attacks. Of course, Pershing could not forget, but he did leave Souilly on the 17th.

Four days later, as Liggett requested, Pershing, the army group commander, gave his First Army commander a general directive to attack on October 28. Afterwards, Pershing would visit Liggett and subordinate commanders but, with one significant exception, he left the conduct of the battle up to Liggett.

For two weeks, Liggett, as he put it, "tightened up" the First Army. He began at headquarters where, to ensure better coordination, he instituted daily meetings of the chiefs of artillery, Air Service, and engineers. He also promoted his former aide, George C. Marshall, to the post of chief of operations—G-3. He relieved worn divisions, such as the Fourth and 32nd, and talked with his generals about their problems. The lull in the battle gave them time to restore their units. Liggett and his staff could suggest solutions but the division commanders had to see that their liaison with adjacent units was firm and that communications and control within their commands were in order.

At this time, the thinned ranks of the infantry regiments worried both Liggett and Pershing. No one knew exactly how many men the army had lost in the battle, but on October 19 Drum estimated it at 119,327. This was an overestimate, yet anyone who visited the divisions could see that they were undermanned. Drum thought that three of them—Third, Fifth, and 82nd—had less than 5000 combat effectives. The replacement program did not supply the men, so GHQ broke up seven divisions and used these troops as replacements. In an attempt to balance the strength of his divisions, Pershing authorized a reduction of the rifle company from 250 to 175 men. While many of the companies at the front had less than this number, this move forced commanders of units which had not suffered so many losses to pare their strength so as to provide replacements.

The men most available to fill the ranks were stragglers. Liggett thought that there were as many as 100,000 in the battle zone. In the confusion of the fighting, men lost their units and passed beyond control when company officers and noncoms became casualties. When the Fifth Division took over a wooded section of the front from the Third, a brigade commander in the Fifth estimated that 1000 of the 2100 infantrymen in the Third remained in their foxholes. Although many attacked with the Fifth, they were considered stragglers in the Third. Of course, some men simply wanted to get away from the battle. They could report that they were slightly gassed and hope for evacuation, or they could get on a rearbound detail and not return. Many wandered openly about the rear areas, while others hid in dugouts. Military police and special details patrolled the roads, searched aid stations, kitchens, and the rear area generally. Punishment was direct: they returned the men to the front and sometimes publicly humiliated them by forcing them to wear placards inscribed "Stragglers from the Front Line" on their backs. In a letter to corps and division commanders in late October, Pershing authorized the most drastic measures to stop straggling: "When men run away in front of the enemy, officers should take summary action to stop it, even to the point of shooting men down who are caught in such disgraceful conduct. No orders need be published on the subject, but it should be made known to younger officers that they must do whatever is required to prevent it." This was a last resort, as Pershing realized. In this same letter, he emphasized that junior officers must maintain discipline and control and make certain that their men were well fed. Most of all, the pause in the battle aided the efforts of commanders to regain control of their units and to find their lost men.

The fighting did not stop in the Meuse-Argonne sector during the lull. North of Cunel and Romagne, the Third, Fifth, and 89th Divisions captured segments of the front which Liggett thought necessary for the coming general attack, but the heaviest and most sustained fighting took place on the extreme left in the vicinity of Grandpré. Here the 78th Division went into the assault as its battalions entered the line on the morning of October 16 and, except for a three day break, elements of the division attacked every day until October 30.

Grandpré and its adjacent area was important because of the terrain and because it was near the boundary between the Americans and the French Fourth Army. At this point, the Aire River had cut a gorge through the rugged plateau that dominated, to the south, the Argonne Forest and, in the north, the Bois de Bourgogne. Grandpré was a formidable objective, as the chief of staff of the 78th, Colonel Herron, said, because it was "very difficult to get at it." An attacking force would have to cross the Aire River, swollen with the steady fall rains, and then capture the thirty-foot high cliff, the edge of the northern plateau, which protruded into the town itself. Even then to control the pass through the plateau, infantry would have to seize the southern rim of the Bois de Bourgogne ridge and the Bois des Loges, a wooden hill, less than a mile square, which lay to the northeast of Grandpré. If the Americans could capture these positions, they would probably help the French to advance, and then they would have an avenue of communications—the first substantial one beyond a road seventeen miles to the rear—with Gouraud's army.

When Major General James H. McRae took his division forward to relieve the 77th on the night of October 15, he could not tell his men exactly where the Germans were. Alexander reported that his division had captured Grandpré, but apparently he did not furnish guides to conduct the incoming troops to their positions. During the night, while the infantry slogged through the cold rain, McRae received orders to attack at 6:00 a.m. There was not enough time to get these orders to all of the units; thus there were disjointed attacks on the next morning in Grandpré, where there were some Germans despite Alexander's claim, and the Bois des Loges. By the end of the day, the 78th had units in the town and on the edge of the Loges woods, but these men were literally fighting for their lives.

For four days, the battle see-sawed in hand-to-hand fighting. McRae, another Pershing classmate, was a man who, as Herron commented, "feared neither God, man, nor the Devil or General Pershing either." He would frighten his aides by getting close to the fighting; yet, despite his personal efforts and the courage and determination of his men, he could not force the Germans out of their defenses. On the night of the 19th, he straightened his front by the withdrawal of his men from Bois des Loges and the slopes of the Bourgogne plateau. This move also strengthened his connection with the 82nd, which was fighting on his right. After three days he sent his infantry forward again. By October 27 he could report—at last—that Grandpré was firmly in American hands— not only the shattered houses but also the cliff, or the "citadel" as it was called, and the southern rim of the Bourgogne plateau. Determined enemy machine gunners, however, still clung to the Bois des Loges. The experience of the 78th, earned at the cost of some 4000 casualties, showed clearly that the German grip had not weakened. There had been some hope that, under pressure, the enemy might pull back. At the end of the month, McRae could testify that this had not been the case on his front.

Despite their stubborn defense, the German units, war weary and understrength, could not hold on much longer. While the soldiers in gray could balance their weakness to a certain extent with the skill developed in four years of war, they could not hope to regain the initiative. As a soldier in the 103rd Division wrote in a contemporary letter: "Germany is standing only on one foot and is already tottering; she will crash down. . . ." Let there be no misunderstanding, however, the German soldier was still a formidable adversary. Any American doughboy who was in the Meuse-Argonne campaign would testify to that.

The Germans knew how to make the most skillful use of terrain; to turn fields, hills, and woods into death traps. In front of the Fifth Division near Cunel, they placed their men in camouflaged foxholes on the open slope of a wooded hill. Naturally, the Americans shelled the woods at the top of the hill and left the hidden machine gunners ready to cut down attackers. And one reason why the 78th Division found the Bois des Loges such a difficult objective was because the Germans had located their machine guns near the high center of the woods, where they could fire over the trees and onto the open fields. The Americans presumed that the gunners were on the edge of the woods, bombarded that section, and then wondered why the infantry came under such heavy fire as they crossed the fields.

The neophytes did fool the experienced Germans on one crucial point. They shielded their preparations for the offensive so well that the Germans misconstrued their intentions. Ludendorff and General Max von Gallwitz, who commanded the army group which fought against the Americans, believed that they would move toward Metz and, at first, thought the attack of September 26 a feint.

The Americans amazed the Germans because of their strongly massed attacks and their seeming lack of concern about heavy losses. Lieutenant General Wellmann, whose I Reserve Corps fought elements of the French Fourth Army and the American First Army in the Argonne and at Grandpré, was impressed by the difference between his two enemies. The French attacks were weak and the poilus appeared to be exhausted, while the Americans possessed "still unused nerves, were fresh, eager for fighting, and brave." But they did lack experience, as Wellmann noted. When they gained a partial success, "they did not understand how to use it to advantage. . . ." When German intelligence officers interrogated prisoners from the 82nd Division, they reported that the Americans showed little interest in military and political affairs, but they did find some resentment toward volunteers on the part of a few draftees they captured from the Rainbow Division. The most impressive fact about the Americans, as far as the Germans were concerned, was that there were so many of them.

Letters which Americans took from prisoners indicated the conditions on the other side of No Man's Land. A reserve infantry lieutenant and company commander wrote on October 16: "Clouded prospects wherever one looks. Really has everything been in vain? Such a piteous finish—I am losing all interest; a quick end is to be hoped for; there is nothing more to be saved." At home, the blockade, the strain of a long war, the many casualties, and the reverses produced an attitude far different from the enthusiasm with which many Germans had greeted mobilization in 1914. In a woman's letter, dated October 27, which the Americans found on a soldier, intelligence officers noted this comment: "It seems apparent that the dawn of peace is drawing nearer, and we dare entertain more hopes that this the most hideous of all wars, this vile murdering, which scorns and derides all humanity; which places us, no matter how highly cultured we pretended to be, lower than the savages, will end sometime and we can feel that we are human beings again."

Despite this disillusionment, there were apparently not very many revolutionaries among the prisoners or, at least, the prisoners did not profess revolutionary tendencies to their interrogators. In the daily Summary of Intelligence of October 19, the First Army G-2 noted that, upon inquiry among recent captives, his men had found only eighteen Bolsheviks, and these were prewar socialists and former Russian prisoners of war who had come to the Western Front as replacements.

October was a terrible month for the Germans in the Meuse-

Argonne and, indeed, for the entire German army. At the most, all they could do was delay temporarily the enemy advance. The military leaders demanded peace yet quailed in the face of harsh terms. Rather than accept such terms, Ludendorff preferred to continue the war, but the realistic German chancellor dismissed him. At the front, generals could award decorations, congratulate their troops on "victoriously" withstanding the onslaughts, and speak of the sacred value of their fighting, but they knew that the enemy blows were shattering their armies. In front of the Americans at Grandpré, Major General Baron von Quadt, in command of the 76th Reserve Division, told his weary troops that they could not expect relief from the front. Even if withdrawn from this sector, Quadt said on October 21: "in view of present circumstances, the result would be that the division would immediately be sent into line at another point, and most likely a worse one."

Manpower was the critical factor. Ludendorff ordered Gallwitz on October 10 to "put into the fighting front every unit which is at all fit for employment in battle." In order to bolster his line, Gallwitz had to send up fragments of divisions, literally any troops he could find, to the front and had to leave remnants of his original divisions in the fight long after these soldiers expected relief. Because of the injection of these regiments or combat teams as well as the intermingling that resulted from the heavy fighting, a German division commander might have men from five other divisions in his sector. Gallwitz found this be the case in the 52nd Division in early October. During the second and third weeks of that month, Gallwitz lost almost 25,000 men. He could not hope to sustain such heavy losses much longer.

Because the Germans did mix men from various divisions, the Americans had difficulty in determining the number and identification of the enemy units. In the period, September 26 to October 20, the American First Army captured 18,591 prisoners from 36 different German divisions and 3 Austro-Hungarian divisions, but 8 of the German units were represented by less than 10 prisoners and only 17 by more than 100. Throughout the entire campaign, Americans believed that the Germans used 43 divisions against them and that they drew 17 of these divisions from the French front and one from the British front.

Since they did not make the spectacular breakthrough that they hoped to make in late September, the Americans emphasized the heavy manpower demands that they forced on the Germans. Later Gallwitz thought that they overestimated the number of divisions he used against them. Perhaps they did: it is difficult to reconcile such figures. Nevertheless, the Germans had to strain their resources to reinforce the Meuse-Argonne front. At this time, however, they were trying to defend against four different offensives. The British were making more progress than the Americans, French, or Belgians. But as Sir James E. Edmonds, the British official historian, pointed out: "Whatever Foch may have intended, the result was attrition pure and simple." Drum seemed to agree with this in a letter he wrote his wife during the last week in October: "The gaining of ground counts for little, it is the ruining of his army that will end the struggle." In this cruel test, the Germans well understood that the Allies had the advantage. And the advantage was the AEF, which on October 31 numbered 1,867,-623 men, with more on the way.

The French viewed the American difficulties in the Meuse-Argonne campaign with a more or less sympathetic "I told you so" attitude. The lack of experienced commanders and staffs which they had emphasized in the long amalgamation argument was now causing the problems they had predicted.

At Pétain's headquarters, various staff officers frankly expressed their views to Pershing's liaison officer, Lieutenant Colonel Paul H. Clark. On the one hand they recognized the difficulties, but, on the other, they indicted the Americans for using too many divisions in the initial assault. One officer told Clark that the French would have used about half the number of troops that the Americans employed. This density of troops at the front brought about the traffic jams and the general transportation crisis. The French also criticized the poor communications within and between units, the lack of proper staff reconnaissance, and other faults which reflected inexperience.

Pétain's aide for operations, Major General Dufieux, did explain to Clark on the last day of September why the Germans would resist stubbornly in front of the French Fourth and the American First: "were they to be forced back there—at the pivot of their whole line to the north, they would be ruined quickly." Dufieux added that, if the French and Americans merely succeeded in holding large masses of the enemy in those sectors, "that alone will be of great service and hasten the cracking at some other point."

A month later, on November 1, General Buat, Pétain's chief of staff, discussed the American role in the fall offensive with Clark:

> When I learned that your army were to undertake the operations you assumed last September, I said it is prodigious. . . . You made mistakes and had difficulties certainly, but why not? Are you supermen? Are you Americans Gods that you can do the miraculous? If you had not had the difficulties that you did have I would certainly have said you were miracle workers . . . given the conditions that existed—enemy—terrain—degree of training there are no other troops in the world who would have given one half the result that the U. S. army did give.

Others were less generous to the Americans.

Sir Douglas Haig, who was still resentful because Pershing had taken those divisions from him, heard an exaggerated account from Foch's headquarters of the Americans' problems: although the Germans were weak in the Meuse-Argonne sector, the American attack had bogged down and front-line divisions were starving. The American leaders were simply too inexperienced to conduct a major offensive. Nevertheless, as the Field Marshal noted in his diary on October 5: "P. won't allow any of his Divisions to be transferred to another sector, where their presence would at once produce decisive results."

Foch also thought that something should be done about the American stalemate. On October 1, he sent Major General Maxime Weygand, his chief of staff, with a suggestion which infuriated Pershing. To avoid congestion between the Meuse and the Argonne, why not withdraw some of the divisions from that area and reorganize the others into two armies: the French Second which would straddle the Argonne Forest and the American First which would be responsible for both sides of the Meuse River? This would mean restructuring the context of the offensive in such a way that the American command would play a lesser role, although as many American troops would be involved as before, yet in different sectors. Acceptance of this recommendation would also mean the casting aside of the First Army plan. Pershing could not tolerate such a drastic change in his organization and plans and thought that Foch overreached his authority by his interference in a tactical matter. After an exchange of views, Foch agreed to withdraw his suggestion if Pershing would continue his attacks. Perhaps Pershing was still irritated about Foch's letter when he remarked to George Van Horn Moseley, his G-4, on the fifth that, when the Americans had the largest force in Europe, the over-all command would go to an American.

Before the month was out, Clemenceau forced Foch into a defense of Pershing. At the time Pershing was only vaguely aware of this move. It was not until 1931 that he saw the extraordinary letter which the Premier sent to Foch on October 21. The American general's "invincible obstinacy" was an anathema to Clemenceau, who believed that Pershing's demand of an independent army had cost French lives. The old man did not rely on reports of American difficulties; he had visited the Meuse-Argonne battlefield on September 29 and had been caught up in the traffic jam near Montfaucon. In this letter, which he sent against the advice of President Poincaré, he sarcastically denigrated the American effort.

> The French Army and the British Army, without a moment's respite, have been daily fighting, for the last three months . . . but our worthy American allies, who thirst to get into action and who are unanimously acknowledged to be great soldiers, have been marking time ever since their forward jump on the first day; and in spite of heavy losses, they have failed to conquer the ground assigned them as their objective. Nobody can maintain that these fine troops are unusable; they are merely unused.

Then, Clemenceau as French Premier strongly advised Foch as a French soldier to appeal personally in his role as Allied supreme commander to Woodrow Wilson in order to overrule Pershing. Foch interpreted this as an effort to relieve Pershing of command. But in his reply he ignored this implication and merely rebutted Clemenceau's view of the American contribution.

Foch was well aware of American difficulties, but he also knew that they were not unique. The French Fourth Army had not broken through either, and in Flanders the Belgian army, supplemented with three French corps and the British Second Army —an army group under the direction of the French general Degoutte—also had suffered from transportation problems during October. They were literally bogged down in a water-logged area and had to have food airlifted because enough supplies could not get through on the ground. Besides, in his view, what was the point in risking an international row and, if he succeeded in getting rid of Pershing, having to bide time while a successor learned the job?

Three weeks after Clemenceau sent this letter, the war would end. While neither Foch nor Clemenceau could know exactly when the end would come, they knew that it was near. Clemenceau was also cognizant of the American achievement. The day after he sent his letter he profusely complimented Pershing on the success of the First Army. Why then, the letter? In his memoir, Pershing considered it a political rather than a military move: "It was obvious . . . that any attempt on his part to discredit our accomplishments would be purely a political gesture designed to minimize America's prestige at the peace conference." At the Supreme War Council, General Bliss, who also did not know of the Clemenceau letter at the time, however, did sense this attitude. On October 14, he wrote General March:

> from various little indications that have come to my notice, it seems to be somewhat evident that the European allies will attempt to minimize the American effort as much as possible. They think that they have got the Germans on the run and that they now do not need as much help as a little while ago they were crying for.

During the first week of October, the new chancellor of Germany, Prince Max of Baden, had initiated a correspondence about peace with Woodrow Wilson. In the course of this crucial exchange, the Allies were suspicious of German motives, worried about Wilson's aims, and, above all, sensitive of being ignored. Before Wilson invited Allied participation, the Allies consulted together and pondered armistice terms while they awaited the results of the American-German correspondence. Although Wilson conferred with military and naval advisers in Washington, evidently he did not think it necessary to ask Pershing for advice or to give the general any instructions about an armistice.

On October 25, Pershing met with Haig and Pétain at Foch's

headquarters to recommend conditions for an armistice. All advocated evacuation of conquered territory and Alsace-Lorraine, but Pétain and Pershing went further than Haig in their suggestion that the Germans give up bridgeheads east of the Rhine. Haig did not want to impose terms of such severity that the Germans would reject them. The Field Marshal overestimated the capability of the German army and did not believe that the Allied and American forces could win a clear-cut victory before the next year. Foch agreed with the more sanguine generals that the Germans were defeated and would accept harsh terms.

The more Pershing thought about matters, the more feasible he considered a demand for unconditional surrender. Although he was ill with influenza for the next few days, he continued to think about the negotiations. On the morning of October 28, his old friend, Charles Dawes, talked with him about his theories. In his diary, General Dawes recorded Pershing's views: "He is convinced that if civilization is to receive the full benefit of this terrible war it must end only with the unconditional surrender of Germany. The military situation is such that in his judgment there can be no excuse for not obtaining unconditional surrender."

Had Colonel E. M. House, the special representative of the President, been willing to brave a visit to the sick room or had Pershing displayed better judgment, the Americans would have been spared an embarrassing display of conflict between political and military leaders. Pershing had cabled promptly a report of the conference at Foch's headquarters. In response, Wilson commented on each of the general's recommendations and indicated that he did not fully approve of them. Nevertheless, he directed Pershing to "feel entirely free" to bring up any matters he thought should be considered and to consult with House. Pershing misinterpreted this to take the license to present his case for unconditional surrender directly to the Supreme War Council. House was as astounded as Prime Minister Lloyd George and Premier Clemenceau. Woodrow Wilson wanted a peace based on his Fourteen Points, while John J. Pershing wanted victory.

When Secretary Baker learned of Pershing's usurpation of authority he prepared for the first time during the war a letter of reprimand; however, on November 7, the President vetoed his sending it. In the interim, Wilson had heard from House that Pershing had explained that he merely meant his recommendation as military advice and did not intend to interfere with the political deliberations. The President accepted Pershing's miscue as a naïve gesture and was willing to forget it. Throughout the war he had allowed Pershing to act virtually as the American proconsul in Europe. In the delicate pre-Armistice negotiations when the general lacked clear-cut instructions, Pershing had gone too far.

Preparations for the renewal of the offensive in the Meuse-Argonne continued during the talk of peace. The plan Liggett adopted was similar to that of September 26, as, indeed, the general configuration of the terrain with heights in the center resembled that the American army faced on the first day. The V Corps, still in the center position, would try to penetrate deeply, while the I and III Corps, on the left and the right, would support the center corps. The objective, however, was more realistic than that of September 26, since Liggett expected the V Corps to make a five-mile advance. Pershing approved this plan and set October 28 as D day.

Three days prior to the jump-off date, Liggett went to see Gouraud in order to coordinate his attack with that of the French Fourth Army. When Gouraud explained that his army could not attack that soon, the two generals agreed on November 1. Apparently, what both Pershing and Liggett construed to be a difference in their plan from that suggested by Foch did not cause any trouble in the discussion. In his general directive Foch had recommended a pincer movement to conquer the Bois de Bourgogne, with the French on the left and the Americans on the right. Liggett did not believe that this maneuver would be as advantageous as a thrust toward Barricourt heights. If he succeeded in capturing the Barricourt heights, he could force a German evacuation of the entire Meuse-Argonne sector rather than merely the Bois de Bourgogne. Besides, he thought that the Germans anticipated the pincer movement.

Since the American front was four miles shorter than the jump-off line of September 26, Liggett employed seven divisions rather than nine. These were all experienced divisions: 78th, 77th, and 80th in Dickman's corps; Second and 89th in Summerall's corps;

and the 90th and Fifth under Hines' command. Although the 78th, 89th, and 90th had been in continuous action for ten days or more, Liggett believed them capable of taking part in the offensive. Ely brought the Fifth Division to the front on October 27, and the others took their places on line a day or two before the attack.

Liggett used the extra time Gouraud's delay had provided to ensure that his army was ready. Behind the front, service troops stockpiled supplies and repaired the roads. In the combat units, officers and men went over their plans and, if necessary, drew new equipment. Liggett called in the corps commanders and coordinated their plans; the corps commanders checked with their division commanders; and on down the chain of command, officers made certain that others understood what to do.

The infantryman needed as much help as he could get. Throughout the campaign, the Germans had used gas effectively, while the Americans had hesitated to use this fearful weapon. Liggett thought it would help the foot soldiers if he ordered gas barrages. He only had fifteen tanks, which he gave to the Second Division, while the air units were ordered to concentrate their support in the center sector. Finally, he gave Summerall 608 guns to blast a path through the German lines.

Proper coordination between artillery and infantry had been a persistent problem. In part this resulted from inexperience, but the fact that the artillery brigades were used interchangeably contributed even more to the difficulties, since it meant few had the opportunity to work together with the same infantry units over lengthy periods. Because of the emphasis on shipment of infantry, some divisions did not have their artillery. On this occasion, only three of the assault divisions would have their integral artillery with them. Liggett and his subordinate commanders did what they could to improve coordination.

In the V Corps, which would lead the attack, Summerall exhorted his men. Day after day in late October, he talked with the troops in his two divisions. In these brief speeches which he gave to each battalion, he resembled a football coach firing up a team before a game. "There is no excuse for failure." "No man is ever so tired that he cannot take one step forward." "The best way to take machine guns is to go and take 'em! Press forward." Such phrases had the desired effect, according to men who were there.

At 3:30 a.m., November 1, the intensive, final preparatory artillery fire began, but this was not the beginning of artillery preparation. For days the huge 14-inch naval guns, mounted on railroad cars, had hurled 1400 pound projectiles some twenty-five miles into German rear areas. Rear Admiral C. P. Plunkett sometimes caused problems in the army chain of command, but his guns did help the army artillery harass the enemy. Then, during the last two days of October, the artillery gassed the Bois de Bourgogne. This deluge of 41.4 tons of gas knocked out nine of the twelve German batteries hidden in the woods and neutralized that area.

The assault battalions of the spearhead divisions—the Second and the 89th—waited in the cold, foggy early morning hours for H hour at 5:30. In the two Marine regiments and the 23rd Infantry, there were not very many left who had been on the Belleau Wood-Vaux front in June, but there were enough veterans to season the ranks. The men in the lead battalions of the 353rd and 354th Infantry Regiments had been fighting for days in this sector and were hopeful that this attack would crack the German line.

In both divisions, the technique of the jump-off illustrated the advantages of experience. In the past the Germans had moved machine guns close to the American line to evade the barrage. To catch these gunners, the Second Division infantrymen withdrew 500 yards behind the front, while the artillery fired for ten minutes on the forward area. The 89th also succeeded in misleading the Germans. Instead of forming the assault troops along the obvious jump-off line at the edge of a woods, these experienced leaders placed the men, under the cover of darkness, in the open field in front of the woods. When the Germans concentrated their counterfire on the woods, they missed the infantrymen.

Once they started, the attackers did not meet as much resistance as they had anticipated. The Marines and infantrymen in the V Corps closely followed the barrage and captured all objectives on schedule. Machine guns did cause temporary delays in some areas, but individuals such as Lieutenant Harold A. Furlong of the 353rd or small groups put them out of action. By nightfall the Second Division had penetrated over five miles, and the 89th on its right made almost as much progress. The III Corps carried its supplementary objectives, as did the extreme right of the 80th Division in the I Corps, but the rest of Dickman's corps did not advance.

Dickman was worried. While his mission was, in part, to stage a holding attack, he expected the 77th to capture Champigneulle and the 78th to drive the Germans out of the Bois des Loges. Despite the terrific shelling—over 16,000 high explosive and phosphorus rounds but no gas—the Germans in the woods were able to stop a brigade of McRae's division. Apparently those in Champigneulle were not subjected to such a heavy concentration, and thus were able to fend off Alexander's attacks. But the success in the center permitted Liggett to discount Dickman's problem. Liggett thought that the penetration would force a German withdrawal.

The Germans had planned to fall back to the Meuse but had not set a time for this retreat. The attack on November 1 made the decision for them. When the Americans overran four divisions (two of them first-class units), the Germans tried to establish a new line. By the time the Fifth Army staff officers had plotted this line on their maps, the American Marines were in possession of part of it. That night, the Germans evacuated Bois des Loges and Champigneulle. On the following days, they withdrew so fast and so far in front of Dickman's corps that, even though he used trucks to carry his infantry, he could not catch up with the Germans.

In the pursuit, the First Army had to make a change of direction. With the Fifth Division as a pivot on the Meuse River, the other six divisions wheeled to the northeast in great concentric arcs toward the Meuse. Private Rush Young in the 80th Division was awed by the devastation: "As we advanced, the roads and fields were strewn with dead Germans, horses, masses of Artillery, transports, ammunition limbers, helmets, guns, and bayonets." Again, the muddy roads were congested and caused delays in supplying the rapidly advancing infantry. In the 309th Infantry Regiment (78th Division), the soldiers lived on "goldfish," as they called canned salmon, for two or three days until regular rations caught up. This was a mere inconvenience for the men who were glad to be moving forward after the stalemate at Grandpré and the Bois des Loges.

The success of the First Army generated enthusiasm in the high command. Pershing and Liggett were pleased; Foch was complimentary; and Lieutenant Colonel Clark noted the great difference in attitude at Pétain's headquarters. Pétain, himself, talked with the liaison officer and remarked on the reports of the observers:

> These officers inform me that a very remarkable improvement has taken place, that there has been a conspicuous absence of difficulties which occur[r]ed in the advance of September 26th; road movements occur in order, orders in all the units are given well and timely, and . . . that the already splendid advance can yet be continued because of the excellent manner in which the whole affair has been managed.

Although Pétain probably did not know of this, an incident on the night of November 3 demonstrated the difference between the American performance at this stage of the battle and that in the initial phase. On September 26, the Americans had failed to take advantage of the Germans when they did have them off balance. This time, though, the Second Division was not bound by restrictive orders and so was able to take advantage of a promising situation.

The Ninth and 23rd Infantry Regiments had made a night march and had relieved the Marines on November 2. After a successful attack in the morning, the infantrymen were near the southern edge of the Bois de Belval. Although the men were tired from lack of sleep and constant marching, the officers thought that they would save lives if they could get through the woods before the Germans had time to establish their positions. The brigade commander, Colonel James C. Rhea, received a hasty clearance from General Lejeune, and then ordered the Ninth to make a night march through the woods and to set up a defense perimeter on the northern edge.

At dusk, Lieutenant Colonel Milo C. Corey formed his men in column of twos behind an advance guard and started across the field toward the woods. He recalled: "One or two machine guns started to open on us but were quickly rounded up or chased away by patrols. . . . Heinie was just sneaking back into the positions our artillery had shelled him out of. But he was about five minutes too late. We had the jump on him." For six and a quarter hours, the silent column marched in the drizzling rain. They could hear the Germans in the woods but ignored them unless they were on the road. The lead battalion under L. T. Janda, a twenty-two-year-old major, did surprise and capture a couple of small German units and just missed seizing a division commander. At 10:45 p.m. the column reached its objective and began digging in. These infantrymen had marched for some four miles into the enemy lines without a single casualty. The men were exhausted, but their spirits picked up when the supply people began distributing the hot coffee and food they had brought along in their carts.

The Ninth had eliminated Belval Woods as an obstacle and, on the next day, the division joined the advance regiment beyond the woods. Lejeune was so pleased with this tactic that he used it successfully on the next two nights. Admittedly, the Germans were demoralized and preparing to withdraw, but the skill and imagination of this veteran division undoubtedly saved lives and speeded up the German withdrawal.

As the First Army pursued the Germans to the Meuse, Sedan became an increasingly attractive goal. Because of its historic significance (no Frenchman could forget the crowning defeat there in 1870), Sedan had great sentimental value. The Americans were aware of this and accepted a change in boundaries which placed Sedan in the zone of advance of the French Fourth Army. Yet, as the pursuit progressed, the First Army approached the town faster than the French, and Pershing received what he considered permission from the French Army Group commander, General Maistre, to disregard the boundary change if the situation justified it.

Pershing wanted the First Army to take Sedan. In what could well be the final move of the war, he wished perhaps to demonstrate in this way the superiority of his army to that of the French. Whatever the reason, he sent Fox Conner, his G-3, to

First Army headquarters to give that army the specific mission of capturing Sedan.

When Conner reached Souilly at 5:30 on the afternoon of November 5, he saw neither Liggett nor Drum but informed George Marshall, his counterpart in the First Army, of the "C-in-C's" desire and dictated a memo to this effect for Marshall to send to Dickman and Summerall. A few minutes after Conner's departure, Drum came in, and Marshall explained the change in plans and showed him the memo. After both Marshall and Drum added to the memo, the former telephoned the message to the two corps headquarters.

Subject: Message from the Commander-in-Chief

1. General Pershing desires that the honor of entering Sedan should fall to the 1st American Army. He has every confidence that the troops of the 1st Corps, assisted on their right by the 5th Corps, will enable him to realize this desire.

2. In transmitting the foregoing message, your attention is invited to the favorable opportunity now existing for pressing our advance throughout the night. Boundaries will not be considered binding.

When he received this, Dickman interpreted it as Pershing, Conner, Drum, and Marshall meant it to be interpreted. He assumed that Pershing had made arrangements with the French and that he should press toward Sedan, which was in the direct path of the I Corps. On his left, next to the French, Dickman had just placed the Rainbow Division. The 42nd would move straight ahead against the town, while his right division, the 77th, would continue toward the Meuse. If necessary he could call on Summerall for help, but he thought that he would not need to do so. The enemy was falling back rapidly and probably would be unable to put up much resistance. Then, the personal element entered the situation: Dickman and Summerall were not friends and, possibly, the older man was somewhat jealous of Summerall's recent successes.

Summerall, however, gave the message a radically different interpretation. Although Sedan was some seven miles distant from his left flank and out of his zone of advance, he assumed because

of the statement—"Boundaries will not be considered binding"—
that Pershing was calling for a race to Sedan, not just between the
French and the Americans but between his corps and Dickman's.
After thinking it over during the night, he went to the headquarters of his left division shortly after two o'clock on the afternoon
of November 6 and ordered his beloved First Division to move as
rapidly as possible on Sedan. Then, he ordered the Second Division to prepare to follow the First. He could not give Brigadier
General Frank Parker, the commander of the First, information
as to the exact location or the plans of the I Corps. In a shocking
lapse of military judgment, Summerall had not contacted Dickman in the twenty hours since he had received the message.

The First Division was tired. During the previous night the infantrymen had gone without sleep as they marched to relieve the
80th Division. Throughout the night of the sixth, they had advanced almost four miles against slight resistance. For 8000 of
these soldiers, the replacements who had joined in the last half of
October, this was their first battle. Some of the men did not share
the enthusiasm of Summerall and Parker for a dash to Sedan.
When Parker took his place at the head of one of the infantry
columns that night, he was disgruntled by the criticizing, swear-
ing, and grumbling he heard from the ranks. Another long march
on muddy roads in the cold rain, another night without sleep, and
the prospects of having to fight on the morrow obviously did
not inspire all these doughboys.

But march they did. Five columns started out after dark in a
northwest direction. A battalion of the 16th Infantry moved along
the Meuse River across the front of the 77th and 42nd Divisions,
while the other four columns trudged on generally parallel routes
through the rear areas of these divisions. Altogether, in the two
sleepless days and nights, beginning with their relief of the 80th
Division, these men marched an average of more than thirty-
three miles.

By daybreak they were beginning to meet men from the 42nd
Division. Apparently Parker did not expect to find anyone but Germans. He had made no provisions for informing either the 42nd
or the 77th Divisions of his march, although he had sent messen-
gers to the I Corps and the Sixth Division. But the Sixth was not
where he thought it was, and apparently no one at corps head-

quarters believed it was necessary to relay this information to Menoher and Alexander, the commanders of the Rainbow and Liberty Divisions.

When the First Division arrived in the 42nd Division area, the Rainbow troops were preparing for the final push to Sedan. Major Cooper D. Winn, the commander of the machine gun battalion of the 84th Brigade, was startled to see unidentified but evidently American infantrymen to his front and was unable to place his guns. Upon inquiry, he learned that they were members of the 16th Infantry. His brigade commander was also surprised. Douglas MacArthur, when he heard that the First Division troops were in his area, informed his subordinate commanders and then went to the front to make certain that there would be no clash. As he crossed a field on his way to the command post of the 168th Infantry, he was stopped by a patrol from the 16th Infantry and had to identify himself. Meantime, General Parker arrived in the area of the 83rd Brigade and set up his command post. He told a lieutenant colonel in the 166th Infantry that he was going to advance on Sedan without regard for the Rainbow plans. By this time, the 26th Infantry Regiment, under Lieutenant Colonel Theodore Roosevelt, Jr., who had recovered from his wound, was in front of the French troops beyond the left flank of the Rainbow.

In the course of the day, the 16th and the 28th Infantry Regiments also fought the Germans, and the former attained the distinction of getting closer to Sedan than did the rest of the First Division. During the morning, the first and second battalions of the 16th drove the Germans off Hill 252 and reached a point about 2500 yards from their goal. There was some intermingling with the Rainbow, and members of the "Fighting 69th" (the 165th) also claimed that they took that hill. At any rate, Americans were in a commanding position in the environs of Sedan, but repercussions of the First Division's remarkable maneuver were piling up.

The French complained; and Menoher reported the situation "intolerable" as he explained in his report of November 8: "The consequent confusion resulting was very great, particularly in view of the already congested conditions of the area, the bad roads and the difficulties of bringing forward ammunition and supplies. . . ." Dickman was furious. He told Menoher to take command of all troops in his sector and then ordered Colonel Henry J. Reilly, the commander of the 83rd Brigade, to find Parker and tell him to get his men out of the area. Before Reilly reached Parker's advance headquarters, Summerall had arrived. He seemed surprised to find Rainbow troops all about and ordered Parker to withdraw his division.

Liggett did not know about the activities of the First Division until the morning of the seventh when he heard about the French complaints. In another surprising lapse of judgment, neither Drum nor Marshall had mentioned Conner's visit and the message which they sent to the corps headquarters. For the only time during the war, by his own admission, Liggett completely lost his temper. When he went to Dickman's headquarters, he regained his own composure as he attempted to calm down Dickman. He did not find Summerall at V Corps headquarters, but he bluntly told the chief of staff that the action of the First Division was "a military atrocity." When the chief of staff tried to blame the memo, Liggett would not accept this argument. According to his aide, P. L. Stackpole, the gist of Liggett's comments were "that no reasonable interpretation of the paragraph about limits would permit of the atrocity of marching one division across the front of another in pursuit of the enemy. . . ." He then left word that Summerall should make a written statement immediately.

Summerall and Parker in their reports pleaded innocent. The corps commander wrote that he thought he was merely complying with orders, while the division commander emphasized his "entirely single-minded purpose to cooperate fully and entirely unselfishly with our comrades of the 42nd and 77th Divisions. . . ." Although Liggett was not satisfied with their statements, the fact that a disaster did not result, combined with the end of the war, caused him to drop any punitive actions. But he later told Stackpole that he would never trust Summerall in a matter in which sentiment was involved and that he thought Parker's limit was a regimental command.

When Pershing visited Liggett and talked about the incident on November 9, he seemed to be amused by the rivalry between the First and 42nd Divisions, and he gave the impression that he did not consider the matter to be serious. In his memoir, he blamed the affair on Summerall's misconception of the order and praised the First Division for its "fine spirit."

What happened on the road to Sedan was that personal feelings and relationships took precedence over professional training and common sense. Pershing wanted to beat the French; Summerall wanted his corps, and the First Division in particular, to beat the rest of the American army; Parker who had successively commanded, within the First, a regiment and brigade and now the division itself, wanted the honor for his division without regard for the rest of the army. In each case, the individual was not placing primary emphasis on the military requirements of the situation. As Clarence R. Huebner, who made the march as a lieutenant colonel, later commented: "Someone was glory hunting. An army officer is dangerous when he begins to be a glory hunter."

Almost twenty-five years later, in July 1943, General Omar Bradley relieved the First Division commander (Major General Terry Allen) and his assistant (Brigadier General Theodore Roosevelt, Jr.) because they, like Summerall and Parker, put the First Division on a pedestal and found it difficult to subordinate their regard for this division to the general interests of the army. The man selected to make the First understand that it was a part of the army was the then Major General Huebner.

In addition to the question of loyalty to a division, there was also the matter of staff loyalty. Drum and Marshall had served under Pershing in the Operations Section of GHQ and while he commanded the First Army. When word came from Pershing they responded directly, without first clearing with their present commander or even later informing Liggett of the rather radical change in mission until trouble resulted. Of course, Pershing was the Commander-in-Chief; nevertheless, as army commander, Liggett should have been told. In this situation Drum was more at fault than Marshall since he was the chief of staff, but evidently both men let their personal relationships with Fox Conner and John J. Pershing cloud their professional judgment.

Fortunately for the Americans the Germans were in no condition to take advantage of their mistakes. General Wellmann, whose corps was opposite the American I Corps, showed no knowledge of the confusion in the American lines. When reports came in that front-line troops had identified the 16th Infantry, he merely assumed that the First Division had come into line and did not speculate beyond that fact. He had too much on his mind anyway. On the afternoon of November 4 he had inspected the defensive positions on the Meuse River line near Sedan and found that there were virtually no preparations made for his infantry. He did not think that he could hold this line after the Americans brought up their artillery.

Farther up the river near Brieulles, the American Fifth Division had already established a bridgehead across the Meuse. This was a particularly difficult operation since they had to cross an open plain, the river (about 82 feet in width), then another plain, and finally a 65-foot-wide canal—all under enemy observation—before they could reach the German positions. Lieutenant Colonel Courtney H. Hodges, who commanded the second battalion, Sixth Infantry, managed to get Company E across the river in the early morning darkness of November 3. But the Germans pinned down these men between the river and the canal for forty hours. After several attempts, Company E, reinforced by Company G, finally forced their way over the canal after dark on November 4. During the following day, the three other infantry regiments aided by the Seventh Engineers joined Hodges's two companies and drove the Germans off the heights. In this attack Captain Edward C. Allworth, Company M, 60th Infantry, found two of his platoons stalled at the canal. He rallied these soldiers, jumped in the cold water, swam the canal, and led his men in a successful attack on Hill 260. He became the second officer in the 60th to win a Medal of Honor; the other was First Lieutenant Samuel Woodfill, who captured three machine guns and killed more than eleven Germans three weeks before near Cunel. Hodges, incidentally, commanded the First Army during World War II.

The Americans were across the river in strength, and there was little hope of stopping them. On November 6, General von Gallwitz watched through his field glasses the infantrymen of the Fifth force their way through the woods between Murvaux and Fontaines more than two miles east of the river. Just the previous afternoon he had received orders from Supreme Headquarters to prevent further crossings "at all costs" and to make every

effort to drive the Americans back across the river. Gallwitz knew
it was pointless to ask with what.

The German armistice delegation crossed the French lines on
the night of November 7. A misinformed public celebrated the
false armistice, but the war continued. The Kaiser abdicated, and
revolution erupted in Germany, while the French and the Americans prepared for another offensive on November 14 toward the
Briey-Longwy area which would pick up where the St. Mihiel
campaign had ended. Meantime, Pershing ordered his armies to
keep up the pressure. The Second, 89th, and 90th Divisions attacked across the Meuse, while the Fifth, reinforced by a regiment from the 32nd, continued its advance. Farther to the southeast, the 79th, 26th, and 81st also pressed forward. Then, on the
last full day of the war, Bullard put his Second Army in motion
with an attack by the 33rd, 28th, Seventh, and 92nd Divisions.

At 5:10 a.m., November 11, the Germans signed the armistice
agreement in Foch's railroad car. No Americans were present—
only French and British officers; yet Americans held 21 per cent
of the front (83 miles) and had two million men in France, more
than the British on both counts.

For once Pershing was not sensitive about being unrepresented.
He spent the morning in his office at Chaumont with Lieutenant
Colonel Lloyd C. Griscom, whom he had known earlier as minister to Japan when he, a captain, was the military attaché. As the
hands of the clock neared eleven he walked to the large map and
described the plans for the Briey-Longwy offensive and mused
aloud: "I suppose our campaigns are ended but what an enormous difference a few days more would have made."

At the front, more men died. By the time word reached the
combat divisions, some attacks were already in progress. When a
II French Colonial Corps staff officer telephoned the news to Colonel Charles D. Roberts, chief of staff of the 81st Division, Roberts
asked what he should do about the attack. He was told: "Continue
the attack and get as far as you can." In at least two divisions, the
Second and 89th, advance units did not get the message until
after eleven o'clock and continued fighting.

In the cities and towns of the United States and the Allied nations, people joyfully celebrated. At the front the reaction was

more subdued, for many men were too tired to cheer or were perhaps too thoughtful. Stunned is probably the best description of
those who actually heard the silence when the guns stopped. Several days later, there would be time to pose for photographs por-
traying the enthusiastic response of the fighting men to the news
—at least that was what happened in the 27th Division, according to General O'Ryan.

There was not supposed to be any fraternization, but in the
124th Machine Gun Battalion, 33rd Division, a lieutenant asked
his men if any of them wanted to go over to see the Germans.
Private Clayton Slack and a German-born soldier volunteered and
crossed No Man's Land. After a pleasant chat and an exchange of
souvenirs, Slack and his buddy started back. A big jack-rabbit
jumped up and, before he thought, Slack pulled out his revolver
and started shooting at it. Fortunately, men on both sides saw
what happened; otherwise, as Slack ruefully admitted: "I could
have started the war all by myself."

During the night men built fires and welcomed their warmth,
for the weather that day was cold and bleak. They marvelled at
the magnificent pyrotechnic display as the artillery fired multicol-
ored flares for hours.

At Souilly, Drum described the exploits of the First Army in a
letter to his wife and concluded: "All the hard hours of study at
Leavenworth & those spent here have borne fruit and my reward
is now at hand."

In the hospitals, Armistice Day was little different from preceding days: casualties still came in, and doctors worked with them.
In a base hospital in Nevers, Captain Charles L. Bolté was recu-
perating from his chest wound of September 29. A man came into
the ward and announced that the war was over. The lieutenant in
the bed next to Bolté made the only comment: "What the hell do
you know about that?"

·XI·

The Stacking of the Arms

While Woodrow Wilson met with Allied leaders at the Versailles Peace Conference, the military forces which gave him that opportunity adjusted to peace. After the Armistice, men who had spent nineteen months developing and maintaining the huge force of 4,800,000 soldiers, sailors, and marines had to consider the complex task of demobilizing most of those men, terminating business contracts, and disposing of the surplus camps, bases, and war matériel. It was 1923 before the last troops left Germany. Despite the plethora of statistics and conjectures, what the war experience meant to Americans is immeasurable in exact terms.

Men returned to civil life rapidly. Within two months after the end of the war, the army had discharged 818,532 of its war strength of 3,703,273, and by the end of June 1919 more than 2,700,000 soldiers had picked up their discharge papers, a uniform, a pair of shoes, a coat, and the $60 bonus. Those who had served overseas also could take a helmet and gas mask as souvenirs. A veteran of the 27th Division, Sergeant Hugh B. Griffiths, summed up the experience:

> We finally returned home—came back to our loved ones
>   and friends.
> We paraded a bit.
> We ate some.
> We partied much.
> We were mustered out.
> *Fini,* Machine Gun Company, 107th Infantry.

During the months following the war, morale was a problem in the AEF. Most of the men would not be able to return home until spring, and army routine became dreary indeed when there seemed no point to it for the civilians in uniform. To keep them busy, GHQ prescribed drills. Raymond B. Fosdick, chairman of the Commission on Training Camp Activities, reported on the results:

> To see a Battery that has fired 70,000 rounds in the Argonne
> fight going listlessly through the movements of ramming an
> empty shell into a gun for hours at a stretch, or training the
> sights on an enemy that does not exist, is depressing enough to
> watch, and its effect on the spirits of the men is apparent. They
> seem to wilt under it. The same is true of infantry drill in the
> muddy roads, up and down which columns of American soldiers
> trudge listlessly and without spirit.

After several weeks Pershing relented and instituted sports contests and educational programs to take up some of the time. The best athletes eventually participated in the Inter-Allied Games in Paris in the summer of 1919. For those soldiers who wanted to learn to read and write or learn a trade or medieval history or a wide variety of subjects from first grade to college level, the army provided instruction. An estimated million and a half took advantage of this opportunity. Many took courses while still on duty with their units. Others went to various schools including the AEF University at Beaune as well as several French and British universities.

There was also a morale problem among the professional officer corps. The War Department stopped promotions on Armistice

Day. Although a few did receive promotions later, most lost their wartime rank when the army deflated to peace strength. Drum and Preston Brown became majors, Hanson Ely a lieutenant colonel, and many generals had to accustom themselves to leaves or eagles after wearing stars. Meantime, boards of officers studied the war and tried to discern its lessons, while staff officers toured the divisions and gave lectures on the achievements of the AEF. Pershing also went on a round of the divisions and inspected his troops at formal reviews.

Schools, sports, and military "spit and polish" still did not drive the dominant thought from doughboys' minds—when do we go home? The mud, the poor accommodations, and the waiting at Brest and other ports, one could endure for a berth on a homeward-bound ship. During May and June more than 300,000 made the voyage each month. In August the last combat division—the First Division—sailed, and on September 1, 1919, John J. Pershing embarked at Brest.

The "C-in-C" was not the last to go. His one-time G-4, Brigadier General William D. Connor, remained as commander of the American Forces in France, now the liquidating agency for the AEF. These people disposed of property, settled claims, and more or less "closed the books" on the AEF. In the process, one overzealous officer sold 15 tons of records as wastepaper, and it took two more years to trace the records. But this was an exception to the generally satisfactory progress of Connor's work. He was able to follow Pershing home in January 1920 and to leave behind 46 officers, men, and field clerks to handle any remaining business questions and a Quartermaster Corps detail to continue work on the cemeteries.

At this time Americans still stood guard on the Rhine. The Third Army, which actually came into existence after the Armistice, had taken up positions in the Coblenz bridgehead (territory within a 30-kilometer radius of the Pfaffendorf Bridge at Coblenz) in December. Until the signing of the peace treaty in late June 1919, these troops, which numbered more than 200,000, initially under Dickman and later under Liggett, prepared for the possibility that the Germans would not sign the treaty. Pershing dissolved the Third Army on July 2, 1919, and turned over the occupation duties to the American forces in Germany. Major

General Henry T. Allen, formerly of the 90th Division, stayed to head the occupation force, which consisted of approximately 16,000 men in 1920. By the end of 1922, Allen had some 1200 under his command, and they came home in January of the next year. Allen stayed a few more days. When his train left on February 19, it was cold and raining—doughboys long since returned to civilian life would have thought the weather appropriate.

On the Emtsa River in northern Russia, a detachment of American soldiers learned of the Armistice from a Bolshevik who shouted the news to them. Other Americans, several miles away, spent Armistice Day and the next three days beating off "Bolo" attacks at Toulgas. Since September 1918 some 5000 Americans, most of them Wisconsin and Michigan draftees in the 339th Infantry Regiment plus support units, had helped British, French, Canadian, and White Russian troops defend a perimeter around Archangel. Under British command, they fought their hardest battles during the winter of 1918–19. At the same time, another 9000 men, with Major General William S. Graves in command, were in Siberia. Graves had orders not to interfere in Russian internal affairs, and he did not allow Japanese and Allied leaders to dissuade him from this position. Nevertheless, in 1919, Woodrow Wilson directed that Graves's men protect shipments of rifles to a White Russian army and that they guard the railroad, so, despite Graves's objections, the Americans did become involved in the civil war to this limited extent.

These Americans were in Russia because President Wilson gave in to Allied pressure to join in the two expeditions. In his Aide Memoire of July 1918, Wilson stated that the two reasons were to guard Allied war stores and to aid Czechs captured by the czarist armies to escape. During the discussions at the Supreme War Council, the Allied leaders also indicated their hope that they might prevent the Germans from moving the bulk of their forces from Russia to the Western Front. Then, on the part of the Americans, there was the belief that a contingent in Siberia would deter Japanese ambitions. The possibility of crushing Bolshevism occurred to some, but it was not the dominant factor in the American decision to intervene. Although Secretary of War Baker and General March strongly objected because of the diversion of effort from the Western Front, the president overruled them and sent the two expeditions.

Within six months Wilson found that it was much easier to commit troops than it was to extract them. He was able to withdraw the "Polar Bears" from North Russia in the summer of 1919. They had morale problems during the preceding winter and, in one instance, a near mutiny. Their casualties—139 killed in action or died of wounds and 266 wounded—indicated the extent of their fighting. It look longer to bring home the 27th and 31st Infantry Regiments and their support units from Siberia. As late as November 18, 1919, Major Sidney Graves, who had led a company in the Fourth of July parade of 1917 in Paris, won his second Distinguished Service Cross by rescuing noncombatants caught in the crossfire between warring factions in Vladivostok. Although the Americans stayed longer in Siberia and there were more of them than there were in North Russia, their casualties—35 battle deaths and 52 wounded—reflect General Graves's success in holding down the American involvement in the fighting. After a passing threat of war with Japan and the collapse of the White Russian forces, the Americans left Siberia in 1920 with General Graves on the last transport, which sailed on April 1.

Although it is difficult for those who grew up during the Cold War to realize, the traditional pattern of American military history was to reduce the large wartime army to a small force which existed largely unnoticed throughout the years of peace. Despite the attempt by military leaders to obtain congressional sanction for peacetime universal military training and a professional army of a half-million men, they were unable to break this pattern after World War I. By 1925, there were only 135,000 in the regular army, and it was 1936 before the strength increased to more than 140,000. During the 1920's, as George C. Marshall recalled, "the cuts, and cuts and cuts came."

But there was a difference. The spectacular row over air power and the development of an armored force in the postwar period were indications of change, but more basic was the new professionalism of the army. In part this was a result of the war experience, but there was a greatly increased emphasis on the schools and professional training. Although a few officers attended the

Leavenworth schools and the Army War College before 1917, many did not think this training essential. After the war, it was. To succeed in the army as a career, officers had to assimilate the new techniques and learn how to use the new weapons. Men lost their lives in World War I because their officers had to learn in battle. While this is always the case to a certain extent, professional training would lessen the chance of error, if the American army had to fight again.

Hunter Liggett never saw a full division of men together until he attended a review of the 81st Division in April 1919; yet he had studied enough to be able to visualize a division, a corps, and a field army. In World War II, American commanders either had seen large units in action or had studied them thoroughly before they had to make decisions. This does not mean that they refought World War I. The men who tried did not stay in power.

By the 1940's, the only American general of the World War I era most people remembered was John J. Pershing. Although he lived until 1948, his last thirty years were anticlimactic. Congress honored him with the rank of General of the Armies and in 1921 President Harding appointed him Chief of Staff. But after three years, Pershing left that post and devoted his time to a diplomatic mission and his memoirs. He also supervised the work of the American Battle Monuments Commission and frequently visited France, until old age and another war halted his journeys. During World War II, the Chief of Staff, George Marshall, the former chief of operations of the First Army and, afterwards, his aide, would visit him and bring news about the war. By this time Pershing lived at Walter Reed Hospital, where he lingered into his eighty-eighth year. In Pershing's funeral procession, Dwight D. Eisenhower and Omar N. Bradley led the generals of a later war in the long march from the Capitol to Arlington.

The international situation and the resulting strategic problems, the extent and the nature of the American involvement, and the American citizen soldiers themselves were different in World War II. The national commitment was greater in the global war of the 1940's, and the United States played a more dominant role in the Allied war councils and on the battlefields. The men who fought were less provincial than their fathers and did not go to war with unshaken beliefs. The disillusionment of the failure to achieve the goals of the earlier war, the Depression, and the increased awareness of the horrors of war made it impossible to recreate the spirit of 1917–18.

Today, the pain and terror of war, which veterans could not communicate to those who had not seen battle, is visible to anyone who watches television. Fifty years ago, young children gaily waved their flags and thought of war in romantic terms. Now, they see the ugliness and ask questions which are increasingly difficult to answer.

The most popular American hero of World War I was the Tennessee mountaineer, Alvin York. After the war he returned to the Valley of Three Forks of the Wolf, but within a few years improved schools, a paved road, radios, and eventually television destroyed the culture he had known until he entered the army. For forty years, the nation honored him as a hero. But, today, young people, born in the 1940's have lived with the threat of war throughout their entire lives. To some of them, York is interesting, as a recent advertisement on a college campus of his movie biography stated, because of "the paradox of a conscientious objector becoming a mass killer."

With Vietnam in the foreground and nuclear weapons and intercontinental missiles balanced precariously in the background, the American involvement in World War I seems almost quaint. The Civil War consumed more people and definitely settled the secession and slavery questions. The enormity of the Second World War eclipsed the First within a quarter of a century. In the course of American history, World War I did not represent the tremendous effort and cost that it did to European nations. Although 50,475 Americans died in battle and another 193,611 were wounded in the AEF, these figures were fractions of the ghastly casualties sustained by the Europeans, who counted their losses of 1914–18 in the millions. The total AEF casualties were 175,000 less than those the British suffered in the Somme in 1916.

For forty years men who experienced this war dominated American life. They matured in an era in which men assumed that to build was to progress. For most of them patriotism was understood and not open to a variety of definitions. Now, a younger generation is more apt to ask why. Now, when the nation

sends a half-million men ten thousand miles to fight an unde-
clared war, questions of the morality of this war and of the meaning of patriotism concern a sizable number of Americans.

The more than 1,888,000 veterans who lived to see the fiftieth
anniversary of Woodrow Wilson's appeal of war in 1917 have wit-
nessed the emergence of their nation as a world power, the tremendous technological developments, the change from a rural to
an urban society, and all of the resulting anxieties. While the beginnings of these developments pre-date World War I, the war
increased the tempo of change and made it virtually impossible to
reverse those trends.

In World War I, within the limited sphere of military activity,
the Americans were successful in mobilizing the nation and making their force a factor on the Western Front. The Allies could not
have won without their help. In 1919, however, the Versailles
Peace Conference caused many to wonder if the results were
worth the effort. Americans expected by their intervention to do
much more than merely act as pawns in an international power
struggle. After all, many did believe that it was the war to end all
wars.

Essay on Sources

MANUSCRIPTS

I found the papers of many of the wartime leaders in the Manuscripts Division of the Library of Congress. The important Newton D. Baker Papers contain the wartime correspondence, including the frequent exchanges with President Wilson, and many postwar letters in which Baker comments on his experiences in the war. Tasker H. Bliss was a detailed letter writer. His papers are essential to an understanding of the early days of the war in the War Department and of the events of 1918 as seen from the vantage point of the Supreme War Council. Hugh L. Scott was not as thoughtful as Bliss and did not write the lengthy letters that his good friend did; yet his correspondence in the spring of 1917 supplements that of Baker and Bliss in providing a view of the War Department's reaction to war.

The John J. Pershing Collection is invaluable. Arranged by correspondent rather than by date, this large collection is easy to use. The unpublished memoir of his life prior to the war gave me a better understanding of the man. The Peyton C. March Collection is a rather small one. Aside from the wartime March-Pershing correspondence, the most valuable letters are those March exchanged with Newton Baker and others in the 1930's when the battle of the memoirs was at its peak. For a much better contemporary insight into War Department affairs during March's wartime service as Chief of Staff, I relied upon the George W. Goethals Papers. His weekly letters to his son and his appointment books, which are virtually diaries, are extremely candid.

The Robert L. Bullard Papers contain his wartime diary but I found little of value in his personal correspondence. The diary is of limited value since he did quote lengthy extracts from it in his book, *Personalities and Reminiscences of the War,* and he left large gaps in it during 1918. In the James G. Harbord Papers, there are several bound volumes of correspondence that are useful—"World War Military Activity," "Personal War Letters," "Personal Letters of Newton D. Baker," and most important of all, his correspondence with Pershing.

Harbord had an overweening suspicion of March and this comes out clearly in his letters and notes to Pershing. Henry T. Allen's wartime letters to his wife were the most interesting part of his collection. Leonard Wood did not spare the vitriol in his diary but he does have a lot to say about the war effort. George Van Horn Moseley saved his wartime correspondence and also wrote a memoir in the 1930's, "One Soldier's Journey," which I found helpful not only in his account of the war but also in the background he provided about the prewar army.

I searched in the Charles P. Summerall and John A. Lejeune Papers but was unable to find any material that I could use. Although I did not make a lengthy search of the Woodrow Wilson Papers, I did find the key to the plan to relieve Pershing of his logistical responsibility in the summer of 1918 in a letter from Colonel House in his collection. This letter, dated June 3, 1918, is in Box 141, File II.

I used several sets of papers in the Naval Historical Foundation Collection, which is in the Manuscripts Division of the Library of Congress. Reginald R. Belknap's letters to his wife and the correspondence in the Albert Gleaves, Mark L. Bristol, William F. Fullam, and John L. Callan Papers were helpful in my chapter on the navy and the section on convoys.

The John L. Hines Collection consists largely of official and semi-official papers; hence I was delighted when the general's daughter, Mrs. Hines Cleland, found the letters the general wrote to his wife while he served on Pershing's staff and as colonel of the 16th Infantry. Mrs. Cleland loaned these, as well as her father's daily record books, to me. The letters were most useful in helping me to understand and to describe the formative period of the AEF. The general did not keep a detailed diary, and throughout 1918 his aide actually wrote up the daily events. The record books, nonetheless, provide a description of what a staff officer, regimental, brigade, division, and corps commander did each day. Eventually these letters and the record books will go to the Library of Congress.

In the State Historical Society of Wisconsin in Madison, I used the George E. Lawrence letters about his experiences on the converted yacht *Nokomis,* and the photostat copy of William D. Leahy's diary in the navy chapter. Edmund P. Arpin's typescript memoir of his service as an infantry officer in the 32nd Division is an excellent account of the experiences of a civilian turned soldier. I am pleased that Ira Berlin is editing and publishing this memoir in the *Wisconsin Magazine of History.* The first section appeared in Vol. 51 #1 (Autumn 1967). Although I examined the William G. Haan Papers, I did not find much that I could use. Several of Haan's letters to his wife were printed in *The 32nd Division in the World War, 1917–1919*.

The Edward M. House Papers and the Sir Willam Wiseman Papers in the Sterling Memorial Library of Yale University were necessary to my understanding civilian-military policy at the highest level and supplemented the Wilson and Baker Papers in this regard. House's diary notes about the pre-Armistice negotiations and Wiseman's notes on the Abbeville conference were particularly helpful. I am indebted to Mrs. Francine Cary for giving me her notes on the Walter Lippmann memo to Colonel House about German prisoners of war which I refer to in Chapter IX. She located this in the House Papers.

The Samuel M. Wilson Papers in the Margaret I. King Library of the University of Kentucky, Lexington, contain his correspondence while training at Plattsburg in 1916 and during the war while he was a candidate in an officers' training camp and, later, judge advocate of the 77th Division. A letter from a fellow Lexington attorney, Clinton Harbison, who was also undergoing officer's training in 1917 gives a very good description of this training.

In the Oral History Research Office at Columbia University, New York City, I examined several reminiscences but used only two in this book. Senator James W. Wadsworth's account helped me describe the period of the Senate investigation in the winter of 1917–18. Gerard Swope's memoir was useful as background for the army's supply situation during the war since Swope was Goethals's assistant.

The George C. Marshall Research Library, Lexington, Virginia, has microfilm of various records relating to General Marshall and the units in which he served. I used Microfilm #4096, which contains documents from the First Division Historical File in the National Archives, in my work on the First Division prior to Soissons. This library also has one of the most valuable sources I found—the typescript diary of P. L. Stackpole from January 25, 1918, to August 2, 1919. This is a detailed and very candid diary which clarifies relationships and situations which are left obscure in published memoirs and in other manuscript sources. I had a much better understanding of the high command of the AEF after I read this diary of Hunter Liggett's aide.

I found Ben H. Bernheisel's excellent unpublished memoir, "Foot Soldiers," in the Cantigny War Memorial Museum, Wheaton, Illinois. In my description of the early days of the First Division, I was fortunate in being able to use this acount, since Bernheisel had such a good eye for human interest detail.

Major General E. N. Harmon loaned me the manuscript of his "History of the Provisional Squadron, 2nd Cavalry Troops B, D, F, H: St. Mihiel and Meuse-Argonne Operations." Since he commanded Troop F and later the Squadron, his acount is of particular aid. An abbreviated version of this history appeared in the *Cavalry Journal*.

Mrs. Charles L. Bolté lent me the diary (May 10, 1918–July 6, 1919) and the typescript memoir "My Experiences in the American Expeditionary Forces 1918–1919" of her father, Benjamin A. Poore. These detailed commentaries by a veteran infantry brigade commander of the Fourth Division were most helpful. I was able to understand better phases of the British-American relationship, the Aisne-Marne, St. Mihiel, and Meuse-Argonne campaigns after I read these accounts. Poore's memoir also contained the story of George H. Cameron's relief.

George B. Duncan's two volumes of unpublished memoirs—"Reminiscences, 1882–1905" and "Reminiscences of the World War"— were invaluable. From the first volume I learned much about the "Old Army"; from the second, I gained insight into the entire AEF period, since Duncan went to France as a regimental commander in the First Division and was later a brigade and division commander. His son, Henry T. Duncan, lent carbon copies of these volumes to me.

Colonel Clifford C. Early, who served on the Operations Division of the War Department General Staff in 1918 and later, gave me his papers. For the most part, these are carbon copies of staff papers he worked on while a member of the staff. Since he wrote several studies about manpower mobilization, I used various ones in my preparation of Chapters II and III.

The most fortunate discovery I made in the course of my research was that of the Hugh A. Drum Papers. I talked with the general's daughter, Mrs. Carroll Drum Johnson, about her father's papers a few weeks before her death in an automobile accident. Later, through the courtesy of her son, Hugh Drum Johnson, and of John Dolan Harrington, I was permitted to search the attic of her home. I found the interesting weekly letters which Drum wrote to his wife, a detailed and thoughtful diary, May 17, 1917–April 30, 1918, and files which Drum had collected apparently with a view toward writing a book. Included in this collection are copies of many records as well as correspondence about controversial events in the AEF, including two large folders on the Sedan incident, postwar lectures, and Fox Conner's succinct printed notes on the various operations of the AEF. Drum also annotated a copy of Frederick Palmer's *Our Greatest Battle*. I relied greatly on this collection in my chapters on the AEF.

NATIONAL ARCHIVES

There are tons of World War I records in the National Archives, so obviously I had to be very selective in my use of them. During my research for *The Hilt of the Sword*, I examined thoroughly the Chief of Staff File, Record Group 165. This is March's office file for 1918–21 and fills more than 200 boxes. I also went through carefully the files of the War Department Cable Section, Record Group 120. Reading third or fourth carbon copies of the cables exchanged between the War Department and GHQ and Bliss is exhausting work but worthwhile if one wishes to understand what went on. The most crucial information is usually in the Confidential Cables, but not always. I used these notes on both the Chief of Staff file and the cables again in writing this book—particularly in Chapter VI.

When I described European attitudes toward the American army prior to the war, I used material from files #6553 and #7267 in the Army War College File, Record Group 165. The correspondence about plans for the expeditionary force is under #10050 in the War College Division File, Record Group 165.

The huge central record file of the army is the Adjutant General's Office Central File, Record Group 94. In the European Expedition section, I found correspondence about the 100-division program #570EE and #055.9EE. Here also is W. D. Connor's report on the American forces in France #370.2EE. The missing records, which I mentioned in Chapter XI, were the cause of correspondence under #314.3EE. There is also a summary of War Department General Staff strength at the close of the war—#321.1—which I used in Chapter II. I found Patrick's letter about Billy Mitchell, which I quoted in Chapter VII, under file #201.6. I also used Pershing's Appointment, Commission, and Promotion File #3849 in working up the description of him in Chapter II.

In the War Department Historical Files, Record Group 120, I found the prewar plans for mobilizing and equipping a large army under #7–12.6 and #7–31 which I relied upon in Chapter II. The History and Weekly Log of the 94th Aero Squadron #2–11.4 is also in this file. William Hayward, who commanded the 369th Infantry Regiment, summarized the history of his regiment in a letter of June 23, 1920, filed under #293–11–4. There is also a Cable History of Colored Soldiers under #7–12.5. These are extracts about Negroes from the cables. A particularly important source for my sections on Negroes in the war was "The Ninety-second Division, 1917–1918: An Analytical Study," prepared in the Historical Section, Army War College in 1923.

I relied upon this in my description of the fighting in the Argonne Forest and in general background of this division. It is filed under #71–20. There is a postwar study, "The Inefficiency of Negro Officers," #16–11.4 in this file. After the war, Colonel C. H. Lanza made some studies of battlefield terrain. I used the one of Cunel #7–18.2 in Chapter X.

Since there has been so much misunderstanding about the actions of the 368th Infantry in the Argonne, I examined not only the material in the 92nd Division Historical File, World War I Organization Records, Record Group 120, but also the headquarters document file of the regiment. In the first I found a history of the regiment under #292–11.4 and the daily intelligence reports, messages, and operations reports under subordinate files in the #292 file. The most interesting documents I located in the headquarters file #1519 were autobiographical summaries by the officers in the regiment.

Although it contains only scattered correspondence (most of it consisting of carbons of outgoing letters), the letterbook of James W. McAndrew, chief of staff of the AEF, in the Chief of Staff/AEF File, Record Group 120, was helpful. The exchange between McAndrew and Benjamin D. Foulois, June 8 and 10, 1918, in which Foulois asked for Mitchell's relief and McAndrew told him that Pershing expected them to work together, was particularly important to me when I wrote Chapter VII.

There are a few collections of personal papers in Record Group 316. I used the copy of the detailed Diary of the Fourth Marine Brigade, May 30–June 30, 1918, in James G. Harbord's Papers. In Chapter VIII, I also referred to the Pétain and Micheler instructional memos which I found in these papers. The John J. Pershing Papers are a particularly valuable source. The original letters from his liaison officer at Pétain's headquarters, Paul Clark, are in this collection. (However, one of Clark's most informative letters about the French reaction to the Meuse-Argonne campaign is in the Drum Papers.) The minutes of the American War Council meetings which George C. Marshall borrowed to do a postwar study for Pershing's use are also misfiled in these papers. Correspondence relative to the preparation of the Report of the First Army is in these papers. The Marshall-Drum exchange in August and September 1919 about the Meuse-Argonne campaign is of particular value. I thought that it was also interesting to see that Pershing received reports on the visiting American generals in the winter of 1917–18 from British commanders. A folder of these reports is in the papers. Pershing also kept dossiers on officers relieved for cause but these are unfortunately closed at the present time.

Timothy K. Nenninger lent me notes that he took on the Tank Corps—History of the 304th (First Brigade) #314.7 Historical Branch, and the Operations Report of this brigade by George S. Patton, November 18, 1918, AEF/G–3 Reports, both in Record Group 120. Mr. Nenninger published Patton's application for the Tank Corps in *Armor*, Vol. LXXVI #6 (Nov.–Dec. 1967). I also borrowed a microfilm copy of "The Colored Soldier in the U. S. Army," Historical Section, Army War College, 1942, from Richard M. Dalfiume. I quoted in Chapter X from C. C. Ballou's letter to the Assistant Commandant of the Army War College, March 14, 1920, which is in an appendix to this study.

Although I did not use the set in the National Archives, I was fortunate in having available a collection of the Summaries of Intelligence which the First Army issued daily. I used W. G. Haan's set, which is in a bound volume filed with government documents and not with Haan's papers in the State Historical Society of Wisconsin. The captured letters, quoted in Chapter X, as well as German comments on American prisoners, are in these mimeographed summaries.

PUBLISHED RECORDS

The basic collection of selected army records is *United States Army in the World War: 1917–1919*, 17 vols. (Washington, D.C., 1948). I used this in my discussion of the amalgamation controversy and throughout the AEF chapters. The compilers also included relevant German documents in the volumes on particular campaigns.

There is much basic information in the War Department Annual Reports, 1914–19. Within the 1919 report is the lengthy Chief of Staff report which describes the General Staff role in the war. The Secretary of War included in his annual report of 1926 a final compilation of World War I casualty figures. Leonard Ayres, *The War with Germany: A Statistical Summary* (Washington, D.C., 1919) has general statistics on the army's war effort. I used it cautiously and tried to check other sources when possible before I decided on which statistic to accept.

In Chapter II, when I discussed mobilization, I depended to a large extent for both statistics and information on the report of the Assistant Secretary of War who was also the Director of Munitions—Benedict Crowell, *American Munitions: 1917–1918* (Washington, D.C., 1919). This is an illustrated encyclopedia about munitions.

The *Second Report of the Provost Marshal General* (Washington, D.C., 1919) and the *Final Report of the Provost Marshal General* (Washington, D.C., 1920) helped me to prepare for the discussion of the draft. I used the former one more because it had more extensive comments. In addition, it covered the operations of the Selective Service System throughout the war period.

Although succinct, the *Final Report of Gen. John J. Pershing: Commander-in-Chief, American Expeditionary Forces* (Washington, D.C., 1920) is a summary which should not be overlooked. For the names and dates of command of various commanders and staff officers, as well as for details on when the units moved, where they were, and what they did, I used the *Order of Battle of the United States Land Forces in the World War: American Expeditionary Forces—Divisions* (Washington, D.C., 1931) and *General Headquarters, Armies, Army Corps, Services of Supply, and Separate Forces* (Washington, D.C., 1937). In the latter volume there is also much information on the American Forces in Germany and the American Forces in France which I used in Chapter XI.

The Personnel System of the United States Army, 2 vols. (Washington, D.C., 1919), I, *History of the Personnel System* and Robert M. Yerkes (ed.), *Psychological Examining in the United States Army,* Vol. XV in Memoirs of the National Academy of Science (Washington, D.C., 1921) were basic sources for my comments on the psychological testing program and personnel system in Chapter III. The Yerkes report includes copies of the various tests.

While Charles P. Summerall was Chief of Staff, many records of the First Division, as well as translations of related French and German documents, were published in a limited edition of twenty-five oversize volumes—*World War Records: First Division, AEF Regular,* 25 vols. (Washington, D.C., 1928–30). Since these volumes have no page numbers, one has to search within such areas as *Operations Reports to September 11, 1918* (Vol. XII) where I found the letter from R. H. Lewis to A. S. Kuegle which I quoted in Chapter VIII about rumors prior to Soissons. I also used Vol. XVI, *War Diaries, Hqs, First Division, First Infantry Brigade, 16th and 18th Infantry Regiments;* Vol. XX, *Training;* Vol. XXV, *French Documents;* and an additional Vol. I, *German Documents,* when I wrote Chapter V.

An essential book for any study of the St. Mihiel and Meuse-Argonne battles is the *Report of the First Army, American Expeditionary Forces: Organization and Operations* (Fort Leavenworth, Kansas, 1923), which George Marshall nourished through publication. In *My Experiences in the World War,* Pershing leaned greatly upon this— his earlier report. For example, compare pages 391–92 of Vol. II with pages 69–70 in the *Report.* The maps also clarified my understanding of plans and operations.

E. J. Price printed without commentary the reports of the Second Tank Brigade, September 27–October 1, and October 8, and the 301st Tank Battalion, October 17, and Sereno Brett's Operations Report of the First (304th) Tank Brigade in the Meuse-Argonne in his *Tank Actions: American Expeditionary Force* (Kansas City, Mo., 1919). I used this material in my discussions of the St. Quentin Canal operation in Chapter IX and the Aire River valley fight during the Meuse-Argonne battle.

In the House Committee on Military Affairs, *Hearings on Army Appropriations Bill, 1919*, 65th Congress, 2nd Session (1917–18), I found detailed information about the mobilization which I used in Chapter II. An example of the detailed material given is the Fort Riley menu and the number of calories in the daily ration, which I mentioned in Chapter IV. George Burr testified about his cornering the leather market in a postwar hearing. Senate Subcommittee of the Committee on Military Affairs, *Hearings on Reorganization of the Army*, 66th Congress, 2nd Session (1919).

For the chapter about the navy, I researched in the Navy Department Annual Reports for 1915–18. A basic source for the early days of the war and the relationship between Josephus Daniels and William S. Sims is the postwar hearings—Senate Subcommittee of the Committee on Naval Affairs, *Naval Investigation*, 66th Congress, 2nd Session, 2 volumes (1920) and a third brief volume which was printed later in the 67th Congress, 1st Session. I depended very much on these reports and even more on the hearings when I wrote that chapter.

I used *Histories of Two Hundred and Fifty-one Divisions of the German Army Which Participated in the War (1914–1918)* (Washington, D.C., 1920) for background and evaluations of the various German divisions. This was compiled from records of the Intelligence Section of GHQ. At Chaumont in 1919, the G–2 section published *The German and American Combined Daily Order of Battle, 25 September 1918–11 November, 1918, Including the Meuse-Argonne Offensive*. I found a copy of this booklet in the Drum Papers and used it together with other sources to determine how many German divisions were in position facing the American troops during the Meuse-Argonne battle.

INTERVIEWS

These conversations helped me to describe historic figures who otherwise were little more than names and to add much of the human interest detail. Most of all, they gave me a "feel" for the human experience of the war.

Mark H. Ingraham rejoiced again as he recalled the thrill of hearing for the first time the song of a skylark on the cliffs above Folkestone in June 1918. Douglas MacArthur was pensive as he discussed the circumstances of his obtaining command of a brigade in the Aisne-Marne campaign. And I was more impressed by the horrible effect of mustard gas when I talked with Joseph G. Stites than by my reading of pages of medical description. As I concluded the interview, I asked Mr. Stites what he thought about his experiences in the war. The reply of this veteran of Bouresches and Belleau Wood was moving: "When I came out of it, I just dismissed it from my mind and have tried to keep out of even thinking about it. It was a rather bad experience and I don't even like to talk about it yet because there were so many of the boys I went in with [who] were killed."

I interviewed Sidney C. Graves on several occasions about his experiences in the First Division as well as in Siberia. I used material from these sessions in the Prologue and in Chapter V. Henry Breckinridge, who was the Assistant Secretary of War from 1913 to 1916, told me about prewar conditions and described Hugh Scott and Tasker Bliss. Major General Benjamin D. Foulois was emphatic about Billy Mitchell and showed me the notches on the pistol he carried as a young officer in the Philippines. Ralph Hayes was Newton D. Baker's private secretary in the War Department. In an interview and in later correspondence, he discussed Baker and various other army figures as well as situations in the War Department. I also used a letter from Baker's wartime stenographer, James H. Durbin, in my description of the Secretary. General of the Army Douglas MacArthur characterized several of the generals and discussed the March-Pershing controversy in addition to reminiscing about some aspects of the war. Major General George Van Horn Moseley was informative in three lengthy interviews about the early days of the First Division and his experience as Pershing's G–4. His recollection of the conversation with Pershing during the Meuse-Argonne about the command of the Allied forces was particularly interesting.

Brigadier General Archibald Campbell remembered Pershing and March at West Point and General Ben Lear served under Pershing in Moro country and with March at Fort Riley. They provided material for my descriptions of these two officers, as did Colonel George T. Langhorne. Brigadier General Beverly F. Browne told me about the early days of the First Artillery Brigade in France and a great deal about March in two interviews.

Dean Mark H. Ingraham and Professor Chester V. Easum of the

University of Wisconsin and General Charles L. Bolté contributed to my descriptions of the training of officers. I also used in appropriate sections their discussions of their service with the 78th Division, 369th Infantry Regiment, and Fourth Division, respectively. General Bolté, in several interviews and in correspondence, gave me much information about General John L. Hines. He was Hines's aide for several years following the war. He also recalled a conversation with George H. Cameron in which Cameron discussed his relief from corps command.

Henry C. Frank, who was in the Guard detachment at Walter Reed Hospital; George E. Transom, a Guardsman in the 27th Division; and Professor Walter R. Agard of the University of Wisconsin, a draftee in 1917, told me about life in the camps. A conversation and a letter from Hughes Combs also contributed to Chapter III. Mr. Transom also talked about service with the British. Professor Agard's article "A Rookie's Reaction" in *The New Republic*, XIII #162 (Dec. 8, 1917) is an excellent contemporary source.

Bishop William P. O'Connor, wartime chaplain of the 120th Field Artillery Regiment, talked about the duties of a chaplain, camp life, and the fighting in the Aisne-Marne, Juvigny, and the Meuse-Argonne campaigns. Brigadier General Charles D. Roberts provided me with material which I used in Chapters III and X. He was chief of staff of the 81st Division and, among other things, was involved in the adoption of the army's first shoulder patch. Clayton K. Slack spent a morning with me as he recalled in detail camp life, the voyage to France, and combat with the 33rd Division.

Sir William Wiseman gave me tea and information about Woodrow Wilson as well as the Abbeville conference. He recalled Clemenceau's comments on the Abbeville conference, which I quoted in Chapter VI. As a British intelligence agent who acted as liaison between the British government and Woodrow Wilson and Colonel House, Wiseman was in a key position during the war.

I interviewed two sailors, Gilbert H. Doane and my father, Howard B. Coffman; two soldiers, Henry C. Frank and Dean William P. Carson of Memphis State University; a second lieutenant, Philip F. LaFollette, and a yeomanette, Miss Azile Wofford, about the flu epidemic.

In the navy chapter, particularly for information about destroyer and subchaser duty, I interviewed Vice Admirals Robert M. Griffin and Leland P. Lovette, Rear Admiral John B. Heffernan, and Captain Frank Loftin, all of whom saw sea duty as junior officers during the war. Admiral Heffernan told me the story about the young officers inspecting the gangway on a destroyer at the Boston Navy Yard, and Captain Loftin was the subordinate who smiled as he started talking about "Juggy" Nelson.

Ralph A. Curtin was Pershing's secretary from 1918 to 1948. He recalled the general's habit of straightening his shoulders if he slouched at the desk. Lieutenant General Clarence R. Huebner discussed the early days of the First Division, Cantigny, and, more briefly, Soissons and the Sedan incident. I used this interview in Chapters V, VIII, and X. When I saw Major General Hanson E. Ely, he talked about Cantigny and emphasized the role of George Marshall in the First Division.

An interview and correspondence with Bernard M. Baruch contributed to my account in Chapter VI. Although he was very old and very deaf when I talked with him in 1958, he expressed his opinion forcibly and clearly recalled incidents of 1918. Brigadier General Robert E. Wood also answered questions in an interview and in a letter about wartime supply problems.

Forrest C. Pogue of the George C. Marshall Research Foundation supplied me with the excerpt about the March-Pershing controversy from an interview he had with General of the Army George C. Marshall.

My work on the air war chapter benefited from interviews with General Carl Spaatz and Douglas Campbell. The general talked about Issoudun, Mitchell, Foulois, and the air war in general, while Mr. Campbell was articulate in his recollection of the spirit as well as the actions of the time. Although he did not talk much about the war, Major General Benjamin D. Foulois did make the comment about Philippine service (chapter I) in an interview.

I have already referred to my indebtedness to Joseph G. Stites, formerly of the 96th Company, Sixth Marines, for the interview about his wartime experiences.

In Chapter VIII, I also used several previously cited interviews to supplement my account of the convoys and the transport experience. I heard the story about the German prisoners' reaction to the arrival of the American convoy from the American who was present—Lee Meriwether, wartime assistant to the ambassador to France.

Colonel Carl Penner and Richardson Browne were the commander and sergeant major, respectively, of the 120th Field Artillery. In a joint interview, we discussed National Guard–regular army relations, training, Aisne-Marne, and Meuse-Argonne campaigns. Colonel Penner was the artillery officer whose comment on the 79th Division I quoted in Chapter X. Colonel Thomas J. Johnson, the G–1 of the 77th Division, characterized Robert Alexander for me. I used a quotation from his interview in Chapter VIII. Johnson, who was Hunter Liggett's aide before the war, helped me to gain an understanding of Liggett.

When I described and analyzed the effect of Leavenworth training on the officer corps and the duties of a division chief of staff in Chapter IX, I relied heavily on an interview with Lieutenant General Charles D. Herron. I used his interview again when I discussed the 78th Division in the fighting about Grandpré.

Chaplain Earl Stover used my questions and taped an interview with General William H. Simpson which I quoted in Chapter X. General Simpson and General of the Army Omar N. Bradley also commented on the impact of the war on the army. Their interviews thus helped me in my preparation of Chapter XI.

In addition to these interviews, I interviewed and corresponded with various other participants. Their comments served as background material or gave me leads to follow. Professor Ralph O. Nafziger of the University of Wisconsin told me about his service with the 339th Infantry in North Russia. Charles J. Petrie, Colonel Gilmer M. Bell, Lieutenant Buford C. Utley, USN, and Professor Victor R. Portmann of the University of Kentucky discussed their experiences with me. Charles Massa who was in Company F, 16th Infantry, wrote me about the raid in which Gresham, Enright, and Hay died. Conversations I had years ago with Colonel Erskine B. Bassett also helped me understand National Guard–regular army relations.

PUBLISHED MEMOIRS, DIARIES, LETTERS, AND SPEECHES

Ray Stannard Baker published selections from Woodrow Wilson's correspondence and included a daily record of Wilson's activities and the events of the day for the period March 1–November 11, 1918, in Volume VIII of his *Woodrow Wilson: Life and Letters*, 8 vols. (Garden City, N.Y., 1927–39). I also used Volumes V, VI, and VII of this biography. In Chapter III, I quoted from Wilson's introduction to Edward F. Allen, *Keeping Our Fighters Fit for War and After* (New York, 1918).

Newton D. Baker, *Frontiers of Freedom* (New York, 1918) is a collection of wartime speeches which includes his informative speech before the Senate Military Affairs Committee in January 1918. In this speech, Baker told about the decision to modify the Enfield rifle—a decision I discussed in Chapter II. In that chapter I also quoted from Baker's introduction to Thomas G. Frothingham, *The American Reinforcement in the World War* (Garden City, N.Y., 1927). Baker reminisced about the war at some length in this essay.

Josephus Daniels left in *The Wilson Era*, 2 vols. (Chapel Hill, N.C.,

1944, 1946) an extensive memoir of his experiences in the cabinet. I used the second volume in particular in my work on the navy chapter. I depended more, however, on Daniels's diary, which was edited and annotated in detail by E. David Cronon, *The Cabinet Diaries of Josephus Daniels*, 1913–21 (Lincoln, Neb. 1963).

Raymond B. Fosdick, *Chronicle of a Generation: An Autobiography* (New York, 1958) is necessary for a discussion of the Commission on Training Camp Activities. I also quoted from this memoir in Chapter XI. Although Frederick B. Keppel did not publish a memoir, he commented on the Secretary of War in "Newton D. Baker," *Foreign Affairs*, XVI (April 1938). Ralph Hayes, in turn, reminisced about Keppel in "Third Assistant Secretary of War," an essay in Harry J. Carman and others, *Appreciations of Frederick Paul Keppel* (New York, 1951). An interesting memoir about Negroes and the YMCA during the war is by Addie W. Hunton and Kathryn M. Johnson, *Two Colored Women with the American Expeditionary Forces* (Brooklyn, N.Y., n.d.).

Other works I used are: William G. McAdoo, *Crowded Years* (Boston, 1931); Robert Lansing, *War Memoirs* (Indianapolis, Ind., 1935); Anne W. Lane and Louise H. Wall (eds.), *The Letters of Franklin K. Lane, Personal and Political* (Boston, 1922); Washington Dawson (ed.), *The War Memoirs of William Graves Sharp: American Ambassador to France: 1914–1919* (London, 1931); Elting E. Morison (ed.), *The Letters of Theodore Roosevelt*, 8 vols. (Cambridge, Mass., 1951–1954), VIII; Henry L. Stimson and McGeorge Bundy, *On Active Service in Peace and War* (New York, 1947); Bernard M. Baruch, *The Public Years* (New York, 1960); and Charles Seymour (ed.), *The Intimate Papers of Colonel House*, 4 vols. (Boston, 1926–28), III.

John J. Pershing, *My Experiences in the World War*, 2 vols. (New York, 1931) is a basic, detailed source. Although Pershing enthusiastically refought his battles with Allied leaders, he glossed over or avoided the intramural AEF controversies such as the relief of generals and showed little understanding of War Department problems. Peyton C. March told the War Department side of the story in a pungent fashion and dealt directly with controversial matters in *The Nation at War* (Garden City, N.Y., 1932).

Robert L. Bullard was able to characterize his fellow generals and events in candid, well-turned phrases. *Personalities and Reminiscences of the War* (Garden City, N.Y., 1925) is his memoir of the war. Later he published biographical sketches of seven of his fellow generals in *Fighting Generals* (Ann Arbor, Mich., 1944), which I relied upon in discussing those officers. With Earl Reeves he wrote a brief history of the war, *American Soldiers Also Fought* (New York, 1936). In the latter, Bullard commented on the relief of commanders during the Meuse-Argonne campaign.

Hunter Liggett was not as talented a writer as Bullard and was more circumspect in his postwar books. *Commanding an American Army* (Cambridge, Mass., 1925) reads like a report. *A.E.F.: Ten Years Ago in France* (New York, 1928) is less formal and has more human interest detail but I had to read Stackpole's diary before I was able to understand some of the points Liggett made in a low-key manner. However, he was very frank about the Sedan incident in the second book.

There are several memoirs of officers who served in the War Department. The best, in that it is the most candid, is that of the Chief of Artillery, William J. Snow, *Signposts of Experience: World War Memoirs* (Washington, D.C., 1941). Henry G. Sharpe, *The Quartermaster Corps in the Year 1917 in the World War* (New York, 1921) and William Crozier, *Ordnance and the World War: A Contribution to the History of American Preparedness* (New York, 1920) are informative about the early days of the war but must be used with caution since they are, to a certain extent, apologias. Enoch H. Crowder, *The Spirit of Selective Service* (New York, 1920) is impersonal in contrast to the very personal chapters on the war in Hugh S. Johnson, *The Blue Eagle from Egg to Earth* (Garden City, N.Y., 1935). Hugh L. Scott, *Some Memories of a Soldier* (New York, 1928) is an accurate reflection of the old Indian fighter's personality. Although John M. Palmer, *Washington, Lincoln, Wilson: Three War Statesmen* (Garden City, N.Y., 1930) is a study of military policy, Palmer included some reminiscences of his experiences as a staff officer in the prewar War Department and at GHQ.

Since he was so close to Pershing officially as well as personally, James G. Harbord's *Leaves from a War Diary* (New York, 1925) and *The American Army in France: 1917–1919* (Boston, 1936) have especial value. The second book, part memoir and part history, was conceived as a rebuttal to March's *The Nation at War*. While it is more than that, nevertheless one should not forget Harbord's strong bias against March when reading passages about War Department–AEF relations.

In *Memoirs of the World War: 1917–1918* (New York, 1931), Robert Alexander answered questions that historians ask more readily than did most memoirists. *Hugh Young:A Surgeon's Autobiography* (New York, 1940) displays the doctor's ability as a raconteur and gives a great deal of information about the venereal disease problem in France. Charles G. Dawes published his wartime diary in Volume I of *A Journal of the Great War*, 2 vols. (Boston, 1921). Since he was probably the only man in the AEF who would call Pershing "John," this diary is an essential source for learning about the C-in-C's moods and attitudes.

Joseph T. Dickman's memoir is prosaic—*The Great Crusade* (New York, 1927)—but since he was involved in so much of the fighting as division and corps commander, I had to consult it frequently. Other memoirs of AEF personages which I used are: John A. Lejeune, *The Reminiscences of a Marine* (Philadelphia, 1930); Johnson Hagood, *The Services of Supply: A Memoir of the Great War* (Boston, 1927); T. B. Mott, *Twenty Years as Military Attaché* (New York, 1937); Avery D. Andrews, *John J. Pershing: My Friend and Classmate* (Harrisburg, Pa., 1939), which included many extracts from his diary; Douglas MacArthur, *Reminiscences* (New York, 1964); Lloyd C. Griscom, *Diplomatically Speaking* (New York, 1940), which was the source for my account of how Pershing spent the morning of November 11, 1918; A. W. Catlin, *"With the Help of God and a Few Marines"* (Garden City, N.Y., 1919); Frederic M. Wise and Meigs O. Frost, *A Marine Tells It to You* (New York, 1929); and Francis P. Duffy, *Father Duffy's Story* (New York, 1919), which is invaluable to anyone interested in the "Fighting 69th."

Although it is semi-fictional, John W. Thomason, Jr., *Fix Bayonets!* (New York, 1926) is also a memoir by a literary Marine who was at Belleau Wood, Soissons, and other battles. Beaumont B. Buck, *Memories of Peace and War* (San Antonio, Texas, 1935) is informative about the early days of the AEF and the battle of Soissons but is silent on the Meuse-Argonne. Omar Bundy, "The Second Division at Chateau Thierry," *Everybody's Magazine*, XL #3 (March 1919) is a succinct report. B. F. Cheatham (the division quartermaster) recalled the First Division Christmas party in "Reminiscences of the World War," *Quartermaster Review*, VIII #5 (March–April 1929). Gustav Stearns, a chaplain in the 32nd Division, published his wartime letters in *From Army Camps and Battle Fields* (Minneapolis, Minn., 1919).

A particularly valuable source for descriptions and analyses of small unit actions is *Infantry in Battle* (Washington, D.C., 1939). Various officers at the Infantry School recalled specific combat situations while others analyzed these actions. I drew upon this for battle details.

W. Kerr Rainsford (a captain in the 307th Infantry), *From Upton to the Meuse with the Three Hundred and Seventh Infantry* (New York, 1920); Jesse W. Wooldridge (a captain and later a major in the

38th Infantry), *The Giants of the Marne: A Story of McAlexander and His Regiment* (Salt Lake City, Utah, 1923); Arthur W. Little (major in 369th Infantry), *From Harlem to the Rhine: The Story of New York's Colored Volunteers* (New York, 1936); Chester D. Heywood (captain in the 371st Infantry), *Negro Combat Troops in the World War: The Story of the 371st Infantry* (Worcester, Mass., 1928) are interesting combination memoir-histories. Maury Maverick, *A Maverick American* (New York, 1937) is a frank memoir of a disillusioned veteran.

One volume of letters and one memoir-history are outstanding because of the authors' unusual abilities to describe their experiences. Both contributed immeasurably to my understanding of the war. They are *Fort Sheridan to Montfaucon: The War Letters of Frederick Trevenen Edwards* (DeLand, Fla., 1954) and Frederick A. Pottle, *Stretchers: The Story of a Hospital Unit on the Western Front* (New Haven, Conn., 1929). Two similar sources which are excellent are Kenneth Gow, *Letters of a Soldier* (New York, 1920) and William L. Langer, *Gas and Flame in World War I* (New York, 1965). Pottle and Langer later became professors at Yale and Harvard respectively.

Donald Davidson briefly reminisced about the war in *Southern Writers in the Modern World* (Athens, Ga., 1958). Alvin York told his story and showed his diary to Tom Skeyhill, who published both in *Sergeant York: His Own Life Story and War Diary* (Garden City, N.Y., 1928). I also used John C. Acker, *Thru the War with our Outfit: Being a Historical Narrative of the 107th Ammunition Train* (n.p., 1920); Rush S. Young, *Over the Top with the 80th by a Buck Private* (n.p., 1933); Irving Crump, *Conscript 2989: Experiences of a Drafted Man* (New York, 1918); John L. Barkley, *No Hard Feelings* (New York, 1930); Robert A. Scudder, *My Experience in the World War* (Dover, N.J., 1921); William E. Roth, *Memoirs of a Private: 1917–1919* (Austin, Texas, 1960); Will Judy, *A Soldier's Diary* (Chicago, 1931); and Charles MacArthur, *War Bugs* (Garden City, N.Y., 1929).

There are also some memoirs about the Mexican border mobilization which I used in the first chapter. They are all by Guardsmen— Roger Batchelder, *Watching and Waiting on the Border* (Boston, 1917); George Brook III, *With the First City Troop on the Mexican Border: Being the Diary of a Trooper* (Philadelphia, 1917), and Irving G. McCann, *With the National Guard on the Border* (St. Louis, Mo., 1917).

In the navy chapter, I used several memoirs. One can easily see why Hugh Rodman and William Sims were not very compatible by reading their memoirs: William S. Sims and Burton J. Hendrick, *The Victory at Sea* (Garden City, N.Y., 1921) and Hugh Rodman, *Yarns of a*

Kentucky Admiral (Indianapolis, Ind., 1928). W. F. Halsey and Joseph Bryan III, *Admiral Halsey's Story* (New York, 1947) and Ernest J. King and Walter M. Whitehill, *Fleet Admiral King: A Naval Record* (New York, 1952), fortunately for my work, did include reminiscences of their World War I experiences. Albert Gleaves, *A History of the Transport Service* (New York, 1921) and Reginald R. Belknap, *The Yankee Mining Squadron or Laying the North Sea Mine Barrage* (Annapolis, Md., 1920) are basically histories with reminiscent comments. I also relied on material from Joseph Husband, *On the Coast of France* (Chicago, 1919); H. Wickliffe Rose, *Brittany Patrol: The Story of the Suicide Fleet* (New York, 1937); Hilary R. Chambers, Jr., *United States Submarine Chasers in the Mediterranean, Adriatic and the Attack on Durazzo* (New York, 1920); Ray Milholland, *The Splinter Fleet* (Indianapolis, Ind., 1936). I learned much about the early days of the destroyer war in the North Atlantic from the series of articles by J. K. Taussig, "Destroyer Experiences During the Great War," *United States Naval Institute Proceedings*, Vol. 48 #12 (Dec. 1922), and Vol. 49 #1–3 (Jan.–March 1923).

There are several good memoirs about the air war. William Mitchell, *Memories of World War I: "From Start to Finish of Our Greatest War"* (New York, 1960) is essential. To balance Mitchell's point of view, one should also read Mason M. Patrick, *The United States in the Air* (Garden City, N.Y., 1928). Charles R. Codman, *Contact* (Boston, 1937); Harold E. Hartney, *Up and At'em* (Harrisburg, Pa., 1940); and Edward V. Rickenbacker, *Fighting the Flying Circus* (Philadelphia, 1947 edition) are good accounts by combat flyers. Hiram Bingham, *An Explorer in the Air Service* (New Haven, Conn., 1920) and H. H. Arnold, *Global Mission* (New York, 1949) were also useful.

I used several memoirs by British leaders. David Lloyd George, *War Memoirs*, Vols. III and IV (London, 1934), Vol. V (Boston, 1936), and Vol. VI (Boston, 1937) and Robert Blake (ed.), *The Private Papers of Douglas Haig: 1914–1919* (London, 1952) were of particular value. Sir Maurice Hankey, *The Supreme Command: 1914–1918*, 2 vols. (London, 1961); Sir William Robertson, *Soldiers and Statesmen: 1914–1918*, 2 vols. (New York, 1926); G. T. M. Bridges, *Alarms and Excursions* (New York, 1939); and Sir John Jellicoe, *The Submarine Peril: The Admiralty Policy in 1917* (London, 1934) were also helpful.

Sir John Monash was in a category by himself as an unusually astute general. I relied much on his memoir-history, *The Australian Victories in France in 1918* (London, n.d.) in Chapter IX.

Georges Clemenceau was a bitter foe in politics, in war, and in memoirs. He gave his definite views about a number of wartime and peacetime matters and chastised Marshal Foch in *Grandeur and Misery of Victory* (New York, 1930). In contrast, Ferdinand Foch, *The Memoirs of Marshal Foch* (Garden City, N.Y., 1931) is rather dull but Foch does provide a great deal of information about the plans and operations. I also consulted J. C. Joffre, *The Personal Memoirs of Joffre*, 2 vols. (New York, 1932), II, for his reaction to the Americans. Pierre Teilhard de Chardin, *The Making of a Mind: Letters From a Soldier-Priest, 1914–1919* (New York, 1965) is impressive because it shows an intellectual's response to the front. This book is the source of his comments on the Americans at Soissons. The French corps commander in that battle, Pierre E. Berdoulat wrote a brief account— "The First and Second Divisions in the Offensive of July 8 [sic], 1918," *Cavalry Journal*, XXXIV #141 (Oct. 1925). This does not add much to what Berdoulat contributed to an account by General Joseph Helle in *As They Saw Us*.

Paul von Hindenburg, *Out of My Life* (London, 1920) and Crown Prince William, *My War Experiences* (New York, 1923) are rather general memoirs as far as the Americans are concerned. Erich von Ludendorff was more specific and detailed in *Ludendorff's Own Story*, 2 vols. (New York, 1919) but Ludendorff hated to admit defeat or error much more than the other two. Walter Görlitz, *The Kaiser and His Court: The Diaries, Note Books and Letters of Admiral Georg Alexander von Müller, Chief of the Naval Cabinet, 1914–1918* (London, 1961) was the source of the story about the Kaiser's vision which I used in Chapter VIII. I found the translation of the memoir of Lieutenant General Wellmann, who commanded a corps in front of the Americans in the Meuse-Argonne battle, a valuable aid when I wrote Chapter X. This manuscript translation is in the Drum Papers.

I depended heavily upon the various accounts in George S. Viereck (ed.), *As They Saw Us* (Garden City, N.Y., 1929). Although Foch and Ludendorff wrote brief essays for this book, those by Walther Reinhardt (chief of staff of the German Seventh Army), Joseph Helle (Mangin's chief of staff), Otto von Ledebur (chief of staff, German Army Unit C), Eugene Savatier (a French division commander), and Max von Gallwitz were of more aid in my preparation of the AEF chapters.

UNIT HISTORIES

These are chronicles compiled to commemorate the role of the particular group of men in the war. They may include orders and reports or collections of brief reminiscences. A few are polemical and all, of course, have to be used with other unit histories and accounts of corps and army commanders, and when possible, of men in the unit, to maintain perspective. Generally, they are more frank and accurate than one might expect commemorative volumes to be. In several cases, I have indicated where I supplemented these histories with documents from the Drum Papers.

History of the First Division During the World War: 1917–1919 (Philadelphia, 1922), compiled by the Society of the First Division, is detailed and impersonal. Oliver L. Spaulding and John W. Wright tried to tell the German side as well as the division's in *The Second Division, American Expeditionary Force in France: 1917–1919* (New York, 1937). The separate brief reminiscences by veterans of the division which they included were also useful. *The Official History of the Second Regiment of Engineers and Second Engineer Train, United States Army in the World War* (n.p., n.d.), compiled by the Regimental Headquarters, reads like a report but has some good pictures. Correspondence about the Ninth Infantry's night march in the last phase of the Meuse-Argonne is in the folder "Ninth Infantry: March through German Lines" in the Drum Papers.

Frederic V. Hemenway, *History of the Third Division, United States Army in the World War for the period December 1, 1917 to January 1, 1919* (Andernach-on-the-Rhine, 1919) consists of separate subordinate unit chronicles.

One of the best written division histories is Christian A. Bach and Henry Noble Hall, *The Fourth Division: Its Services and Achievements in the World War* (Garden City, N.Y., 1920). For my account of the Fourth Division and the controversy over Montfaucon, I also used correspondence in the Drum and Hines Papers. The Roy Winton and James A. Stevens letters are in the folder "4th Division-Montfaucon" of the Drum Papers. Much of the Booth, Bach, and Hines correspondence in this folder is duplicated in the Hines Papers.

Kenyon Stevenson, *The Official History of the Fifth Division U.S.A.* (Washington, D.C., 1919) is another well-written account.

The 26th was a controversial division and three histories which I used are naturally partisan. The best is by a division staff officer, Emerson G. Taylor, *New England in France, 1917–1919: A History of the Twenty-sixth Division U.S.A.* (Boston, 1920). Frank P. Sibley, as a correspondent for a Boston newspaper, was with the division in France. His book, *With the Yankee Division in France* (Boston, 1919), reflects his intense loyalty to the division. Harry A. Benwell, *History of the Yankee Division* (Boston, 1919) is neither as complete as Taylor nor as polemical as Sibley. Two subordinate unit histories I used are

James T. Duane (captain in 101st Infantry), *Dear Old "K"* (Boston, 1922) and Daniel W. Strickland (an officer in the 102nd), *Connecticut Fights: The Story of the 102nd Regiment* (New Haven, Conn., 1930).

The division commander, John F. O'Ryan, showed a sense of human interest detail in his *The Story of the 27th Division*, 2 vols. (New York, 1921) and Gerald Jacobson included some interesting reminiscences in the form of company chronicles in his *History of the 107th Infantry U.S.A.* (New York, 1920). This is the source of Sergeant Griffiths's summing up of the demobilization which I quoted in Chapter XI.

H. G. Proctor wrote a rather slight history of the 28th Division— *The Iron Division: National Guard of Pennsylvania in the World War* (Philadelphia, 1919).

The 32nd Division in the World War: 1917–1919 (Madison, Wis., 1920) is complete yet concise. The inclusion of excerpts from the division commander's [W. G. Haan] letters to his wife add to the value of this history. G. R. Garlock, an officer in the division, wrote *Tales of the Thirty-Second* (West Salem, Wis., 1927). I found the full story of Captain Strom and the Côte Dame Marie fight in Garlock and corroborated it with the briefer account in the history. Carl Penner, Frederic Sammond, and H. M. Appel put together *The 120th Field Artillery Diary: 1880–1919* (Milwaukee, Wis., 1928)—a collection of diaries and commentaries by veterans.

I depended upon *Illinois in the World War: An Illustrated History of the Thirty-third Division*, 2 vols. (Chicago, 1921) for my descriptions of actions of this division.

Clair Kenamore is polemical in *From Vauquois Hill to Exermont: A History of the Thirty-fifth Division of the United States Army* (St. Louis, Mo., 1919). I found the Inspector General's report, together with interviews with various participants, in a folder "35th Division #1" in the Drum Papers.

Although I did not go into the role played by the Americans with the French Fourth Army and the Belgian Army, I did consult the histories of two of the divisions: Ben H. Chastine, *Story of the 36th: The Experiences of the 36th Division in the World War* (Oklahoma City, Okla., 1920) and Ralph D. Cole and W. C. Howells, *The Thirty-seventh Division in the World War: 1917–1918*, 2 vols. (Columbus, Ohio, 1929). A facsimile of King Albert's tribute, which I quoted, is in Volume II.

Henry J. Reilly was an artillery regimental commander and an infantry brigade commander in the Rainbow during the war. In his

Americans All, The Rainbow at War: Official History of the 42nd Rainbow Division in the World War (Columbus, Ohio, 1936) he included acounts of many participants. At times, these range somewhat far afield from the Rainbow, such as Colonel O. P. M. Hazzard's story of the calvary squadron at St. Mihiel. William H. Amerine, *Alabama's Own in France* (New York, 1919); John H. Taber, *The Story of the 168th Infantry*, 2 vols. (Iowa City, Iowa, 1925); and R. M. Cheseldine, *Ohio in the Rainbow: Official Story of the 166th Infantry, 42nd Division in the World War* (Columbus, Ohio, 1924) are other regimental histories consulted.

The 77th Division is amply commemorated by the *History of the Seventy-seventh Division: August 25th, 1917–November 11, 1918* (New York, 1919); Frank B. Tiebout, *A History of the 305th Infantry* (New York, 1919); *History of the 306th Infantry* (New York, 1935); L. Wardlaw Miles (the Medal of Honor winner), *History of the 308th Infantry, 1917–19* (New York, 1927); and the previously cited Rainsford memoir-history of the 307th. The Miles and Rainsford books are particularly well written. In his book, Miles included Whittlesey's recollections of the Lost Battalion episode.

Thomas F. Meehan, *History of the Seventy-eighth Division in the World War, 1917–18–19* (New York, 1921) and J. Frank Barber, *History of the Seventy-ninth Division A.E.F. during the World War: 1917–1919* (Lancaster, Pa., n.d.) were helpful. Barber's is the more detailed history.

Four other division histories I used during my preparation are G. Edward Buxton, *Official History of 82nd Division, American Expeditionary Forces: "All American" Division* (Indianapolis, Ind., 1919); George H. English, Jr., *History of the 89th Division, U.S.A.* (Denver, Colo., 1920); George Wythe, *A History of the 90th Division* (n.p., 1920); and *The Story of the 91st Division* (San Francisco, Calif., 1919). In Chapter IX, I used some quotations from captured German letters which English included in his history.

I also used three other histories of this genre: Daniel P. Morse, Jr., *The History of the 50th Aero Squadron* (New York, 1920) and *History of the U.S.S. Leviathan* (New York, n.d.), prepared by a history committee on board the ship. The first book has an interesting section on the Meuse-Argonne while the second has facts and figures about the voyages of the *Leviathan* as a transport. An important source for logistical information is William J. Wilgus, *Transporting the A.E.F. in Western Europe, 1917–1919* (New York, 1931).

A SELECTIVE BIBLIOGRAPHY OF OTHER SOURCES

Frederic L. Paxson, *America at War: 1917–1918* (Boston, 1939), Volume II in his three-volume series, *American Democracy and the World War,* is the standard history. Paxson provides an excellent summary of the American role in this political, diplomatic, economic, social, and military history. Laurence Stallings, as a young Marine officer, was badly wounded at Belleau Wood. In *The Doughboys: The Story of the AEF, 1917–1918* (New York, 1963), he mixes personal reminiscences with a great deal of research in published sources to come up with an interesting account. On the one hand, he was there and understands the doughboys; on the other, he was limited by his dependence on published sources in his knowledge and understanding of what transpired at the high command level. There are many good photographs and lengthy quotations from assorted letters, diaries, and memoirs in Frank Freidel, *Over There: The Story of America's First Great Overseas Crusade* (New York, 1964). For portraits of AEF figures, see Joseph C. Chase, *Soldiers All* (New York, 1920).

For general background and to gain perspective, I used Sir Basil H. Liddell Hart, *The Real War: 1914–1918* (Boston; Little, Brown, and Company paperback edition, copyright 1930); Cyril Falls, *The Great War: 1914–1918* (New York, Capricorn Books paperback edition, 1961); and Sir James E. Edmonds, *A Short History of World War I* (London, 1951). I relied on Sir Basil's perceptive essays in *Reputations: Ten Years After* (Boston, 1928) and *Through the Fog of War* (New York, 1938) to help me understand personalities and situations of the war. Barrie Pitt, *1918: The Last Act* (London, 1962) was also of aid.

Anyone who attempts to write about the American military role in the war becomes acquainted with Frederick Palmer. An experienced war correspondent and a member of Pershing's staff, Palmer wrote extensively and knowledgeably about the war. *America in France* (New York, 1918) and *Our Greatest Battle* (New York, 1919) are journalistic accounts based on his observations and his access to some records. In his two-volume work on *Newton D. Baker: America at War* (New York, 1931), he used Baker's Papers, the cable file, and a few other records. *Bliss, Peacemaker: The Life and Letters of General Tasker Howard Bliss* (New York, 1934), as the title indicates, is based on the Bliss Papers. In these two works, Palmer also relied on interviews and correspondence with many of the figures of the period. Although he was not in the inner circle, he was close enough to Pershing to write a biography—*John J. Pershing: General of the Armies* (Harrisburg, Pa., 1948)—based, to a great extent, on personal observation. Finally, he has some interesting comments to make on World War I in his autobiography, *With My Own Eyes: A Personal Story of Battle Years* (Indianapolis, Ind., 1933). Although Palmer never took the time to do exhaustive research or, apparently, to think about his material at length, his experience as a newsman and his acquaintance with American military men, together with the fact that he was often recording first-hand observations, give a special value to his books.

In the 1950's, the Chemical Corps sponsored a research project on gas warfare in World War I. Rexmond C. Cochrane and his assistants thoroughly researched the records in the National Archives in preparation of a series of studies on the AEF and gas warfare. I depended greatly upon Cochrane's excellent discussions and analyses of various units in combat situations. All of these are in U. S. Army Chemical Corps Historical Studies: Gas Warfare in World War I: *The 1st Division at Ansauville, January–April 1918* (Study #9, Aug. 1958), *The 1st Division at Cantigny, May 1918* (Study #11, Jan. 1959), *Gas Warfare at Belleau Wood, June 1918* (Study #1, June 1957), *The 3rd Division at Château-Thierry, July 1918* (Study #14, July 1959), *The 26th Division in the Aisne-Marne Campaign, July 1918* (Study #4, Sept. 1957), *The End of the Aisne-Marne Campaign, August 1918* (Study #13, June 1959), *The Use of Gas at Saint Mihiel (90th Division in September 1918)* (Study #5, Dec. 1957), *The 78th Division at the Kriemhilde Stellung, October 1918* (Study #2, July 1957), *The 1st Division in the Meuse-Argonne, 1–12 October 1918* (Study #3, Aug. 1957), *The 33rd Division along the Meuse, October 1918* (Study #8, July 1958), and *The Use of Gas in the Meuse-Argonne Campaign, September–November 1918* (Study #10, Dec. 1958).

When I did my research for *The Hilt of the Sword,* I paged the *New York Times* and *The Evening Star* of Washington, D.C. for the period January to mid-November 1918. I also went through the *Army and Navy Journal,* a weekly newspaper, for the entire period. I used these notes for general background but looked up other events, such as the July 4, 1917, parade in Paris in the specific *New York Times.* For the sections on the Negroes, I researched the NAACP periodical, *The Crisis* (Vols. 14–18 #2), for the war period.

I used various books to establish the political and diplomatic context of the military effort. Some of them are: Arthur S. Link, *Woodrow Wilson and the Progressive Era: 1910–1917* (New York, 1954) and *Wilson: The Struggle for Neutrality, 1914–1915* (Princeton, N.J., 1960); Ernest R. May, *The World War and American Isolation: 1914–*

1917 (Cambridge, Mass., 1959); and Arthur W. Walworth, *Woodrow Wilson*, 2 vols. (New York, 1958), II. I have previously cited Ray Stannard Baker's and Frederic L. Paxson's works.

Francis W. Halsey provided a contemporary description of the foreign missions in *Balfour, Viviani and Joffre* (New York, 1917). One of the junior officers who accompanied Joffre, Edouard J. Réquin, described the war effort in *America's Race to Victory* (New York, 1919). I found this most valuable about the period of the mission.

There are several books which provide information about the army generally and the policy debate prior to the war. The experiences of a young officer in the prewar period are well handled by Forrest C. Pogue, *George C. Marshall: Education of a General, 1880–1939* (New York, 1963). This is also excellent for Marshall's work during the war. Otto L. Nelson's history of the General Staff, *National Security and the General Staff* (Washington, D.C., 1946) and *American Military Policy: Its Development since 1775* (Harrisburg, Pa., 1955) by C. J. Bernardo and E. H. Bacon are useful for the information on those particular topics. John M. Dickinson in *The Building of an Army* (New York, 1922) discusses the failure of Garrison's Continental Army plan. Marvin A. Kriedberg and Merton G. Henry, *History of Military Mobilization in the United States: 1775–1945* (Washington, D.C., 1955) provide perspective as well as specific details about World War I manpower mobilization. The best history of the army—Russell F. Weigley, *History of the United States Army* (New York, 1967)—has three chapters on the prewar and war periods.

Ralph B. Perry, *The Plattsburg Movement: A Chapter of America's Participation in the World War* (New York, 1921) is a sympathetic discussion. The enigmatic General Leonard Wood has an extremely laudatory biography. I used volume II of Hermann Hagedorn, *Leonard Wood: A Biography*, 2 vols. (New York, 1931). Floyd Gibbons described in a prejudicial vein what he saw in the camps on the Mexican border in second part of *How the Laconia Sank and the Military Mobilization on the Mexican Border: Two Masterpieces of Reporting* (Chicago, 1917).

A "unit history" of the Council of National Defense and the War Industries Board is Grosvenor B. Clarkson, *Industrial America in the World War: The Strategy Behind the Line: 1917–1918* (Boston, 1923). Clarkson, who was secretary and later director of the Council, has provided a good starting point for research about industrial mobilization in this book. Bernard M. Baruch, *American Industry in the War* (New York, 1941) contains Baruch's report on the work of the

WIB. The best biography of the chairman is Margaret Coit, *Mr. Baruch* (Boston, 1957).

Daniel R. Beaver, *Newton D. Baker and the American War Effort, 1917–1919* (Lincoln, Nebr., 1966) is an excellent work of scholarship. C. H. Cramer in his general biography *Newton D. Baker* (Cleveland, Ohio, 1961) did not cover the war period as thoroughly or as perceptively as did Beaver. Beaver's "Newton D. Baker and the Genesis of the War Industries Board," *Journal of American History*, LII #1 (June 1965) and an unpublished manuscript by Paul A. C. Koistinen, "The 'Industrial-Military Complex' in Historical Perspective: World War I," forced me to rethink Baker's role. While our interpretations differ, this results in part from the fact that my book has a different focus from that developed by these two scholars.

Two contemporary articles which I found to be of particular value in my work on Chapter II are Edward G. Lowry, "The Emerging Mr. Baker," *Colliers*, LX (Oct. 6, 1917) and George Soule, "The Brain of the Army," *The New Republic*, XIII #164 (Dec. 22, 1917). A scholarly article by H. A. DeWeerd, "American Adoption of French Artillery: 1917–1918," *Journal of the American Military Institute*, III (Summer 1939) was also helpful.

David A. Lockmiller, *Enoch H. Crowder: Soldier, Lawyer and Statesman* (Columbus, Mo., 1955) is a well-researched biography of this powerful bureau chief.

Relevant sections of three government-sponsored histories helped me to understand the logistical situation in World War I. They are: James A. Huston, *The Sinews of War: Army Logistics 1775–1953* (Washington, D.C., 1966); Erna Risch, *Quartermaster Support of the Army: A History of the Corps 1775–1939* (Washington, D.C., 1962); and Constance M. Green, Harry C. Thomson, and Peter C. Roots, *The Ordnance Department: Planning for War* (Washington, D.C., 1955).

Emmett J. Scott published many documents as well as his comments in *Scott's Official History of the American Negro in the World War* (n.p., 1919). To balance this, one should see W. E. B. Dubois's brief "An Essay Toward a History of the Black Man in the Great War," *The Crisis*, Vol. 18 #2 (June 1919). Charles H. Williams, *Sidelights on Negro Soldiers* (Boston, 1923) is the best book-length account. The entire Summer 1943 issue of *The Journal of Negro Education*, XII #3, is devoted to Negroes in World Wars I and II. Articles by Scott, DuBois, Campbell C. Johnson, William H. Hastie, Charles H. Garvin, John W. Davis, and Charles H. Houston were all informative; the one by Howard H. Long was particularly helpful. The title of Long's article,

"The Negro Soldier in the Army of the United States," does not hint that it is in part a memoir of his wartime service. I used this in my account of the 368th Infantry's experience in the Argonne.

Fred D. Baldwin's doctoral dissertation, "The American Enlisted Man in World War I," which he completed at Princeton University in 1964, is a work of solid research. I found it particularly helpful when I wrote Chapter III. I am also indebted to this work for leading me to Frederick T. Edwards's and Frederick A. Pottle's books and Walter Agard's *New Republic* article. Mark Sullivan, *Over Here: 1914–1918* (New York, 1933), a volume in Sullivan's *Our Times*, provided background for Chapter III also.

The Medical Department of the United States Army in the World War, 15 vols. (Washington, D.C., 1921–29) is encyclopedic in its coverage of the activities of the Medical Department. I used Volume IV, Albert S. Bowen, *Activities Concerning Mobilization Camps and Ports of Embarkation;* Volume IX, Joseph F. Siler, *Communicable and Other Diseases* when I researched for the flu epidemic section of Chapter III. I also used the statistics in Volume XV. A. A. Hoehling wrote a popular history of the epidemic—*The Great Epidemic* (Boston, 1961).

There is much of human interest as well as basic information in Benedict Crowell and Robert F. Wilson, *The Road to France*, 2 vols. (New Haven, Conn., 1921). I used these books for material about the transportation of drafted men to camp and the troop movements to ports of embarkation.

For my discussion of conscientious objectors, I used, in addition to some previously cited sources, Norman Thomas, *The Conscientious Objector in America* (New York, 1923); H. C. Peterson and Gilbert C. Fite, *Opponents of War: 1917–1918* (Madison, Wis., 1957); and Donald Johnson, *The Challenge to American Freedoms: World War I and the Rise of the American Civil Liberties Union* (Lexington, Ky., 1963). Although Thomas was very much involved in the issue during the war, his book is more objective than some would expect. The other two works of sound scholarship have good sections on the COs. I discovered F. Scott Fitzgerald's method of dealing with a CO and the novelist's officers' training camp experience in Andrew Turnbull, *Scott Fitzgerald* (New York, 1962).

Various chronicles of the wartime service agencies which I used are William H. Taft (ed.), *Service with Fighting Men: An Account of the Work of the American Young Men's Christian Association in the World War*, 2 vols. (New York, 1922); Katherine Mayo, *"That Damn Y": A Record of Overseas Service* (Boston, 1920); *The Jewish Welfare*

Board: *Final Report of War Emergency Activities* (New York, 1920);
Maurice F. Egan and John B. Kennedy, *Knights of Columbus in Peace
and War*, 2 vols. (New Haven, Conn., 1920); and Evangeline Booth
and Grace Livingston Hill, *The War Romance of the Salvation Army*
(Philadelphia, 1919).

There are sections about the work of chaplains in World War I in
Daniel P. Jorgensen, *The Service of Chaplains to Army Air Units:
1917–1946*, Volume I in *Air Force Chaplains*, 2 vols. (Washington,
D.C., n.d.) and Roy J. Honeywell, *Chaplains of the United States Army*
(Washington, D.C., 1958).

In my preparation of the navy chapter, I used Elting E. Morison's
excellent biography of Sims—*Admiral Sims and the Modern American
Navy* (Boston, 1942). It is difficult to be neutral about Sims. Although
Morison is sympathetic, he fully understands Sims's faults. I based
my comment on the navy's reluctance to give up the convoy system
in World War II on an essay "The Pertinence of the Past in Computing
the Future" in Morison's *Men, Machines, and Modern Times* (Cambridge, Mass., 1966). This collection of essays is a valuable introduction to the problem of the impact of technology on society.

Josephus Daniels chronicled in detail the activities of the navy in
Our Navy at War (New York, 1922). Harold and Margaret Sprout,
The Rise of American Naval Power: 1776–1918 (Princeton, N.J.,
1939) and *Toward a New Order of Sea Power: American Naval Policy
and the World Scene, 1918–1922* (Princeton, N.J., 1943) are scholarly
works which helped me place the war in the context of American
naval policy. E. B. Potter and others, *The United States and World Sea
Power* (Englewood Cliffs, N.J., 1955) and Dudley W. Knox, *A History
of the United States Navy* (New York, 1948) are broad surveys.

Tracy B. Kittredge's strong partisanship for Sims lessens the value
of *Naval Lessons of the Great War* (Garden City, N.Y., 1921) which
is a review of the postwar Senate investigation.

Archibald D. Turnbull and Clifford L. Lord, *History of United States
Aviation* (New Haven, Conn., 1949) was informative. Thomas G.
Frothingham, *The Naval History of the World War: The United States
in the War, 1917–18* (Cambridge, Mass., 1926) was not very helpful.
E. Keble Chatterton, *Danger Zone: The Story of the Queenstown Com-
mand* (Boston, 1934); John L. Leighton, *Simsadus: London—The
American Navy in Europe* (New York, 1920); and Ralph D. Paine,
The Corsair in the War Zone (Boston, 1920) are popular histories I
found useful. Frank Freidel has a section on FDR as Daniels's Assistant Secretary in *Franklin D. Roosevelt: The Apprenticeship* (Boston,

1952). I referred to Henry Newbolt's volume, V (London, 1931) in Sir Julian S. Corbett, *History of the Great War: Naval Operations*, for the British point of view.

I used several articles from the *United States Naval Institute Proceedings*. They are: William S. Sims, "Military Conservatism," Vol. 48 #3 (March 1922), Captain A. Gayer (German Navy), "Summary of German Submarine Operations in the Various Theaters of War from 1914 to 1918," Vol. 52 #4 (April 1926), Maurice Prendergast and R. H. Gibson discussion of Gayer's article in Vol. 52 #8 (Aug. 1926), Rear Admiral Spindler (German Navy), "The Value of the Submarine in Naval Warfare Based on the German Experience in the War," Vol. 52 #5 (May 1926). Two scholars explored aspects of submarine warfare in *Military Affairs*. They are James M. Merrill, "Submarine Scare, 1918," XVII #4 (Winter 1953) and Philip K. Lundeberg, "The German Naval Critique of the U–Boat Campaign, 1915–1918," XXVII #3 (Fall 1963).

A good brief summary of the American air effort in World War I is in the appropriate section of Volume I of Wesley Frank Craven and James Lea Cate (eds.), *The Army Air Forces in World War II*, 8 vols. (Chicago, 1948). I. B. Holley, Jr., *Ideas and Weapons* (New Haven, Conn., 1953) is a scholarly analysis of the air program. Holley has also provided an annotated guide to pertinent records in the National Archives. This book is essential to anyone who wishes to study the air programs.

Arthur Sweetser, *The American Air Service* (New York, 1919) is a contemporary history with an introduction by Newton D. Baker. A former staff officer, H. A. Toulmin, Jr., in *Air Service, American Expeditionary Forces: 1918* (New York, 1927) helped clarify for me the tangle of AEF Air Service administrative problems. Two air pioneers, Charles D. Chandler and Frank P. Lahm, provided background in *How Our Army Grew Wings: Airmen and Aircraft Before 1914* (New York, 1943).

Two booklets literally crammed with information are Edgar S. Gorrell, *The Measure of America's World War Aeronautical Effort* (Northfield, Vt., 1940) and Charles G. Grey, *The History of Combat Airplanes* (Northfield, Vt., 1941). The former chief of staff of the AEF Air Service, Gorrell provides many statistics in this brief account. His booklet was much more important to my work than was Grey's.

The publication of the Society of World War I Aero Historians, *Cross and Cockade,* contains reminiscences and articles about the subject. In Volume VI (1965) there is an interview with Douglas

Campbell by A. J. Lynch and part of a series on the Air Service by Sam
H. Frank, who wrote his doctoral dissertation on this topic at the Uni-
versity of Florida. In *The Airpower Historian*, IV #2 (April 1957),
Bruce C. Hopper has an article on "American Day Bombardment in
World War I."

Anyone who studies the American battles in World War I is indebted to the American Battle Monuments Commission for its *American Armies and Battlefields in Europe: A History, Guide, and
Reference Book* (Washington, D.C., 1938). It is what the subtitle
indicates. As I attempted to determine who was where and what the
significance was, I constantly referred to the maps, descriptions, and
photographs of the terrain in this book. I also used two of the Commission's division histories: *30th Division: Summary of Operations in
the World War* and *80th Division: Summary of Operations in the
World War*, both published in Washington, D.C., in 1944.

Shipley Thomas, *The History of the A.E.F.* (New York, 1920) is a
competent survey history written by the former intelligence officer of
the 26th Infantry Regiment. In Chapter VIII, I found Jennings C.
Wise, *The Turn of the Tide* (New York, 1920) of help in my attempt
to determine what happened in the Soissons battle. Wise was a staff
officer at GHQ.

For the early days of the AEF, Heywood Broun, *The A.E.F.: With
General Pershing and the American Forces* (New York, 1918) was
useful. Another journalist who stayed longer with the AEF than Broun
—and who lost an eye in the battle of Belleau Wood—was Floyd
Gibbons. His book is *"And They Thought We Wouldn't Fight"* (New
York, 1918). Emmet Crozier, *American Reporters on the Western
Front: 1914–1918* (New York, 1959) is an interesting account of the
correspondents' problems in covering this war.

In *The United States in the Supreme War Council: American War
Aims and Inter-Allied Strategy, 1917–1918* (Middletown, Conn.,
1961), David F. Trask presents a thorough, yet brief, scholarly discussion of the American role on the Council.

Robert B. Asprey, *At Belleau Wood* (New York, 1965) is an excellent account of the battle, with proper attention given to the background
on the Second Division prior to June 1918. The quotation of Sergeant
Thomas which I used in Chapter V is from this book. Aspery did more
research and goes into more detail than does Richard Suskind, *Do You
Want to Live Forever!* (New York, 1964). The German side of the
battle is given by Ernst Otto in "The Battles for the Possession of
Belleau Wood, June, 1918," *United States Naval Institute Proceedings,*

Vol. 54 #11 (Nov. 1928). Robert D. Heinl, Jr., *Soldiers of the Sea* (Annapolis, Md., 1962) and Clyde H. Metcalf, *A History of the United States Marine Corps* (New York, 1939) have sections on World War I. Both are Marine officers but Heinl is the better writer.

In my book *The Hilt of the Sword: The Career of Peyton C. March* (Madison, Wis., 1966), I dealt with the problems of the Chief of Staff in the last eight months of the war as well as the entire career of March. My work on this book helped me when I wrote Chapter VI.

An American correspondent during the war, Thomas M. Johnson did not rely merely on his own observations in his book about the St. Mihiel and Meuse-Argonne battles—*Without Censor* (Indianapolis, Ind., 1928); after the war, he queried many of the key figures about the events. Copies of some of his correspondence are in the Drum Papers.

Samuel T. Moore, "The General Died a Major," *The American Legion Magazine*, Vol. 25 #3 (Sept. 1938) is the only published account that I could find about Henry Hill. Apparently, Moore based this article on interviews with some of Hill's acquaintances and correspondence with the division chief of staff, William K. Naylor. Since Hill became Arpin's battalion commander when he left the 33rd and joined the 32nd, there is some information about the former brigadier general in Edmund P. Arpin's memoir in the State Historical Society of Wisconsin. General William H. Simpson attempted to find out more about Hill's relief for me but was unable to do so. Although he was the division commander's aide and later the G–3 of the 33rd, General Simpson was on detached service at the time of Hill's relief; hence, he does not know the circumstances. In his interview, however, he made it clear that he thought that General Bell gave Hill a fair chance to succeed.

John Terraine has tried to rehabilitate the reputation of Field Marshal Haig in *Douglas Haig: The Educated Soldier* (London, 1963). I used this biography, together with Blake's edition of Haig's diary, to obtain the Field Marshal's views in his relations with Pershing and the AEF. In Chapter IX, I also used Volumes III, IV, and V of the official British history—Sir James E. Edmonds, *Military Operations: France and Belgium, 1918*, 5 vols. (London, 1939, 1947)—to keep the attached American units in perspective. Edmonds seemed to be scrupulously fair in his sections on the American forces.

The French political-military scene was complicated. I depended upon Jere C. King, *Generals and Politicians* (Berkeley, Calif., 1951) as a guide through this maze. Harry R. Rudin, *Armistice: 1918* (New

Haven, Conn., 1944) was useful when I came to that topic. Dixon Wecter, *When Johnny Comes Marching Home* (Cambridge, Mass., 1944) is a good history of demobilization.

Finally, I want to comment on the problem of accurate statistics. The men who compiled the records of this period were very conscious of recording statistics; frequently they were more zealous than exact in this regard. At any rate, anyone who wants to go to the trouble of corroborating a figure for men, guns, planes—anything—will find, more often than not, two, three, or even more different figures in each case. Although any one of the sources could be considered authoritative, the historian must rely on his background knowledge to take the calculated risk involved in the choice of a particular statistic. In fact, he is making an educated guess. The Chief of Field Artillery, William J. Snow, pointed up the problem when he recalled using an Ordnance chart which showed anticipated gun production. A major told him that the chart was worthless; that two offices within the Ordnance Department put out such figures; and that one was accurate and the other was unreliable. For the historian, however, both would be primary material from presumably equally authoritative sources. Unfortunately, General Snow, in his memoir, did not specify which was the reliable source.

Index

Abbeville, 172, 176, 177, 180, 263
Acker, John C., 65, 81
Adams, Harry J., 280
Admiralty, 92, 96, 103, 113
Agard, Walter R., 79, 85
Aguinaldo, Emilio, 162
Air Service (AEF), 39, 332; coordination problems, 193, 196; administrative difficulties, 194–5; plans, 195–6; training, 197–200; pilot's attitude, 202, 204; at St. Mihiel, 207–208; in Meuse-Argonne offensive, 208–10, 344
Air Service (AEF) units:
  First Pursuit Group, 198
  First Pursuit Organization, Training Center, 200
  94th Pursuit Squadron, 200–202
  96th Daylight Bombardment Squadron, 206
Aircraft: British, 189; French, 189; Curtiss "Jennies," 199; Nieuport, 199, 200; Pfalz, 201; Fokker, 203; Halberstadt, 203; Spad, 203; DeHaviland-4, 206; Handley-Page, 210
Aircraft Production Board, 191, 193, 196
Aire River, 300, 311, 313, 321, 324, 333
Aisne-Marne campaign, 158, 251–261, 283, 297, 327
Aisne province, 212
Aisne River, 259
Albany (N.Y.), 233
Albert, King of the Belgians, 284
Alcedo, 114
Alexander, Robert, 258, 259, 323, 334, 351
Allen, Henry T., 26, 275, 360
Allen, Terry de la Mesa, 280, 353
Allenby, Viscount, 249
Allied missions, 8, 43, 47, 51; instructors, 66
Allied Naval Council, 103
Allworth, Edward C., 354
Alsace-Lorraine, 342
Alsace sector, 259
Alvord, Benjamin, 138

Amalgamation issue, 9–11, 48–9, 168–71
Amberger, Gustav, 113
American Battle Monuments Commission, 362
American Expeditionary Forces (AEF): initial planning, 42–43, 47–9; controversy over size of, 127–8, 177–82; relations of soldiers with French people, 132–5; schools and training, 137–8; first actions, 139–40; coordination with Allies, 142–4; transatlantic crossing, 182–3, 227–31; *see also* Air Service; Amalgamation issue; Army; National Guard; Navy
American Expeditionary Forces University, 358
American Library Association, 77, 78
American Psychological Association, 59
American Red Cross, 48, 77, 228, 322
American Social Hygiene Association, 77
Amherst College, 79, 85, 319
Amiens, 248
Andrews, Avery D., 126
Annapolis, *see* U.S. Naval Academy
Ansauville sector, 144, 146, 147, 148, 155
Antietam Creek, 215
Antigone, 110
Archangel, 360
Argonne Forest, 125, 270, 272, 298, 300, 303, 305, 321
Armistice, 166, 341–3, 355–6
Armour Institute of Technology, 57
Army, British, 19, 80; American troops attached to, 285–98
   Second Army, 291, 340
   Fourth Army, 288, 291, 292, 297
   Fifth Army, 130, 154, 155
   III Corps, 289
   Guards Division, 250
   15th Scottish Division, 245
   46th Division, 295
   Royal Welsh Fusiliers, 123
Army, French: mutiny, 19
  Armies:
   First, 292
   Second, 152, 270, 272

Fourth, 223, 284, 291, 303, 315, 327, 333–5, 338, 340, 343, 348
Sixth, 224, 234, 239, 248
Tenth, 234, 239, 259, 273
Corps:
  II, 248
  VII, 248
  XVII, 325, 326
  XX, 234–7
  XXI, 213
  XXXVIII, 255, 257
  II Colonial, 273, 355
Divisions:
  18th, 138
  47th, 135
  153rd, 240, 243, 244
  157th, 233
  167th, 250, 252, 253
  15th Colonial, 278
  First Moroccan, 144, 234, 237, 239, 240, 243, 244, 245
Regiments:
  Ninth Cuirassiers, 316
Army, German: American rating of unit effectiveness, 158; morale, 280–81, 335–7
  Armies:
   Fifth, 346
   Seventh, 223, 227, 235, 237, 243
   18th, 222
   Detachment C, 279, 283
  Corps:
   I Reserve, 335
  Divisions:
   First Guard, 311, 321
   Fourth Guard, 253
   Fifth Guard, 321
   Tenth, 219, 223, 226, 281
   28th, 219, 221
   36th, 224, 226
   52nd, 337
   76th Reserve, 337
   77th Reserve, 279
   78th Reserve, 145
   82nd Reserve, 158
   87th, 219
   103rd, 335
   237th, 219
  Regiments:
   Fifth Grenadier, 226, 227
   Sixth Grenadier, 226, 227
   Seventh Bavarian Landwehr, 140
   271st Reserve, 157

Army, German (*cont.*)
 272nd Reserve, 157
 461st, 219
Army, United States
 Armies:
  First, 205, 207, 262–4, 267–70,
   272, 278, 282, 291, 300, 301,
   303–5, 311, 315, 317, 327,
   329, 331, 332, 335–9, 341,
   346–9, 356, 362
  Second, 210, 318, 329, 355
  Third, 359
 Corps: size, 153, 250
  I, 248, 257, 263, 275, 304, 310,
   315, 323, 343, 346, 349, 350,
   353
  II, 171, 286, 292, 296, 298
  III, 257, 263, 308, 310, 325,
   330, 343, 344, 346
  IV, 275, 330
  V, 275, 304, 321, 330, 343, 344,
   345, 349, 352
 Divisions: size, 48, 152; numbering system, 61
  First, 132, 134, 135, 137, 138,
   141, 144, 146–8, 151, 153,
   155, 156, 158, 168, 215, 227,
   229, 234–7, 239, 242–5, 248,
   258, 266, 276, 282, 312, 321,
   323, 324, 350–54, 359
  Second, 147, 151–3, 155, 175,
   214, 215, 217, 221, 222, 234–
   237, 239–43, 248, 276–8,
   281, 284, 291, 343, 344–7,
   350, 355
  Third, 213, 224, 257, 261, 321–
   323, 330, 332, 333
  Fourth, 64, 66, 68, 229, 248,
   253, 255, 257, 275–8, 286,
   304–6, 308–10, 314, 321, 332
  Fifth, 275–7, 327, 328, 330,
   332, 333, 335, 344, 346, 354,
   355
  Sixth, 350
  Seventh, 355
  26th, 147–9, 155, 250–53, 275,
   276, 278, 330, 355
  27th, 64, 68, 171, 287, 289, 291–
   293, 295–8, 356, 358
  28th, 227, 253, 257, 258, 286,
   304, 305, 312, 321, 323–5,
   355
  29th, 325
  30th, 171, 286, 287, 289, 291–
   293, 295–8
  32nd, 64, 80, 81, 153, 155, 228,
   229, 255–7, 259, 276, 291,
   321, 327, 328, 332, 355
  33rd, 66, 286, 287, 289, 290,
   301, 304, 305, 307, 321, 325–
   327, 355, 356
  35th, 286, 304, 305, 311, 312,
   314
  36th, 284
  37th, 284, 304, 305, 308, 311
  41st, 153, 250
  42nd (Rainbow), 84, 147, 149–
   151, 155, 223, 253, 255, 258,
   259, 276, 279, 327, 328, 336,
   349, 350, 351, 352
  77th, 66, 258, 285, 286, 304,
   305, 316, 321, 323, 325, 334,
   343, 346, 349, 350, 351, 352
  78th, 64, 67, 264, 285, 287, 290,
   333, 334, 335, 343, 344, 346
  79th, 304–11, 314, 355
  80th, 287, 289, 290, 304, 305,
   321, 343, 346, 350
  81st, 68, 355, 362
  82nd, 66, 67, 275, 278, 286,
   323, 324, 325, 332, 334, 336
  89th, 275, 276, 278, 280, 333,
   343–6, 355
  90th, 275, 277, 280, 344, 355,
   360
  91st, 284, 304–6, 311
  92nd, 72, 73, 231, 232, 314,
   315, 317–20, 355
 Brigades: size, 48
  First, 144, 147, 236, 240, 243–5
  Second, 147, 239, 240, 243, 244
  Third, 222, 241
  Fourth (Marine), 152, 214–17,
   276, 345, 346
  Sixth, 257
  Seventh, 256
  Tenth, 277
  52nd, 251, 252
  56th, 257
  58th, 325
  65th, 290
  83rd, 351, 352
  84th, 351
  164th, 324
  180th, 277
 Regiments, Cavalry:
  Second, 281, 312
  Seventh, 22
  Ninth, 69
  Tenth, 45, 69
 Regiments, Engineer:

Army, United States (*cont.*)
First, 244
Second, 214, 220, 242
Sixth, 213
Seventh, 354
Regiments, Field Artillery:
Fifth, 132
Sixth, 145
18th, 261, 322
120th, 80, 256, 314
129th, 311
149th, 255
Regiment, First Gas, 278
Regiments, Infantry: size of, 48
Fourth, 64
Sixth, 354
Seventh, 214, 219, 224
Ninth, 152, 216, 236, 240, 241,
278, 347, 348
16th, 3, 131, 136, 139, 141,
144, 146, 156, 157, 240, 321,
350, 351, 354
18th, 131, 139, 145, 146, 156,
225, 240
23rd, 152, 216, 222, 240, 241,
245, 347
24th, 69, 70, 72
25th, 69
26th, 131, 132, 137, 240, 244,
245, 351
27th, 361
28th, 131, 137, 147, 156, 157,
240, 244, 246, 282, 321
30th, 224–6
31st, 361
38th, 225, 226
39th, 255, 309
47th, 253, 309
58th, 64, 256
59th, 65
60th, 354
102nd, 148, 253, 277, 282
104th, 148, 251
106th, 293, 296
107th, 295–7
126th, 328
127th, 328
128th, 256, 291, 327, 328
131st, 289, 290
132nd, 289
139th, 312
145th, 308
165th, 150, 253, 255, 351; see
also 69th New York Infantry
Regiment
166th, 150, 255, 279, 351

167th, 150; *see also* Fourth Alabama Infantry Regiment
168th, 150, 351
305th, 305
307th, 287, 304
309th, 285, 346
313th, 307
314th, 307
327th, 324
328th, 324
332nd, 284
339th, 284, 360
353rd, 345, 346
354th, 345
368th, 314–20
369th, 223, 232, 233, 320; see
also 15th New York Infantry
Regiment
370th, 233, 320; see also Eighth
Illinois Infantry Regiment
371st, 73, 233, 320
372nd, 73, 233, 320
Regiments, Marine:
Fifth, 151, 152, 214, 236, 237,
240, 241
Sixth, 152, 219, 221, 242, 243
Regiments, State:
Fourth Alabama, 84; see also
167th Infantry Regiment
First Illinois, 289; see also 131st
Infantry Regiment
Eighth Illinois, 73, 233; see
also 370th Infantry Regi-
ment
15th New York, 73, 232; see
also 369th Infantry Regi-
ment
69th New York, 62, 84, 151;
see also 165th Infantry Regi-
ment
Hospitals,
Base #4, 227
Evacuation #8, 22
Machine Gun Battalions,
Seventh, 213
124th, 326, 356
107th Ammunition Train, 81
301st Tank Battalion, 295
World War II units:
First Army, 354
Ninth Army, 307
XXII Corps, 282
First Division, 137, 280, 353
First Armored Division, 282
Second Armored Division, 282
Army Schools Center, 137

Army War College, 9, 11, 46, 47, 249, 265, 276, 291, 306, 362
Army War College, Historical Section, 317
Arnold, H. H., 193, 196, 210–11
Arpin, Edmund P., Jr., 256, 257, 327
Artillery, 40
  British 18-pounder, 40–41
  14-inch naval railroad guns, 119–120, 345
  French 75, 40–42, 137
  French 155, 40, 137
  Model 1902, three-inch gun, 40–42
  Model 1916, three-inch gun, 41–42
  37 mm gun, 136
Artois, 139, 140, 146
Association for National Service, 14
Astor Battery, 162
Atlantic Fleet, 91, 92–3, 95, 97, 104, 106
Atterbury, William W., 129
Australians, 285, 292, 296
Automatic rifles: Chauchat and Browning, 39, 136
Aviation: effect on signal Corps, 31; navy, 100, 188, 197; American pre-war development, 187–9; initial planning, 189–192; see also Aircraft

Babcock, J. V., 101, 106
Bach, Christian A., 308, 310
Bacon, Robert, 15
Bacon, Robert H., 47
Bagley, David W., 114–15
Baker, Chauncey B., 127
Baker, Newton D., 9, 23, 29, 34, 35, 41, 50–52, 54, 59, 67, 75–80, 107, 130, 132, 133, 146, 149–151, 159, 162–4, 191, 192, 196, 197, 250, 276, 282, 360; biographical sketch, 20–22; and draft, 24–8; and mobilization, 29–31, 33, 38; and Pershing, 43–5, 47–9, 169–186, 342–3; attitude toward Negroes, 69–70; attitude toward conscientious objectors, 74; reorganizes General Staff, 160–61; and March, 162, 167, 179, 186
Baldwin, Frank D., 249
Balearic Islands, 113

Balfour, Arthur J., 8
Ballou, Charles C., 58, 72, 317–18, 320
Baltic, 122, 125
Bantry Bay, Ire., 101
Barkley, John L., 64
Barricourt, 300, 343
Baruch, Bernard M., 159, 163–6, 179
Basilisk, 114
Bassens, 125
Bastedo, Paul H., 117–18
Bataan, 324
Bathelémont, 139
Bayly, Lewis, 103, 108
Bay of Biscay, 110–11
Bazoches, 258
Bearss, Hiram I., 277, 282
Beatty, David, 101, 104
Beaune, 358
Beaurevoir Line, 292, 297
Beauvais, 154
Belfort, 269–70
Belknap, Reginald R., 99, 118–19
Bell, George, Jr., 290–91
Bell, J. Franklin, 75
Belleau Wood, 214–22, 237, 251, 277, 345
Benson, William S., 89, 93, 95, 101, 104–7
Berdoulat, Pierre E., 234, 242–3
Berehaven, Ire., 104
Berlin, 275
Bernheisel, Ben H., 135–6, 140, 144, 246
Berrien, Frank D., 113
Berzy-le-sec, 243–5
Biddle, John, 52, 162, 168
Binarville, 316
Bingham, Hiram, 198
Bischoff, 219
Bjornstad, Alfred W., 308–9, 310
Blakely, C. A., 112
Blanc-Mont ridge, 284
Bliss, Tasker H., 9, 10, 23, 25, 33, 34, 36, 38, 42, 49, 50, 52, 143, 151, 154, 168, 171, 172, 173, 174, 179, 181, 250, 341
Blois Classification Depot, 330
Boehn, von, 223
Böhm, 221
Bois Brulé, 148
Bois de Belval, 347–8
Bois de Bourgogne, 333–4, 343, 345
Bois de Brieulles, 309–10
Bois de Cuisy, 307
Bois de Grimpettes, 257

Bois de Loges, 325, 334–5, 346–7
Bois de la Planchette, 255
Bois de Remières, 145–6, 148
Bois de Vaire, 287
Bois Pelger, 255
Bolling, Raynal C., 194–5
Bolsheviks, 284, 336, 360
Bolté, Charles L., 57, 256, 356
Bony, 297
Booth, Ewing E., 308, 310
Bordeaux, Paul E. I., 138, 140, 213
Boston, 82, 95, 108
Boston Navy Yard, 107
Bouconville, 144
Bouillonville, 280
Boulogne, 123
Bouresches, 217, 219
Boyce, William E., 224
Bradley, Omar N., 18, 353, 362
Bragg, Braxton, 57
Breckinridge, Henry, 16–17
Brest, 97, 103, 110–11, 114, 359
Brewster, André W., 205
Bridges, G. T. M., 9–10, 47
Brieulles, 300, 354
Briey-Longwy, 126, 283, 301, 355
Brindisi, 117–18
Bristol, Mark L., 104
Brown, Fred R., 315–17
Brown, Preston, 216–17, 236, 258,
    260, 330, 359
Brown, Robert A., 255
Browne, Ralph, 99
Browning, John M., 39
Browning machine gun, 39
Browning, Montague E., 95, 105
Bruchmuller, 154
Buat, Edmond A. L., 339
Buck, Beaumont B., 244–5, 330
Bullard, Robert L., 46, 49, 51, 137,
    152, 209–10, 249; as First
    Division commander, 142,
    144–5, 155–7; as III Corps
    commander, 257–8, 263, 304,
    321; as Second Army com-
    mander, 318, 329, 355
Bundy, Omar, 216–17, 269–70
Bureau of Aircraft Production, 196
Bureau of Military Aeronautics, 196
Burnham, William P., 275
Burr, George W., 34
Butts, Edmund L., 225
Buzancy, 243–5

Cadorna, Luigi, 130
Callan, John L., 197

Cambrai, 270, 291
Camellia, 115
Cameron, George H., 256–7, 275,
    281, 304, 321, 330
Camp Alexander (Va.), 71
Camp Cody (N.M.), 82
Camp Colt (Pa.), 313
Camp Devens (Mass.), 79, 85
Camp Dix (N.J.), 64
Camp Funston (Kan.), 64, 72, 75
Camp Grant (Ill.), 64, 73
Camp Greene (N.C.), 64, 68
Camp Hill (Va.), 71
Camp Jackson (S.C.), 73
Camp Lee (Va.), 70–71
Camp life, 64, 77–9
Camp Logan (Tex.), 66, 73
Camp MacArthur (Tex.), 64, 80,
    228
Camp Meade (Md.), 74
Camp Merritt (N.J.), 228
Camp Mills (N.Y.), 84
Camp Shelby (Miss.), 83
Camp Sheridan (Ala.), 75
Camp Sherman (Ohio), 82
Camp Stuart (Va.), 73
Camp Zachary Taylor (Ky.), 58
Camp Upton (N.Y.), 30–31, 72, 75
Camp Wadsworth, (S.C.), 64, 68, 73
Campbell, Douglas, 199–202, 204
Canadians, 285
Cantigny, 156–8, 237, 241
Cantonment Division, 29–31
Cantonments, 31
Caporetto, 19, 143, 153
Carignan-Sedan-Mézières   Railroad,
    299
Carnegie Corporation, 70
Carnegie Institute of Technology, 59
Carpenter, A. S., 113
Carson, William P., 134
Caserta, 231
Cates, Clifton B., 221
Catholic Athletic Clubs, 62
Cavalry, 257, 281–2, 312
Cazaux, 199
Central Officers Training Camps, 58
Chamberlain, George E., 160–61,
    164
Chambers, Hilary R., Jr., 116, 118
Champagne, 200, 233, 284, 320
Champigneulle, 346
Chaplains, 79–80
Charlevaux Mill, 323
Châtel-Chéhéry, 324

Château-Thierry, 204, 206, 214, 216, 221, 224, 234, 263
Château du Diable, 258
Chaudun, 240
Chaumont, 131, 137–8, 150–51, 172, 175, 177, 213, 250, 266, 355
Chazelle ravine, 237, 243
Cheatham, Benjamin F., 135
Chemical Warfare Service, 142
Chemin des Dames, 147, 158, 222
Chickamauga (Ga.), 56
Chillicothe (Ohio), 82
Chiperfield, Burnett M., 26
Chipilly Ridge, 290
Churchill, Winston, 123
Civil War, 18, 21, 25, 29, 44, 56–7, 215, 249, 363
Clark, Paul H., 222, 247, 338–9, 347
Clark University, 318
Classification tests, 59–61
Cleland, John R. D., 244
Clem, John, 18
Clemenceau, Georges, 133, 143, 146, 154, 169, 172–4, 177–9, 263, 282, 340–42
Cleveland (Ohio), 21, 164
Coblenz, 206, 359
Codman, Charles R., 199
Coffin, Howard E., 15, 191
Cole, Charles H., 147
Colonia Dublan, 45
Colt-Marlin machine gun, 39
Columbia (S.C.), 73
Columbia (S.C.) Record, 73
Columbia University, 51
Columbia University Law School, 75
Combs, Hughes, 64
Comfort, Willis E., 139
Commission on Training Camp Activities, 77–8, 358; prohibition, 80; suppression of venereal disease, 80–81
Committee on Classification of Personnel in the Army, 60
Committee on Supplies, 34
Compiègne, 124, 126
Conger, A. L., 270
Congress, United States, 7, 8, 16–17, 23, 25–7, 32–3, 45, 50, 87, 89, 92–3, 160–61
Conner, Fox, 12, 47, 126, 263, 266–267, 269, 348–9, 352–3
Connor, William D., 126, 359
Conscientious objectors, 74–6
Conscription, see Draft

Consenvoye, 326
Construction Division, 31
Construction and Repair Division, 29
Conta, von, Lt. General, 217
Continental Army plan, 17
Convoy system, 96–7, 109–10
Corey, Milo C., 347
Corfu, 116
Cornell University, 56
Corregidor, 324
Corsair, 97
Côte de Chatillon, 329
Côte Dame Marie, 327–9
Council of National Defense, 15, 17, 164, 190, 196
Craig, Malin, 251, 266, 323
Crampton, Harry E., 15
Crise ravine, 243–4
The Crisis, 69
Cromwell, Oliver, 235
Cronkhite, Adelbert, 305
Crowder, Enoch H., 12, 25–6, 28–9, 162
Crowell, Benedict, 63
Crozier, William, 32–4, 38–9, 41–2
Cruiser and Transport Force (American navy), 229
Cukela, Louis, 240–41
Cunel, 300–301, 321–2, 333, 335, 354
Cushing, C. A., 112
Custer, George A., 22

Daly, Dan, 217
Damvillers, 209
Daniels, Josephus, 77, 80, 88, 90–93, 95, 97, 101, 104–7, 114
Danville, Virginia, 64
Davidson, Donald, 56–7
Davis, Jefferson, 56
Dawes, Charles G., 129, 182, 262, 342
Deeds, E. A., 192
Degoutte, Joseph, 213, 216–17, 224, 234, 257–8, 260, 264, 271, 340–41
Demobilization, 356–9
Dennis, George A., 279–80
Depth charge, 95
Destroyers, 92, 107–9
Dewey, George, 87, 102
Diaz, Armando, 284
Dickman, Joseph T., 224, 275, 281, 329–30, 346, 349–52, 359
Dilboy, George, 251

Distinguished Service Cross: award of, 233, 291, 317, 361
Dixie, 109
Dodd, Townsend F., 193, 195
Dodge, Horace E., 111
Donaldson, James H., 244–5
Donovan, William J., 255–79
Doullens, 154
Dowell, Cassius M., 27
Doyen, Charles A., 152, 216
Draft, 22–9, 63–4; *see also* Selective Service Act
Dreadnought, 87, 100
Drum, Hugh A.: 150–51, 212, 266, 272, 305, 315, 325, 359; as a member of Pershing's staff, 125–6, 246–7, 263; characterized, 267; chief of staff, First Army, 267–9, 300–301, 303, 323, 327, 329–30, 338, 349, 352–3, 356
Duane, James T., 148
DuBois, W. E. B., 69, 320
Duffy, Francis P., 151, 253
Dufieux, 338
Duncan, Donald, 217
Duncan, George B., 136, 142, 146, 226, 258, 323–4
Durazzo, 117
Duval, Maj. General, 247

East St. Louis race riot, 70
Easum, Chester V., 57, 223
Edison, Thomas A., 91
Edmonds, James E., 338
Edwards, Clarence R., 148, 250–252, 259, 277, 282, 330–31
Edwards, Frederick T., 54–6, 58, 62, 84, 261, 322
Eisenhower, Dwight D., 18, 57, 155, 266, 313, 362
El Paso, Texas, 45
Eltinge, LeRoy, 263
Ely, Hanson E., 157, 241, 330, 344, 359
Embarkation Service, 182
Emergency Construction Committee, 29
Emergency Fleet Corporation, 182
Emtsa River, 360
Enfield rifle, 38, 48
Engineer Corps, 31
Enlisted men (army): typical recruit, 59; physical examination, 62; training problems, 66–67; classification, 67

Enright, Thomas F., 140
Escadrille Lafayette, 189, 200
Europe, James Reese, 232
Evans, E. R. G. R., 108
Exermont, 312, 321

Fairview, Kentucky, 64
Fanning, 112–13
Farnsworth, Charles S., 305
Farragut, David, 102
Federal Council of Churches of Christ, 70
Fire Island, (N.Y.), 114
Fiske, Bradley A., 88
Fiske, Harold B., 126
Fismes, 258
Fismette, 258
Fitzgerald, F. Scott, 57, 62, 75
Flanders, 19, 130, 143, 222, 291
Fleury-sur-Aire, 322
Fléville, 321, 323
Flu epidemic, 81–4, 321
Foch, Ferdinand, 130, 154–5, 173, 176–8, 183, 213, 234–5, 247–258, 263–4, 269–73, 282, 284, 286, 321, 325, 331, 338, 340–43, 347, 355
Food, U.S. army: daily ration and typical ration, 65
Food Administration, 36
Fontaines, 354
Forest of Compiègne, 236
Forest of Fère, 253
Forest of Retz, 236–7, 245
La Forge, 323
Forges Brook, 307
Forrestal, James, 197
Fort Benjamin Harrison (Ind.), 56–57
Fort Benning (Ga.), 225
Fort Des Moines (Iowa), 58
Fort Leavenworth: School of the Line and Army Staff College, 11, 57, 125–6, 264–6, 356, 362
Fort Oglethorpe (Ga.), 56–7, 68
Fort Riley (Kan.), 65, 75
Fort Sheridan (Ill.), 55, 57–8
Fort Sill (Okla.), 42
Fosdick, Raymond B., 21, 77, 79–80, 133, 358
Foulois, Benjamin D., 19, 188–90, 194, 197, 205
Frankfurter, Felix, 127–42
Franklin, P. A. S., 180
French, John, 123

Fresnes, 329
Freya Stellung, 300
Friedenstürme, 222
Friedrich Wilhelm (German Crown Prince), 237
Friends Reconstruction Unit, 74
Fuchs, Lt. General, 279, 283
Fullam, William F., 89
Fullinwider, S. P., 99
Furlong, Harold A., 345

Gallipoli, 223
Gallwitz, Max von, 283, 335, 337–338, 354, 355
Garrison, Lindley M., 16–17
Gas (as weapon), 145–6, 156, 221, 288, 326, 344–5
Gay, James H., 225
General Board (navy), 87, 92
General Munitions Board, 33, 164
General Purchasing Board (AEF), 182
General Staff (army), 12, 23–5, 37, 42, 47, 49, 51–2, 83, 161–3, 166–7, 178–9, 185
General Staff (navy), 89
General Staff College (AEF), 137
General Theological Seminary, 55
George V, King of England, 101, 123
George Washington, 319
Gettysburg, battle of, 215
Geyer, 154
Gibraltar, 96–7, 102, 110, 116
Gièvres, 129
Gleaves, Albert, 229
Godfrey, Hollis, 15
Goethals, George W., 32, 166–7, 175–6, 179, 182, 184–5
Golfe de Malancourt, 307, 310
Gompers, Samuel, 30
Gondrecourt, 132, 135, 137
Gorfu, 303
Gorrell, Edgar S., 197, 206, 208
Gouraud, Henri, 223–4, 343–4
Governor's Island (N.Y.), 122
Gow, Kenneth, 68, 297
Goybet, M. F. J., 233
Grandpré, 300, 325, 333–5, 337, 347
Grant, U. S., 44
Grant, Walter S., 268–9
Grasset, R. A., 95, 105
Graves, Sidney C., 3, 141, 144–5, 361
Graves, William S., 360–61
Greenlaw, Albert, 147
Greer, Allen J., 72

Gresham, James B., 140
Gressaire Wood, 290
Griffiths, Hugh B., 358
Griscom, Lloyd C., 355
Guadalcanal, 115
Guantanamo, 91–2
Guillemont Farm, 293

Haan, William G., 259
Haessler, Carl, 74
Haig, Douglas, 10, 130, 154–5, 264, 269–70, 272, 285, 288, 290, 339, 341–2
Hall, E. J., 192
Hall, James N., 200, 202
Halsey, William F., 93, 109–10
Hamel, 287, 295
Harbison, Clinton, 56
Harbord, James G.: 26, 122, 124, 130, 132, 167, 258, 276; characterized, 46; as Pershing's chief of staff, 46, 49, 126, 142, 183–4; commanding general, services of supply, 129, 175–6, 182, 185; commander of Marine Brigade, 216, 219–21; commander of Second Division, 235–6, 241–2
Harding, Warren G., 362
Harmon, Ernest N., 282
Hartney, Harold E., 202, 298
Harvard University, 59, 69, 202, 319
Hattonchâtel, 282
Hawaii, 57
Hay, Merle D., 140
Hayes, Ralph, 21
Hayward, William, 233
Hazzard, O. P. M., 281
Heintzelman, Stuart, 329
Hellé, Joseph, 237
Herron, Charles D., 264–6, 333–4
Hesse, Kurt, 227
Hill, Henry R., 290–91
Hindenburg, Paul von, 57, 222, 247–8, 283, 297–8
Hindenburg line, 292, 293; see also Kriemhilde Stellung
Hines, Frank T., 182
Hines, John L., 123–4, 131, 141, 144, 240, 245, 277, 310, 329
Hirschauer, 152
Hoboken (N.J.), 228
Hodges, Courtney H., 354
Hodges, Henry C., Jr., 36

Hoffman, Charles, 221
Holcomb, Thomas, 221
Holden, Missouri, 64
Holley, I. B., Jr., 192
Hoover, Herbert, 9
Hostess Houses, 78
Hotchkiss machine gun, 39, 136
Hough, Benson W., 255
House, Edward M., 9, 169, 174–5, 281, 342–3
Houston race riot, 70, 73
Howard, Oliver O., 44
Howze, Robert L., 26
Hubbard, Samuel T., Jr., 158
Huebner, Clarence R., 137–8, 141, 156–7, 240, 243, 353
Huffer, Jean, 200
Hulit, Mrs. Hazel Leroy, 65
Hurley, Edward N., 52, 179–80
Husband, Joseph, 107
Hutier, von, tactics, 154

Indianapolis (Ind.), 56
Indians and Indian Wars, 22, 28, 44, 69, 249
Industrial Preparedness Committee, 15
Influenza, see Flu epidemic
Ingalls, David S., 197
Ingleside, 114
Ingraham, Mark H., 56, 64, 285
Intelligence tests, 60–61
Inter-Allied Games, 358
Invergordon, 119
Inverness, 119
Irish County Societies, 62
Issoudun, 198, 199, 200, 202

Jackson, Stonewall, 56, 235–6
Jacob Jones, 114
"Jacobsbrunnen," 140
Jacoby, Maclear, 118
Janda, L. T., 348
Janis, Elsie, 276
Jellicoe, John, 94–7, 103, 119, 123
Jervey, Henry, 179
Jewish Welfare Board, 77–8
Joffre, Joseph, 8–9, 43, 47–8
Johns Hopkins University, 21, 133
Johnson, Henry, 233
Johnson, Hugh S., 25, 27–8, 31, 34
Johnston, William H., 306
Les Jomblets, 255
Juilly, 221
Jutland, 100
Juvigny, 259, 327

Kahn, Julius, 27
Kaiser Wilhelm II, 57, 248, 355
Kelly Field (Tex.), 200
Kelton, Robert H. C., 257
Kenly, William L., 195–6
Keppel, Frederick P., 22, 51, 69, 70, 75, 76
Kerensky, Alexander, 142
Kernan, Francis J., 49, 129, 175
Kilmer, Joyce, 151, 255
King, Ernest J., 89, 93, 101, 107
Kingery, James R., 224–5
Knights of Columbus, 77–8
Knoll, the (St. Quentin), 293
Kocak, Matej, 241
Korean War, 37, 39, 152
Kriemhilde Stellung, 300, 301, 303, 309–10, 321, 327, 329; see also Hindenburg Line
Kuhn, Joseph E., 24, 33, 306

Laclede (Mo.), 44
Lafayette College, 162
Lafayette Flying Corps, 200
LaGuardia, Fiorello H., 191, 197
Lane, Franklin K., 22
Langer, William L., 278
Langres, 137
Lansing, Robert, 170
Lawrence, George E., 111
Leahy, William D., 90, 230
Lee, Robert E., 56
Legge, Barnwell R., 245
Lejeune, John A., 276–8, 347–8
Lenin, 142
Leviathan, 230
Levinsky, "Battling," 79
Lewis, Edward M., 291
Lewis, R. H., 235
Lewis machine gun, 39
Liberian Frontier Force, 319
Liberty engine, 192, 197
Liddell Hart, B. H., 130, 287
Liggett, Hunter: 209–10, 255, 257, 264, 313, 315, 359, 362; biographical sketch, 248–50; as commander, I Corps, 250–52, 256, 258, 275, 278, 283, 304, 321, 323, 325; commander, First Army, 329–33, 343–4, 346–7, 349, 352–3
Ligny-en-Barrois, 270, 272
Linard, J. L. A., 231, 232
Lindsey, Julian R., 324–5
Line of Communications, see Services of Supply

Lippmann, Walter, 30, 281
Littell, Isaac W., 29–31
Little Big Horn, battle of, 22
Liverpool, 123
Lloyd George, David, 95–6, 123, 143, 154, 168–71, 173–4, 177, 285, 342
Logan, James A., 125–6
London, 94, 123
Long, Howard H., 318–19
Longwy-Briey, see Briey-Longwy
Loomis, David D., 112
Lorraine, 125, 131, 134, 135, 141, 147, 151, 258
Lost Battalion, 323–4
Lovett, Robert A., 197
Ludendorff, Erich von, 153, 213, 222, 248, 260, 289, 298, 335, 337
Lufbery, Raoul, 200–201
Luke, Frank, 203
Lunéville sector, 150–51
Lusitania, 15–16
Lydonia, 110, 113–14

McAlexander, Ulysses G., 225–7, 277, 281
McAndrew, James W., 126–7, 137, 268, 323, 330–31
MacArthur, Douglas, 12, 22, 46, 149–50, 184, 186, 255, 268, 283, 329, 351
McCain, Henry P., 25
McCardle, Tommy, 151
McDougal, 108
Machine guns, 38–9; see Browning, Colt-Marlin, Hotchkiss, Lewis, and Vickers
McKinley, William, 11, 267
McMahon, John E., 276, 330
McRae, James H., 334–5
Madison (Wis.), 64
Madison Barracks (N.Y.), 56
Mangin, Charles, 234, 259–60
Manila, battle of, 162
Manila Bay, battle of, 6, 102
Maistre, 348
Malone, Paul B., 126, 222, 277
Mann, William A., 149–50
Marbache sector, 320
March, Peyton C.: 12, 49–50, 61, 67, 75, 82–3, 164–8, 172, 174–86, 341, 360; biographical sketch, 162–3; see also Baker and Pershing

Marine Corps, officers training, 91; see Fourth (Marine) Brigade and Fifth and Sixth Marine Regiments under United States Army
Marne province, 131, 212
Marne River, 58, 214, 224, 226, 257, 281
Marne salient, 222, 239, 248, 260, 264
Marr, Kenneth, 200
Marshall, George C., 13, 135, 138, 140, 167, 186, 264, 266–9, 303, 332, 349, 352–3, 361–2
Marshall, Richard C., Jr., 31
Martin, Thomas S., 8
Maverick, Maury, 321–2
Max, Prince of Baden, 341
Mayo, Henry T., 94, 104, 106
Medal of Honor, award of, 203, 217, 221, 233, 241, 249, 251, 258, 289, 297, 326, 354
Medical Department (U.S. army), 31, 55, 59
Melville, 109
Menoher, Charles T., 150, 351
Merrill, John N., 316
Merritt, Wesley, 44
Metz, 12, 126, 206, 270–72, 283, 301, 335
Metz-Sablons, 210
Meuse-Argonne offensive, 64, 68, 183, 198, 208–9, 233, 272, 283–4, Chapter 10
Meuse River, 270, 272–3, 291, 298, 300, 303, 305, 325, 349, 354–355
Mexican border mobilization, 13–14, 17, 32, 36, 62, 77, 267, 291
Meyer, George von L., 89
Mézières, 270
"Michael" offensive, 154, 213
Michel line, 282–3
Middleton, Troy, 253
Miles Wardlaw, 258
Milholland, Ray, 115–17
Mills, Ogden, 128
Milner, Lord (Alfred Milner), 172, 176–7
Milwaukee Sentinel, 320
Missy ravine, 237, 239, 243
Mitchel, John P., 14
Mitchell, William, 187, 193–5, 197, 201, 204–9, 211, 249
Mobile Bay, battle of, 102

Mobilization, 29–37, 51; *see also* Draft
Moldavia, 229
Monash, John, 287–9, 292–3, 296–298
Montdidier sector, 155–6, 222
Montfaucon, 300–301, 305, 307–10, 314, 322, 340
Montreuil, 130
Montsec, 144, 273
Moore, Dan T., 47
Mordacq, Jean-Henri, 213, 217
Moros, 19, 22, 45–6
Moscow, 275
Moseley, George Van Horn, 12, 26, 126, 132, 340
Moselle River, 329
Muir, Charles H., 258, 330
Mulhouse, 269
Müller, George A. von, 248
Mullin, John, 151
Murvaux, 354
Myrdal, Gunnar, 70

Nancy, 139
Nantillois, 308, 310
Nashville, battle of, 229
National Advisory Committee of Aeronautics, 189–90
National Army, 24, 29, 30, 31, 35, 36, 61–3, 67
National Association for the Advancement of Colored People, 58, 69
National Defense Act of 1916, 16, 17, 23
National Guard, 13, 14, 17, 18, 27, 29, 31, 36, 54, 61–3, 65, 67, 69, 77, 84
National Research Council, 14
National Security League, 14
Naval Consulting Board, 14
Naval War College, 23, 90, 93, 94, 102
Navy, British, 92; Grand Fleet, 100, 103; Adriatic Force, 118; *see also* Admiralty
Navy, United States: preparedness, 87, 91–2; strength at beginning of the war, 90–91; initial plans, 92–3, 95; Sixth Battle Squadron, 100; U.S. Naval Forces Operating in European waters, 101; strength at the end of the war, 119–20; *see also*

Atlantic Fleet; Aviation; Convoy system; Josephus Daniels; Destroyers; William S. Sims; Subchasers
Navy League, 14
Negroes, 58, 69–73, 78, 171, 231–3, 314–20
Nelson, Charles P., 116–18
Neufchâteau, 264
Nevers, 356
Neville, Wendell C., 221
Newport (R.I.), 92, 114
Newport News (Va.), 228
New Orleans (La.), 80
The New Republic, 52, 85
New York, 17, 62, 160, 228
New York, 93
New York Port of Embarkation, 229
New York Times, 4, 161, 222
Niblack, Albert P., 102
Nicholson, 112–13
Nokomis, 111
Nolan, Dennis E., 126
North Sea, 270
North Sea mine barrage, 99–100, 104, 118–19
Northern Bombing Group, 100, 197
Northwestern University, 59

O'Brien, 112
O'Connor, William P., 80, 256
Officers: army, 54–8; navy, 90–91
Oise-Aisne sector, 320
Ordnance Department, 32, 33, 37, 38, 40–42
Orduna, 227
Orkney Islands, 104
Orlando, Vittorio, 173, 177
Orleans, 198
O'Ryan, John F., 77, 291, 293, 356
Otranto Barrage, 116, 118
Ourcq River, 253, 255, 259, 260, 279
Overman Act, 161, 167

Painlevé, Paul, 124, 143
Pallice, La, 125
Palmer, Frederick, 134, 141, 216
Palmer, John McAuley, 12, 13, 24, 47–8, 126–7
Panama, 57
Panama Canal, 142, 166
Paris, 3, 6, 123, 130–31, 158, 212, 236, 358
Paris-Avricourt railroad, 282
Parker, Frank, 350–53

Patrick, Mason M., 195, 205, 207, 209
Patton, George S., Jr., 123, 312–13
Penner, Carl, 314
Pershing, John J., 4, 12, 31, 52, 68, 72, 78, 82, 102, 104, 107, 121, 143, 146, 149–53, 156, 158, 175–6, 202, 207, 213, 216, 226, 231–2, 235, 249–250, 258, 260, 266–7, 276, 281, 282, 284, 358–9; biographical sketch, 43–6, 362; selects staff, 46–7, 127; organizes AEF, 48–50, 126–7; opinion of Negro soldiers, 69, 319; goes to France, 122–5; plans for large AEF, 128–30; at Chaumont, 131; and venereal disease in AEF, 132–133; and schools and training in AEF, 137–8; relieves officers, 141–2, 330–31; aids Allies during spring offensives, 154–5, 215; relations with Peyton C. March, 162, 167–8, 183–6; and amalgamation controversy, 168–174; and 100 Division program, 177–82; and Air Service, 193–5, 205, 208, 211; forms First Army, 262–264, 268; and St. Mihiel plan, 269–73, 278; and Americans serving with British, 285–6, 288, 290, 339; and Meuse-Argonne, 299, 304, 310, 313–14, 320–21, 323, 325–7, 330–34, 340–41, 347–50, 352–3, 355, 358–9; forms Second Army, 329; on Armistice terms, 341–3
Pétain, Henri Philippe, 124–6, 130, 153–5, 213, 215, 222, 234–5, 247, 263–4, 269, 271–2, 282, 284, 301, 304, 331, 338, 341–342, 347
Peterson, David M., 200
Pfaffendorf Bridge, 359
Philippines, 18–19, 22, 45, 57, 87, 110, 275
Philippine Insurrection, 69, 162
Piave River, 143
Pigeons, 31
Plattsburg (N.Y.), 14–15, 17, 43, 55–6, 324
Ploisy ravine, 237, 243–4

Plunkett, C. P., 345
Plymouth, 116
Pogue, Forrest C., 186
Poincaré, Raymond, 124, 270, 282, 340
Poore, Benjamin A., 256
Pope, Thomas A., 289
Port-sur-Seille, 329
Pottinger, Hiram B., 219
Pottle, Frederick A., 68, 221, 228, 231
Pouyraguin, de, A., 138
Pratt, William V., 106
Preparedness, 14–18, 87, 91–2
Princess Matoika, 230
Pringle, J. R. P., 103
Public Health Service, 81
Puckle, Colonel, 122
Puerto Rico, 57
Pulkowsky, 154
Punitive Expedition, 13, 43, 45, 188

"Q" ships, 100
Quadt, von, Baron, 337
Quantico (Va.), 91
Quartermaster Corps and Department, 29, 32, 34–7, 167, 359
Queenstown (Ire.), 97, 103, 108–110, 112, 114–16
Quennemont Farm, 293
Quincy (Ill.), 291

Railroad Administration, 37
Rainsford, W. Kerr, 286
Ransom, John Crowe, 57
Rau, George J., 253
Rawlinson, Henry, 288, 292–3, 295, 297
Read, George W., 286–8, 291–2, 297–8
Reading, Lord (Rufus Isaacs), 172, 174
Réguin, Edouard J., 40, 47–8
Regular army, 17, 18, 27, 53, 55
Reilly, Henry J., 150, 255, 352
La Reine sector, 148
Reinhardt, Walther, 227, 235, 237
Remington, Frederic, 286
Replacements, 67–8
Reserve Officers Training Corps, 17
Reynaud, Claud F., 113
Rhea, James C., 347
Rheims, 200, 222–3, 234–5, 291
Rhine River, 342, 359
Ribot, Alexandre, 190, 191, 196

Rickenbacker, Edward V., 122, 199–200, 202–3
Rifle, see Enfield; Springfield
Roberts, Charles D., 68, 355
Roberts, Needham, 233
Robertson, William, 123, 130, 171
Rock Island Arsenal, 34, 38
Rockenbach, Samuel D., 313
Rockford (Ill.), 73
Rodgers, Thomas S., 101
Rodman, Hugh, 90, 101–3
Romagne, 301, 321–2, 327–9, 333
Roosevelt, Franklin D., 90, 93, 99, 106, 267, 276
Roosevelt, Quentin, 199, 205
Roosevelt, Theodore, 6, 11, 26, 45, 74, 89, 93, 160
Roosevelt, Theodore, Jr., 136–7, 243, 351, 353
Root, Elihu, 11, 13, 18, 89, 160
Rose, Hans, 114
Rosenwald, Julius, 34
Rosyth, 100
Rough Riders, 27
Royal Flying Corps, 198
Rudd, H. W. Dwight, 113
Rupt de Mad, 279
Russia: American intervention in north Russia, 284, 360–61; see also Siberia
Russo-Japanese War, 12, 162
Ryan, John D., 196

Saar, 126
St. Benoit, 280
St. Mihiel offensive, 125–6, 144, 198, 201, 207–8, 262–84, 300–301, 303–4, 313, 324, 329, 355
St. Nazaire, 3, 125, 131
St. Quentin, 124
St. Quentin Canal attack, 292–8
St. Thibaut, 258
Salvation Army, 77–8
Sanborn, Joseph B., 289–90
San Diego, 114
San Juan Hill, battle of, 45
Santee, 100
Sarajevo, 5
Savatier, Eugene, 152
Scanlan, Anthony, 146, 240
Scapa Flow, 100
Schmidt, 250
Scilly Islands, 115
Scott, Emmett J., 70

Scott, Frank A., 164
Scott, Walter D., 59–60
Scott, Hugh L., 9, 22–5, 33, 38, 43, 47, 51–2, 128
Scott, Norman, 115
Scudder, Robert A., 65, 68
Sedan incident, 348–55
Seicheprey, 144, 146, 148
Selective Service Act, 74, 77, 80
Selle River, 297
Sergy, 253
Services of Supply (AEF), 129, 175–176, 181
Sharpe, Henry G., 29, 32, 35
Shearer, Maurice, 214, 219–20
Shell shock, 224
Shepard, Lemuel C., Jr., 221
Sheridan, Philip H., 44
Sherman, William T., 44
Shipping Board, 16, 52, 182
Shipping Control Committee, 182
Siberia, 284, 360–61
Sibert, William L., 134–5, 141–2
Signal Corps, pre-war supply needs of, 31
Simpson, William H., 307
Sims, William S., 90–91, 95–96, 102, 110, 113, 116, 119, 123; characterized, 93–4; relations with British, 94, 103–104; forces under his command, 101, 119; relations with Daniels, 104–7
Slack, Clayton K., 64, 231, 286, 289, 326, 356
Smith, Holland M., 221
Smuts, Jan Christian, 123
"Snoopy," 187
Snow, William J., 40–42, 58
Snyder, Herbert, 278
Society of World War I Aero Historians, 187
Soissons offensive, 136, 205, 234–248, 257, 259, 304
Soissons–Château-Thierry highway, 242, 244
Soissons–Paris Railroad, 244
Solly-Flood, Arthur, 286
Somme campaign, 363
Somme River, 287, 290
Sommedieue, 151
Sommerviller sector, 139, 147, 225
Souain, 223
Souilly, 304, 327, 329, 331, 349, 356
Soule, George, 52
Spaatz, Carl, 199, 209–10

Spanish-American War, 18, 45, 55, 69, 86–7, 162, 267, 275, 319
Spingarn, Joel E., 58
"Splinter Fleet," see Subchasers
Springfield Arsenal, 38
Springfield rifle, 11, 37–8, 146
Stackpole, P. L., 331, 352
Stanton, C. E., 4
Stark, Harold R., 110
Starrett, W. A., 29
Stettinius, Edward R., 161, 175
Stevens, James A., 309–10
Stimson, Henry L., 18
Stites, Joseph G., 221
Stone, Harlan F., 75
Stragglers, 332–3
Strauss, Joseph, 99, 104
Strickland, Daniel W., 149
Strom, Edward B., 328
Student Army Training Corps, 58
Subchasers, 99, 115–18; Subchaser #95, 117; Subchaser #128, 118; Subchaser #129, 117–118; Subchaser #215, 117–118
Submarines, 7, 86–7, 94–100, 229–230; AL-2, 100; U-53, 92, 114; U-58, 113; UB-70, 114
"Suicide Fleet," 110
Summerall, Charles P., 128, 235, 239, 242–4, 329–30, 344, 349–50, 352–3
Supreme War Council, 143, 153, 171–3, 176, 213, 250, 285, 341–2, 360
Sweetser, Arthur, 191
Sweezey, Claude B., 307–8

Taft, William H., 89, 94
Tampico, 188
Tank Corps; see Tanks
Tanks, 39, 239, 241, 242, 287, 312–313, 344; Mark V tank, 295; Renault tank, 312
Tarawa, 217
Tardieu, André, 178
Taussig, Joseph K., 103, 108–10
Teilhard de Chardin, Pierre, 245, 246
Terraine, John, 155
Thiaucourt, 281
Thomas, Gerald C., 152
Thomas, Norman, 76
Thomason, John W., Jr., 215, 236, 241
Ticonderoga, 229

Todd, Henry D., Jr., 66
Toul sector, 148, 201, 203, 206, 248
Toulgas, 360
Toulmin, H. A., Jr., 195
Tours, 129
Traub, Peter E., 305
Trenchard, Hugh, 204, 205
Truman, Harry S, 311
Tuscania, 229
Tuskegee Institute, 70

U-boat; see Submarines
Underwater listening device, 99
United States Military Academy (West Point), 17, 22–3, 44, 55, 138, 185, 249, 264, 266, 276, 316
United States Naval Academy (Annapolis), 91
University of Nebraska, 44

Valdahon, 137
Vanderbilt University, 56
Vanquois Hill, 311
Varennes: in Marne offensive, 224; in Meuse-Argonne offensive, 313
Vaterland, see Leviathan
Vaux, 222, 237, 345
Vauxcastille, 240
Venereal disease, 80–81, 132–4
Vera Cruz, 188, 267
Verdun, 203, 300, 304
Versailles, 170, 176, 177, 180, 213
Versailles Peace Conference, 357, 364
Vesle River, 255, 257–60, 263, 264
Vickers machine gun, 39
Vierzy ravine, 237, 240, 241
Vietnam and Vietnamese, 215, 363
Vigneulles, 282
Villa, "Pancho," 13, 45
Villeneuve-les-Vertus, 200
Vincent, J. G., 192
Virginia Military Institute, 267
Viviani, René, 8
Vladivostok, 361
Vosges Mountains, 125, 275, 315

Wadsworth, 108–9
Wadsworth, James W., 40, 160, 166
Wainwright, Jonathan M., 324
Waldon, S. D., 192
Walker, Fred L., 225
Walter Reed Hospital, 82, 362

War Camp Community Service, 77–
    78
War Council, 161
War Industries Board, 161, 163–5
Ward, Ralph T., 323
Washington, Booker T., 70
Wavell, Archibald, 249
Wellmann, 335–6, 353
Wells, Briant H., 47
Westminster Abbey, 123
West Point, see U.S. Military Acad-
    emy
Weygand, Maxime, 339
Weymouth, 118
Whittlesey, Charles W., 324
Wilder, John T., 56
Wilhelm II, see Kaiser
Willard, Daniel, 164
Williams, Charles H., 70–71
Williams, Clarence C., 32, 41, 163
Williams, Raymond R., 296
Wilson, Henry B., 93, 95, 103
Wilson, Samuel M., 56
Wilson, Woodrow, 23, 29, 47, 62,
    74, 83, 92, 133, 174–5, 177,
    180, 191, 196, 320, 357, 364;
    and events leading to war,
    7; asks for declaration of
    war, 7–8; and Joffre, 9, 43;
    and preparedness, 13–14, 16–
    17, 87; attitude toward the
    military, 20, 76; relations
    with Baker, 20–21, 160–61;
    and draft, 25, 27–8; and
    Pershing, 45, 46, 48–9, 127,
    171, 340, 342–3; and Dan-
    iels, 88; and naval affairs,
    92, 96–7; and Supreme War

    Council, 143; and Baruch,
    163–5; and amalgamation
    controversy, 168–72; and
    pre-Armistice negotiations,
    340–43, 360–61
Winn, Cooper D., 351
Winslow, Alan F., 201
Winton, Roy W., 309
Wise, Frederic M., 220, 277
Wiseman, William, 173–5
Woëvre Plain, 273, 284
Wolf, 140
Wood, Leonard, 14–15, 43, 49, 51,
    75, 142, 276
Wood, Robert E., 162–3
Woodfill, Samuel, 354
Wooldridge, Jesse W., 226
Work, Marjorie L., 322
World War II, 363
Wright, Orville, 188, 191, 205
Wright, Wilbur, 188
Wright, William M., 276

Yale University, 198, 216
Yaphank (N.Y.), 30
Yerkes, Robert M., 59–60
York, Alvin C., 61, 66–7, 74, 324,
    363
Yorktown (Va.), 106
Young, Charles, 69, 72, 319
Young, Hugh, 133
Young, Rush S., 304, 346
Young Men's Christian Association,
    77–8
Young Women's Christian Associa-
    tion, 77–8

Zimmermann note, 7